THE COMPLETE ILLUSTRATED GUIDE TO

EVERYTHING
SOLD IN
MARINE SUPPLY
STORES

THE COMPLETE ILLUSTRATED GUIDE TO

EVERYTHING SOLD IN MARINE SUPPLY STORES

Steve Ettlinger with
Caroline Ajootian and Tom Gannon

Illustrations by Robert Strimban

Hearst Marine Books
New York

This book is dedicated to all of us who have ever walked into
(or been sent to) a marine supply store
and asked for a whatchamacallit or a thingamajig.
Or a doo-hickey.

Copyright © 1995 by Steve Ettlinger

All rights reserved. No part of this book may be reproduced or utilized in any form or
by any means, electronic or mechanical, including photocopying, recording, or by any
information storage or retrieval system, without permission in writing from the Publisher.
Inquiries should be addressed to Permissions Department, William Morrow and Company, Inc., 1350 Avenue of the Americas, New York, N.Y. 10019.

It is the policy of William Morrow and Company, Inc., and its imprints and affiliates,
recognizing the importance of preserving what has been written, to print the books we
publish on acid-free paper, and we exert our best efforts to that end.

Library of Congress Cataloging-in-Publication Data

Ettlinger, Steve.
    The complete illustrated guide to everything sold in marine supply
stores / by Steve Ettlinger with Caroline Ajootian and Tom Gannon;
illustrations by Robert Strimban.
      p.   cm.
    Includes index.
    ISBN 0-688-13300-2
    1. Boats and boating—United States—Equipment and Supplies—
Catalogs. 2. Boats and boating—Terminology. I. Ajootian,
Caroline. II. Gannon, Tom. III. Title. IV. Title:
Everything sold in marine supply stores.
VM12.E88 1994
623.8'3—dc20   94-34757
                                   CIP

Printed in the United States of America

First Edition

1 2 3 4 5 6 7 8 9 10

CONCEIVED AND EDITED BY ETTLINGER EDITORIAL PROJECTS

BOOK DESIGN BY MM DESIGN 2000, INC.

CONTENTS

Neither the authors nor the publisher can be held responsible for any accidents caused by the tools or products described herein. Use tips are by their very nature incomplete and not intended to be fully instructive.

PREFACE

Anyone who has ever gone into a marine supply store or riffled through the pages of a mail order catalog has probably come across a good number of items that seemed rather mysterious. Certainly that's the case with me. And like me, many of you are very curious as to what these things actually *are*.

This book, like its predecessor, *The Complete Illustrated Guide to Everything Sold In Hardware Stores,* was written partially to address that problem, but also because so many of us need particular things that we don't necessarily know by name. Furthermore, many times boat repair becomes a social act, with advice coming from everyone in the boatyard. By the time you get to your local store, you've got opinions on every aspect of your prospective purchase from magazines and advertisements too. It's downright confusing.

To add insult to injury, when you actually do get into the store, there is usually a bewildering array of choices. The sales clerks are not always informed or present, and then of course they start asking *you* all the choices one could make about a piece of equipment—choices that you probably would not consider if it weren't for this book. That's where *The Complete Illustrated Guide to Everything Sold In Marine Supply Stores* can help.

What we've tried to do here is to sort out all the buying advice, all the various names, all the various materials, and give some straightforward help to you, the consumer. We've also tried to write and illustrate it so that you might want to browse during your off-water days, or use it to explain to a helper (willing or reluctant) exactly what it is you want them to go pick up for you, so that they won't bring back a coupler pin when you sent them for a cotter pin.

ACKNOWLEDGMENTS

I am very lucky to have been able to work with two able and dedicated writers, Caroline Ajootian and Tom Gannon. I am very grateful to BOAT/U.S. and Practical Sailor for supporting Caroline and Tom's extracurricular activities. (Please note that neither company is officially involved with this book.) As always, it was terrific to work with illustrator Bob Strimban, whose work never fails to elicit compliments. Caroline Ajootian thanks her parents, who taught her to love books and boats; her children and crewmates, Matthew, Maria, and Catherine; and David Stein, for his support and encouragement.

Bill Griffin of Fawcett Boat Supplies, Annapolis, Maryland, gave me some essential research assistance early on, which was greatly appreciated. A big thanks to my various assistants who helped prepare the manuscript and illustrations—Sharon Guskin, Carol Murashige, and Sean Sullivan.

Hearst editor Michael Mouland provided excellent editorial guidance and was the initiator of this project; Megan Newman enthusiastically carried it through. Thanks go to fellow book producers Ella Stewart and John Smallwood of Smallwood and Stewart for making the original contact on my behalf.

A special thanks to Dylan and Gusty—your support makes it all worthwhile. Marge Ettlinger and Betsy Chotin were of great help guiding me to various Annapolis marine supply stores. Ralph Ettlinger would have loved this one, for sure. This one's for you, Dad.

INTRODUCTION

HOW THIS BOOK IS ORGANIZED

We've tried to organize *The Complete Illustrated Guide to Everything Sold in Marine Supply Stores* much the way a good store or catalog is organized, but also by function. Unfortunately there is always some overlap. For example many stores and catalogs lump all their electronic devices together under "Electronics," whereas we split some of those items up into various chapters better defined by function, such as "Communication" (Chapter 1) or "Navigation" (Chapter 2). There are electronics in both. In our case function prevails. The chapters themselves are grouped by general function into two parts, Part I for things that make a boat go and Part II for things that simply go into or onto a boat for all other functions.

WHAT IS NOT INCLUDED

Though you might find them sold in marine supply stores, we have tried to avoid including anything that is not specifically nautical, such as sports equipment, cooking equipment, common tools and materials, common hardware, or custom-made items such as sails. Brand names and unique gadgets are not included here either, except on rare occasions where the name or item has become generic or could not be described by any other name. Inclusion of either is by no means an endorsement.

HOW TO USE THIS BOOK

Readers are best served if they read through this book prior to a shopping expedition. It should help you anticipate the questions having to do with choices that arise whenever you make a purchase, such as different sizes, shapes, materials, or quality.

This is not a buying guide for specific products. This book is intended only to orient the consumer to the various categories of products available. Descriptions are meant to be generic in all cases. Every effort has been made to use brand names and trademarks properly. Sample brand names appear from time to time but do not imply any endorsement of any kind. Lack of mention does not imply a negative review.

CHAPTER ONE

COMMUNICATION

FLAGS

ABOUT FLAGS

Few customs relating to boats are as colorful or as steeped in tradition and etiquette as the display of flags. Here's where boat owners have a chance to express their patriotism and their personalities, as well as that *joie de vivre* essential to having fun on the water.

Although flags come in standard sizes, a few guidelines will help choose the right one for your boat. Flags displayed from the stern—the U.S. Ensign, Yacht Ensign, U.S. Coast Guard Auxiliary Ensign, or U.S. Power Squadron Ensign, for example—should be 1" on the *fly* (the length) for each foot of overall boat length. The *hoist* (the height) should be two thirds of the fly. Flagstaff height is determined by the length of the boat, as follows: to 18', 24"; 19'–24', 30"; 25'–30', 36"; 31'–36', 48".

Flags such as club burgees, officers' flags, and private signals flown on sailboats should be ½" for each foot of the highest mast. On powerboats these flags should be roughly ⅝" on the fly for each foot of overall length.

the skull-and-crossbones Jolly Roger is a good example—and *yacht club officer flags.*

USE: The only national flag considered appropriate for all boats. While on the high seas, it is necessary only to fly the ensign when meeting or passing other vessels. While in foreign waters, it's customary to fly the U.S. National Ensign above a *courtesy flag,* the flag of the country you're visiting.

USE TIPS: Whether at anchor or under way, both power and sail boats fly the ensign from the stern. If the flagstaff has to be off center, it should be on the starboard side. Some sailors like the tradition of displaying the ensign from the leech of the aftermost sail while under way, about two thirds of the length of the leech above the clew. The ensign should never be displayed while power *or* sail boats are racing.

NOTE: Though not official, flying the U.S. flag upside down is recognized as a distress signal.

BUYING TIPS: Better-quality ensigns have embroidered stars and sewn stripes. Look for extra stitching on the edges, fade-resistant nylon, and brass grommets. Less-expensive dyed flags are also available but they won't last long when exposed to constant sunlight and salt spray.

MARINE FLAG

ALSO KNOWN AS: Old Glory; Stars and Stripes; the Red, White, and Blue; ensign

DESCRIPTION: Available either as *U.S. National Ensign,* with 50 white stars on dark blue ground, 13 alternating red and white stripes, or the *Yacht Ensign* (Betsy Ross flag) with a circle of 13 white stars on blue ground surrounding a fouled anchor, 13 alternating red and white stripes. *State flags* are also commonly found in catalogs, as well as novelty flags—

SPECIAL-PURPOSE FLAG

DESCRIPTION: Rectangular, square, triangular, or swallow-tailed flags of various size, color, and markings.

TYPES:

Diver-down flag: Diver's flag or diver-down flag is a red triangle with a white diagonal stripe. The *International Alpha,* or *Code A,* flag is a blue-and-white swallow-tail pennant, sometimes stiffened with a

batten or made itself of rigid material. Diver-down flag alerts boaters that diving operations are going on; the Alpha signals that a boat's movement is limited because of diving operations.

 Quarantine flag (also known as the *International "Q" flag*) and *Request practique:* Yellow rectangle, typically 12" × 18", flown when entering a foreign port or reentering the U.S.; signals that a boat is "healthy" and requests clearance.

Protest flag: Angry red rectangle or swallow-tail, flown to inform race officials that you intend to lodge a protest. Not to be confused with such marginally humorous nonstandard protest flags bearing such messages as "Thanks for the Wake, You Jerk," used to criticize other boaters' bad manners.

Man-overboard flag: Battened square "Oscar" with yellow and red diagonal halves.

Waterski flag: Light-red flag denotes waterskiing activity going on.

USE: To convey specific information for the information of other boaters.

USE TIPS: Have the proper flag on hand if you expect to be engaged in a given activity, i.e., entering a foreign port or engaging in sport diving or salvage work.

BUYING TIPS: Look for brass grommets and fade-resistant fabric that won't deteriorate in salt spray.

INTERNATIONAL CODE FLAGS

ALSO KNOWN AS: International Code signal flags

DESCRIPTION: Flags and pennants representing letters of the alphabet, numerals, "repeaters," and decimal point ("Code" or "Answering" pennant). "Repeaters" or substitute flags are used as replacements for flags or pennants already in use, since each set has only one flag for each letter and number. The "Code" pennant is used as a decimal point. International Code signal flags may be rectangular or swallow-tailed (26 for the alphabet), pennants (10 for numerals, plus one "Code") or triangular (3 repeaters) in various combinations of red, white, blue, yellow, and black.

spells "boat"

USE: Besides being decorative, code flags are displayed alone, in pairs, or in groups of three for communicating messages often related to safety. When signal flags are used for decoration, the boat owner is said to be "dressing ship." *Prestrung* flags are available for this purpose.

USE TIPS: A rudimentary knowledge of visual signaling is invaluable, particularly when radio communication isn't available. Refer to Publication 102, "International Code of Signals," published by the Defense Mapping Agency Hydrographic/Topographic Center, 6500 Brooks Lane, Washington, D.C. 20315, for specifics. A handy *self-adhesive international code flag* chart is available for quick reference.

BUYING TIPS: May be purchased as a set of 40 separate flags with storage bag or as a prestrung set for easy decorating.

INTERNATIONAL DISTRESS FLAG

ALSO KNOWN AS: Distress signal

DESCRIPTION: Rectangular orange flag with black square and ball.

USE: To signal true emergency situations only.

USE TIPS: Other ways to signal distress using flags are: International Code flags November (above) and Charlie (below) or square black flag flown above a ball or disk. Never use unless in serious trouble. For daytime use only.

BUYING TIPS: Distress flag should be large (3' sq.) for maximum visibility.

Fun Flag

ALSO KNOWN AS: Novelty flag

DESCRIPTION: An unofficial flag, including aforesaid "Wake" statement, and various symbolic tributes to special interests, such as fish species and martinis.

USE: To express yourself; similar to applying bumper stickers to your automobile or thinking up cute names for your vessel.

USE TIPS: Flying your martini glass upside down might be construed as an urgent request for more ice.

BUYING TIPS: Available, alas, everywhere.

Steaming Cone

ALSO KNOWN AS: Day shape

DESCRIPTION: Black conical form made of nylon fabric displayed with point down.

USE: For sailboats over 12 m (39.4') when under power with sails raised.

USE TIPS: Indicates that vessel is not entitled to right-of-way normally given to sailboats.

BUYING TIPS: Not required for coastal or inland sailors.

FLAG ACCESSORIES

Flagstaff

ALSO KNOWN AS: Flagpole

DESCRIPTION: Teak, chrome, or anodized aluminum, 14"–48" long, fits up to 1¼" sockets. Teak pole is slightly oversized to fit snugly into socket (see below). Also available in the *flagpole and rail mount kit,* which includes a stainless steel or chrome-plated zinc socket that clamps onto any ¾"–1"-diameter bow or stern rail.

USE: To display flags. Fits into permanently mounted or clamp-on flagstaff socket.

USE TIPS: The teak pole gives a more traditional "yacht" look, especially when used with the Betsy

Ross Yacht Ensign. Use clamp-on socket when you don't want a permanent installation, for example on a trailered boat.

BUYING TIPS: Teak pole may require some sanding to fit into socket. Stainless steel components are more likely to last longer than chrome-plated zinc.

Flagpole Socket

DESCRIPTION: Short, chrome-plated zinc clamp-on style or stainless steel cylinder that attaches to deck or rail by screws or through-bolts. Stainless

socket is either standard mount, which rises above a flanged base, or flush mount, which is recessed into the deck or mounting surface.

USE: To provide a base for the flagstaff.

USE TIPS: Permanent mount creates the most finished appearance.

BUYING TIPS: If you have a metal flagstaff, match it with the material of the base.

FLAG COVER

ALSO KNOWN AS: Burgee cover

DESCRIPTION: Water-resistant acrylic canvas cover that slips over the top of flagstaff.

USE: To protect flag when not in use.

USE TIPS: Cuts down on sun-fading and stains.

BUYING TIPS: An inexpensive item. Flag will probably last longer than cover, particularly if it's stowed away when the boat is unoccupied.

FLAG CLIP

ALSO KNOWN AS: Flag grip, flag tender, flag attachment, flag holder

DESCRIPTION: A variety of stainless steel, vinyl-coated metal and nylon springlike clips. Some come with screw eyes for mounting onto wood, metal, and fiberglass. Different sizes fit cables from ⅛" to ½".

USE: To attach flags to cylindrical objects, such as antennas, halyards, and shrouds. Makes removing flags easy and allows flags to rotate 360° without fouling.

USE TIPS: Use two clips per flag. May not be suitable in high winds or with heavy flags.

BUYING TIPS: Inexpensive and may come in handy for other purposes, so keep a few extras in your toolbox.

HALYARD RUNNER

DESCRIPTION: Small nylon cylinder that fits around wire stay or halyard.

USE: Used with nylon flag tender or hoisting line to send flags above arm's reach.

USE TIPS: Use with ⅜" or ½" tenders for loose fit on wire up to ¼" diameter.

BUYING TIPS: Inexpensive, sold in pairs.

BACKSTAY FLAG HALYARD KIT

DESCRIPTION: Kit includes polyester line, small block and cleat with wire clamps, and two bronze snaps. Fits 5/32"–⅜" wire.

USE: To enable sailors to fly flags from the backstay.

USE TIPS: An alternative to attaching flag to the leech of the aftermost sail.

BUYING TIPS: A simple solution to jury rigs, which usually do not work.

HORNS, BELLS, AND WHISTLES

electric trumpet horn

ABOUT HORNS AND BELLS

The U.S. Coast Guard requires that all boats carry a mechanical "means of making an efficient sound signal" to alert other boats of their position or possible dangers. It's not enough just to have a loud, commanding voice! Bells, whistles, horns, and/or gongs are appropriate. Stringent rules apply to boats over 12 m (39.4') and to tug and tow boats, but smaller vessels merely need to be capable of audibly signaling to their neighbors on the water.

Bells were also used to tell time aboard sailing vessels in the old days, when few sailors owned or wore watches. Time was kept by the ship's quartermaster, who turned a 30-minute hourglass at the beginning of each watch. With each half hour a bell was struck. An odd number of bells spelled the half hour and an even number marked the hour. Eight bells signaled the welcome end of each four-hour watch. With the advent of compressed-air devices and with virtually all boats having some electrical system and digital timekeeping devices, the traditional brass bell and rustic boatswain's whistle are outmoded.

Horn

ALSO KNOWN AS: Air horn, foghorn, sound signal

DESCRIPTION: A device that produces a loud sound either by forcing air through a reed system in a trumpet or by electronic means. May be activated by an electric motor, by a compressed-air canister, or by lung power. Air horns have long (about 18"), trumpetlike bells made of stainless steel or chrome or they may be made of high-impact plastic. Permanently installed horns, such as the *compact horn* (fits in the palm), the mini *hidden horn* (about 4" sq.), and the *electric trumpet horn* with bells up to 18" long, operate when electromagnets cause an internal diaphragm to vibrate loudly, giving off a loud sound. *Compressed-air horns* sometimes come with mounting brackets but are more typically handheld units the size of a soft-drink can, with plastic bells attached. Many of these contain CFCs, a gas that is harmful to the ozone layer of the atmosphere. An environmentally correct version of the compressed-air horn is the *rechargeable signal horn,* a device that comes with a minipump for building up pressure in the air canister. The traditional lung-powered *foghorn* is a foot-long aluminum or brass cone with a nylon or brass mouthpiece.

USE: Sound signaling. All these horns meet Coast Guard sound-signal requirements for boats under 12 m. Whether you choose a permanently mounted electric horn or the simple foghorn will be determined by your boat's configuration and where you go boating. Simpler, smaller boats need less-sophisticated horns.

USE TIPS: Electric and compressed-air horns have the highest decibel ratings, up to 120dB (normal conversation may register at 60dB, a twin-engine cruiser running wide open would be about 110dB, while painful is the only way to describe a noise level of 140dB). As with all signal devices, proper use at appropriate times goes without saying. Though tempting, refrain from "blasting" another boater simply because you don't like "the cut of his jib."

BUYING TIPS: Replacement canisters are available for compressed-air horns. Traditional foghorns, which are blown by people, are good backups to mechanical or electrical horns.

Fog Bell

ALSO KNOWN AS:
Brass fog bell

DESCRIPTION: 6"–8"-diameter brass bell with arm that slides into wall-mount bracket. Clapper may have lanyard eye.

USE: May satisfy Coast Guard sound-signal requirement, but mostly just a salty or decorative accessory.

USE TIPS: Slide-in bracket makes it easy to remove bell for storage. Remember to keep brass polish on hand if you want to keep your bell shipshape.

BUYING TIPS: A handmade lanyard would make a nice gift to go with this bell.

Tritone Whistle

ALSO KNOWN AS: Plastic whistle

DESCRIPTION: Yellow plastic device with one mouthpiece and three pipes.

USE: To hail water taxis, launches, or other boats in close quarters.

USE TIPS: Practice a few hornpipes while waiting (and waiting) for the water taxi.

BUYING TIPS: Probably doesn't meet sound-signal requirements for horns.

Boatswain's Whistle

ALSO KNOWN AS: Bo'sun's whistle

DESCRIPTION: Curved brass whistle fits in your hand and, when played correctly, produces an impressive and truly nautical series of sounds. Comes with instructions on how to pipe the calls.

USE: Fun. Order the crew to hoist the sails! Weigh anchor!

USE TIPS: Once the technique is mastered, you'll think of all kinds of uses.

BUYING TIPS: An inexpensive gift, not an essential item.

RADIOS AND ELECTRONIC COMMUNICATIONS

ABOUT RADIOS

Aside from being a convenient means of communication with the outside world, a marine radio is an important safety-equipment item. For most coastal or inland boaters, VHF (very high frequency) radios, installed or portable, are the most useful. VHF waves are short, confining the signals to line-of-sight, or about 25 miles. Power output is limited by law to 25 watts. Boaters who make long passages or go offshore frequently will want a more powerful radio, such as a single-sideband model. Comparing VHF models can be confusing in regard to numbers of channels, scanning functions, and power output. Most callers use only a few channels, including Channel 9, the Coast Guard–designated hailing channel, and Channel 16, which is reserved for emergency calls. Some models boast ten weather channels, but in reality there are only three U.S. weather channels operating. Scanning functions range from the simple, in which the receiver stops at a given frequency when it "hears" a message, to priority scanning, which focuses on a particular channel or two.

How strongly a VHF receives and transmits depends on its antenna and also its power output. For powerboaters, who often must speak over a loud engine, greater power (and speaker size) is desirable. Most boat owners install their VHFs at the helm or nav station; sailboaters often prefer to have one in the cabin and a second, portable unit for use in the cockpit or dinghy. Recently the Coast Guard has begun enforcing an FCC law that requires VHF radios to be licensed. Dealers should provide the appropriate Form 506. A handheld unit is considered an adjunct to the main radio (and referred to as Unit 1 on the air) and does not require an additional license unless it is the sole radio on board.

V HF RADIO

DESCRIPTION: FM radio transceiver with power output up to 25 watts that operates on a wavelength between 30 MHz and 300 MHz. The internal circuit, downsized considerably in modern radios, consists of a double-conversion superheter-

handheld VHF

odyne, which converts incoming signals to a lower frequency for better amplification.

TYPES:

Handheld VHF: Portable handset with built-in antenna and mike; measures anywhere from 6½" to 16½" in height (with the average about 12") and under 3" in width and 2" in depth. Weighs from 2 lbs. to 4 lbs. Ranges in power from 1 watt to 5 watts and operates on single rechargeable Nicad battery. Has an audio output between ¼ watt and ½ watt.

Full-size VHF: Larger, more powerful (25 watts) version of the handheld. Typically 5¾" wide, 2⅜" high, 7½" deep, weighing 7–12 lbs. Detachable hand mike. Average audio output of 4 watts.

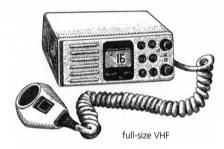
full-size VHF

USE: For short-range radio communiciation.

USE TIPS: For marine business, not chatter. Be brief.

BUYING TIPS: Because of confusing manufacturers' claims, check for a strong warranty on such things as waterproofness and durability.

S INGLE-SIDEBAND RADIO

ALSO KNOWN AS: SSB

DESCRIPTION: 150-watt, 12-volt AM radiotelephone that transmits on just one of three parts of its radio wave, concentrating its power in that single band, designated the AJ3 sideband by the FCC. Measuring about 11½" × 3½" × 9" deep and weighing 12 lbs. or more, a single sideband is slightly larger than but half again as heavy as most VHF radios.

USE: For long-distance transmitting and receiving.

USE TIPS: Can be operated at 20 or 60 watts to save power.

BUYING TIPS: Some models also function as shortwave receivers.

Mayday mike™

DESCRIPTION: Hand mike containing a voice chip; can be programmed numerically and alphabetically to record boat's name, registration, or documentation number. A red distress button (protected by a plastic cover) activates Channel 16 and broadcasts programmed message in synthesized voice through ship's VHF radio.

USE: No-hands, automatic method of broadcasting a continuing distress message on Channel 16.

USE TIPS: Will hook up to loran or GPS unit and broadcast your position simultaneously.

BUYING TIPS: Great idea, but this only works with one brand, called Shakespeare, at present.

Radar reflector

ALSO KNOWN AS: Collapsible radar reflector, passive radar reflector

DESCRIPTION: Complex three-dimensional grouping of circles or squares roughly the size of a basketball with surfaces perpendicular to each other. Lightweight, no more than a pound or two, made

of or clad with aluminum or other metal mesh. Rings or eyes at outermost edges provide attachment points for halyard. Some models fold flat for easy storage.

Circle version looks like a model of an atom; square version like a camping stove. Another radar reflector has the appearance and size of a white inflatable fender, 20" long × 8" in diameter with eyes at either end. Round shape keeps reflector from damaging rigging, sails, or mast.

USE: To catch and reflect—"echoes"—radar waves from passing vessels or airplanes, increasing your visibility to rescuers. A helpful safety device, the reflector does not require the vessel carrying it to be equipped with radar—it merely takes advantage of other boats' equipment.

USE TIPS: Hoist aloft on a three-point harness from above and a single one below for maximum effectiveness.

BUYING TIPS: Buy a collapsible model. Very inexpensive, very worthwhile.

Hailer

DESCRIPTION: Electronic gizmo about the size of a shoebox that is part intercom, part PA system, and part fog signal. Some models can be connected to as many as four remote intercom speakers.

USE: To communicate with other onboard "stations" or to meet Coast Guard Inland Rule that vessels must carry a bell and/or horn capable of making an "effective sound signal."

USE TIPS: An intercom is a good peace-of-mind device for keeping tabs on any kids aboard—if you have a very large boat.

BUYING TIPS: As a signal, a simple (non-CFC) aerosol horn or traditional ship's bell is cheaper, doesn't draw power, and can be heard at much greater distance than a hailer.

Hailer Speaker

DESCRIPTION: Remote loudspeaker, ranging in size from 5" × 5" to 9" × 11" and in power from 8 to 40 watts.

USE: To amplify talking and listening capability of a hailer.

USE TIPS: As sparingly as possible, please.

BUYING TIPS: Ask yourself, "How often will I need to shout across 250 yards?"

International Shortwave Receiver

ALSO KNOWN AS: Ham radio

DESCRIPTION: Radio that receives (and transmits) high-frequency shortwaves (from 1.6 MHz to 30 MHz). Memory can hold up to 500 frequencies and sometimes comes preprogrammed to most-used international frequencies. About the size of a portable radio. Runs on D-cell batteries or 120/220 AC power.

USE: To receive international news, weather, or other programming transmitted via shortwave.

USE TIPS: Transmitting requires an amateur radio license.

BUYING TIPS: More for entertainment than practical use these days.

Weather Radio

DESCRIPTION: FM crystal set with retractable antenna dedicated to receiving one of three NOAA weather channels. Small (as small as 5½" × 3½" × 1½") and powered by a 9-volt battery.

USE: To receive local and regional weather reports.

USE TIPS: Best source of marine weather.

BUYING TIPS: At $25 or less, this is an excellent investment.

— ENTERTAINMENT ELECTRONICS —

ABOUT MARINE STEREO EQUIPMENT

As with all marine electronics, there has been rapid improvement recently in the quality and variety of marine entertainment systems. Previously choices were limited to automobile/RV 12-volt equipment or their marinized equivalents. *Marinized* generally refers to gear made of noncorrosive metal parts and coated electronics components. New stereo equipment, including CD players, are often made specifically for the marine market and offer such features as buffers and shock mountings, "bump" bars to protect the controls, waterproof covers, and remote controls.

AM/FM CASSETTE PLAYER

ALSO KNOWN AS: Cassette receiver

DESCRIPTION: A sound reproduction system in which two or more channels (and multiple speakers) are used to simulate real-life sound. Combines AM and FM radio bands and stereo cassette player. Ranges in RMS (continuous output per channel) from 7.5 watts to 30 watts. Optional features include weather channels, Dolby noise reduction, fader controls (automatic balancing of front and rear speakers), and outlets for portable CD players.

USE: To receive AM and FM radio transmissions and to enjoy taped music.

USE TIPS: The nav station, with its ready source of power, is the most convenient location for stereo equipment.

BUYING TIPS: Because sound dissipates on board a boat more so than in the enclosed space of a car, go for the most powerful unit you can afford. Units with jacks for CDs will make it easier to join the current entertainment format.

COMPACT DISC PLAYER

ALSO KNOWN AS: CD player

DESCRIPTION: Stereophonic sound reproduction device that uses a low-intensity laser beam to "read" digital information on a compact disc and reconvert it to analog mode, in this case sound. Used in conjunction with an amplifier and speakers.

USE: To play CDs for listening pleasure.

USE TIPS: CDs are not indestructible; keep them in their plastic "jewel box" covers when not in use.

BUYING TIPS: Better suited for the gentler confines of a sailboat than a powerboat—unless at the dock.

CD CHANGER

DESCRIPTION: CD player that uses a carousel or cartridge to "stack" multiple CDs, usually from 6 to 12. Two types: Regular CD changer that operates through controls on certain models of cassette players; or, for those who do not want to buy a new cassette deck, there is a permanent "add-on" CD changer that operates through the FM radio, sending a signal to a preselected FM frequency by a patch through the antenna connection.

USE: To program hours of continuous play.

USE TIPS: Install in an out-of-the-way but easily accessible location.

BUYING TIPS: Add-on is an excellent way of adding CD capability to a still-good AM/FM cassette system.

STEREO AMPLIFIER

DESCRIPTION: Electronic device, 80 watts, with three-way input for hooking up to most marine stereos.

USE: To power up your marine stereo; also protects against circuit overload.

USE TIPS: Be sure your speakers can handle the extra power.

BUYING TIPS: You will need one if you decide to go the CD route.

Radio COVER WITH LATCH

waterproof cover

ALSO KNOWN AS: Radio waterproof faceplate

DESCRIPTION: Plastic or Lexan™ rectangular cover of various designs, 7½"–9" × 3½"; different models fit shafted, shaftless, and pull-out chassis radios. Some models have gaskets and some have pop-open latches.

USE: To provide waterproof protection for in-dash marine stereo radios.

USE TIPS: The more waterproof protection, the better.

BUYING TIPS: Make sure the cover fits your type of radio.

Noise SUPPRESSOR

ALSO KNOWN AS: Noise filter

DESCRIPTION: Combination coil and capacitor that blocks, respectively, AC and DC current. Installed between fuse and radio receiver.

USE: To filter noise conducted from engine, alternators, ignition system, etc.

USE TIPS: While suppressing noise to improve listening quality, be sure the radio is not interfering with other electronics, especially the loran, which may require their own suppressors.

BUYING TIPS: Before buying, determine when and where you use the radio (the cassette player gets the most use) and whether a filter is needed.

Stereo SPEAKER

DESCRIPTION: Transducer that converts electromagnetic energy to physical, in this case vibrations that re-create recorded sound.

USE: For remote transmission of sound from a stereo receiver.

USE TIPS: If you want cockpit music as well as sound down below, pair speakers with a four-channel stereo. Beware the magnetic field that many speakers give off—it can easily disrupt your compass. Interference can be neutralized by epoxying a second, smaller magnet to the speaker magnet.

BUYING TIPS: In terms of pure sound, speakers are the most important component of a stereo system; don't stint. Also, speaker cones must be of polypropylene or similar moisture-resistant material to stand up to the marine environment.

Tinned SPEAKER WIRE

ALSO KNOWN AS: Speaker wire

DESCRIPTION: Two-strand 20-gauge wire; the ends extending from insulation have been "bathed" in tin. Sold in red or black.

USE: To prevent corrosion in wires that run from receiver to speakers.

USE TIPS: Essential for marine entertainment equipment.

BUYING TIPS: Available in 100' lengths.

Stereo MOUNTS

DESCRIPTION: Various design containers and brackets, usually molded plastic, sized to accommodate most marine stereo sets.

TYPES:

Underdash radio housing: Boxlike molded plastic container, typically 9¾" × 8¾" × 4 ³⁄₁₆," that will accommodate most standard-shaft radios.

Gimbal stereo mount: White plastic casing mounted on U-shaped gimbal brackets that allow radio to stay balanced in a seaway. Smoked waterproof lift-up cover with neoprene gasket permits use of automobile (nonmarinized) radio. Accepts standard two-knob or rectangular DIN (Euro-style) chassis.

Weatherproof in-dash mount: Plastic frame with slide-open door with neoprene seal that mounts around hole in dashboard. About 9" × 4¼" × 1⅞"; stainless steel mounting hardware included.

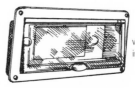

weatherproof
in-dash mount

USE: To install marine stereos in-dash, under the dash, or on a flush surface without requiring holes to be cut into the dash or bulkhead.

USE TIPS: Matter of space and personal taste whether you use separate brackets or in-dash mounting.

BUYING TIPS: Some stereo/radios come with their own pull-out antitheft bracket for easy removal.

ANTENNAS AND ANTENNA
ACCESSORIES

ABOUT ANTENNAS

The strength and quality of a radio's reception and transmission are determined more by the height, size, and type of antenna you use than by any other factor, including radio watts. Sailboat owners favor shorter antennas, 3'–5' long, mounted high on the masthead for maximum elevation. Powerboats generally use a longer, 8' whip, mounted on the transom or bridge. That is not the only difference. Because sailboats heel, they require an antenna whose signal is less powerful but emanates in a broader cone toward the horizon. The commonest sailboat antenna, in radio jargon, has a 3dB (decibel) *gain;* powerboats, which do not heel, do best with a 6dB- or 9dB-gain antenna, which has a more concentrated signal, beamed horizontally toward the horizon.

VHF ANTENNA

ALSO KNOWN AS: VHF whip

DESCRIPTION: Stainless steel whip or fiberglass pole (enclosing a solid copper conductor) often coated with urethane, with a band width compatible with the range of frequencies (30 MHz–300 MHz for VHF) built into the VHF transceiver. A marine antenna usually has a gain, measured in decibels, of 3dB to 6dB, with an occasional 8dB or 9dB version available. A whip may come in one-, two-, and three-piece sections and range in length from about 3' to almost 20', with one-piece, 3'–8' models enjoying the most popularity. While some can accept a maximum input as high as 50 watts, marine VHF radios are limited by law to 25 watts, providing a maximum range of about 25 miles. The female bottom fitting (*ferrule*) of the whip, which threads onto a mount, is made of plastic, nylon, or metal (often brass), and has 1-14 thread (1-14 refers to 14 threads per inch).

USE: To receive and transmit VHF radio signals (156 MHz–163 MHz for marine use) to and from a VHF radio.

USE TIPS: Powerboaters should install a whip where it has a clean line of sight to the horizon, but away from locations where it becomes a convenient handhold for passengers. Antennas should be wiped down regularly to clean off salt spray, and metal parts should be checked for corrosion.

BUYING TIPS: Racing sailors who do not want a masthead-mounted antenna should consider getting a lower 3dB-gain 8' whip to mount on the transom; the "fatter" signal will have a better chance of reaching its target when the boat heels.

Emergency VHF Antenna

ALSO KNOWN AS: Emergency antenna

DESCRIPTION: Backup antennas of various design, 10"–19" whip, or sometimes a simple stainless steel coil connected to a PL-259 cable connector (see page 18). While most are designed to hook into existing coaxial cable, some models are meant to be attached directly to the VHF radio. Limited range—about 15 miles maximum.

USE: To provide an emergency backup in the event your main antenna fails.

USE TIPS: If you do not have an emergency antenna, a 19" length of coat hanger or similar wire can be inserted into the antenna socket. Be careful not to short it out by contact with other metal fittings at the back of the radio.

BUYING TIPS: Because higher is better, the kind that comes with its own length of cable and/or a PL-259 connector is superior to the kind that plugs directly into the radio. Direct plug-in type may also interfere with transmission.

AM/FM Antenna

ALSO KNOWN AS: Radio antenna, aerial

DESCRIPTION:
Metal coil, either stainless steel or other conductive metal, that attracts radio signals. Can be bare metal or metal enclosed in fiberglass or some other protective coating.

TYPES:

Steel whip: Slim, lightweight 17-4PH stainless steel (see Appendix A) whip, 34" or 56" in length, mounted to nickel-plated post. Coil is base-mounted in a stainless-steel housing sealed with an O-ring. Rated at 250 watts, 3dB gain on AM. Comes with L-shaped mounting bracket and can be mounted on the mast, stern pulpit, or cabin top. Coaxial cable is extra.

Fiberglass whip: Familiar white fiberglass antenna with coil sealed inside one-piece casing. Ranges from 36" to 39" in length. Comes with polycarbonate "lift and lay" mount (U-shaped bracket on a round base) and stainless steel hardware for deck mounting. Rated at 3dB gain on AM. Comes with 7' or 12' coaxial cable.

Flexible antenna: Small black antenna, rubber with stainless steel base, 11" or 14" in length. Comes with 4'–6' of cable and stainless-steel mounting hardware. Can be adjusted for top or side mounting. Nearly unbreakable.

USE: To receive AM and FM radio signals.

USE TIPS: For sailboats, one good antenna, mounted at the top of the mast, is the best way to go. Powerboats, with more mounting surfaces and, often, more electronics, can carry two or more, which provides a measure of safety in the event one is broken or disabled.

BUYING TIPS: The sealed fiberglass whip is more weatherproof but not as efficient as the stainless steel whip—the type used on Coast Guard rescue vessels.

GPS ANTENNA

ALSO KNOWN AS: Mushroom antenna

DESCRIPTION: Encapsulated boxed or mushroom-shaped antenna, about 8½" high, 5" in diameter, with receiver capable of tracking, usually, five satellites, with updates every second or so. Most can interface with NMEA 0183 lorans (see page 45), fish finders, plotters, etc. Fits standard 1" antenna mounts. Some models include 30' or so of connecting cable.

USE: To receive satellite transmissions and transmit them to a GPS receiver for three-way fix.

USE TIPS: Because GPS antennas like to be level, some operators fix them to adjustable mounts or radar brackets on the stern rail or (on a sailboat) the backstay.

BUYING TIPS: As with any electronics, your best bet for compatibility is to stick with a single brand.

LORAN ANTENNA

DESCRIPTION: Small whip antenna, 3', 4', or 8' in length, either stainless steel or white fiberglass, with ⅜" 24-thread base fitting; will fit on standard 1" antenna mount with a loran antenna adaptor (see page 17).

USE: To pick up radio transmissions from loran-C radio transmitters and convey them to loran receiver for position finding and route plotting.

USE TIPS: Smaller stainless steel whips are almost as effective and less obtrusive than 8' fiberglass antennas; mount on stern pulpit or rail.

BUYING TIPS: Because the loran-C system may be phased out as early as 1998, a big investment in loran equipment is not recommended.

MARINE TV ANTENNA

ALSO KNOWN AS: Television antenna, VHF/UHF antenna, aerial

DESCRIPTION: Metallic device that attracts (and sometimes amplifies) electromagnetic waves. Usually circular with diameter ranging from 10" to 25" and base, or ferrule, several inches long with 1-14 female thread that fits on standard marine antenna mount. Some makes come with coaxial cable (75-ohm minimum) and own mounting gear.

TYPES:

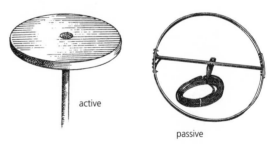

active

passive

Active: The most common type of marine TV antenna is electric-powered; a coupler feeds 12 volts DC (and/or 110 volts AC) power up the antenna feedline to an amplifier. Power consumption is low—83 mA at 12 volts DC. Antenna is encased in ABS UV-resistant plastic housing 1 ¾"–6" thick. Some models contain rotator (of dubious value while swinging on a mooring); others, such as Shakespeare's Seawatch 2030, are omnidirectional.

Passive: Non-electric-powered, often hoop-shaped aluminum antenna, which feeds signal directly down its feedline to a television. Can be fixed on standard 1-14 mount or hoisted up the mast of a sailboat. Improves VHF (Channels 2–13) reception, but is less effective for UHF.

USE: To receive VHF and UHF waves for transmission to a television receiver.

USE TIPS: Getting good TV at sea can be difficult; many boaters use their TV primarily to show videos. Passive, hoistable antennas are popular with those who prefer a temporary, rather than permanent, antenna.

BUYING TIPS: Get one that has been thoughtfully designed for marine use, with strand cable (if included), corrosion-resistant base (preferably nylon), and a solid housing (no vents to admit moisture).

CELLULAR PHONE ANTENNA

ALSO KNOWN AS: Cellular antenna

DESCRIPTION: Smaller, 4' and under, antenna, either stainless steel or urethane-coated fiberglass (with brass and copper radiators) capable of receiving and sending on a frequency range between 806 MHz and 900 MHz. Various shapes and designs, including whip with 1-14 chrome-plated ferrule for standard mounts and rail-mount version with plastic clamp and thumbscrews on the base. Gain of 3.5dB or 6dB. Also available in a 12" portable model with a suction-cup base for easy mounting. Some require special mounts. Coax lead-in is RG-8X cable.

USE: To receive and transmit telephone waves.

USE TIPS: Many models also work with regular 800 MHz radio telephone.

BUYING TIPS: As with any antenna, buy one specifically designed for the marine market.

SAILBOAT MAST MOUNTING BRACKET

ALSO KNOWN AS: Sailboat mast mount

DESCRIPTION: Wedge-shaped aluminum bracket, 15¾" × 3" × 4". Flange with holes at inboard (thicker) end permits bolting to mast; 1-14 male-thread fitting topside of outboard end accepts female thread on antenna ferrule.

USE: To mount TV antenna off the deck.

USE TIPS: As with most antennas, the higher the better.

BUYING TIPS: For smaller (under 15" diameter) antennas.

ANTENNA MOUNT

DESCRIPTION: Standard mount has 1" male-threaded post, about 4" high, on base of varying design, for mounting to flush surfaces or ⅞" or 1" rails. Made of stainless steel, aluminum, chrome-plated brass, or nylon.

TYPES:

Rail antenna mount: Rail mounts of various designs and materials permit antenna installation without drilling. Most common type, made of aluminum, stainless steel, or nylon, is a threaded (1") post with band or U-bolt that fits around ⅞" or 1" rails

rail antennna mount

(metric sizes are available for foreign-made boats) and is secured by screws. A second version, made of white polypropylene, is either round or rectangular and consists of two halves (that make a hole) that snap over rail and are secured with a wing nut.

Fixed antenna mount: Stainless-steel pedestal mount (circular base with 4" tube); 1-14 pitch threads accepts standard antennas. For affixing to radar arch, flying bridge, or any flush surface. Works with TV, VHF, loran, GPS antennas. Also available in larger version to accommodate 1½" SSB-type antenna. 12" and 24" tube extensions are available as options.

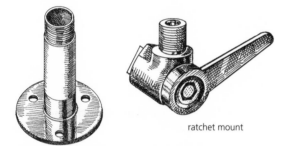

ratchet mount

fixed antenna mount

Ratchet mount: Rail or fixed mount base of various materials (nylon, stainless steel, chrome-plated brass) with ratchet feature that allows threaded post, and an antenna, to be adjusted to one or more angles. Most fit either ⅞" or 1" rail or have base measuring about 3¾" × 2" for permanent installation. Most ratchets have handles; some, adjustable by Allen wrench, do not.

Swivel antenna mount: Chrome-plated brass or zamac (see Appendix A) mount that installs permanently on deck or other vertical surface. Has dual-joint swivel base that permits antenna to be raised and lowered (laid down) and threads for standard 1" antenna. Comes with stainless steel hardware.

Loran antenna mount: Many all-purpose mounts take loran antennas. The necessary feature is an internal feed and cable exit hole. Portable aluminum loran mount has stainless steel wing nut for fixing to ¾"–1" rail.

Loran antenna adapter: White nylon reducer that permits attaching of ⅜" 24-thread loran whip on a standard 1" × 14" mount.

USE: To attach an antenna to the boat.

USE TIPS: Match the mount material with the antenna base material as closely as possible to avoid corrosion.

BUYING TIPS: Some mounts are rated for antennas 8' and under; if yours is longer, make sure the mount will support it.

Laydown Hook

ALSO KNOWN AS: Laydown antenna hook, antenna hook

DESCRIPTION: Stainless-steel hook, 3½" long, 1½" wide with two predrilled holes for mounting to vertical surface.

USE: To mount in cockpit to hold antenna lowered by swivel mount.

USE TIPS: Also keeps lowered antenna secure during trailering.

BUYING TIPS: Best means of securing a lowered antenna. A natural complement to a swivel mount.

Antenna Standoff

ALSO KNOWN AS: Standoff bracket, upper antenna bracket

DESCRIPTION: Molded plastic bracket with U-shaped depression in outboard end and detachable fastening latch. Sized to take either 1"- or 1½"-diameter antenna; some come with insert for larger-size antenna. Fastening hardware included.

USE: To fasten to flying bridge or other high structure to provide additional support to longer antennas.

USE TIPS: Helps keep antenna vertical for maximum efficiency.

BUYING TIPS: Extra support is advisable for longer VHF antennas and on high-powered speedboats.

Antenna Extension

ALSO KNOWN AS: Extension mast

DESCRIPTION: Lightweight but strong fiberglass insert; 1½" diameter, with 1-14 male and female and female threads at lower and upper ends, respectively. Comes in 4', 8', and (in heavy-duty version) 13' lengths.

USE: To insert between antenna base and mount for added antenna height.

USE TIPS: Some extensions require special mounting kits.

BUYING TIPS: You could just buy a longer antenna.

Antenna Cable

ALSO KNOWN AS: Coax, coax cable, coaxial cable

DESCRIPTION: High-frequency transmission cable consisting of an inner core of tinned-copper conducting wire made of either solid or multiple strands inside an insulating sleeve (the dielectric),

which, in turn, is surrounded by a tinned-copper braid topped by a vinyl or PVC jacket. An incoming signal is carried between the inner conductor and the braid, which also blocks out foreign signals.

USE: To transmit antenna signals to the proper receiver.

USE TIPS: Coax comes in a bewildering array of sizes, materials, and resistances. Generally the larger the size (diameter), the less the signal loss. Much electronic equipment comes equipped with RG-58 or RG-8x cable (also known as RG-8 *"mini"*), which is adequate for runs of 25' or less. For longer runs, larger (and lower loss) RG-8AU works better. Highest quality is RG-213U, which has a thoroughly waterproof and UV-resistant jacket, but is expensive and difficult to work with.

BUYING TIPS: Buy the best marine coax you can; when in doubt, follow the manufacturer's (electronics or antenna) recommendations. Some cable comes with a foam inner insulating sleeve, which will not do for a marine environment because it attracts moisture; buy only cable with a solid polyethylene dielectric. Also unacceptable is a vinyl outer jacket, which will soon begin to crack; make sure the jacket is PVC, which is designated a *noncontaminating jacket*. Tightness of the weave in the copper braid is also important. 95% is adequate, but 98% is preferable. Finally most marine cable is rated 50-ohm, which is fine. TV antennas, however, require 72-ohm coax.

Coax Connectors

PL-259 connector

ALSO KNOWN AS: PL-259 connectors, coaxial connectors

DESCRIPTION: Thimble-sized and shaped fittings made of brass with alloy (nickel, silver) coating;

various designs about 1" long, ½" in diameter, with male and/or female connection features.

TYPES:

PL-259: Standard connector for RG-8U and RG-213U cable, with hole for soldering to cable. Also available as *solderless connector,* which crimps on but will eventually corrode and thus is best used for temporary connections.

Barrel connector (Also known as *PL-258* or *double-female connector*): this joins two standard PL-259 connectors.

Cable adaptor: Reducing connector for joining PL-259 connectors and RG-8X or RG-58 cable.

90° antenna connector: Right-angle joint eliminates bends in coax, which can cause signal loss; for use where turns are necessary, such as at the back of a radio.

USE: To connect coax cable to electronics or to another length of cable.

USE TIPS: For the best-protected connection, solder the joint, coat the connector with a waterproof silicone treatment, and top off with heat-shrink tube.

BUYING TIPS: Always match the connector to the cable size. If you cannot find what you need in a marine outlet, try an electronics store.

THROUGH-DECK/ BULKHEAD CONNECTORS

ALSO KNOWN AS: Through-deck fittings, cable fittings, deck feed-throughs, coax fitting, coax connector

DESCRIPTION: Various design circular fittings of coated brass or plastic with openings sized to pass through most coaxial cable, although some are for a specific size cable. Most have rubber seals for waterproofing.

TYPES:

radio connector through-deck fitting

drill through-deck fitting

Cable outlet: Chrome-plated brass fittings with either rubber seal or grommet for waterproof passage of cable; various sizes to accommodate different cable sizes. Usually have three predrilled holes for fastening with #4 or #5 flathead bolts.

Radio connecter through-deck fitting: Brass tube, 2½" long, ½" in diameter, with rubber gaskets for sealing at each end. Upper (deck-side) end is a reducer that accepts standard antenna coax; lower (inboard) end accepts male-to-male cable extending from a radio. You can get an optional cap with chain to plug the fitting when it is not in use.

Plastic cable fitting: Various size circular hard plastic plugs, 1"–2½" in diameter with openings for different sizes of cable from ¾" to 1½" (for passing cable with factory-installed connectors). Standard color is white, but available in black as well.

Drill through-deck fitting: White plastic mount with solid rubber diaphragm that can be drilled to accommodate various diameter cable.

USE: To create a waterproof conduit to run coaxial cable from topside through a deck or through a bulkhead to the appropriate electronics device.

USE TIPS: Plastic fittings with rubber diaphragms work well and are the choice of most boat owners, although some might prefer the brass outlet for aesthetics. Some experts recommend against the radio connector as an unnecessary additional break in the cable and advise using a plastic fitting instead.

BUYING TIPS: Get the plastic kind.

CABLE CAP

ALSO KNOWN AS:
Deck receptacle cap

DESCRIPTION: Various design circular plastic or nylon plugs with holes for one or two cables.

USE: To plug (and cover up) holes in deck or bulkheads drilled to pass coaxial cable.

USE TIPS: Not needed with drill-through or perfectly sized deck and bulkhead connectors.

BUYING TIPS: Some through-deck fittings come with their own caps.

CABLE FEEDER

ALSO KNOWN AS: Cable feed-through

DESCRIPTION: Small stainless steel or plated brass bracket measuring 1½" × ¾" with raised groove that accommodates either RG-58 or RG-59 coaxial cable. Has predrilled holes and two #6 screws for mounting.

USE: To mount to bulkhead or other flat surface to pin down cable as it feeds through an access hole.

USE TIPS: Handy replacement in the event cable comes loose from back of a radio set, etc.

BUYING TIPS: Inexpensive item—get two just in case.

ANTENNA GROUNDING SYSTEM

ALSO KNOWN AS: Lightning arrestor

DESCRIPTION: Alloy-coated brass cylinder, 2" long, ½" diameter, with a screw penetrating one side

(for attaching a side cable leading to the boat's grounding system). Installs in-line along the coaxial cable.

USE: To prevent static buildup and thus theoretically protect antennas from a lightning strike. Also, again theoretically, to divert electrical energy from your coax cable (and electronics) to a ground in the event of a strike.

USE TIPS: Many antennas have a built-in ground. Lightning experts tend to doubt the efficacy of lightning arrestors in diverting an actual strike. An overall grounding system is the best protection for persons and the boat hull. The arrestor may prevent static buildup, but, as another interruption of the coax, may cause some signal loss.

BUYING TIPS: On balance, a device of dubious value.

VHF ANTENNA ADAPTER

ALSO KNOWN AS:
Handheld adapter, jack connector, BNC plug to UHF jack connector

DESCRIPTION: Coated brass reducing connector; one end fits into the "rubber duck" antenna mount on the handheld, the other is compatible to receive a PL-259 connector.

USE: To improve reception/transmission by permitting a handheld VHF to be connected to an existing deck- or mast-mounted antenna.

USE TIPS: The likeliest use would be if your permanent VHF or electrics have been disabled. Otherwise the rubber duck or an optional telescoping antenna should do the job.

BUYING TIPS: Some brands, including ICOM and Motorola, require their own connectors.

Antenna Switch

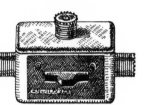

ALSO KNOWN AS:
Coaxial switch

DESCRIPTION: Single-pole, double-throw switch.

USE: To allow switching between two units and one antenna or two units and two antennas.

USE TIPS: Provides the capability for using a backup antenna, either for better reception or in the event one gets damaged. If it is two units and one antenna you are after, go with the band separator (see this page), which has an isolater to protect your AM/FM radio during VHF transmission.

BUYING TIPS: Requires separate purchase of RG-58 coax jumper, which includes 3' of cable with PL-259 fittings on each end.

FM/VHF Switch and Antenna

ALSO KNOWN AS: Two-way switch

DESCRIPTION: Switch with output for one AM/FM radio and one VHF radio plus an emergency backup antenna.

USE: To connect radios to both the main antenna and the emergency antenna.

USE TIPS: Extra insurance that your radios are always connected to one antenna or another.

BUYING TIPS: Good idea for single-antenna boats.

Band Separator

ALSO KNOWN AS:
Antenna splitter

DESCRIPTION: In-line device, with coil, that isolates VHF from AM/FM signal. Inserted in feedline from VHF antenna. Comes with 3' of VHF cable, 10' of AM/FM cable, and connectors to VHF and AM/FM stereo radio.

USE: To permit use of one antenna for both VHF and AM/FM functions; isolator is necessary to protect radio during VHF transmission.

USE TIPS: For those (especially sailors) who do not want to clutter their masthead with antennas.

BUYING TIPS: Cheaper than buying two antennas.

Splashproof Junction Box

ALSO KNOWN AS: Quick-connect junction box

DESCRIPTION: Water-resistant aluminum box with white enamel finish and screw-down lid, com-

monly 2" × 2" × 13/16" (six terminal blocks) or 2⅜" × 4⅜" × 1¼" (ten terminal blocks); smaller version has ports for two ¼" cables, the larger has holes for ten ⅜" cables.

USE: For belowdecks wiring connections. Stripped wire ends are inserted into block and screwed down.

USE TIPS: For light-duty wiring, such as for lights or an external GPS unit, and not for power-intensive uses, such as running a windlass.

BUYING TIPS: Anticipate and buy a junction box with sufficient terminal blocks to meet your future needs.

RADIO ACCESSORIES

HANDHELD VHF CADDY

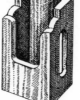

ALSO KNOWN AS: VHF case, VHF rack

DESCRIPTION: PVC or teak holder open on top, some with U-shaped cutout on front panel; mounts to bulkhead or other vertical surface with two screws. Sized to hold most VHF handhelds (see page 8).

USE: To secure handheld VHF in cockpit or down below when not in use.

USE TIPS: Make a habit of always returning radio to its caddy.

BUYING TIPS: Some PVC models have a slot for storing the antenna when it is removed.

ELECTRONIC-EQUIPMENT MOUNTING BRACKET

DESCRIPTION: Fixed or swiveling mount, often goalpost-shaped, with slots for receiving various electronic devices. Made of rust-resistant plastic or Teflon®-coated aluminum.

TYPES:

VHF/CB/Depth finder rail mount: Viselike polypropylene clamp that fastens most bracket-mounted electronics to either ⅞" or 1" rail. Sold in pairs.

Screwless windshield bracket: Plastic bracket, sometimes known as *Console Mate,* that adheres to powerboat windshield via suction cups.

Swivel mount: Triangular nylon base with round socket that accepts the pedestal of an existing bracket mount; ratchet action permits 360° turning. Fastens to horizontal surface with stainless steel screws.

swivel bracket

Swivel bracket: Brackets of various design with a swivel base; made of plastic or Teflon®-coated aluminum. Some have locks to secure electronics and most require drilling for fasteners.

USE: To permit swiveling of electronics for best viewing angle.

USE TIPS: Best for powerboaters; sailors can go with more permanent installations at the nav station.

BUYING TIPS: Look for models with locks and quick-release features so that gear can be removed for safekeeping.

Waterproof PVC Pouch

DESCRIPTION: Clear plastic bag with rollover seal on bottom; safety lanyard attached.

USE: To protect a handheld VHF from weather or a wet hand while permitting operation.

USE TIPS: Always wrap the lanyard around your wrist.

BUYING TIPS: One size fits all, but custom pouches can be bought for some radio models.

TELEPHONE ACCESSORIES

Telephone Cable Cordset

ALSO KNOWN AS: Phone cord

DESCRIPTION: Yellow vinyl three-conductor cord with male and female connectors with large, moisture-resistant covers. Sold in 12', 25', and 50' lengths.

USE: To connect dock phone outlet to hull phone inlet.

USE TIPS: If you berth at a marina, measure the distance between the dockside outlet and your boat to determine the length you need; 12' might be too short, 50' too long.

BUYING TIPS: Marine-quality telephone cord comes with a 5-year warranty.

Television Cable

DESCRIPTION: Standard 75-ohm RG-59 coaxial cable consisting of solid copper conductor and tinned-copper braid in a white PVC plastic jacket.

Includes slip-on connections for hull-inlet and dock-outlet ends and heavy-duty boots, or covers, at each end. Sold in 250' reels.

USE: To connect a boat's cable TV inlet to the dockside cable TV outlet.

USE TIPS: Although 250' might seem too much for some boats, any extra can be used as a backup where RG-58 coax cable is used.

BUYING TIPS: As with all coax, buy marine-grade cable for your TV.

Telephone Plug

DESCRIPTION: Plastic and metal fitting at the end of a telephone cord with either prongs or receptacle.

TYPES:

Male plug: Three-pronged plug, two of which have flanges for "locking" in a dockside outlet.

Female connector: Fitting with three receptacles for connecting to a boat's telephone inlet.

USE: To connect a telephone cord to either an inlet or an outlet; as replacements or making your own custom cordset.

USE TIPS: As with other dockside connections, plugs should have flanges that lock with a slight sideways turn.

BUYING TIPS: For watertight connection, purchase the optional cover for each plug and connector.

WATERPROOF TELEPHONE CONNECTOR COVER

ALSO KNOWN AS: Plug and connector cover

DESCRIPTION: Bullet-shaped plastic capsule open at both ends and sized to fit standard telephone plugs and connectors.

USE: To slip over plug or connector to seal out moisture.

USE TIPS: Any outdoor connector should have a waterproof covering.

BUYING TIPS: Must be bought separately from plugs; one or two spares might be a good idea.

TELEPHONE ADAPTER

DESCRIPTION: Short cord with either a male plug or a female connector at one end and a standard modular telephone jack at the other.

TYPES:

Male adapter: Cord with three-pronged locking plug at one end and modular jack at the other.

Female adapter: Cord with three-slot female connector at one end and a modular jack at the other.

USE: Male adapter permits a phone to be plugged directly into a dockside cordset without an inlet; female adapter permits a modular phone line to connect to a boat inlet.

USE TIPS: Male adapter allows you to use a phone aboard a boat that does not have an installed inlet, and the female adapter connects a phone to an inlet.

BUYING TIPS: The male adapter could help as a backup, but why use the temporary link provided by the female adapter when you can just direct-wire to a permanent jack?

TELEPHONE/ CABLE TV HULL INLET

DESCRIPTION: Waterproof inlet made of either 316 stainless steel (see Appendix A) or plastic resin with stainless steel trim containing both telephone and cable TV connections. Cover snaps down for waterproof seal when not in use. Meets FCC and UL standards for boats and RVs.

USE: To hook up telephone and cable TV at dockside.

USE TIPS: Combination telephone/TV inlet requires just one through-hull.

BUYING TIPS: Be sure the inlet you select is approved for marine use—not all are.

CHAPTER TWO

NAVIGATION

COMPASSES

ABOUT COMPASSES

Navigating, getting from point A to point B, requires a fixed reference point. Early travelers, including the ancient seafaring Phoenicians (and the Three Wise Men), relied on the stars, which were found to have a repeatable pattern according to the season. One in particular, Polaris, the North Star, became a favorite of sailors because of its dependability and year-round visibility. Some millennia later humans began to explore the earth's magnetic forces, invisible but as predictable as the firmament. Lodestone, a mineral found in Mesopotamia, was magnetic and, when floated on a piece of wood, aligned itself on a north-south axis, one end pointing closely toward the North Star. Lodestone could impart its magnetism to iron filings rubbed against it, and sailors began magnetizing these slivers, attaching them to a stick, and floating them in a container of water. These crude compasses operated on the same principle as today's mariner's compass. Like the lodestone, a compass needle does not point to geographic, or true, north, but rather along the magnetic meridian. (The exception is an imaginary line, called the *agonic line,* that runs from a point off the west coast of Florida up through the Great Lakes.) The angular difference between the direction of magnetic and true north and a given position on earth is called variation, which is measured in degrees and which is either added to or subtracted from a compass reading to determine real north as recorded on maps and charts.

COMPASS

DESCRIPTION: Spherical container, consisting of a solid (often plastic) bowl filled with fluid (generally an oil), topped by a clear glass or plastic watertight dome for viewing. Fixed inside, on a horizontal plane, is a circular compass card, or dial, of aluminum or baked enamel marked off in 360° and gradations thereof, as well as the cardinal points (north, northwest, etc.). A magnetic needle, suspended on a pivot, rotates atop the card. The whole unit is mounted to either an interior or an exterior gimbal to remain level at sea. A lubber line, a marking on the bowl parallel to the boat's keel, enables the helmsman to steer a course. Except for some handheld compasses, most have 12-volt powered lighting.

TYPES:

Binnacle-mount compass: Compass mounted on a pedestal, often part of the helm, with stainless steel base and *dish* (or back-read) compass card; common on larger, wheel-steered boats. Some are removable, and many have hoods to protect against spray.

Bracket-mounted compass: Midsize (5" diameter) compass mounted in a bracket rather than permanently installed in a bulkhead or binnacle. Two thumbscrews can be loosened for easy removal.

Bulkhead-mount compass: Common on sailboats, this compass is installed vertically on interior or exterior bulkhead, usually facing the tiller or wheel. Has ei-

binnacle-mount compass   bulkhead-mount compass

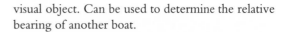

ther *dome* (direct-reading) card or a combination back- and front-reading dial.

Flush-mount compass: Low-profile compass that is mounted horizontally, usually with a direct, or front-reading, card.

Fluxgate compass: Electronically senses earth's magnetic field. Provides either analog or digital readout of magnetic direction; can be integrated with other onboard electronics.

fluxgate compass

Powerboat compass: (W 194/BUS 144,145) Standard compass, but with low viscosity fluid and modified card suspension to dampen agitation and vibration from a pounding hull at high speed; often has oversized numerals for easier reading.

USE: To determine magnetic direction (and, by deduction, true direction) at sea.

USE TIPS: Also handy for checking how quickly and efficiently your sailboat tacks through the wind under different sail.

BUYING TIPS: This is an important piece of equipment—don't scrimp, but don't feel compelled to buy the most expensive, jewel-pivoted model either. Any good mid-range model will give the same dependable service.

HAND-BEARING COMPASS

DESCRIPTION: Handheld compass, either regular or fluxgate, that often can be locked onto a single bearing; sometimes contains stopwatch.

USE: To find the bearing (direction) of a distant

visual object. Can be used to determine the relative bearing of another boat.

USE TIPS: Helpful for keeping an eye on the competition during a race.

BUYING TIPS: Nice to have one as an emergency backup. Conventional type doesn't require batteries.

ABOUT CORRECTING COMPASSES

Correcting your compass, or swinging ship, as it's called, is a good idea, especially for long-distance cruisers, anytime a compass is installed or reinstalled, a new boat purchased, or just as a periodic check. Error, or deviation, is often introduced via magnetic interference from metal or electronic gear (or something as simple as a tool placed in the vicinity of a compass) or can occur during installation if a compass is not lined up with the boat's keel. There are several ways boaters can check their own compasses. One is to align a boat with a range, consisting of two or more shoreside structures, running on an east-west and north-south axis, and compare the known bearing with that measured by the compass. Another is to check the ship's compass by means of a smaller handheld compass. If consistent or significant error is found, it's best to call in a professional compass adjuster. However, some of the professional's tools are available, in downsized form, to the regular boat owner.

PELORUS

ALSO KNOWN AS: Compass corrector

DESCRIPTION: Device of various designs that resembles a handbearing compass, but with a card that is not magnetized and can be turned manually. Dial is fitted with a movable U-shaped sighting arm.

USE: To take horizontal bearings of charted objects for comparison with magnetic compass reading.

USE TIPS: Best left to skilled navigators or compass adjusters.

BUYING TIPS: It's more cost-effective to rent one—along with the professional adjuster.

COMPASS COVER

DESCRIPTION: Plastic or rubber dome-shaped snap-on cover in various sizes, parallel to compass sizes and models.

USE: To protect marine compass from weather and UV degradation.

USE TIPS: Keep the cover on unless actively using the compass.

BUYING TIPS: Many compasses have covers specifically designed for them, but generic equivalents are available; look for one, possibly with a hole for a lanyard, that is easily removed.

—— NAVIGATION EQUIPMENT ——

KNOTMETER

ALSO KNOWN AS: Speed/log, speedometer, speed indicator, knotlog

DESCRIPTION: Device of various design that measures and displays boat speed. Consists of knotmeter dial, with readouts from 0 to 15 knots or 20 knots up to 40 or even to 99 knots (and sometimes in mph as well). Some have resettable log or tripmeter, similar to an automobile odometer, and some display other functions, such as water temperature.

TYPES:

Hydraulic: Simplest and most common type of log. It uses a pitot device, an open-ended tube, with a smaller hole on one end that points into a boat's slipstream and measures the pressure of water flowing through it.

pitot tube

Mechanical/electronic: Knotmeter with sensor consisting of a paddle wheellike device on the hull bottom that translates movement of water into an electrical impulse that is measured and converted to speed in knots or miles per hour.

USE: To tell you how fast a boat is moving through the water (but not necessarily over the ground), a necessary ingredient in piloting.

USE TIPS: Check the accuracy of your knotmeter by running a measured mile (some charts will have one designated) on a day when there are few or known variables, such as current. If there is a problem, it might be attributable to location of the log on the hull.

BUYING TIPS: The hydraulic type is cheaper and about as reliable as the mechanical/electronic kind.

KNOTSTICK

ALSO KNOWN AS: Knot log, sailboat speedometer

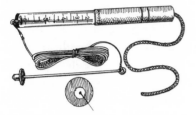

DESCRIPTION: Calibrated clear plastic 12" tube (called a read head) connected to trolling unit by 20' nylon cord with swivels at either end. The trolling unit consists of a calibrated disk dragged behind the boat. The nylon cord attaches to the spring-balanced read head on which speed is indicated by hatch marks similar to a thermometer.

USE: A simple device for measuring sailboat speeds that is supposed to be accurate within 0.2 knots.

USE TIPS: Handy for checking the calibration of electronic speedometers.

BUYING TIPS: The knotstick may not be high-tech enough for serious racers, but is fine for the curious sailor who does not need exact speed readings.

MULTIDATA DISPLAY

ALSO KNOWN AS: Multifunction display, tri-data, bidata

DESCRIPTION: Instrument that combines two or more functions, such as wind direction/speed or depth/speed. Sometimes incorporates data from another instrument via connector.

USE: To combine information on one display for more convenience and better comprehension.

USE TIPS: Find one that combines the information you use most. A sportfisherman, for example, might want a mulitdata system that combines depth, speed, log, and water temperature.

BUYING TIPS: Avoid mixing brands despite claims of electronic compatibility.

DEPTH SOUNDER

digital depth sounder

ALSO KNOWN AS: Fishfinder, depth meter, echo sounder

DESCRIPTION: High-frequency transducer connected to a sounder and an instrument panel with readouts (either digital or analog) measured in feet, fathoms (6' increments), or meters. The transducer receives a burst of AC energy from the sounder, converts it into a sonic beam that bounces off the sea bottom or other submerged objects, such as fish, then reconverts the reflection to AC energy and transmits it to the sounder for a reading. There are several kinds of transducers, but the most common is the piezoelectric, which is usually made of a polycrystalline ceramic (synthetic crystal) within a protective coating and which is attached to the boat—on the transom, through-the-hull, or inside the hull bottom. Available in various frequencies (and beam diameters), from 50 kHz to 200 kHz. Effective, depending on frequency, from about 2⅕' to 400'.

USE: To determine the distance between the underside of the boat or keel and the sea bottom (some models have programmable shoal alarms), or to locate underwater objects or fish.

USE TIPS: Lower frequencies are absorbed less by the water and thus are more effective for deep-water applications. Sailors looking for hazards to navigation and the average fisherman looking for fish should use the higher, more focused frequencies, closer to the 200 kHz range.

BUYING TIPS: A godsend to fishermen, and a safety and navigation tool for both powerboaters and sailors.

TRANSDUCER BUBBLE

DESCRIPTION: Clear plastic half-globe, 7½" diameter, 3¼" depth, that fits over most transducers. Fastens by epoxy glue to inside bottom of hull.

USE: To permit mounting of a transducer without drilling holes in the hull.

USE TIPS: For solid fiberglass hulls only.

BUYING TIPS: What may be lost in signal sensitivity is more than compensated for by lack of wear and tear on the transducer. Bubble is essential to protect any inboard-mounted transducer from water and kicks, etc.

DATASCOPE

DESCRIPTION: Grenade-shaped (4½" × 1¾" × 2⅜") handheld monocular (5 × 30 power) that incorporates fluxgate compass (page 27) and rangefinder (see this page). Also contains chronometer in a waterproof housing with rubber buttons, grip, and eyecup.

USE: To magnify distant object while simultaneously giving its bearing or range.

USE TIPS: Telescopic effect is helpful for identifying a good range-bearing mark amid the clutter ashore.

BUYING TIPS: Gadget lovers love this kind of thing.

ABOUT RANGEFINDING

Ex–Boy and Girl Scouts will remember a rudimentary exercise in rangefinding: holding up a stick to determine the height or distance of a far-off tree. The same technique—finding distance to an object of known height, or the height of an object at a known distance—is a helpful aid to mariners attempting to get a rough fix (position) while piloting. The calculations involve some geometry and some simple trigonometry. Rangefinders enable you to take the height of an object as measured by the device, divide it into the known height, and multiply the result by 1,000 for distance in feet. This can be useful, not only for getting a fix but for determining how far off you are—or should be—from a lighthouse, for example, or a rocky shore.

RANGEFINDER

DESCRIPTION: Handheld device, either optical or electronic, with reticule (grid or scale) for measuring the angle of a distant object and converting it to measured height or distance.

TYPES:

Rangefinder: Inexpensive (about $10) handheld optical device resembling a hand mirror, with vertical scale that enables you to calculate distance manually. You do the work, but don't need battery or electric power.

Waterproof Rangefinder: Plastic puck-shaped device that provides an electronic readout, in yards or statute or nautical miles, of distance to a sighted object; accurate to within 1%.

USE: To sight on a distant object of known height to determine its distance (and a boat's relative position).

USE TIPS: Good practice in keeping a fix for budding navigators.

BUYING TIPS: If you are interested in rangefinding but do not want to spring for a datascope, the puck is a good alternative.

Tacking Angles Chart

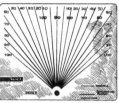

DESCRIPTION: Stick-on Mylar™ sheet measuring 9¾" × 7¾" that is marked with prefigured angles fanning out from the inboard end and extending from 0° at the layline (perpendicular to the centerline of the boat) to 100° fore and aft in 10° increments. Has self-adhesive backing.

USE: Attached to the hull or deck and aligned with the centerline of the boat, the diagram allows the skipper or crew to determine the angle of a boat in relation to other boats and to the laylines for a particular mark or point.

USE TIPS: By measuring off the length of a boat against degrees on the diagram, you can also determine how many boat lengths it is ahead or behind your position.

BUYING TIPS: Most useful for racers who wish to know the exact angle to a layline or the relative position of other boats. Also helpful to cruising boaters for determining port-starboard crossing positions (and potential collisions) and for taking bearings as you would with a hand-bearing compass.

Starscope

DESCRIPTION: Battery-run handheld monocular with electronic light amplifier; provides 1:1 magnification.

USE: To enable night vision.

USE TIPS: Helpful in a crowded anchorage or while crossing fish-trap grounds.

BUYING TIPS: Be sure to carry extra batteries for this. Most require the AA size.

Binoculars

ALSO KNOWN AS: Marine binoculars, glasses, binocs

DESCRIPTION: Small, parallel telescopes joined on a common frame. Each barrel consists of at least two lenses, a clear front (objective) lens and a magnifying rear (ocular) lens capped with an eyepiece, and also two prisms, which reinvert the image as seen by the lenses and shorten the distance needed between front and back lenses. A central focusing wheel adjusts both telescopes, while individual focus rings on many models permit independent adjustment of each scope. Modern prism binoculars are reasonably light (1 lb.–5 lbs.) and are made of such lightweight materials as aluminum (often coated with rubber) or plastic. Sizes are stated in combination figures, such as 7 × 50 (the image is magnified seven times; the "50" refers to the size of the ojective lens in millimeters).

USE: To provide an enlarged stereoscopic image of a distant object.

USE TIPS: Marine binoculars are sturdy, but should be handled with care. Always keep the neck strap on while using.

BUYING TIPS: Most authorities agree that 7 × 50–strength binoculars are the optimum power and size for mariners, providing a sharp, bright image. They are sufficiently large to admit enough light for dusk or dawn use; larger front lenses would admit more light, but the binoculars would be too heavy for sustained use.

BINOCULAR ACCESSORIES

BINOCULAR BAG

DESCRIPTION: Nylon or plastic case, either rigid or soft, with straps.

USE: To store binoculars.

USE TIPS: Always keep binoculars in a case while not in use.

BUYING TIPS: Many binoculars come with case included. If not, be sure to get one specifically designed for your make. It is good insurance.

BINOCULAR BULKHEAD BOX

DESCRIPTION: UV-resistant rubber case, with cover, sized to take binoculars 10 × 50 or smaller. Mounts on any vertical surface; has a drain hole in the bottom.

USE: To provide weather protection for binoculars stored onboard.

USE TIPS: Handy for storing binoculars in cockpit or lazarette, where they can be retrieved from the helm.

BUYING TIPS: Good for short-handed cruisers.

BINOCULAR RACK

DESCRIPTION: Wooden or plastic open-topped box, often with U-shaped cutout in front panel for easier grasping of binoculars, sized to accommodate most 7 × 50 and 10 × 50 (a second version is for 7 × 35) binoculars. Mounts with screws (not included) to any vertical surface.

USE: To store binoculars within easy reach.

USE TIPS: Also handy for storing other small shipboard items and, at home, for mail or bills.

BUYING TIPS: Go for the teak, which looks much more nautical.

FLOATING BINOCULAR STRAP

DESCRIPTION: Padded cotton-covered neoprene strap (44" long), with metal connectors for clamping onto binoculars; international orange for easy spotting.

USE: To keep binoculars afloat if they are dropped overboard.

USE TIPS: This padding is more comfortable than the usual leather/plastic strap.

BUYING TIPS: A worthwhile purchase if you use your glasses often.

Floating duffel bag

DESCRIPTION: Water-repellent nylon binocular case with closed-cell flotation.

USE: To keep binoculars afloat and dry if they are dropped overboard or into the bottom of a flooded cockpit. Also handy to keep them dry in driving rain.

USE TIPS: Convenient means of carrying binoculars (plus wallet or personal papers) between ship and shore.

BUYING TIPS: Not essential, as it only works if binoculars are in the case when lost overboard.

SEXTANTS

ABOUT SEXTANTS

Despite the electronic tools available to the modern navigator, a knowledge of celestial navigation is a must for offshore sailors, who do not have available to them the navigation aids and landmarks that serve as a backup for coastal sailors when the electricity or electronics fail. Celestial navigation makes use of the known, fixed order of celestial bodies to gain a three-way fix much as you would using three identifiable landmarks. The *sextant* is used to measure the angle between a celestial body and the horizon. With that angle and the precise time, the navigator can refer to the appropriate *sight-reduction table,* or specialized electronic calculator, to determine a line of position (LOP). Celestial navigation takes the proper tools, a certain ease with mathematics, and above all practice.

Sextant

ALSO KNOWN AS:
Quadrant, octant, quintant

DESCRIPTION:
Handheld optical device consisting of an aluminum or plastic frame, roughly triangular in shape with an arced bottom marked with graduations in degrees (originally 60, hence the name *sextant,* but now commonly up to 120). Other features include a fixed horizon mirror attached to the front of the frame, a telescope lens for sighting through the horizon mirror, and an index arm, which is pivoted by hand along the curve of the arc and is topped with an index mirror. Weight ranges from just under 1 lb. to 2-plus lbs. Usually sold with a carrying case.

USE: To determine position (latitude and longitude) at sea by measuring the angle of elevation of a celestial body above the horizon at a specific time and cross-referencing with data from a navigation almanac that contains sight-reduction tables (see this page).

USE TIPS: Primarily for offshore use when there are no visible land objects from which to calculate a fix. A sextant may be used in place of a compass for inshore piloting by taking horizontal angle readings on three fixed objects.

BUYING TIPS: A good thermoplastic sextant is fine for learning celestial navigation, but the serious navigator is better off with a sturdy metal instrument that is more finely calibrated and will last longer.

Nautical Almanac

DESCRIPTION: Almanac of about 300 pages published annually in hardcover by the U.S. Naval Observatory. Contains locations of the sun, moon, four planets, many stars, abbreviated sight-reduction tables, and correction tables.

USE: Used in conjunction with sight-reduction tables for celestial navigation.

USE TIPS: A nautical almanac can be used on its own for locating stars to steer by and for limited practice of celestial navigation.

BUYING TIPS: Privately printed versions of this government publication are sold, including at least one with a spiral binding that makes it more practical for onboard use (it opens flat).

Sight-Reduction Tables

DESCRIPTION: Reference tables issued jointly in several volumes by the U.S. Naval Oceanographic Office and the British Admiralty, containing azimuths, computed altitudes, and interpretration data and tables for certain navigational stars, the sun, moon, and planets.

USE: To determine a line of position by referencing tables with sextant sights and the time the sights were taken. A necessary companion to the tables is the *Nautical Almanac,* published annually by the U.S. Naval Observatory, which gives you the daily GP (ground position) of the sun, moon, stars, and primary navigation stars.

USE TIPS: As with using a sextant, practice with the tables is necessary.

BUYING TIPS: For the celestial navigator, the appropriate volume (by latitude and the celestial bodies that will be used) is a must.

Sextant Prism Leveler

ALSO KNOWN AS: Prism-Level℠

DESCRIPTION: Patented optical device consisting of coated glass lens measuring 1¼" × 4/10" in a rigid plastic frame. Clips to a sextant. Includes separate plastic alignment device and instructions.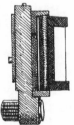

USE: To reduce tilt error to less than 1° during celestial sighting by providing a second horizon. Eliminates the need to "swing the arc" to approximate touching the horizon with the bottom of the celestial body in the sight.

USE TIPS: Simply line up the prism horizon with the natural horizon seen through the sextant mirror the same way you would focus a single-lens reflex camera.

BUYING TIPS: Especially helpful on a rolling deck. Sold in two models—one for Davis Instruments plastic sextants, the second for metal sextants that have a larger circular horizon mirror frame with outside measurements from 2.44" to 2.56".

ARTIFICIAL HORIZON

ALSO KNOWN AS:
Artificial horizon with sunshades

DESCRIPTION: Plastic box, 6" × 4" × 1½", shaped like a house with a sharp-peaked roof. Includes a reflecting surface and two sunshades. Folds flat when not in use.

USE: To measure the angle of the sun, which is reflected off the inside bottom of the box (which you cover with water). Half your sextant reading from this artificial horizon is the sun's angle over the true horizon.

USE TIPS: For use on foggy days when the horizon is obscured; also handy for backyard practice sessions when there is no sea horizon in sight.

BUYING TIPS: At less than $30, this is an inexpensive and excellent aid for the budding celestial navigator.

NAVIGATION COMPUTER

ALSO KNOWN AS: Celestial navigation calculator

DESCRIPTION: Pocket-sized calculator whose software replaces many of the functions of the sight-reduction tables noted above; also contains a 200-year almanac for sun, moon, and Aries.

USE: Various navigational uses, including computing lat/lon (latitude/longitude) from sights you input, route plotting, and calculating your dead-reckoning position from time sailed and heading changes.

USE TIPS: You will still need sight-reduction tables (see page 34) for planet positions. A plastic pouch for waterproofing is recommended. Because the computer makes navigating easier, you may find yourself shooting more sights.

BUYING TIPS: Nice to have, if a bit pricey, but you will still need your sight-reduction tables and almanac when the batteries give out.

STAR FINDER

DESCRIPTION: White plastic disk (9" diameter) marked with fixed positions and names of major celestial bodies used in navigation. Disk has small pin in the center for holding one of seven clear plastic altitude and azimuth templates marked in 10° increments. Sold with plastic pocket pouch with Velcro closure.

USE: To locate the altitude and azimuth (bearing) of any of 57 primary navigation stars.

USE TIPS: Helpful for presetting your sextant.

BUYING TIPS: If you do not want to buy another gizmo, the same information is available from the Defense Mapping Agency Hydrographic Center's publication, HO 249, Vol. 1, which also lists star groupings that lend themselves to shooting.

ABOUT COURSE PLOTTERS, PROTRACTOR/PLOTTERS, AND PLOTTERS

This group of items has more nomenclature confusion than any other in this book. Both common usage and manufacturers' imaginations have served the consumer badly in that general terms have been appropriated incorrectly as specific item names. This creates the kind of problem we would have if some large restaurant chain decided that the term "sandwich" would now be used to designate their peanut butter and jelly concoction—it would not be totally inaccurate, but it sure would be confusing to newcomers. Furthermore, while all of these devices are used to plot a course, each is designed for different techniques and results. Finally, the worst case is that some catalogs use two different names for the same item, right on the same page. Now *that's* confusing!

The bottom line is that the better items are hybrids—innovative combination products that feature both protractors' degrees and plotters' straight edges. The most accurate term for the item on page 38 is *protractor/ plotter.* Many people call it a *course plotter* as well as the other names noted below, even though *course plotter* could be applied to any device for transferring courses, such as the *parallel ruler* and *protractor triangle.*

COURSE PROTRACTOR

ALSO KNOWN AS: Protractor

DESCRIPTION: Device of many confusingly similar designs made of transparent or transluscent plastic and marked with distance scales and an angle-measuring scale marked in degrees, usually 360°. Although the terms *protractor* and *plotter* are often used interchangeably, and hybrid models do exist, a distinguishing feature of a course protractor is that it contains its own compass scale and can be used to

determine direction in degrees without reference to a chart's compass rose.

TYPES:

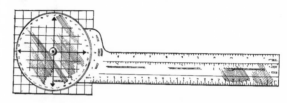

One-arm protractor: What people generally think of as a protractor, the one-arm device consists of a clear plastic square or circle representing a compass rose (diameter from 3½" to 5½") and a rotating rulerlike arm usually between 9" and 15" long. The device is aligned with a meridian on a chart and the arm rotated to lay off the desired course.

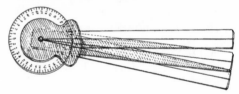

Three-arm protractor: Similar to the one-arm protractor but with three 15" rotating arms. Used by taking bearings on three recognizable land features marked on the chart. After measuring the angle between the first and second mark and second and third mark with a sextant (see page 33) or pelorus (see page 27), the navigator arranges the arms accordingly and lays them on the chart so that they intersect the marks. Your position is at the center of the hinge. (Of course after taking all those bearings you should be well aware of your position, three-arm protractor or not.)

USE: To measure angles in general. Specifically, to determine and plot course and distance and true bearings directly without the need to refer to the compass rose on the chart.

USE TIPS: The one-arm protractor is the most useful for coastal piloting, although the circular plotter is workable.

BUYING TIPS: Navigators tend to be partial to the tools they used to learn the craft, but you might want to consider a combination protractor/plotter (see page 38), which is easier to use and does away with the need for separate tools.

Parallel Ruler

ALSO KNOWN AS: Parallel rules

DESCRIPTION: Traditional plotting device consisting of two rules (once wood, now clear acrylic) with small handles, usually about 15" long, joined by metal hinges (often brass), which keep them parallel.

USE: Once a bearing or course is established, usually to or from the compass rose, the rules are "walked" across the chart by alternately spreading and closing them, and then used to draw the course in the new location.

USE TIPS: This walking is not an easy feat in rough seas. Better suited to the relatively stable chart room of a ship than the tossing cabin of the average small craft.

BUYING TIP: Old stand-by that many people like to have, but not an essential tool.

Protractor Triangles

ALSO KNOWN AS: Marine triangles, drawing triangles, drafting triangles

DESCRIPTION: Clear acrylic triangles with or without a small handle in the middle; 45°-45° or 30°–60°. Sold in pairs for the navigation market.

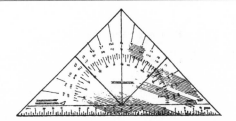

USE: Used in pairs as a plotter to transfer a course from one portion of a chart to another, usually to or from the compass rose. The long sides (hypotenuses) are placed together and a shorter side of one triangle is lined up in a specific direction (course, bearing, etc). With the second triangle acting as a base, the pair is moved across the chart to the desired location.

USE TIPS: Simple, inexpensive, but a little difficult to do without practice.

BUYING TIPS: Will do in a pinch.

Plotter

ALSO KNOWN AS: Course plotter

DESCRIPTION: Device of various designs and shapes but always with a straightedge for drawing. The typical plotter also contains a 180° protractor drawn onto or within a ruler. A *rolling plotter* or *gliding plotter* has a roller attached for easier movement across a chart.

USE: Transferring a line (or course) on a chart to or from a chart's compass rose to mark off a true or magnetic bearing.

USE TIPS: Works well with smaller charts found in chart books or kits, but can take some gymnastics to reach the compass rose on a full-size chart and mark off a course in the desired location.

BUYING TIPS: Better to get the more convenient protractor/plotter (see page 38).

PROTRACTOR/ PLOTTER

ALSO KNOWN AS: Course plotter, course protractor, course protractor plotter

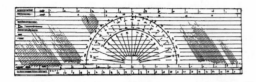

DESCRIPTION: Strip of clear plastic with parallel lines running lengthwise and, on top or at or near the center, two semicircular scales, one reading 000°–180° and the other, usually main scale, reading 180°–360°. Combines both its own compass rose and a straightedge.

USE: To determine and draw a course and bearing *without* referencing the chart's compass rose.

USE TIPS: Try one—they are much easier to use than the various enhanced, but single-purpose protractors and plotters, as well as the intricate hybrids that add in other functions, such as solving vector triangle problems, estimating fuel consumption, and balancing your checkbook—gadgets that usually disappear quickly from the marketplace.

BUYING TIPS: Best bet for combining uses of various protractors/plotters.

DIVIDERS

DESCRIPTION: V-shaped metal (brushed aluminum alloy or nickel-plated brass) device measuring 5"–7", consisting of two hinged arms that can open almost 180°. Very similar to an artist's compass for drawing circles but with stainless steel needle points instead of a pencil at the tips of both arms. Also available as *one-hand dividers,* an eighteenth-century British Navy design in which the arms cross and can be adjusted with the use of one hand.

USE: To measure distance on a nautical chart.

USE TIPS: A vital navigation tool; take good care of your dividers and keep them in a water-resistant pouch when not in use.

BUYING TIPS: Available in different sizes and weights; try out several for comfort and be sure they are of high-quality, corrosion-resistant metal.

CHART TABLE/KIT

ALSO KNOWN AS: Chart table and plotter, chart board

DESCRIPTION: High-impact plastic board of several makes and designs measuring about 16" × 21", with movable ruler (marked with three nautical mile scales for use with different charts) and sliding stainless-steel compass dial attached. Ruler moves up and down the chart on sliding bar with nylon gears and may also be angled (another version has the plastic plotter attached to a hinged arm that can be adjusted and locked at the desired angle).

USE: To hold charts and plot courses.

USE TIPS: The board permits direct reading of a course without computations.

BUYING TIPS: Many pilots swear by the tables as a convenient and easy way to navigate.

Speed/Time/Distance Calculator

ALSO KNOWN AS:
Nautical slide rule

DESCRIPTION: Circular plastic calculator marked with speed in knots or mph; time in hours, minutes, and seconds; and distance in nautical or statute miles. Smaller overlaid disk with cutouts can be turned to highlight the appropriate speed, time, or distance.

USE: To calculate speed, time, distance problems—the essence of dead reckoning—with the input of any two of the three variables.

USE TIPS: There is a conventional and fairly simple formula (available in any navigation guide) for making the same calculations—one worth learning in the event your calculator gets lost or broken. It is: $60D = ST$, or 60 multiplied by the distance in nautical miles (D) is equal to the speed in knots (S) multiplied by time in minutes (T). The U.S. Power Squadron suggests using the following mnemonic: 60 "D" Street.

BUYING TIPS: Handy tool for those who cannot or do not want to do the math.

Vectormaster

ALSO KNOWN AS:
Vector calculator

DESCRIPTION:
Clear plastic circular rule with outer disk marked in degrees, a rotating inner compass rose, and a rotating grid. Includes instruction manual.

USE: To determine the effects of current and true or apparent wind on a boat as it makes its way along

a true course plotted by chart or electronic device. A current on the nose or tail will affect *speed over ground,* while a crosscurrent will move a boat to one side or another of its intended course. In the latter case there will be a divergence of lines, in effect setting up a triangle; a vector is the *directed quantity,* a certain amount of speed in a given direction, in this case both the motion of the boat and that of the water. A vectormaster will calculate these quantities and also compute time, speed, distance, and fuel-consumption problems.

USE TIPS: As with the speed/time/distance calculator, you may want to learn the simple current diagram formula (available in *Chapman Piloting: Seamanship and Small Boat Handling,* and similar publications) in the event your vectormaster is unavailable. While using the device, you may want to construct a simple diagram on a piece of paper or a chart.

BUYING TIPS: Helpful reference tool for the nonmathematically inclined.

Electronic Charting System

ALSO KNOWN AS: Electronic plotter, electronic navigating system

DESCRIPTION: Patented device that consists of a digitizing pad about the size of a small chart table ($21\frac{1}{8}$" × $21\frac{1}{2}$"), which can accommodate a regular chart folded in quarters or a chart book, plus an electronic "hockey puck" with keyboard and display that is hooked to your loran or GPS set. Memory will store lat/lon identification for up to 1,000 charts and reference points for 100 waypoints. Draws less than 1 amp of electric power.

USE: Pad creates an electronic grid over which a paper chart is laid; the moving puck, using data from loran or GPS, pinpoints your position on the chart.

USE TIPS: The good thing about the plotter is that it makes use of conventional paper charts and chart kits, which are always available for old-fashioned navigating should the plotter go on the blink.

BUYING TIPS: Although developed to be integrated into the Quadro brand electronic charting system, the plotter will accept data from virtually any loran or GPS using the NMEA 0183 protocol (see page 45).

CHARTS AND NAVIGATION
PUBLICATIONS

ABOUT CHARTS

Although charts are not Coast Guard–required safety equipment, they nonetheless are extremely important navigation and safety tools. Taking to the water without an approved chart is like driving at night without your headlights. Charts are published by a number of sources, including government agencies, most commonly the National Ocean Survey (NOS) in the U.S., and also by private companies. Many privately printed charts are cheaper than the government versions and also smaller, making them more convenient for onboard use; however, they frequently are less detailed, less accurate, and often carry the disclaimer "not for navigational purposes," which should give any navigator pause.

Official charts contain a wealth of information, not the least of which is how much water is under your keel and how much air there is between the top of your boat and the bridge you are about to pass under. Besides delineating various natural and man-made obstructions, a chart pinpoints buoys, lights, and other navigation markers and outlines navigable channels. They bear studying, not only to learn the features of a particular cruising ground but also to understand the significance of the myriad symbols used. Charts cover areas of varying size in different degrees of detail, described as *scale*. A scale of 1:50,000, for example, translates to 1" = 0.8 mile. The most common scales for recreational vessels are: 1:20,000 (large scale, for offshore passages); 1:40,000 (medium scale, for coastal cruising); and 1:50,000 (small scale, for close navigating, as in harbors). The scale is noted at several points on an official chart, and latitude inches are ruled on the borders.

CHART

DESCRIPTION: A Mercator projection map in which meridians are drawn parallel to each other and at right angles to the parallels of latitude. NOS (National Ocean Survey) maps are printed with one or more compass roses denoting true north and, in the center, a full rose showing magnetic north. They range in size from 42" × 29" or slightly smaller for NOS charts to as small as 10" × 14" for some privately printed charts.

USE: To find your way on the water, lay courses, plot positions, and avoid hazards.

USE TIPS: Official government charts fray when folded, but folded they must be in the small confines of a boat. A chart holder (see page 42) for storing rolled charts is recommended. Fraying charts can be backed in the creases with duct or similar tape or, when coming apart, cut into sections and laminated (you can do it yourself with clear self-adhering shelf paper).

BUYING TIPS: Although alternatives exist, there is nothing as reliable as an official chart, and you should have one or more of your prime cruising or fishing area. Be sure to keep them up to date by subscribing to the weekly (in season) *Notice to Mariners,* issued by your local Coast Guard district commander's office. The notices are free and the updated information is especially important in areas where flooding and silting and the like can create major changes in navigable channels.

CHART KIT

ALSO KNOWN AS: Chart book, chart guide

DESCRIPTION: Privately printed compilation of government charts, sometimes with additional information, such as magnetic courses and distances, loran waypoints, and aerial photos of harbors. Bound as books that range in size from 8½" × 12" to 17" × 22" and in number of charts from 15 to more than 80. There are also special-use kits that show such things as fishing or diving areas.

USE: Same as regulation charts (above), but only a kit combines multiple charts, covering a particular region or waterway, at a somewhat reduced size.

USE TIPS: Supplementing a chart kit with a cruising guide to a given area is the best means of obtaining all the information you will need.

BUYING TIPS: A single chart kit not only saves space at the nav station, it can save you hundreds of dollars over a series of NOS or similar charts. But kits vary greatly in quality and amount of detail depending on the publisher. Generally the larger-format kits are better. One check is the quality of the binding—a solid wire spiral or plastic comb binding will hold up best.

CHART CATALOG

DESCRIPTION: Catalog listing official government charts, including NOS, CHS (Canadian Hydrographic Service), and DMA (Defense Mapping Agency), by identifying number. There are also privately printed catalogs with diagrams depicting the area covered by a specific chart.

USE: To order charts for a given geographic area.

USE TIPS: A cruising guide (see page 42) will also often tell you which charts, by number, you need for a given area. Many general marine-gear catalogs list numerous charts by region and number.

BUYING TIPS: Always refer to a chart by number when ordering.

NOS COAST PILOTS

ALSO KNOWN AS: Coast pilots

DESCRIPTION: Paperbound books distributed by the National Ocean Survey (NOS) containing detailed descriptions and locations of harbors, their physical characteristics, and shoals, rocks, and other hazards to navigation.

USE: To supplement data contained on regular charts.

USE TIPS: Distances and recommended courses between points are handy for plotting courses or cruises and more accurate and reliable than what you may find in a privately printed cruising guide.

BUYING TIPS: Published in nine versions covering various sections of the U.S. Coast; updated annually.

CRUISING GUIDE

ALSO KNOWN AS: Cruising almanac

DESCRIPTION: Book, usually paperbound, containing port and marine supply information, dockage facilities and prices, reproductions (not for navigation) of chart sections, plus sundry other relevant information. Not to be confused with official government-published nautical almanacs (see page 34).

USE: Similar to using a Mobil or AAA guide on land—a directory of services for those traveling by water.

USE TIPS: Handy for planning a trip. Allows you to compare services and prices and to call ahead for reservations. Local cruising tips are a helpful addition to nonofficial charts.

BUYING TIPS: Although updated frequently, a guide usually retains its usefulness for several years.

CHART HOLDER

ALSO KNOWN AS: Chart tube, waterproof chart tube

DESCRIPTION: Polyethylene tube, 40" long × 3" in diameter, with removable caps at either end. Stick-on reference label included.

USE: To store charts and protect them from moisture.

USE TIPS: Rolling instead of folding a chart also prevents fraying at the fold lines.

BUYING TIPS: Fits all but the largest-format NOS charts.

PORTABLE CHART-VIEWING TABLE

DESCRIPTION: Pair of acrylic sheets, each measuring 19" × 15½" (and .098" thick), hinged at one end with adhesive tape; includes four stainless steel clips to secure other sides.

USE: Charts are slipped between the plastic sheets, clipped down, and kept dry while visible from both sides. The device will accommodate many charts folded in quarters—you may have to do some fiddling—or in eighths.

USE TIPS: Convenient means of reading a chart while at the helm; the weight also prevents a chart from blowing around.

BUYING TIPS: Works with standard charts; will not handle chartbooks unless you are willing to tear out a page. Handy sailors can custom-fashion their own portable chart holders out of acrylic.

WATERPROOF CHART SLEEVE

ALSO KNOWN AS: Chart envelope, chart cover, chart slicker

DESCRIPTION: Clear vinyl plastic envelope measuring 35" × 23" and sized to fit most standard charts and chart kits. Vinyl material permits drawing course lines and erasing them with a damp rag.

USE: To protect charts from moisture and rips.

USE TIPS: Holds charts up to 35" × 45" when folded in half, which permits reading from both sides.

BUYING TIPS: Some chart-kit publishers sell custom sleeves.

Waterproof Chart Coating

DESCRIPTION: Clear liquid consisting in part of petroleum distillates with a drying time of 24 hours; sold in 16-oz. quantities.

USE: For applying a waterproof film to existing paper charts.

USE TIPS: Also suitable for coating fabric footwear.

BUYING TIPS: One pint covers about 100 sq. ft., or eight charts, but this seems an anachronistic way of going about things. Better to purchase already-coated charts or to use a plastic chart sleeve for older charts than to add more petroleum distillates to the environment.

Light list

DESCRIPTION: Paperbound book published by the U.S. Department of Transportation covering various regions of U.S. and foreign countries and containing detailed information about aids to navigation, including lights, sound signals, buoys, daybeacons, racons, and radio beacons.

USE: To supplement navigation data found on a chart with much more detail.

USE TIPS: Not to be used for navigation, but handy for plotting and verifying coordinates for electronic navigation purposes.

BUYING TIPS: Extremely useful tool for those who do extended cruising. A must for those who navigate with a radio direction finder (see page 47).

Tide and Plotting Guide

ALSO KNOWN AS: Tide guide, nautical almanac

DESCRIPTION: Variety of paperbound books ranging from tiny annual booklets with high and low tides for a specific region to larger works of up to 1,000 pages, containing tidal and tidal current information for many specific points for the entire East or West coasts. Two of the best known are the *Eldridge Tide and Pilot Book,* which is kind of the *Old Farmer's Almanac* of the boating world, and *Reed's Nautical Almanac.*

USE: To provide annual tide and current tables as well as light lists for region covered. Some almanacs contain celestial navigation tables.

USE TIPS: Times in *Eldridge* are given in standard time; be sure to correct by one hour for daylight saving time.

BUYING TIPS: Indispensable references. *Eldridge* covers the Northeast coast only; *Reed's* is available in separate editions for the East and West coasts.

Tide and Current Tables

ALSO KNOWN AS: Tide tables

DESCRIPTION: Paperbound book ranging in length from 200 to 300 pages. Issued annually in regional editions for U.S., Canada, South America, and Europe.

USE: To provide daily tide rise and fall information as well as data about localized tidal currents, including time, speed, and duration.

USE TIPS: Handy reference if cruising in unfamiliar waters.

BUYING TIPS: For local boating, an *Eldridge* or *Reed's* is more compact and generally useful.

COMPUTERIZED TIDE AND CURRENT GUIDE

DESCRIPTION: Software compatible with IBM and/or Apple Macintosh computers containing tidal data usually based on NOAA tide tables and good for specific regions or nationwide. Program lengths vary from 1 year to 5 years and range from hundreds to thousands of reporting "stations"; some also programmable by inputting lat/lon for creating a custom station.

USE: To obtain tidal information (time, height, duration) and tidal current data (time, speed, direction) for specific places at specific times by computer.

USE TIPS: Unless you bring your laptop with you, these are best for planning cruises ahead and making printouts to bring aboard, or for just plain armchair cruising.

BUYING TIPS: In many parts of the country tidal current data are more useful than rise and fall of the tide. Buy a program that includes both types of information. Programs vary in sophistication and user-friendliness, so get a demonstration if possible.

TIDAL-CURRENT CHARTS

ALSO KNOWN AS: Current charts

DESCRIPTION: NOAA reprint of nautical charts in an 18" × 9" format. The 15-page booklets, sold in seven editions ranging from Boston Harbor to Puget Sound, consist of a single chart marked with speed and direction of various currents at high water, then successively 1 hour to 12 hours later.

USE: To visually depict information contained in tidal current tables.

USE TIPS: Tidal currents change daily. Chart booklet shows you how to take the mean and high and low for the day (from an almanac or tide book) and compute the current for a given day.

BUYING TIPS: NOAA has reprinted these because of public demand, so boaters must find them useful.

ABOUT ELECTRONIC NAVIGATION EQUIPMENT

Electronic navigational devices provide the contemporary boater with the information sailors have been seeking for millennia—where am I, and how do I get from here to where I want to go? *GPS* (global positioning system) devices, which provide the mariner with the ultimate in navigational information—the three-way fix—are the most accurate equipment available, using multiple satellite signals to pinpoint position 24 hours a day, anywhere in the world, to within 6–10'. By the year 2000, GPS will be the standard means of navigation for both coastal and offshore sailors, due in part both to falling prices and shrinking sizes and to its inherent superiority to loran, which may soon be phased out anyway.

Loran-C (from "long-range navigation"), the most common position-finding electronic device on boats, relies on a chain of land-based radio transmitters to determine lat/lon. Also useful, especially at night, but less accurate is the *RDF* (radio direction finder), which receives signals from radio beacons positioned along the coast as part of the government's aids-to-navigation system. Despite the reliability and accuracy of electronic devices, the sailor must still possess basic navigational skills to fall back on when either a unit or the boat's power fails. After all, the single most important piece of navigational gear on the boat, despite all the electronic advances, remains the ancient compass.

Integrating the various electronic devices on a boat greatly enhances their use to the boat owner, combining data (speed, direction, depth, lat/lon, etc.) that otherwise would have to be read and interpreted separately. To that end the National Marine Electronics Association (NMEA) has developed an industrywide standard or protocol called *NMEA 0183*. The 0183 format denotes compatibility, but in reality some manufacturers go by their own standards or meet only part of the industry standard, nonetheless claiming adherence. While compatibility, also described as full integration, is improving, the safest route for the consumer is to stick with a single brand when connecting various electronic devices. Or you can check with the various manufacturers when considering different brands. One tip-off is the type of connecting cable a maker uses for coupling purposes: the standard calls for two-conductor shielded cable rather than ordinary coaxial still favored by some manufacturers.

Loran

ALSO KNOWN AS: Loran-C

DESCRIPTION: A low-frequency radio receiver that picks up multiple transmissions from land-based transmitters in the form of synchronized pulses at exact time intervals and measures the time differences (TDs) between them in microseconds. The TD between the main, or "master," station and one or more secondaries is displayed as a five-digit number on the receiver and also on many sets as lat/lon. Most lorans can also be preprogrammed with 100–250 locations, called *waypoints*, as well as "routes" linking waypoints, and many will display range, bearing, and VMG (velocity made good). Correction for automatic secondary factors (ASF), distortions created as signals move across landmasses, is standard. Available in both permanent and handheld models.

USE: To determine position by matching TDs on the receiver screen with those printed on a loran-C chart, a regular chart overlaid with a grid of TD numbers, which remain constant for a given location. Will also lead you along preprogrammed route, providing you with range, bearing, and distance-to-go information as you proceed.

USE TIPS: Loran has excellent "memory" and is better able to find a location once it has actually been there, a trait known as repeatability. So, lock in your coordinates when you are physically at a place you want to return to, such as a fish trap or mooring.

BUYING TIPS: Some loran units are fairly inexpensive and of great use for coastal applications. However, with GPS soon to displace loran as the standard nav tool, a big investment in expensive loran gear is no longer a wise choice.

Loran Filter Set

ALSO KNOWN AS: Power conditioner

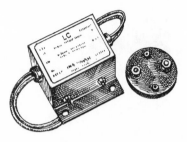

DESCRIPTION: 5-amp power conditioner in an anodized aluminum case measuring 2¾" × 2" × 2" for 6–48-volt DC systems. Installed in-line in the loran input power leads. Includes a blocking capacitor (condenser) that is installed in the ground lead to the coupler.

USE: To reduce noise interference by isolating loran from the electrical system (as opposed to conventional noise filters that are installed at the alternator output to suppress noise at the most common source).

USE TIPS: Check for loran signal interference by turning it on at a known location with the engine and all other electronic and electrical devices off; turn them on, one by one, to determine what, if anything, is degrading the signal.

BUYING TIPS: If your loran antenna is properly installed and the system well grounded, continued interference calls for installation of a filter.

Loran Crash Protector

ALSO KNOWN AS: Loran startup guard

DESCRIPTION: Device of several kinds that consist of a small lead acid battery (about 2.5 amps)

that maintains or injects voltage into the loran circuit when the engine is cranked or power supply interrupted. Some models include a noise filter. Sold in 12-volt and 24-volt versions.

USE: To prevent loran crash from power drain (as during engine startup), surges, or other power interruptions.

USE TIPS: Should not be necessary if you have battery(ies) dedicated to engine starts.

BUYING TIPS: Before investing in one, test your loran circuit during startup to see if there is any power drain or surge.

GPS

ALSO KNOWN AS: Global positioning system

DESCRIPTION: Receiver, either handheld or mounted, that accepts high-frequency signals from 3 to 5 satellites, either sequentially or simultaneously, on anywhere from 1 to 5 tracking channels. Like loran, GPS can be preprogrammed with multiple waypoints and routes and provide routing and VMG information.

USE: To obtain a three-way position fix. With older *sequencing units,* position reports are slightly outdated, although less so than with loran (as noted above), because of the reduced time difference between signals; the difference is reduced by sets that feature *multiplexing,* or rapid sequencing. Newer five-channel sets that offer *parallel tracking* receive signals from three satellites simultaneously, pinpointing the exact location your receiver can be on earth at a given moment (a fourth satellite provides altitude information, which is more useful for airplane pilots).

USE TIPS: Despite its accuracy, GPS should not be used for close-quarter navigation in such places as crowded harbors. An old-fashioned lookout is still needed. GPS, which can provide an initial fix within seconds, is especially useful for powerboaters because it updates position information far more rapidly than loran.

BUYING TIPS: While the serious cruiser or electronics enthusiast may not want to wait to join the world of GPS, those with working loran sets might be better off sticking with their older, perfectly adequate nav system and waiting for further GPS improvements and (inevitably) falling prices.

DIFFERENTIAL BEACON RECEIVER

ALSO KNOWN AS: DBR, DBR box, Differential GPS, DGPS

DESCRIPTION: Supplemental receiver that reads DGPS (Differential GPS) signals from a Coast Guard ground station and relays corrected information to GPS receiver (above).

USE: To unscramble GPS signals that have been deliberately degraded by the Department of Defense to frustrate our enemies (a phenomenon called *selective availability),* correcting them to the degree of accuracy (within about 6') an undistorted GPS signal provides. (This degradation technique assumes that potential enemies do not have the wherewithal or savvy to buy one of these gadgets for themselves.)

USE TIPS: Even distorted GPS signals provide fairly accurate positions. (The degree of distortion varies from place to place.)

BUYING TIPS: Not all GPS receivers are compatible with DBRs; make sure yours is before investing. Also, the day may come when the DOD

stops degrading GPS signals and the Coast Guard ceases to spend millions connecting them.

RADIO DIRECTION FINDER

ALSO KNOWN AS: RDF

DESCRIPTION: Portable or permanent radio receiver with a directional antenna, usually mounted on the top

over a 360° azimuth scale ring. Receives radio beacon frequencies between 275 kHz and 335 kHz and AM broadcast bands. Front panel features tuning and band selection knobs and a meter or digital readout that shows signal strength and, by deduction, signal direction.

USE: To determine position by taking readings of two or more beacons (radio beacons are often clustered along the shore and identified in light lists). When a signal is picked up, the antenna is rotated manually until it reaches a *lull,* a position at which the signal is weakest or silent and which indicates its source; with the azimuth scale lined up so that the 0° and 180° marks parallel the boat's centerline, relative bearings can be taken.

USE TIPS: Obtaining accuracy within 5° takes practice. Avoid using at dusk and dawn when signals are least reliable. RDF is also useful as a homing device (offshore sailors have been locating Bermuda this way for years), with a boat heading directly toward the source of a signal until its identifying light is sighted.

BUYING TIPS: Difficult to find these days except in manufacturers' catalogs. Considered obsolete by some but a valuable backup navigational tool by others, especially for those making long passages or traveling at night. The portable model is the best buy, because it is both cheaper and nondependent on the boat's electrical system.

Radar

DESCRIPTION:

Electronic device consisting of two parts, an LED display unit and an antenna, connected by shielded cable. An oscillator/transmitter at the base of the rotating antenna sends out short bursts of high-frequency radio waves, then switches to receiving mode to catch any echo; the cycle is repeated within fractions of a second. A recreational boat radar ranges in power from 1.3 kW to 4 kW and in range from about 15 to 32 nautical miles. Units typically have from 7 to 10 different ranges, measuring from ⅛ mi. to the maximum radar range. Many interface with loran or GPS to provide waypoint navigational data.

USE: To detect distant objects and determine their position, size, speed, and other characteristics. Another use is to determine the position of a boat by taking measurements on two distant objects.

USE TIPS: Unless you are an electronics whiz, have an expert install or at least fine-tune your set.

BUYING TIPS: Radar is not cheap, but it is an excellent safety/navigation tool for serious boaters, especially those who sail often in fog or at night. Range depends not only on power of the unit but on antenna height—radar is a line-of-sight device. A radar antenna in a dish-shaped plastic housing is best for sailboats because it will not snag on rigging, while the familiar bar-shaped antenna (called "open array") has a narrower-width cone and better target resolution.

CHAPTER THREE

LIGHTING

NAVIGATION LIGHTS

ABOUT LIGHTS

All recreational boats must carry navigation or running lights that comply with the U.S. Inland Navigation Rules or Unified Rules. Lights are used at night or in poor visibility to indicate course and position, as well as the type, size, and propulsion of the vessel. In international waters, boats must meet international collision regulations (known as Colregs) that are similar to the Inland Rules.

HIGH-VISIBILITY STEAMING LAMP

ALSO KNOWN AS: Steaming light, masthead light

DESCRIPTION: White light, often in a chrome-plated brass or zinc housing, that is installed at or near the masthead on sailboats or on a short staff on the cabin roofs of powerboats. Clear lens provides the required 225° visibility, with the dark area toward the aft end of boat.

USE: Lit when under way at night to indicate position and heading of boat. Meets running light requirements for boats under 12 m (39.4').

USE TIPS: Some steaming lamps have floodlight features for illuminating the deck, which should not be used under way because floodlight reduces skipper's ability to see. Masthead lights should be the best quality you can get—the top of the mast is a hard place to do repair work.

BUYING TIPS: Brightness and visibility requirements vary with size, type of boat. Be sure light has shield underneath to prevent blinding glare. Spare lenses, bulbs available.

GLARE SHIELD

DESCRIPTION: Black, flat teardrop-shaped plastic slab that installs under masthead light.

USE: To prevent glare from masthead light from interfering with skipper's ability to see at night.

USE TIPS: Slots allow shield to be installed without removing light.

BUYING TIPS: An inexpensive must for nighttime boating.

TRICOLOR/STROBE ANCHOR LIGHT

ALSO KNOWN AS: Tricolor anchor light

DESCRIPTION: Combination white, red, and green running light, anchor light (see page 65), and strobe. May have quick-release mount for easy removal.

USE: Combines running and anchor lights with an emergency strobe.

USE TIPS: Best for smaller powerboats; sailboats, which could lose their mast or otherwise have power interrupted, might not want to have all their lighting capability in a single unit.

BUYING TIPS: Quick-release mount is useful for transportation, trailering, and storage. Spare lenses and bulbs available.

WHITE ALL–AROUND LIGHT

ALSO KNOWN AS: 360° white light

DESCRIPTION: Cylindrical white lamp with 360° visibility, secured to a 7"-high rod with a screw-in flange base for mounting.

USE: To indicate position and heading of boat when under way at night.

USE TIPS: On boats less than 12 m (39.6') this light need only be 1 m (3.3') higher than the sidelights.

BUYING TIPS: Look for lights with glare shields to avoid blinding the pilot. Spare lenses and bulbs available.

Bicolor light

ALSO KNOWN AS: Combination bow light, combination sidelight, pole light

DESCRIPTION: One chrome-plated zinc or stainless steel housing contains red port and green starboard lenses illuminated by a single light bulb. May have plastic base for permanent installation on deck. A similar model, the *bicolor plug-in light,* consists of a removable light attached to a pole that fits into a permanently mounted socket on deck.

USE: Deck-mounted lights are installed at the bow of powerboats less than 12 m (39.6') and on sailboats where low clearance is crucial.

USE TIPS: A single bicolor lamp will draw about one-half the power (2 amps) of two individual sidelights.

BUYING TIPS: Removable or plug-in combination light is also available with rear-facing white utility lamp. Spare lenses and bulbs are available.

Plug-in base and light

ALSO KNOWN AS: Removable light

DESCRIPTION: Permanently installed deck-mounted electrical base for lamp pole. Has water-

proof plastic cap for protection when pole is not in place. Plug-in light may be attached to a pole that plugs into the base, or the lamp unit itself may plug in.

USE: To permit use of portable, removable navigation lights.

USE TIPS: To eliminate costly replacements due to breakage, plug-in lights can be removed when boats are in storage or being trailered.

BUYING TIPS: System provides a backup in the event permanently installed lights fail.

Double-contact bayonet socket

ALSO KNOWN AS: Bayonet socket

DESCRIPTION: 1"-long brass with 6" wire lead. Two L-shaped slots on barrel sides.

USE: Bayonet base bulbs have two "knobs" on their sides, which fit into slots. One-quarter twist locks bulb in place. May be used for low-amperage lighting applications.

USE TIPS: Accepts most plug-in lights, but check to be sure yours fit.

BUYING TIPS: Handy to carry spares.

Clamp-on bow and stern lights for small boats

ALSO KNOWN AS: Removable running lights

DESCRIPTION: Small plastic light about the size of a flashlight, powered by two D batteries, with red and green lenses for bow, and a clear acrylic lens for the stern. Anodized aluminum C-clamp attaches to bow rail or gunwale of small boats. Stern light has 24" aluminum pole and 360° visibility.

USE: Running lights on small craft such as jon boats, inflatables, or dinghies without electrical systems.

USE TIPS: For emergency lighting only. Do not meet Coast Guard visibility requirements.

BUYING TIPS: Light bulbs (9-candlepower) included. Have spare batteries on hand.

Light pole storage clips

ALSO KNOWN AS: Pole storage clips

DESCRIPTION: Nearly triangular black rubber forms with circular indentation on outer point or cylindrical plastic shells with slot. Predrilled for permanent mounting. Used in pairs.

USE: To hold light poles against the wall.

USE TIPS: Useful on the boat or at home. Holds mops and boat hooks too.

BUYING TIPS: Inexpensive, sold in pairs. After extended use, may lose their grip.

Stern light

DESCRIPTION: Stainless-steel or chrome-plated brass helmet-shaped horizontal mount or headlamp-style vertical mount with clear lens and a predrilled

base. Vertical version may also be found in a flush-mount style that installs flat against the transom. All use 8-candlepower bulbs. By law must provide 135° arc of visibility.

USE: For sail or power boats under 20 m (65.6').

USE TIPS: Vertical style is probably the most suitable for powerboats with high transoms. The low-profile horizontal-mount style works well on sailboats where clearance may be a problem.

BUYING TIPS: Choose stainless steel with gaskets for watertightness whenever possible. Order spare lenses.

Vertical-surface-mount light

ALSO KNOWN AS: Port and starboard lights, sidelights

DESCRIPTION: Chrome-plated brass lamps with red or green lenses. Bases are predrilled for mounting.

USE: Port and starboard running lights for operating under way at night.

USE TIPS: Provides longer (about 3 miles) visibility than deck-mounted lights.

BUYING TIPS: Sailboaters especially should make sure they have the clearance to install a vertical light.

Lamp bracket

ALSO KNOWN AS: Bracket

DESCRIPTION: Flat (*deck-mount bracket*) or angled (*mast-mount bracket*) stainless steel plate with var-

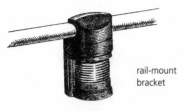

rail-mount
bracket

ious predrilled holes, or a clamp-on version that fits on ¾"–1" rail (*rail-mount bracket*).

USE: To hang running lights from these when you don't want to drill holes in deck, bow or stern pulpit, or mast.

USE TIPS: Clamp-on rail-mount bracket installs and adjusts easily.

BUYING TIPS: Presents a logical alternative to plug-in and permanent lights.

CABIN AND UTILITY LIGHTS

ABOUT CABIN AND UTILITY LIGHTS

A boat's interior lighting can be a strictly utilitarian arrangement intended only to make it easier to locate gear stowed below. But when boats are used for weekend getaways or extended cruising, most people want some ambience and illumination in the cabin. There are many types of lamps and lighting fixtures to choose from, such as oil, incandescent, halogen, or fluorescent, as well as many different styles ranging from traditional salty brass lanterns to modern streamlined spotlights. Owners can also select utility lights for work areas such as chart tables, the engine compartment, and the galley.

HURRICANE LAMP

ALSO KNOWN AS: Hurricane lantern

DESCRIPTION: Brass or glass base holds votive candle or lamp oil (more traditional), and a pear-shaped glass chimney to shield the flames. May have brass glare shield encircling chimney as well as han-

dle that doubles as hanging loop. Typically about 8" high and 3" wide.

USE: To provide very low light. A nice addition on the table at dinnertime.

USE TIPS: May not give enough light for reading or doing close work. Look for lamp with wide base so that it doesn't tip over easily.

BUYING TIPS: A nice gift. Prices range widely, but start low.

BRASS OIL LAMP

ALSO KNOWN AS: Trawler lamp, cargo oil lamp, yacht lamp, Atlantic oil lamp, wall lamp

DESCRIPTION: A variety of solid brass lamps and lanterns fueled by lamp oil featuring glass chimneys or globes (replacements available), woven cotton wicks, and, in some cases, brackets to hang from the wall. All should have a broad flat base for resting on a table. Some lamps are equipped with smoke bells (wall-mounted, flat bell-shaped disks) suspended a few inches over the chimney to prevent soot buildup and hot spots on the cabin ceiling.

USE: Lamp oil emits a bright flame, so any of these lamps would be suitable for a reading light.

USE TIPS: While oil lamps cast a romantic glow, the oil itself is highly flammable. Don't leave lamps unattended while they're lit, especially when children are around. Be careful not to hang or place close to the cabin ceiling, since the heat emerging from the chimney will be hot enough to cause a burn. Since most boats are fitted out with electrical systems, oil lamps may be too much of a nuisance—and possibly dangerous—to make them a practical answer to lighting needs.

BUYING TIPS: Choose brass rather than glass lamps for durability. Lacquered brass lamps require less polishing.

CANDLE LANTERN LAMP

ALSO KNOWN AS: Candle lantern brass lamp

DESCRIPTION: All-in-one candle, canister and Pyrex chimney telescopes open to 6¾" high, 2" shorter when collapsed. Has leather storage pouch.

USE: Good emergency lighting. Candle lasts for up to 9 hours. Replacements commonly available.

USE TIPS: More suited for ambience than for practical use.

BUYING TIPS: Handy for home, camping, or the boat.

CHART LIGHT

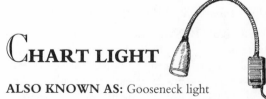

ALSO KNOWN AS: Gooseneck light

DESCRIPTION: Shaded incandescent or halogen lamp at end of 12"–14" flexible neck. Includes red lens for night vision, may have dimmer control and quick-disconnect mount.

USE: To illuminate chart table.

USE TIPS: Flexibility is a plus over fixed-mount lamps for navigators who want to concentrate on a particular section of a chart.

BUYING TIPS: Red lens makes it easier to make transition from lighted chart table to relative darkness on deck (although some recent research suggests low-intensity white light produces the same effect).

INTERIOR AND EXTERIOR DOME LIGHT

ALSO KNOWN AS: Night-vision two-way dome light, surface-mount dome light

DESCRIPTION: Circle of polished brass, brass and teak, or chrome-plated zinc with clear or faceted lens. May have two bulbs, one red and one white. Built-in toggle switch controls light.

USE: For overhead light in cabin, helm station, or cockpit under canopy.

USE TIPS: Just to be sure, switch on red light when under way to reduce glare and help preserve night vision.

BUYING TIPS: Look for water-resistant features (switches and sockets) for exterior applications.

UTILITY LIGHT

ALSO KNOWN AS: Fixed utility light, adjustable utility light, bulkhead light fixture, shallow recessed light, portable nonmagnetic dimmable light

DESCRIPTION: Various functional designs with plastic or chrome-plated zinc housings. Some swivel to change direction of the light. Lit by incandescent or halogen bulbs.

USE: To illuminate work areas such as lockers, engine compartments, and storage spaces.

USE TIPS: Portable dimmable light has clip-on base and coiled cord and thus can double as work-area lamp and chart light.

BUYING TIPS: Most are surface-mounted, but a few require cutouts. Plan carefully. Incandescent bulbs are inexpensive and easy to obtain, but are short-lived. More expensive halogen bulbs emit brighter light and last far longer, but they are extremely fragile and must be handled with care.

FLUORESCENT LIGHT FIXTURE

DESCRIPTION: One or two straight fluorescent bulbs or ring-type bulb housed in plastic or enameled aluminum case. The plastic-faceted diffuser covering bulb prevents glare and spreads light evenly. Line filters are included to cut down on interference with electronic gear. Varying dimensions between 3" wide × 15" long make installations possible in tight spots. A handy variation is the *stick-up fluorescent light,* which operates on four AA batteries and attaches to surfaces with Velcro tabs.

USE: Provides more light, draws less power, and lasts longer than incandescent lamps.

USE TIPS: The glare of fluorescent lights in a boat cabin may be overwhelming to some. More important, the transformers used in fluorescent lights sometimes interfere with electronic gear such as radios. For aesthetic and practical reasons, experiment before making a permanent installation.

BUYING TIPS: Stick-up lights are great for emergencies, whether on the water or on shore, and are inexpensive enough to keep several for the boat,

home, and car. Look for a fixture that has a built-in interference filter.

WATERPROOF FLASHLIGHT

ALSO KNOWN AS: Heavy-duty flashlight, compact flashlight, floating lantern

DESCRIPTION: Heavy-duty bright yellow plastic body is waterproof and chemical-, grease-, and impact-resistant. May have three-way switch that includes a flashing signal mode. Other features are hanging ring and recess for spare bulb. Uses two or three D batteries. Normally under a foot long, but compact style is small enough to hang from key ring. Floating lantern is not only waterproof, but its 6-volt battery is housed in a buoyant box that includes a flashlight/spotlight with luminous ring and a handle.

USE: To provide a dependable source of light in an emergency.

USE TIPS: Flashlights have a way of getting lost on a boat; better to have several sizes and types, including one with a squared-off head or body that won't roll in the cockpit.

BUYING TIPS: Look for sparkproof switches, especially if you plan to use flashlight in engine compartment or when gasoline fumes are present. Batteries and light bulbs should be replaceable; don't choose inexpensive throw-aways.

FLOOD/SPOT/TROUBLE LIGHT

ALSO KNOWN AS: Emergency light

DESCRIPTION: Torch-shaped light with combination spotlight and floodlamp. Runs on 12-volt

DC power, using cigarette lighter plug with 10' cord. Has hanging ring. Uses 12-volt 25-watt or 50-watt bulb.

USE: Use spotlight mode for searching (or signaling) and floodlamp mode for illuminating work areas at night.

USE TIPS: Cigarette lighter plug-in connections should not be relied upon for permanent installations.

BUYING TIPS: It is better to invest in a heavy-duty battery-operated flashlight that does not require outside electrical power in an emergency.

SPOTLIGHT

ALSO KNOWN AS: Marine spotlight, power beam

DESCRIPTION: Any of various handheld or permanently mounted intensely bright (250,000–400,000 candlepower) lights. May run on batteries, 110 AC current, or boat's 12-volt system. Some have built-in on-off switch. 6"–7" reflector cone in housing augments brightness of halogen or incandescent bulb. Coiled cord or swivel mount makes it easy to aim these lamps.

USE: To search and signal in darkness, fog, and other low-visibility situations.

USE TIPS: When entering a crowded harbor at night, avoid aiming spotlights at boats already at anchor. This is highly annoying to those onboard.

BUYING TIPS: Shorthanded boaters or those, such as trap fishermen, who frequently use a spotlight are best off with a remote-controlled permanent lamp; for others a portable will do.

FLOODLIGHT

ALSO KNOWN AS: Spreader light, deck/bow floodlight, cockpit floodlight

DESCRIPTION: Weatherproof incandescent or halogen lamp with clear lens and adjustable bracket. Mounts on spreaders, mast, or in cockpit area.

USE: To illuminate work areas on deck. Should not be used while under way, as night vision may be impaired.

USE TIPS: Sailboats may use spreader lights to illuminate sails momentarily to alert other boats to their position (smaller boats can use the time-honored method of shining a flashlight beam on their sail).

BUYING TIPS: Not essential, but useful.

WINDVANE LIGHT

DESCRIPTION: Electric light mounted adjacent to windvane at masthead. Has threaded mounting.

USE: To illuminate the windvane at night, but is dim enough not to be mistaken for a navigational light or to cause night blindness.

USE TIPS: May be helpful during a shifty night at sea; otherwise you can steer by your compass or the feel of the helm.

BUYING TIPS: Go for a night sail and see whether you really need windvane illumination before adding another light to the masthead.

LIGHTING ACCESSORIES

12-VOLT DC BULB

ALSO KNOWN AS: Incandescent light bulb, incandescent lamp bulb

DESCRIPTION: Familiar inverted teardrop-shaped bulb that may have either standard screw-in base or bayonet mount (with small knobs on the sides that fit into slots on bayonet sockets).

USE: Screw-in bulbs are used in interior lights; bayonet mount are used for exterior lights because they make better contact with the socket.

USE TIPS: Sold in 15-, 25-, and 50-watt versions; to save power and your eyesight, use the lowest possible wattage that serves your needs.

BUYING TIPS: On the water, as at home, you can never have too many spare light bulbs. Look for break-resistant glass bulbs and bases of nickel-plated brass to resist corrosion.

LIGHT COVER

ALSO KNOWN AS: Spotlight cover

DESCRIPTION: Tubular weatherproofed acrylic canvas cover with hook-and-loop closures. Usually blue.

USE: To cover spotlights permanently mounted on deck.

USE TIPS: Keep it covered until you plan to use it.

BUYING TIPS: Sized for different makes and models of lights.

FLASHLIGHT HOLDER

ALSO KNOWN AS: Flashlight pocket

DESCRIPTION: 8" long, white flexible rubber pocket with predrilled flanges for mounting on walls or bulkheads, and sized to accommodate D battery–size flashlight.

USE: To store and secure a flashlight.

USE TIPS: Especially helpful in the cockpit, where flashlights tend to roll with the boat.

BUYING TIPS: Not necessary below unless you don't have adequate storage.

CHAPTER FOUR

ANCHORING, MOORING, AND DOCKING

ANCHORS

ABOUT ANCHORS

The earliest anchors were simply stone weights, tied to a line and tossed overboard. Metal anchors, similar in concept to those of today, have been traced back to the Bronze Age. The effectiveness of an anchor—its holding power—depends both on its weight and on its ability to hook itself into the bottom. An anchoring system consists of a metal weight with flukes, or arms, to dig into the sea bottom, a shank, or shaft, to keep it horizontal and increase its digging power, and a ring, or eye, for attaching a line. Some models feature a crossbar at the base of the flukes, called a stock, to add stability.

Most variations in design are an attempt to increase penetrating ability in different types of bottoms or to economize in size and weight. Many are better known by their brand name than by their type, and the brand name is used, confusingly, as if it were a generic term for a type of anchor. This is noted on page 61.

Aside from providing temporary mooring, an anchor is an essential safety item that enables you to stop or slow a boat in the event of emergency, such as engine or rigging failure.

ABOUT ANCHOR MATERIALS

Most anchors are steel and vary in grade from untreated cast steel to heat-treated premium alloy steel. Some of the newer lightweight models are aluminum. Untreated steel and even some "stainless" steel can rust, so it's wise to choose a higher-grade, high-tensile alloy that will last many years. Because some countries just don't have the technology at present to produce the best marine-grade steels, you might be safer sticking with domestic or Western European makes. Also check that your anchor of choice has been hot-dip galvanized, which provides a protective zinc coating.

GRAPNEL ANCHOR

ALSO KNOWN AS: Folding dinghy anchor, fold-up anchor, collapsing anchor

DESCRIPTION: Small (under 7 lbs.) anchor with four or five curved arms called flukes. Usually offered in a folding version. Made of galvanized steel or cast iron.

USE: Commonly used for temporary dinghy mooring; once designed, in a larger version, for anchoring in coral.

USE TIPS: Also handy for dragging for lost objects. Not to be used where serious holding power is required.

BUYING TIPS: Get the folding kind for easy storage. Good choice for inflatables because it lacks sharp, pointed flukes. The most compact anchor made.

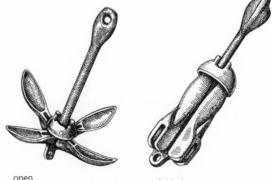

open   folded

LIGHTWEIGHT ANCHOR

ALSO KNOWN AS: Danforth, fluke anchor

DESCRIPTION: Lightweight steel or aluminum construction, with two long, thin hinged flukes, relatively long shanks, and a stock at the base for stabilization. Ranges in weight from 4 to 40 lbs.

TYPES:

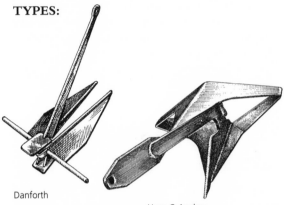

Danforth

Hans C-Anchor

Danforth®: The original lightweight anchor, developed in 1938 by Richard Danforth, this term is now used generically by many people to denote an anchor that has long flukes for digging in and a rounded bar that serves as a stock and keeps it from capsizing as a boat swings on its rode (anchor line). Many other makes, similar in design, are as reliable as the actual Danforth.

Fortress® anchor: High-tensile aluminum version of the lightweight anchor, with relatively wide flukes. Pound-for-pound, it has twice the holding power of a steel lightweight and it won't rust. Can be disassembled for storage.

Hans C-Anchor®: Resembling a cross between a lightweight and a single-bladed plow anchor, the Hans-C has two broad arrow-shaped flukes that are joined together at the open end, creating, in effect, a doubled-sided plow anchor. The flukes can be adjusted to create holding angles from 24° to 30°, for

progressively softer bottoms. Made of galvanized steel, the anchor weighs between 3.3 lbs. and 20 lbs. (for boats up to 30' in length) and has relatively strong holding power for its weight.

USE: To anchor smaller pleasure boats where storage space and ease of handling are priorities.

USE TIPS: Two flukes provide the best holding on sand, clay, or muddy bottoms. Anchor of choice for most boaters.

BUYING TIPS: Check quality of construction by looking for even welds and symmetrical eyes. Follow manufacturer's recommendations for finding the right size of anchor for your size of boat.

MUSHROOM ANCHOR

DESCRIPTION:
Small (8 to 15 lbs.) dish-
shaped anchor, with a short shank, usually made of iron coated with vinyl (PVC). This is a miniature version of the (much) larger 200–500-lb. mushrooms used to permanently anchor moorings.

USE: Temporary anchoring for inflatables and small craft.

USE TIPS: Use only in calm waters and don't leave the boat unattended.

BUYING TIPS: Look for one with drain holes in the bottom.

PLOW ANCHOR

ALSO KNOWN AS: CQR® anchor (popular brand name)

DESCRIPTION: Single, plowshare-shaped fluke and no stock. Some are one-piece construction with no welds. Often made of cast steel, sometimes manganese steel, and usually galvanized. Ranges in weight from 11 to 75 lbs., slightly more than double-fluke anchors.

TYPES:

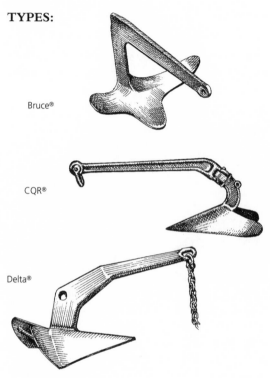

Bruce®

CQR®

Delta®

Bruce® anchor: One-piece heat-treated galvanized cast-steel plow. The single fluke has two protruding wing tips, curved up slightly at the ends. Ranges in weight from 11 to 44 lbs. and is capable of anchoring boats up to 40' in length.

CQR®: Best known of the plow anchors, the CQR ("Sea-Cure") has a broad hinged single fluke. Weighs from 25 to 75 lbs. and will hold boats up to 70'.

Delta®: Single-piece galvanized manganese steel plow with a ballasted tip, or shoe, that helps it drop directly to the bottom. At 14 to 55 lbs., the Delta is lighter than the CQR and is intended for boats 50' and under.

USE: To anchor boats over 20' long in unfamiliar grounds with a variety of surfaces or where grass or rocks impede penetration.

USE TIPS: Best stored on boats with anchor rollers or specially designed chocks. Avoid using on muddy bottoms.

BUYING TIPS: Best all-purpose anchor. Many people swear by their CQRs, while others wax equally enthusiastic about their Deltas and Bruces. Whatever the make, every boat over 20' should have one to complement its lightweight anchor. Follow the manufacturer's recommendations for choosing the right size anchor for your boat.

TROLLING SEA ANCHOR

ALSO KNOWN AS: Drift anchor, drag anchor

DESCRIPTION: Lightweight cone-shaped bag, open at both ends, usually made of nylon and sometimes coated with vinyl. Generally less than 2' long with diameters from 10" to 30" at the wider end. Two to four short lines, joined at a ring, keep the wide end open when deployed.

USE: Trailed off the stern to slow a vessel's speed.

USE TIPS: Use only in light wind and wave conditions.

BUYING TIPS: Since they are small anyway, get the largest version for the most versatility.

STORM ANCHOR

ALSO KNOWN AS: Drogue, sea anchor, storm sea anchor

DESCRIPTION: Larger, stronger version of trolling sea anchor and made of heavy-duty canvas or

parachute material. Some storm anchors are closed at the pointed end. A trip line, attached to a ring at the closed end, allows water to be spilled and drag reduced for easy hauling in.

USE: To slow speed while running before a storm or keeping a boat's head to the wind and slowing drift while lying ahull. The effect is similar to, but more efficient than, trailing warp lines or pouring oil on troubled waters.

USE TIPS: Practice deploying from various hull positions in less-than-storm conditions to learn a boat's behavior under sea anchor.

BUYING TIPS: Primarily for offshore sailors. Get a model with a ring for a trip line.

YACHTSMAN'S ANCHOR

ALSO KNOWN AS: Fisherman anchor, kedge anchor

DESCRIPTION: Traditional style (kedge type) anchor with long shank and two relatively short fixed flukes curved upward at the ends.

USE: Primarily for kedging, where weight can be a factor. Otherwise mostly decorative, especially on larger classic yachts, where it is historically correct.

USE TIPS: Not generally useful for smaller boats, because of the size and weight needed to achieve the holding power of modern designs. Using the rule of thumb of 2 lbs. per foot of waterline length, a 30' boat would require a 60-lb. anchor (a 35-lb. CQR would do the same job).

BUYING TIPS: Don't get one unless your boat has a long bowsprit for raising and stowing. Extra-large models make great lawn ornaments.

ROCKER STOPPER

ALSO KNOWN AS: Flopper stopper, stabilizer

DESCRIPTION: Available in several very different models: vertically stacking, slightly concave high-impact plastic disks approximately 14" in diameter; 24"–36" stainless-steel hinged wings; a collapsible bag 20" or 24" in diameter with trip line, and steel-framed polyethylene sheet measuring 432 sq. in., all attached to ropes.

USE: Suspended from the sides of a drifting or anchored boat to reduce rocking-and-rolling motion by using the resistance of the water.

USE TIPS: Not to be confused with sea anchors or drogues. Use three to twelve of the smaller plastic models, depending on the length of your boat.

BUYING TIPS: Might be useful while fishing or at anchor. At anywhere from $10 to $200 depending on type, try before you buy.

ANCHOR ACCESSORIES

ANCHOR SHACKLE

ALSO KNOWN AS: Shackle, screw-pin anchor shackle

DESCRIPTION: U-shaped steel fastener with holes at each open end to receive screw-in pin; pin diameter ranges from 5/16" to 5/8" for anchoring systems, although shackles can be larger or smaller. (A whole range of shackles designed for use on running rigging are described in Chapter Five.)

USE: To connect the eye (closed loop) of a line to the anchor ring.

USE TIPS: To increase your safety margin, always use a shackle one size larger than the chain (it will still fit).

BUYING TIPS: Get the best-quality stainless steel kind.

SWIVEL CHAIN CONNECTOR

jaw & eye

DESCRIPTION: Double-link swiveling connector; variations include combination shackle (jaw) and closed loop (eye), eye and eye, or jaw and jaw. Ranges in size from 1/4" to 3/4" (relative to chain size) with safe working loads of between 1,000 and 8,000 lbs.

USE: To help prevent twisting between chain and rope sections of anchor rode.

USE TIPS: Good protection against chafing of rope portion of the rode. Choose type depending on whether or not you'll want to disconnect either (or both) chain or rope ends at some point. Jaw and eye is weakest of the connections, probably because of the dissimilar parts.

BUYING TIPS: As with shackles, go up one size larger than the chain. And pick the highest-grade metal—in this case 316 stainless steel.

LOCKING WIRE

ALSO KNOWN AS: Seizing wire

DESCRIPTION: Spooled corrosion-resistant stainless steel or monel (nickel, copper, iron, manganese alloy) wire with diameters from .020" to .041", in lengths from 30' to 60'.

USE: For threading through the eye of the shackle pin to secure it to the shackle.

USE TIPS: Don't be afraid to use lots of wire—just wrap tightly and don't leave a loose end. Also useful for securing turnbuckles on standing rigging.

BUYING TIPS: Get the smallest spool available—it'll be plenty.

THIMBLE

DESCRIPTION: Teardrop-shaped insert, either metal (galvanized or stainless steel) or nylon, that is spliced into the eye (loop) of a rope or wire rope line.

USE: To prevent chafing of the line.

USE TIPS: For rope, wrap duct tape around the eye to prevent chafing of the outer side of the loop.

BUYING TIPS: Get a metal thimble for anchoring systems (nylon is suitable for dock lines), but be sure to match a galvanized thimble with galvanized wire, likewise with stainless.

ANCHOR ALARM

DESCRIPTION: An electronic motion sensor contained in a small steel or plastic waterproof box that is clamped on or near the bow pulpit. Two systems are available: one that is a self-contained noise alarm and one that is hooked into the loran alarm system.

USE: To detect shifting or dragging of anchor.

USE TIPS: Get one with a remote alarm speaker that can be heard anywhere on the boat.

BUYING TIPS: Only for the exceptionally nervous.

ANCHORING BALL

ALSO KNOWN AS: Day signal

DESCRIPTION: Inflatable plastic ball, approximately 16" in diameter, often black in color. Fitted with grommets for hoisting on a halyard.

USE: Required by U.S. Coast Guard as a day signal advising others that a boat is anchored outside a designated anchorage area.

USE TIPS: When in use, hoist up to lower spreaders for maximum visibility. Deflate for easy storage.

BUYING TIPS: This is a required item that is rarely used. Reserve purchase unless you plan extensive cruising to unfamiliar areas.

ANCHOR LIGHT

ALSO KNOWN AS: Riding light

DESCRIPTION: Small lamp, either battery-run portable or permanent 12-volt fixture, that shines a

bright white light 360°. Made of either polycarbonate or chrome-plated brass base and a glass or plastic lens. Some have built-in hooks for installation; others require special brackets.

USE: Required by Coast Guard as night signal to indicate a boat at anchor outside of a designated anchorage.

USE TIPS: Also helpful for finding your way back to your boat at night or in a fog.

BUYING TIPS: Be certain the light meets Coast Guard standards of 360° of illumination and 2 mi. of visibility. If you anchor infrequently, consider a cheaper, clamp-on portable or one that is incorporated as part of a permanent running-lights system.

DAY-GLO ANCHOR RODE MARKER

DESCRIPTION: Numbered yellow, green, and orange plastic tab that sticks onto an anchor rode. It is actually just a more colorful version of the knot used to "mark twain" in days of yore.

USE: To stick on rode at regular intervals, from 20' to 200', to mark off how much line you've played out while anchoring.

USE TIPS: Tend to get frayed or lost after a while.

BUYING TIPS: Duct tape will do the same job.

Anchor Rode Bag

DESCRIPTION: Solid fabric or mesh bag, either open or duffel shape, sized to accommodate 150'–300' of ½"–⅝" anchor rode and chain, with an opening anywhere from 12" × 15" to 28" by 19".

USE: To store anchor rode without snags or tangles.

USE TIPS: The kind with at least partial mesh hastens drying of wet rodes (which should be rinsed off frequently).

BUYING TIPS: A spare bucket will suffice while doing double duty as—a bucket.

Anchor Chock

DESCRIPTION: Chrome-plated metal (usually brass or bronze) plastic, or nylon wedge plus brackets (four to five pieces in all) designed to be installed on the deck. Two sizes—one for anchors under 21 lbs., the other for anchors 22 lbs. or more.

USE: Hold an anchor firmly in place on the foredeck.

USE TIPS: Best for those with smaller boats or who sail shorthanded.

BUYING TIPS: Most chocks are designed for lightweight-type anchors. Special makes, such as Bruce or CQR, are best secured with a roller or roller/mount (see page 67).

Anchor Holder

ALSO KNOWN AS: Anchor rail chock, rail bracket

DESCRIPTION: Small stainless steel bracket with jaws for holding an anchor; has clamps for fastening, either vertically on a stanchion or horizontally on a rail.

TYPES:

Bow rail chock (also known as *bow pulpit anchor holder*): Either single flat unit with two curved sides or else two stainless steel strips with notches, both designed to be fastened or hooked over the bow rail; accommodates anchors from 8 to 22 lbs.

Stanchion anchor holder: Single-unit bracket with clamps for fastening to ⅞" or 1" vertical tubing; accommodates lightweight anchors from 8 to 22 lbs.

USE: To secure anchor off the deck to either the bow rail or a stanchion.

USE TIPS: Good way for frequent anchorers to keep their tackle abovedecks, out of the way but ready for quick deployment.

BUYING TIPS: The double strips, which hook over the rail (and which can be removed) are best for smaller boats with smaller anchors. Security-minded sailors might want a single-unit version with predrilled holes for a padlock.

Anchor Roller

ALSO KNOWN AS: Bow roller

DESCRIPTION: Scoop-shaped stainless steel device, anywhere from 12" to 20" in length, and fitted with a Marithane™ or similar plastic wheel, or roller, capable of handling rodes from ⅜" to 1½". Some are fitted with a bail, or metal bridge, over the roller to keep line from slipping. Has predrilled holes for bolting to bow or deck.

USE: Used like a pulley to hoist anchor and rode at bow (occasionally at the stern).

USE TIPS: Makes raising anchor much easier than hand-over-hand. Especially good for shorthanded or family cruising.

BUYING TIPS: Get the higher-grade model with a bail.

Anchor Roller/ Mount

ALSO KNOWN AS:
Storage roller

DESCRIPTION: Anchor roller fitted with means of securing anchor after hoisting.

USE: To store an anchor over the bow in a ready position.

USE TIPS: Best suited for larger boats whose bows won't be weighed down by a hanging anchor.

BUYING TIPS: Only larger vessels require a roller/mount. Most are designed for lightweight anchors (see page 61). "Universal" mounts will accommodate both plow and lightweight anchors. Also available are special mounts to hold plows or specific brands, such as a Bruce (see page 62).

Chainstopper

DESCRIPTION: Small (6" × 3¾" or slightly larger) stainless-steel gripping device capable of handling ¼"–⅜" anchor chain. Has a working strength up to 5,000 lbs.

USE: To take the tension off the rode of an anchored boat to prevent strain on the windlass.

USE TIPS: Also serves as a chain lock.

BUYING TIPS: Some anchor rollers offer custom chainstoppers as an option. Good item that protects your windlass while providing an extra means of securing an anchor rode to the boat.

Anchor Lock

DESCRIPTION: Small stainless steel channel with interlocking pin that fits through anchor shackle (see page 64) or link of rode chain. Mounts on foredeck.

USE: To secure anchor to prevent accidental dropping while under way.

USE TIPS: Lock's ¼" pin is not strong enough for holding a boat at anchor.

BUYING TIPS: Good insurance for smaller boats that store an anchor on deck.

Anchor Tensioner

DESCRIPTION: Hinged stainless steel locking device, about 7" long, 1⅜" wide, that has an adjustable hook that fits through anchor shackle or chain link. Creates 200 lbs. of tension and can handle anchors weighing up to 90 lbs.

USE: To snug anchor to roller to prevent rattling around on deck.

USE TIPS: Can be used with a roller, roller/mount, or windlass.

BUYING TIPS: Must buy your own #12 fasteners (two required).

WINDLASSES

ABOUT WINDLASSES

In earlier times—back to the Middle Ages at least—ship's crews weighed anchor or hoisted heavy cargo by means of a line wrapped around a capstan, a vertical drum that acted as a pulley. Even with the aid of a capstan, raising anchor was hard work, so some early efficiency expert invented sea chanteys, which were sung in rhythm with the job at hand. Modern pleasure-boat windlasses are a down-sized adaptation of the capstan, with the difference that the drum or barrel is usually mounted horizontally rather than vertically. They make hoisting anchor so effortless that sea chanteys have become a relatively obscure folk art form, though you can still sing them as you push the "on" button with firmness and seagoing resolve.

A windlass is simply a kind of winch, operated either manually or electrically, used for handling anchors and anchor rodes. Most wrap vertically and are deck-mounted. Though compact in size, ranging in weight from 14 lbs. to just under 100 lbs., windlasses have tremendous pulling power—an average of 500 lbs., for boats under 30', to 1½ tons for boats between 50' and 70' in length. Depending on the load, windlasses can pay out or retrieve rodes at speeds of 50'–100' per minute. A windlass (or winch) drum with a smooth surface is called a *gypsy;* one with a machined surface for handling chain is called a *wildcat.* Some electric models are self-contained units, while others have their motors and transmissions located belowdecks for less clutter. And some models are remote-controlled, allowing them to be activated from the helm. Better models have bronze innards and gears and stainless-steel or aluminum casings, sometimes coated with polyester for extra protection from the weather.

ELECTRIC WINDLASS

DESCRIPTION: Electric-powered (12-volt) barrel or drum, similar to a winch mounted on its side, but larger and more powerful. The electric windlass does its work with minimal power drain (about 100 amps over 5 minutes) by running a small motor quickly while rotating its drum slowly.

TYPES:

Free-fall windlass: Deck-mounted, self-contained power unit that allows anchor and rode to fall as fast as nature allows. Can handle up to ½" three-strand rope line and anchors from 10 to 35 lbs., with a maximum working load of 500 lbs.

Rope windlass: Windlass capable of handling the rope, but not the chain, section of the anchor rode.

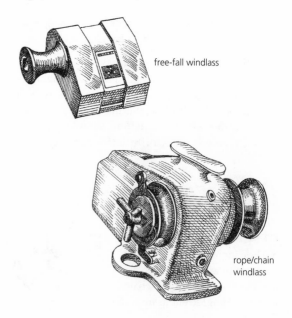

free-fall windlass

rope/chain windlass

Rope/chain windlass: Windlass that can hoist both the rope and the chain sections of an anchor rode.

USE: To lower and retrieve anchors and anchor rodes, substituting electric for muscle power.

USE TIPS: For cruising sailboats over 30' or powerboats 25' and up. Despite the pulling power of these devices, anchors should be broken free of the bottom by moving the boat (under power or sail), not by using a windlass.

BUYING TIPS: Refer to manufacturers' charts for aid in choosing the right size winch for a given boat. Be sure to factor in the extra weight of an all-chain rode—⅜" galvanized steel chain, for example, weighs 1.7 lbs./ft. Windlasses that permit either powered or free-fall deployment of the anchor are a best bet—they permit faster dropping, when conditions permit, which creates a better initial grab on the surface.

Manual Rope/Chain Windlass

DESCRIPTION: Smaller hand-operated winches that provide anywhere from 12:1 to 40:1 mechanical advantage. Most are double-action (taking in line on both fore and aft stroke), and some have two gears, high for no-load hauling, low for when there is weight on the line.

USE: To ease and speed up the retrieval of anchor and rode.

USE TIPS: Preferred for smaller cruising sailboats up to 35'. Two-speed kind is best in crowded anchorages or where there is strong tidal current.

BUYING TIPS: Excellent choice for smaller boats that can't afford the power drain of electrical windlasses.

ANCHOR RODES AND CHAINS

Anchor Chain

ALSO KNOWN AS: Mooring chain

DESCRIPTION: A series of interlocked steel rings or links welded together. Marine chain, usually galvanized steel, has link diameters from ³⁄₁₆" to ⅝" and link lengths 10%–20% shorter than standard industrial chain (for better gripping by a windlass). Chain is rated by its WLL (working load limit), which is the maximum recommended load, which is about ¼ its ultimate, or breaking, strength.

TYPES:

Proof-coil chain: The most commonly used chain for anchor rodes, proof coil is made from low carbon steel and has slightly longer link length than other marine chain. Link diameter from 3/16" to ⅝" and working load ranging from 750 lbs. to 6,900 lbs. Identifiable by G3 stamped on each link. *Coated proof-coil chain* is regular galvanized proof coil with a thick polymer coating on each link to protect hulls and decks during anchoring.

BBB chain: Also called *Triple B chain,* this is similar in composition and strength to proof coil chain, but with shorter links, which makes it slightly stronger and heavier per foot. Smaller links are best suited for windlasses. Identified by 3B embossed on each link.

High-test chain: High carbon steel, which has been surface-hardened, gives high-test chain greater strength per weight and is the choice for many with all-chain rodes. WLL is one third, rather than one quarter, of breaking strength. Identified by G4 stamped on each link.

Stainless steel chain: Stronger and more corrosion resistant than other types, but four to five times more expensive than high test.

USE: To join anchor to nylon anchor rode or make up the entire length of the rode, from anchor to deck. To join mooring ball to mooring mushroom.

USE TIPS: While some recommend one-half chain, one-half rope for rodes, 12'–15' of chain will do for most anchoring purposes. As a rule of thumb, link size can be one half the diameter of the rope being used, i.e., ¼" chain with ½" rope. Follow manufacturers' recommendations for size needed for your size boat.

BUYING TIPS: Galvanized chain varies greatly in quality—for anchor chain buy domestic marine grade only. Proof-coil chain will do for most recreational boaters, while serious long-term cruisers might choose high-test for all-chain rodes. The great expense of stainless-steel chain makes it a poor choice for anchor rode.

CONNECTING CHAIN LINK

ALSO KNOWN AS: Connecting link

DESCRIPTION: Galvanized, drop-forged steel link, oval in shape consisting of two mirrorlike parts; each has rivet projections and countersunk rivet holes, and the halves are fastened by peening the rivets flat.

USE: To join two sections of chain rode more or less permanently.

USE TIPS: Handy for emergencies; for long-term use you are better off getting a full-size welded section of chain or using a shackle (unless you have a windlass, which will better accept the connecting link).

BUYING TIPS: You can buy connecting links at a hardware store, but for anchoring purposes get a galvanized connector at a marine outlet.

LAP LINK

DESCRIPTION: Oval or heart-shaped ring with two overlapping ends. Galvanized steel but generally weaker than comparable-sized chain link.

USE: To temporarily join two sections of chain.

USE TIPS: Light duty only.

BUYING TIPS: You could use a spare shackle to do the same job.

MOORINGS

ABOUT BUILDING A MOORING

From the ground up, a mooring system consists of the following: a mushroom or similar heavy weight as a permanent anchor; two sections of chain, the *primary* chain or *ground chain*, and the *secondary chain* or *riding chain;* for overall chain length, the rule of thumb is two to two and one half times the maximum depth of the water. Depending on local conditions, a scope of

2:1, using equal lengths of ground and riding chain, may be sufficient. The ground chain is heavier and has larger links than the riding chain. The rule of thumb for size is that the ground chain links should be twice the diameter of those in the riding chain (i.e., if the ground chain has ½" links, the riding chain has ¼" links); local ordinances may also govern minimum link size. The chain is connected to the mushroom by a shackle; a shackle should also be used to connect the two lengths of chain. Although some experts recommend using a swivel to connect the riding chain to the mooring ball, others believe a simple shackle, which is stronger, is the best way to go. The mooring ball, preferably a hard-shell one, is connected to the boat via another shackle and a mooring pennant (or pendant), preferably three-strand nylon rope.

Mooring Buoy

ALSO KNOWN AS:
Mooring ball, mooring

DESCRIPTION: White spherical float marked with blue horizontal band to comply with U.S. Coast Guard and state waterway marking requirements enacted in recent years. Made of closed-cell foam or polyethylene, sometimes covered with seamless hard plastic shell. PVC tube through center holds through bolt with eyes at either end for attaching anchor chain below and mooring pennant above. 12"–24" diameter.

USE: Mooring buoys carry the load of light anchor chain from the bottom to the water's surface. They mark the location of moorings and relieve vertical stress by providing a floating attachment point between the anchor chain and the mooring pennant. This allows the boat's bow to move freely in heavy seas.

USE TIPS: Strain should be transmitted directly through the buoy by means of a chain or rod.

BUYING TIPS: Mooring buoys with solid shells are less likely to get waterlogged. Also look for a through-bolt arrangement that moves freely through the buoy. *Ropehole buoys* are also available but should be used only as markers for temporary anchorages, since they have a single eye and may not meet state marking requirements.

Three-Strand Twist Dock Line

DESCRIPTION: Nylon (sometimes polyester) line made of three twisted strands. Called *laid* line in the industry. Sold in diameters from ¼" to ⅞", with breaking strength ranging from 1,500 to 18,000 lbs. (popular sizes ½" and ⅝" have respective breaking strengths of 5,750 and 9,350 lbs.).

USE: Flexibility and abrasion resistance make this best for mooring, anchoring, and dock lines.

USE TIPS: Wear gloves if your hands are sensitive—nylon fibers can sting.

BUYING TIPS: White nylon is less prone to abrasion than sportier black line. Because nylon can lose up to 40% of its strength when wet, a marine coating, such as SeaGard®, is advisable. Polyester three-strand better resists mildew and UV rays, but has about one-half the stretch.

POLYPROPYLENE ROPE

DESCRIPTION: Three-strand twisted cordage made of polypropylene, the lightest of the synthetics. Diameter ranges from ¼" to ½".

USE: Because it floats (and is thus less likely to foul propellers), polypropylene rope is excellent for towing dinghies or water skiers.

USE TIPS: Because it's vulnerable to UV rays, limit its exposure to sunlight.

BUYING TIPS: Often sold in 100' lengths.

LINE ACCESSORIES

CHAFING TAPE

DESCRIPTION: Plastic-coated fabric tape in spools 1" × 25'.

USE: To protect dock or mooring lines at points vulnerable to chafing.

USE TIPS: Also good for quick repairs and to seal off hatches during storms or winter layup. Use acetone to remove any residue.

BUYING TIPS: Duct tape will do the same job—go for the best deal.

LEATHER CHAFE-GUARD KIT

DESCRIPTION: Kit contains two 10"-long leather strips with prepunched holes along the edges, waxed twine, and sewing needle. Available in sizes for ⅜"–¾" lines.

USE: To sew semipermanent protective sleeves over mooring lines at the points where they go through chocks (see page 66).

USE TIPS: Finish by duct-taping over the ends to prevent slipping and also water from getting underneath the sleeves.

BUYING TIPS: Go up a size if one end will be over the tail of an eyesplice.

RUBBER CHAFE GUARD

DESCRIPTION: Snap-on UV-resistant rubber tube, 14" long and in sizes for lines with diameters from ⅜" to ¾". Small holes in ends for tying on.

USE: Snap over dock or mooring lines to prevent chafe at chocks, etc.

USE TIPS: Tie—then tape.

BUYING TIPS: Sold in pairs.

MOORING SNUBBER

ALSO KNOWN AS: Mooring compensator

DESCRIPTION: Highly flexible solid rubber tube, commonly 17", 19", and 22" in length, with

holes at either end for threading ⅜", ⅝", or ¾" nylon line. Line either wraps around the tube or forms a loop between the holes at either end, essentially creating a shunt.

USE: Is wrapped along length of either dock or mooring line to absorb shocks that might be caused by waves, wake, or wind and would otherwise be borne by the line. In this respect, acts as kind of spring line.

USE TIPS: Take no more than three turns around the wrapping type, similar size loop for the non-wrapping kind.

BUYING TIPS: Get two or more for big boats (over 40') or where wakes or surge are a particular problem.

RUB RAIL

DESCRIPTION: Extruded vinyl, aluminum-vinyl combination, annodized aluminum, brass or stainless steel molding. May be solid half-round or hollow raised shape in cross section. Aluminum and vinyl rub rails sometimes have channel for vinyl or rope insert. May or may not be predrilled with countersunk screw holes for flush mounting. Vinyl is sold in lengths up to 70', aluminum in 6' lengths.

USE: Apply to exterior hull surfaces that come in contact with or chafe against docks, pilings, dinghies, and other boats. Prevents dents, scratches, and cosmetic damages but will not protect boats involved in collisions or other high-impact contact. *Vinyl inserts* add an extra measure of protection.

USE TIPS: Rub rail can also be used for a neat, trim finishing touch. For example *overlap rub rail* has

a hook edge that covers over sharp edges or end grains. Tapered *stainless steel rub-rail ends* are available. Use brass and stainless steel for a traditional look where vinyl rub rails would not be appropriate.

BUYING TIPS: Shop around, as there is a wide variety of styles available.

STAINLESS RUB STRAKE

ALSO KNOWN AS: Rubwale, rubbing strake, steel guard

DESCRIPTION: Polished stainless steel strip, usually ¾" wide and from 12" to 24" in length. Attaches to flat surface with #8 flat or oval head fasteners.

USE: To fasten fore and aft to gunwale, caprail, or other surface and runs over which a mooring or dock line passes in order to protect against chafe.

USE TIPS: When installing, use a polysulfide sealant as a bedding compound to prevent leaks.

BUYING TIPS: Protects against chafe but will not hold a line in place the way a chock will.

SECURING STRAP

ALSO KNOWN AS: Line hanger and organizer

DESCRIPTION: Double-looped vinyl strap, approximately 1⅜" by 10", with snaps or buttons.

USE: Hanging a coil of line from a railing.

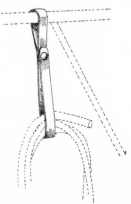

USE TIPS: Handy for keeping dock or heaving line at the ready.

BUYING TIPS: Usually sold in pairs.

LINE HANGER

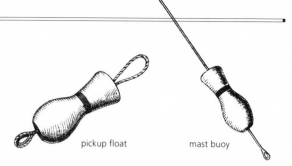

ALSO KNOWN AS:
Hang-up strap

DESCRIPTION: Small hooks of various designs that can be mounted to a bulkhead, stanchion, or just about anywhere about the boat.

TYPES:

Bulkhead mount hanger: Plate with single hook at the top and hole at the bottom that holds a loop of shock cord; pull the loop over the hook and you've closed the circle. Shock cord and ¼" fasteners not included.

The Snapper: Molded plastic with spring-release clasp. Mounted with either ¼" fasteners or epoxy, included.

Stainless steel line holder: Wire rack with four 4¾" hooks, similar to kitchen utensil holder. #8 fasteners not included.

USE: To secure coils of line to horizontal surfaces, such as bulkheads.

USE TIPS: Stanchion-mount hanger is handy for keeping dock line coiled and at the ready but off the deck. Also handy for clothes, towels, and as general belowdecks organizer.

BUYING TIPS: Boats tend to accumulate many coils of line, so several hangers for above and below are a worthwhile investment.

PICKUP BUOY

ALSO KNOWN AS: Mast buoy

DESCRIPTION: Lightweight float about a foot high with either a bight (rope loop) for boathook pickup (*pickup float*) or flexible 4'–6' fiberglass mast for pickup by hand (*mast buoy*). Galvanized eye connects pickup buoy to mooring pennant.

pickup float   mast buoy

USE: To make it easy to pick up a mooring. Once the pickup buoy is on board, the mooring pennant is tied to a cleat.

USE TIPS: In a crowded harbor a distinctive pickup buoy makes it easier to identify your mooring.

BUYING TIPS: *Mast buoys* are less likely to be run over and easier to grab.

BOATHOOK

DESCRIPTION: Wood or metal pole, usually telescoping, with a hook fitting at one end. A handy alternative is the *telescoping paddle/boathook* with a hook at one end and plastic paddle at the other. Many innovative designs are available that feature complex hook fittings, some with spring-loaded jaws.

USE: To pick up or place lines on moorings or piles or to retrieve objects in the water. May also be used to fend off from docks or other boats.

USE TIPS: *Telescoping boathooks* are probably the weakest, but they store more easily.

BUYING TIPS: A solid wood pole is stronger than a metal one, which may crease in an inopportune moment. Boathooks go over the side frequently, so find one that floats or buy a spare. The new, complex hook designs are generally helpful improvements over the old standard.

Boathook holder

DESCRIPTION: J-hooks made of stainless steel with predrilled holes.

USE: To hold any tubular object up to 1½" in diameter.

USE TIPS: Boats with stanchion-mount spinnaker-pole chocks (see page 114) could use these instead. Best not to leave your boathook on deck unless singlehanding.

BUYING TIPS: Sold in pairs.

— DOCKING ITEMS AND ACCESSORIES —

Fender

ALSO KNOWN AS: Rafting cushion, bumper

DESCRIPTION: Cushionlike devices, usually cylindrical, made of vinyl stain-resistant material. Some have rings at one or both ends for attaching ropes; through-hole fenders have a hole through which a rope is passed. *Rafting fenders* have lateral tubes connected by a flat rectangle, a design that allows them to lock onto the rub rail. *Inflatable fenders* come with inflation needle for adjusting internal pressure according to temperature changes. Oval *polyform fenders* or round *polyform buoys* are heavy-duty, made for commercial use. Another style is the *fender pad,* which is a flat rectangular sandwich of foam with a tough outer surface and has attached hanging lines. The fender pad can double as a cockpit cushion, knee pad in work area, or as a swim float (caution: these do not meet USCG personal-flotation-device requirements), but it is probably not as good a fender as the more typical white vinyl cylinder. A new entry on the fender market is the *waffle-like* disk (15"–25" diameter) made of rubbery white plastic (it floats) that looks for all the world like a huge rippled snack chip. Holes are placed around the perimeter so that it can be hung with the ripples vertical, horizontal, or diagonal.

USE: Placed between boat hull and docks, pilings, or other boats, fenders help prevent scratches, dents, and damage during normal wind, weather, and sea conditions.

USE TIPS: Inspect fenders for stains from oil, fuel, and pollution, which could mar the boat's topsides. It is an inexcusable gaffe to have fenders hanging over the side while a boat is under way or to call a boat fender a bumper.

BUYING TIPS: You will need a variety of shapes and sizes depending on where you keep your boat.

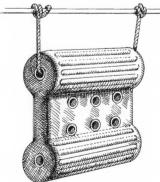

FENDER LINE STORAGE REEL

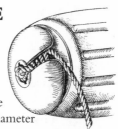

DESCRIPTION:
Plastic-threaded spool device that fits on the ends of 8"-diameter through-hole fenders.

USE: To keep fender lines neat while fenders are in use or being stored.

USE TIPS: Allows you to pile your fenders in a locker without the lines tangling.

BUYING TIPS: Sold in pairs.

FENDER LINE

ALSO KNOWN AS: Fender rope, fender whip

DESCRIPTION: 6'-long nylon line with pre-spliced eye.

USE: To attach to fenders with end eyes.

USE TIPS: Not recommended for use with through-hole fenders. Can double as (very) short dinghy painter.

BUYING TIPS: If you know how to splice, you can make your own.

FENDER PUMP

ALSO KNOWN AS: Plastic bicycle pump

DESCRIPTION: Plastic cylinder body with depression-type pump handle at one end and flexible hose with inflation needle at the other. Smaller than familiar bicycle pump.

USE: To adjust pressure of inflatable boat fenders.

USE TIPS: Fender pressure varies with temperature. Be sure to monitor.

BUYING TIPS: Very inexpensive; probably not durable enough to double as a bicycle pump.

FENDER HOLDER

ALSO KNOWN AS: Self-stowing fender holder

DESCRIPTION: Rail-mounted stainless steel collapsible rack consisting of two oval hoops mounted horizontally between upright posts.

USE: To store fenders up to 7" diameter on deck when not in use.

USE TIPS: Can be easily removed from rail and folded flat when not in use.

BUYING TIPS: Buy *fender basket brackets* separately for attaching to rail.

FENDER BENDER

ALSO KNOWN AS: Fender hook

DESCRIPTION: Ingenious bent-wire design has one end that loops over lifeline with a hook for fender line at the other end. Sold in pairs.

USE: To hang fenders from lifeline. Can be moved easily anywhere along the lifeline.

USE TIPS: Also useful for hanging up wet towels and bathing suits.

BUYING TIPS: Inexpensive. Or you could use an S-hook with a closed eye.

FENDER HOOK

ALSO KNOWN AS: Fender lock, snap-type fender hook

DESCRIPTION: 1" hook on flat base for wall mounting. *Open-* or *snap-types* are most common. *Fender lock* has mount with keyhole opening into which slides a ring attached to the fender line. Hooks hold up to ⅜" lines and are usually made of chrome-plated zinc.

USE: To mount on cabin of hull when you want a permanent mounting point for your fenders.

USE TIPS: Handy when fenders are always used in the same place.

BUYING TIPS: Tying a knot is simpler and cheaper.

FENDER CLEAT

DESCRIPTION: Small, lightweight chrome-plated zinc cleat for ¼" line.

USE: To hang and adjust fenders.

USE TIPS: Don't rely on this cleat for high-load sailing purposes.

BUYING TIPS: When installed precisely where you need it, helps keep a docked boat free of clutter.

FENDER BOARD

DESCRIPTION: Short lengths of wood or other durable material sometimes with cushioning attached along the length.

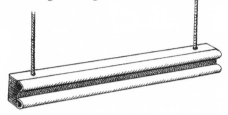

USE: Suspended horizontally between two or more vertically hung fenders to keep boats from hitting against narrow, vertical obstructions, such as pilings.

USE TIPS: Good for protecting your boat at dockside during stormy weather.

BUYING TIPS: Ready-made fender boards have synthetic rubber casings, but do-it-yourself kits are available with rubber guards that fit over standard 2 × 4s.

PORTABLE DOCK RING

DESCRIPTION: Zinc-plated bar with round eye at one end and flattened oval eye at the other. Less than a foot long.

USE: To provide a temporary dock-fastening point for a lightweight boat.

USE TIPS: Insert oval end between dock planks and twist 90° so that oval end locks device in place. Be sure to place ring inboard of perpendicular dock bracing so that ring does not slide off end of dock planks.

Store safely because the portable dock ring could puncture inflatables.

BUYING TIPS: Inexpensive and useful item.

DEICER

ALSO KNOWN AS:
Bubbler system

DESCRIPTION:
Water-circulating pump or
submerged air pump runs
on 110-volt AC current at
the boat dock. Suspended beneath or adjacent to
boat by polypropylene lines usually tied to dock.

USE: During winter weather deicers keep water
circulating around boat to prevent ice buildup that
would otherwise damage hull.

USE TIPS: The deicer's flow can be adjusted according to the angle by which it is hung in the water.

BUYING TIPS: Different models are available,
depending on winter climate. You may also want to
buy a deicer thermostat that switches the deicer on
and off as needed.

DOCK HOOK

ALSO KNOWN AS: Rope hook, piling hook

DESCRIPTION: Giant plastic hook that mounts
to top of wooden dock piling, hook extended over
one side. Similar in function is the *line caddy*, a
6'-long canelike pole that mounts on pilings or
docks and swings out of the way when not in use.

dock hook

line caddy

USE: Coil unused dock lines over hook as leaving
slip to keep lines dry and from fouling propeller.
Rotate hook out of the way when you leave the
dock.

USE TIPS: Handy for people who have their own
slips.

BUYING TIPS: Inexpensive, probably not crucial
if you're careful with your dock lines.

DOCK LADDER

ALSO KNOWN AS:
Boarding ladder

DESCRIPTION: Four- or five-step
angled ladder with steel or aluminum
frame. Arched top extensions have
predrilled plates for attaching to
dock. *Quick-release ladder* has latching mechanism for
easy removal. Up to 250 lb. capacity.

USE: Makes boarding boats or getting into or out
of the water much easier, especially in areas with
extreme tides.

BUYING TIPS: Check with your marina for permission before you install a dock ladder. Compared
with a full vertical model, it is much easier and requires less strength to climb a ladder that angles
slightly away from the dock.

PILING AND DOCK BUMPER AND PROTECTION SYSTEM

DESCRIPTION: Extruded vinyl or PVC form
with hollow center, usually white.

TYPES:

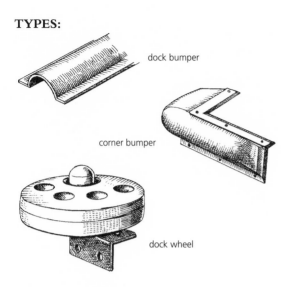

dock bumper

corner bumper

dock wheel

Dock bumper: Several-inches-wide strip that can run the length of the dock.

Corner bumper: Large L-shape that attaches to sharp convex angles.

Dock wheel: 10"-diameter wheel that mounts vertically and allows the boat to ride up and down without hitting the dock or getting rub marks on its side—a very gentle bumper.

USE: To attach to docks, piers, floats, and pilings, to prevent scratches and other damage to boats alongside.

USE TIPS: Install with rust-proof fasteners, such as galvanized nails with rubber washers (see this page).

BUYING TIPS: Bumpers have limited shock-absorbing qualities. You can never have too much.

CONEHEAD PILING CAP

DESCRIPTION: Shallow black polyethylene cone with vertical flange that fits over the top of dock pilings. 6½"–11" diameter, also available in

"flat-top" style. Traditional piling cones are made of copper cut in half circle, bent into place and fastened with copper nails.

USE: Nailed to top of pilings to prevent birds from perching and protect from rot.

BUYING TIPS: Polyethylene is cheaper than copper, but may not last as long and will not develop an attractive patina.

GALVANIZED NAIL WITH RUBBER WASHER

ALSO KNOWN AS: Galvanized nail

DESCRIPTION: Steel nail with galvanized coating and a rubber washer beneath nail head. Usually 1¾" long; other sizes available. Sold in boxes of 140.

USE: Galvanized nails withstand rust and are used in high-exposure areas for attaching bumpers to pilings, for example.

USE TIPS: For utility applications only.

BUYING TIPS: Inexpensive.

WOOD DOCK HARDWARE

DESCRIPTION: Heavy-duty ¼" hot dipped galvanized steel or medium-duty 7- and 10-gauge PVC-coated steel plates in various configurations (*inside* and *outside* corners, *male* and *female T's, backing plates, pipe holders, chain retainers*), predrilled for ⅜" bolts.

USE: Do-it-yourself dock construction, along with flotation, wood, galvanized nuts and *carriage* or *lag* bolts. The possibility for shapes and configurations is endless. Medium-duty hardware should be used only in fresh water; it will corrode in saltwater environments.

USE TIPS: Video instructions for dock building, along with plan kits, are available.

BUYING TIPS: Use only galvanized fasteners.

Float Drum

DESCRIPTION: Large rectangular sealed polyethylene box filled with foam will support 400 lbs. weight. Chemical-, oil- and gasoline-resistant. Typically 4' × 2' × 1'.

USE: Mounting flange around perimeter and predrilled holes make this easy to use when constructing a dock or float with wood dock hardware (see page 79).

USE TIPS: Can be used for main or finger docks.

BUYING TIPS: Best makes come with a 5 to 8-year warranty.

Dockside Canopy

DESCRIPTION: Polyester rectangular awning cantilevers from dock on stainless-steel frame. Available from 16' to 24' long, and in blue, gray, or green.

USE: To shield docked boat from UV rays, leaves, bird droppings, and rain.

USE TIPS: Manufacturer says canopy will stand up to wind and snow, but don't expect much in high winds or in areas with heavy snowfall.

BUYING TIPS: Unless you want shade while you are aboard, a boat cover is cheaper and more effective.

Dock Box

DESCRIPTION: Heavy-duty fiberglass lidded box with hasp and ring for padlocking. May have hydraulic mechanism for holding lid open. Dock boxes range in size from 11 cu. ft. to 20 cu. ft.

USE: To serve as a dockside locker for storing lines, fenders, life jackets, and equipment. *Boat step dock boxes* do double duty as boarding steps.

USE TIPS: Do not store portable fuel tanks or dirty rags in dock boxes. The buildup of heat, as well as paint and gas fumes, could cause an explosion or fire. Some marinas don't even allow these materials to be stored dockside.

BUYING TIPS: If you need a padlock, be sure to buy a corrosion-resistant one made for marine use.

Ship's Snake and Owl

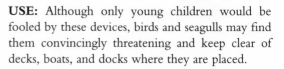

ALSO KNOWN AS: Inflatable snake, sentinel owl

DESCRIPTION: 6'-long flexible plastic snake and 16"-tall molded plastic owl.

USE: Although only young children would be fooled by these devices, birds and seagulls may find them convincingly threatening and keep clear of decks, boats, and docks where they are placed.

USE TIPS: To maintain the effect, snake and owl should be moved from time to time.

BUYING TIPS: Inexpensive fun even if the word is out among today's birds.

GULL SWEEP

DESCRIPTION: Six-foot wide, horizontal spinner made of wire with two red metal "flags" on the ends. Mounted on a small base designed for temporary installation on boat tops and decks. Wire and flags spin in even the gentlest of breezes.

USE: Chasing away seagulls.

USE TIPS: Not intended for use while under way. Remove when using your boat.

BUYING TIPS: Good idea effectively executed.

BOARDING BAR

DESCRIPTION: Canelike stainless steel bar with handle that fits into socket permanently mounted in boat or on dock.

USE: To help you keep your balance climbing into or out of the boat.

USE TIPS: For powerboats. Rigging and lifelines usually provide sufficient handholds on sailboats.

BUYING TIPS: Spare sockets available so that bar can be used in different locations.

CANVAS ICE BAG

ALSO KNOWN AS: Canvas tote bag

DESCRIPTION: Large, heavy canvas bag with two strong loop handles, each secured down the entire side, with a reinforced bottom. Some models have zipper-closed top flaps.

USE: Hauling heavy gear, such as foul weather gear and boots, or small appliances. Originally designed to haul large blocks of ice, hence the name.

BUYING TIPS: One of the handiest things to have around: tough, well-made, and not too expensive.

DOCK CART

ALSO KNOWN AS: Cargo hauler, dock caddy

DESCRIPTION: Two-wheeled cart with push-bar handle and wheelbarrowlike stands. *Collapsible folding carts* have sides that fold for storage on board boat. Available accessories include bicycle and tractor hitches, as well as two types of rear gates.

USE: To carry gear, groceries, and other supplies to or from boat. Some have up to 330 lb. capacity.

USE TIPS: Buy the collapsible folding cart if you are going to be cruising. Many stores are located a long way from the wharf.

BUYING TIPS: In the U.S. many marinas provide dock carts for renters and guests.

FOLDING BICYCLE

ALSO KNOWN AS: Folding bike, travel bicycle

DESCRIPTION: Stainless steel and aluminum-alloy two-wheel cycle whose crossbar between seat and handlebar fork comes apart so that bike can be

folded in half, front wheel next to rear wheel. Three-speed, six-speed, and even eighteen-speed mountain versions are available specially treated to stand up to the marine environment. Compact 16"-wheel models often have elongated steering forks, making the bike look like a circus cycle, but models with 20"- and 26"-diameter wheels have traditional proportions.

The smallest version, the 16"-wheel model, folds to 28" long × 18" high × 10" wide, while the full-size 26"-wheel model folds to 34" long × 14" high × 14" wide.

USE: Stored onboard to provide on-shore transportation while cruising, particularly handy when shopping, sightseeing attractions, and taxis are at a distance.

USE TIPS: Because of the additional hardware required to make folding bikes meet Consumer Product Safety Commission standards, they are considerably heavier than most bikes on the market.

Availability of storage space is a major consideration before you buy a folding bike. Although they take up less space than a conventional cycle, they are nevertheless bulky and heavy.

BUYING TIPS: If you plan to store your folding bike on board all summer or throughout a long cruise, be sure to buy one that is meant to withstand exposure to the elements. Economical folding-bicycle models are available for about half the price,

but they are not marine grade and will definitely rust.

A variety of accessories, such as luggage racks, bells, baskets, toolsets, and sheepskin seat covers are sold separately.

REGULATORY BUOY AND CHANNEL MARKER

DESCRIPTION: Cylindrical (can) or cone-shaped (nun) buoy made of impact-resistant plastic rises 40" out of the water, having eye ring for mooring chain. Buoys bear symbols and inscriptions indicating restricted travel areas, underwater obstructions, controlled areas, exclusion areas, or dangers and hazard, etc.

USE: To provide an unofficial means of marking channels, hazards, or slow-wake areas, for example. Used by yacht clubs, marinas, waterfront property owners, among others.

USE TIPS: Only state waterway agencies and the U.S. Coast Guard have the authority to require compliance with navigation aids or regulatory markers. All others placing regulatory buoys or channel markers on the waterways should consider these only to be suggestions to their fellow boaters. Out of courtesy, boaters should comply with such markers whenever reasonable.

BUYING TIPS: Over 200 standard markings are available. Custom markings may be special-ordered.

DINGHIES

ABOUT RIGID-HULL AND INFLATABLE DINGHIES

The traditional dinghy or rowboat is a small (6'–10') rigid-hulled vessel propelled by oars, a low-horsepower outboard motor, or sometimes a simple mast-and-sail arrangement. Hulls are made of wood, fiberglass, or aluminum with a fairly wide beam and slight V-bottom and can usually carry four to six passengers safely.

Increasingly common versions sold in marine supply stores are inflatables with coated-fabric hulls, sometimes complemented by a fiberglass hull shell for rigidity. (This latter type is called a Rigid Inflatable Boat, RIB for short.) Inflatables are easy to deflate and can be easily stowed.

The primary use for a dinghy is as a tender for a larger boat, although it can also be a great vehicle for exploring sheltered harbors and inlets. A dinghy's size and low freeboard design, however, make it unsuitable and unsafe for open- or rough-water use. Towed, dinghies create considerable drag. On larger boats it is common to hang dinghies on davits over the transom.

INFLATABLE BOAT

ALSO KNOWN AS: Inflatable

DESCRIPTION: Horseshoe-shaped system of separate airtight inflatable coated-fabric tubes, roughly a foot in diameter, with fabric floor stretched between the tube arms. Wooden stringers and/or floorboards make floor more rigid. Rigid plywood or plastic transom completes the aft end of the boat. May be equipped with removable plywood or plastic seats, oarlocks, rigid or inflatable keels, and rope "rails" on sides. Base fabric for tubes is polyester or nylon made airtight by a coating of hypalon, PVC, or neoprene.

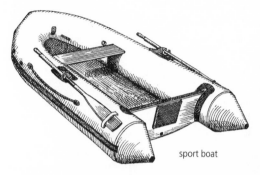

sport boat

Rigid inflatable boat (RIB) has a fiberglass hull attached to inflatable tubes on the sides. A *sport boat* typically has a rigid transom for mounting an outboard motor. The *inflatable dinghy* is smaller and lighter than a sport boat and has a soft transom, actually a continuation of the same inflatable tubes on the sides, on which a small outboard motor, up to 2 hp, can be mounted.

USE: To serve as a tender for larger boats, as a recreational boat for fishing and waterskiing, or as a diving platform. Rigid transom makes it possible to mount an outboard motor.

USE TIPS: Although inflatables are virtually unsinkable, all models have specific ratings for maximum passenger and gear capacity, as well as maximum horsepower capacity. Do not overload!

Because they are so lightweight, inflatables are ideal to bring along on cruises. They are also great for kids to operate, since they are stable and sturdy and will not ding your primary boat when coming alongside. Their lightweight features, however, make inflatables unwieldy for towing since they tend to "skate" across the surface. Allow enough length on the painter so that the boat floats relatively level, not bow-up.

Inflatables are not life rafts and should not be relied upon as such (see "Life Rafts," page 333)!

BUYING TIPS: Inflatables get crowded fast. Do not underestimate the amount of room you will need. Also, a good air pump is an essential accessory (see page 87).

DINGHY ACCESSORIES

Net float

DESCRIPTION: Doughnut- or lozenge-shaped hollow hard plastic or solid-foam float with rope hole through the center for up to ½" line. Fits in the hand. Comes in a variety of solid colors and multiculor combinations. Buoyant up to about 2 lbs.

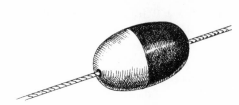

USE: Fishermen use these to float the edges of their nets, but on a pleasure boat they can be used to float rescue lines, dinghy painters, and the like. Keep floats evenly spaced by tying a small knot at each end of line where it passes through a float.

USE TIPS: In some areas where skim ice forms occasionally in winter, net floats can be strung on a long line like a necklace that is then floated around the boat's waterline to break up ice and prevent it from damaging the hull.

BUYING TIPS: Net floats can be purchased inexpensively from chandleries serving commercial fishermen. They cost more if you buy them at a store catering to recreational boaters.

Inflatable boat and dinghy bottom coating

DESCRIPTION: Cuprous oxide-laced antifoulant paint that dries flexible thanks to a vinyl base. Black. Cleans up easily with water.

USE: To prevent buildup of barnacles, algae, and other marine growth on inflatable boats. For use in fresh or salt water.

USE TIPS: Coating will not crack when boat is rolled up for storage.

BUYING TIPS: One quart is enough for applying two coats to the average 8'–10'-long inflatable boat.

Oar

ALSO KNOWN AS: Paddle, scull

DESCRIPTION: A long shaft (known as the loom) handle-shaped at one end and flat blade at the other. Traditionally made of ash, but more modern, lightweight versions are made of a combination of plastic, aluminum, and/or plywood. Wooden oars are coated with polyurethane or varnish. Sold singly or in pairs.

Common sizes of *one-piece oars* are 5' to 6½' long,

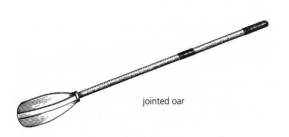

jointed oar

but longer sizes are also available. *Jointed oars* have plastic snap-in joints so that they can be taken apart for easy storage. Typical length is 6'.

USE: To row, row, row your boat, gently or otherwise. A simple example of lever-and-fulcrum cooperation, rowing is great exercise and an energy-efficient way of getting around on the water.

Although oars are most often used in pairs, you can also propel your boat with a single oar—this is called sculling—while standing at the stern. The technique of moving the oar from side to side in a figure-eight pattern takes some practice.

USE TIPS: To make sure the oars fit your boat, sit at the rowing station, usually the middle seat of the boat, and place the oar blades in the water. The handles should not overlap. It is virtually impossible to row without oarlocks and sockets. Prevent chafe on oars by slipping on leather oar protectors; prevent oars from slipping overboard with rubber oar sleeves.

Manufacturers of some dinghies and rowboats make oars specially sized for their models.

If you want your oars to last, do not use them to fend off from docks or other solid objects. Also, it is considered good etiquette to "ship your oars" (pull them inboard) to avoid damaging the hull of the boat you are approaching.

BUYING TIPS: Prices can vary significantly. Cheaper models are probably going to wear out just when you need them most. Yearly maintenance of wooden oars includes a light sanding and a coat of polyurethane.

ONE-PIECE WOODEN PADDLE

ALSO KNOWN AS: Paddle, canoe paddle

DESCRIPTION: Lightweight oar with short loom (see "Oar," page 84), flat triangular handle and large, flat blade. Made of solid fir or ash, finished with polyurethane. 3'–5' long.

USE: To provide auxiliary propulsion for small outboard motor-propelled boat or sailboat. Primary propulsion for small inflatables, kayaks, and canoes.

USE TIPS: Unlike rowers who sit with their backs to the bow, paddlers sit facing forward and paddle from one side of the boat at a time. One paddle is used at a time.

BUYING TIPS: Sold individually.

DAVIT FOR RIGID AND INFLATABLE DINGHIES

ALSO KNOWN AS: Dinghy davit

DESCRIPTION: Reinforced upright arm made of hollow stainless-steel tubing or wood (traditional) installed over transom or on deck on larger boats. Davits extend as much as 36" and may fold when not in use.

USE: To provide a support system for storing inflatables and dinghies out of the water.

USE TIPS: Once davit is in place, rig a *hoisting kit* consisting of rope, cleats, blocks, and snap hooks. You will need to tailor the hoist to fit the needs of your particular boat.

Optional angled bracket kits are also available and provide additional support strength.

BUYING TIPS: Rated for static loads up to 500 lbs. Measure and weigh your dinghy or consult davit manufacturer for proper size. For larger boats only.

Portable Pulley

ALSO KNOWN AS:
Pocket block

DESCRIPTION: L-shaped cast-aluminum frame with a ½"-diameter stainless-steel pin on the bottom and a 2½" nylon block, or pulley, cradled in the outboard end. Unit is 7½" high, weighs 12 oz., and handles lines 3/16"–⅜" diameter. Has a cast-in crease that acts as a jam cleat for tying off a line.

USE: To slip into standard oarlock and serve as a portable block for easier handling of line during retrieval of lobster pots, crab pots, small anchors, etc.

USE TIPS: Not for use with motor-driven winches.

BUYING TIPS: Especially useful for those pulling up pots or anchors from a dinghy or small boat.

Boat dolly

DESCRIPTION: Tubular aluminum (1" diameter) rack consisting of upright pole with cleat, and base with adjustable width (15"–20"), as well as two 12" semipneumatic wheels and two 5" rubber caster wheels. Handles loads up to 150 lbs. A simpler version that consists of an upright horseshoe loop of 1" aluminum tubing and an adjustable horizontal bracket handles loads up to 250 lbs. and is mounted on two 7" rubber wheels.

USE: Larger version is used for on-land transportation and storage for small rigid or inflatable boats. Smaller version is used only for transportation.

USE TIPS: Maneuver large dolly alongside dinghy that is lying flat on the ground. Tip the dolly over, slide the boat in place onto the adjustable base, and stand upright. With the smaller version the boat must be turned keel-up. The dolly is clamped onto the stern and the boat is rolled like a wheelbarrow.

BUYING TIPS: Very handy if your dinghy is stored up a ramp or far from where your boat is docked. The smaller version costs about half the price of the larger dolly system.

Mounting Chock

DESCRIPTION: Rectangular plastic plate with quarter-circle cutout and rope holes on top end.

USE: To store inflatable boats off the ground by resting tubes in circular cutouts. Secure boat by passing shock cords or tie-downs through the rope holes.

USE TIPS: Circular cutout can handle tube diameters of up to 15". To store inflatables on edge, put two chocks together so that cutouts make a half circle.

BUYING TIPS: Sold in sets of four.

Dinghy sealant pack

DESCRIPTION: Liquid solution in plastic squeeze bottle with long pointed spout.

USE: To seal porous areas and leaks that cannot otherwise be reached. To prevent leaks from developing.

USE TIPS: Inject sealant into buoyancy chambers of inflatable boat through the valves. Some injected sealants require forced air to cure. The ones that do not are easier to use. May take as long as 24 hours to cure. Check with the manufacturer of your inflatable before using this kind of solution.

BUYING TIPS: If you bring your dinghy with you, bring along a sealant pack as well.

INFLATABLE-BOAT REPAIR KIT

ALSO KNOWN AS: Patch kit

DESCRIPTION: Plastic pouch contains 1 oz. cleaning solvent, 1 oz. adhesive and 12" × 6" strip of reinforced fabric.

USE: To use like a Band-Aid to seal leaks and tears on all types of nylon inflatable boats and life rafts.

USE TIPS: Cleaning the surface prior to applying patch is essential for a successful repair. With life rafts safety is absolutely critical. Though patch kits may save the day in an emergency, have damages assessed and repaired by a professional.

BUYING TIPS: Inexpensive insurance.

PRESSURE GAUGE

DESCRIPTION: Similar in style and size to automobile tire-pressure gauge, with readings to 50 psi. Sensor end consists of black rubber device that fits into inflatable boat valves, ½" tip for depressing valve to deflate air chamber.

USE: To indicate whether boat is properly inflated.

BUYING TIPS: Fairly expensive, considering some inflation pumps have a built-in pressure gauge and could therefore be a better buy.

HAND PUMP

ALSO KNOWN AS: Bicycle pump

DESCRIPTION: Plastic bicycle-style pump with plunger handle and flexible fill hose with clamp-on valve. Some versions include adapters so that pump can be used with all sizes of valves.

USE: To inflate inflatable boats and other air-filled items.

USE TIPS: You may be exhausted before you can successfully inflate an entire boat.

BUYING TIPS: A power pump is more efficient for inflating an entire boat, but the hand pump is okay for topping off drooping tubes.

INFLATER/DEFLATER

DESCRIPTION: Resembles small electric hand drill in size and configuration. Instead of drill, 12-volt DC motor pumps 17 cu. ft. of air per minute, at a maximum pressure of 1.1 psi. Can either inflate or act as a vacuum to remove air. Comes with alligator clips for connection to battery, but can also be adapted for use with cigarette lighter. ABS plastic housing.

USE: To inflate or deflate inflatable boat.

USE TIPS: Use suction mode only with air. This pump is not made to move water or dirt.

BUYING TIPS: Inexpensive, handy, and easy to use.

Boat cover

ALSO KNOWN AS: Dinghy cover, sport-boat cover

DESCRIPTION: Polyester-cotton canvas treated with water and mildew repellent; sold with shock-cord hem and tie-down loops. Sewn with polyester thread. Designed for dinghies and sport boats from 8' to 11' long, but virtually any size is available. Some dinghy styles include a special hood for the outboard.

USE: With shock cord hem, fits like a shower cap to protect small boats from water, dirt, and debris, as well as harm from UV rays.

USE TIPS: Tie-down loops are more durable than grommets.

BUYING TIPS: All styles cost around $100.

CHAPTER FIVE

RUNNING RIGGING

ABOUT RUNNING RIGGING

Sailors call the ropes, wires, and mechanical devices used to handle sails the *running rigging*. There are specific names for each, depending on its function: *Halyards* are the rope-and-wire combinations used for hoisting sails, while *sheets* are those lines used to adjust the sails' trim in relation to the wind. Once sails have been raised, it's rarely necessary to adjust the halyard, but sail trim needs constant slight adjustment according to wind shifts and heading changes. For both there is a wide array of devices and equipment to choose from.

ROPE AND LINE

ABOUT ROPE AND LINE

Rope is the material that makes up rope, or cordage, which is called *line* for most of its uses aboard ship. Both material and construction should be factors in which type of rope is chosen for a specific job. Synthetics have almost completely replaced natural fibers, such as cotton and manila, which degrade quickly and are relatively weak. Rope technology has continued to advance rapidly in recent years, giving rise to confusing terminology and (often) meaningless marketing jargon. Generally, stretchable nylon is favored for anchor and mooring lines and, often, for dock lines, where some give is desirable. Lower stretch synthetics, especially Dacron, are the materials of choice for sail controls, such as sheets and halyards. Polypropylene, which is buoyant, makes a good tow rope or dinghy painter. New super materials, such as Kevlar® and Spectra,® provide core strength many times greater than a comparable measure of steel, but are expensive and have a number of shortcomings, including ultraviolet sensitivity, and ultimately aren't really necessary for the average cruising boat. Rope, whatever its onboard use, is usually sold by the foot; dock lines often come in precut lengths, anywhere from 12' to 60', and may come with a prespliced eye on one (usually) or both ends.

BRAIDED ROPE

ALSO KNOWN AS: Cordage

DESCRIPTION: Rope whose fibers are interwoven rather than twisted. Often made of Dacron (polyester) and sometimes of nylon.

TYPES:

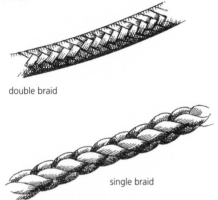

double braid

single braid

Double braid (also known as *braid-on-braid*): Braided core overlaid with a braided cover for extra abrasion resistance and strength. Easy on the hands.

Single braid: Single, uncovered line that is made up of anywhere from six to twelve strands braided together; twelve strands is best, creating a compact but very strong line.

Yacht braid with SeaGard®: Double braided line treated with Allied Chemical trademark coating that resists water (which saps strength) and prevents abrasion.

USE: Low stretch and high strength of braided, especially double-braided, rope make it ideal for halyards and sheets; single braid is best for dock or tow lines.

USE TIPS: Although braided line is strong—a ⅜" double braid might have a breaking strength of 4,000 lbs.—thicker ½" or ⁷⁄₁₆" diameter line feels better in the hand.

BUYING TIPS: Chafe resistance, not breaking strength, is the main consideration on boats, so go with double braid for lines, such as halyards, that see heavy use.

WIRE/ROPE HALYARD

ALSO KNOWN AS: Wire rope

DESCRIPTION: Spliced line consisting of (about) one-half 7 × 19 stainless steel wire and (about) one-half braided low-stretch polyester rope. Wire comes in diameters from ⅛" to ⁷⁄₃₂", rope from ⅜" to ½". The "7" in wire rope refers to the number of strands in the wire; the "19," to the number of wires per strand.

USE: Used so that the wire part is the top half of the halyard for greater strength, with less stretch and more chafe resistance than synthetic rope. Fiber rope is lighter and permits use of smaller winches on the deck top.

USE TIPS: Check periodically for "meathooks," tiny breaks that indicate the wire is fraying. Do this by running your fingers (lightly) or a cloth (old pantyhose is excellent) the length of the wire, feeling for snags.

BUYING TIPS: Make sure the wire is stainless, not galvanized, steel, which can rust.

NYLON SOLID BRAID

ALSO KNOWN AS: Braided utility cord

DESCRIPTION: "Braided" is something of a misnomer in this line, which consists of a minimal core covered with multiple strands wound over and over to create something much like a clothesline. Available in ⅛", ³⁄₁₆", and ¼" diameters.

USE: Good for sail tie-downs and other simple lashing jobs.

USE TIPS: Low strength and the inability to be spliced limit its use. Don't use nylon solid braid for any high-stress functions, such as towing or docking.

BUYING TIPS: Sold in 50' hanks.

ABOUT SPLICING

Even in this day of prespliced lines, the art of splicing, or marlinspike, as it's sometimes called, is a handy thing for a sailor to know. Among other things it enables you to convert ordinary line into dock lines or an anchor rode, ready to receive a shackle. In a way it's the means of making permanent knots by interweaving the strands of a piece of rope. Almost always, splicing means working with three-strand rope, which is much more simply constructed than braid. A minor cousin to splicing is whipping, the sealing off of a rope end so that it will not unravel. Both practices involve some special tools and materials.

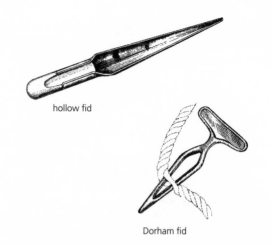

hollow fid

Dorham fid

Dorham fid: Bronze T-shaped fid from West Marine with open blade; splices three-strand up to 1".

Splicing fids: Kit of two solid and narrow nylon fids, for splicing polypropylene rope, from ¼" to ⁵⁄₁₆".

Fid Kit: Kit-in-a-tube contains two knitting-needlelike aluminum fids, one for ¼"–⅜" line, the other line ⁷⁄₁₆" and up; designed for braided line.

USE: To separate and weave rope strands.

USE TIPS: Read up on splicing, or get an old salt to show you how.

BUYING TIPS: Heft it in your hand to test for comfort.

F**ID**

DESCRIPTION: Hand tool, originally made only of hardwood, from about 6"–12" long, thick (1½"–2") and rounded at one end and tapering to a near point.

TYPES:

Hollow fid: Hardwood handle and stainless-steel point, hollow and open on one side to cradle strands as they are fed through the lay.

R**OPE DIP**

ALSO KNOWN AS: Rope end dip

DESCRIPTION: Liquid vinyl or similar sealer, sold in 4-oz. can.

USE: To seal ends of rope or strands so that they won't unravel.

USE TIPS: Best combined with whipping for double protection against unraveling.

BUYING TIPS: Worth having a can on hand for other possible uses, such as sealing an electrical-wire connection.

Whipping Thread

ALSO KNOWN AS: Whipping twine, sail twine, sailing thread

DESCRIPTION: Brown or white Dacron thread, sometimes prewaxed, in 150' spool.

USE: To tie off, or seize, the ends of lines to prevent them from unraveling. To whip a rope means that you have bound its end with fine-gauge twine so that the rope's various strands do not fray. The completed binding is called a whipping. Finer types can be used in sail repair.

USE TIPS: There is no end of uses for strong thread aboard ship.

BUYING TIPS: Get the prewaxed kind so that you won't need a ball of beeswax; also, some brands come with sailmaker's needle included. A good item to keep on hand.

Sail Palm

ALSO KNOWN AS: Sewing palm, leather palm

DESCRIPTION: Leather insert that fits over the palm of your hand and is fastened by a strap and buckle; most offer a thumb shield and all have a built-in reinforced thimble.

USE: Protects the sewing hand against burns when mending sails; the thimble enables the wearer to bear down and force a large needle through thick material.

USE TIPS: Handy for sewing other recalcitrant materials at home, such as canvas or leather.

BUYING TIPS: A must to protect the hands. Specify left or right palm when ordering.

Sail Needles

ALSO KNOWN AS: Sailcloth needles, sailmaker's needles

DESCRIPTION: Forged cast steel sewing needles, usually sold in packages of a half-dozen or more, with special edges designed not to damage sailcloth; kits usually contain semicircular needles for quick-stitching on flat surfaces.

USE: Repairing or reshaping sails and general repairs involving sailcloth, canvas, and other heavy cloths.

USE TIPS: Don't try to sew sails without heavy-duty needles made for the purpose.

BUYING TIPS: Sail needles vary in quality—only use the best.

Sewing Awl

DESCRIPTION: Speed-stitching device with hardwood handle and steel tip that holds a sail needle; usually sold with spare needles and 80 yards or so of nylon thread.

USE: Making a quick line of lock stitches in heavy fabric.

USE TIPS: Great device for making emergency repairs at sea; excellent alternative to sail repair tape.

BUYING TIPS: All sailors who go on long passages or offshore should have a sewing awl as part of their on-board sail repair kit.

SAIL ACCESSORIES

BATTEN

ALSO KNOWN AS: Sail batten

DESCRIPTION: Thin strip of flexible fiberglass, ABS plastic, or wood (traditional) that slips into pockets sewn into the leech of a sail. Can be as small as 24" long × ⅝" wide or as large as 36" long × 2" wide. *Full battens,* two to four per sail, run the width of the sail from luff to leech.

USE: To support and give stiffness to keep the roach of the sail flat. The roach is the aerodynamic curve in the side of the sail that makes it work as an efficient wind foil.

USE TIPS: Keep a supply of spare battens in case they get lost or broken. Different-size battens are sometimes used in the same sail.

BUYING TIPS: Measure carefully for the closest fit. ABS plastic battens are easy to trim to size. If yours don't come with protective vinyl tips, tape the ends to avoid sail tears.

SAIL COVER

DESCRIPTION: Fitted protective fabric, preferably weather- and UV-resistant, that is tied, snapped, or laced over a sail furled against a spar.

USE: To prevent damage from sun, wind, and dirt when sails are not in use.

USE TIPS: Make covering the mainsail your first task after you are securely moored or docked. Hot sun is a sail's worst enemy; even a day or two without the cover on ages the sail.

BUYING TIPS: A custom-fitted sail cover looks the best and fits like a glove, but can be expensive. Ready-made covers are available for considerably less, however do not expect the same ease of adjustment or fit.

SPINNAKER SCOOP

ALSO KNOWN AS: Chute scoop

DESCRIPTION: Dacron-reinforced nylon sleeve with internal guidelines and down-haul bridle encloses spinnaker or can be raised aloft into a tight bundle when sail is set. Available 25'–44' long.

USE: The scoop is an easy, efficient way to set or douse your spinnaker. When the sail is in use, the scoop is raised to the sail's head. When it is time to drop the sail, the scoop is pulled down, making it easy to control the lightweight spinnaker and bag it.

USE TIPS: Get used to using your sleeve—you'll soon be flying your chute more often.

BUYING TIPS: Buy a scoop 3'–6' shorter than the luff of the sail.

SAIL FEEDER

ALSO KNOWN AS: Feeder

DESCRIPTION: Palm-sized C-shaped stainless steel device with hard-coated ball rollers on arms. Has backup slug or thumbscrew that tightens into mast slot.

USE: To prevent luff from jamming in mast groove as sail is being hoisted, eliminating the possibility of damage to the sail. Allows rapid raising of the sail.

USE TIPS: Can be used on headsail or main. Fits bolt rope up to ⁷⁄₁₆" and a minimum mast slot of ³⁄₁₆".

BUYING TIPS: Excellent alternative for those with lazy-jack system or fully battened mainsails who do not want to invest in a batten traveler system (see page 115).

SAIL TRACK STOP

DESCRIPTION: Knurled brass knob or thumbscrew threads through a flat, postage-stamp-sized aluminum plate that fits into sail track. Different versions and sizes for round or flat grooves.

USE: With the flat or rounded base inserted into the end of the sail track or slot, the knob is tightened, pulling up the base snugly so that it cannot move. Placed at the end of the track or slot, this keeps the sail from falling out of the track while being lowered or pulling out from the boom.

USE TIPS: Insert one in the boom as well to prevent foot of sail from pulling loose.

BUYING TIPS: Knob should be at least ½" diameter, to give a good tractive grip. Look for anodized aluminum or plated brass.

SAIL SLUG

ALSO KNOWN AS:
Sail slide

DESCRIPTION: White nylon cylinder, 5⁄16" or ½" diameter × 1" long, called a *bail sail slide* or flat rectangle, 5⁄8" or 7⁄8" wide × 1" long, known as an *internal slide*. Both types have squared stainless-steel or nylon eyes projecting about ½" from the side. Solid bronze slides (rare) are a very shallow V-shape in cross section. Often sold in packs of five.

USE: To attach main and mizzen sails to masts equipped with internal or external sail tracks. The nylon cylinder or rectangular types slide into hollow channel in aluminum masts, while the bronze types insert into the corresponding bronze channel mounted externally on wooden masts. Allows sails to slide up and down easily.

USE TIPS: Shackle for slide (see below), sold separately, bolts through grommet on luff or vertical edge of sail.

BUYING TIPS: This is an area where quality counts (and where boatbuilders and sailmakers often scrimp). Buy the best and keep some spares on hand.

SHACKLE FOR SLIDE

ALSO KNOWN AS:
Slug shackle

DESCRIPTION: Nylon or stainless steel shackle with stainless steel bolt through arms. Clear plastic oval hood is bent inside stainless steel shackles. Sold in packs of five.

USE: To attach sail to sail slug (see above). Insert shackle through grommet in luff side of main, mizzen, genoa, or jib.

USE TIPS: The plastic hood on stainless shackles protects sails from chafe.

BUYING TIPS: Sized to fit variety of sail slugs. Get the stainless models for longer wear.

SAIL TIE

ALSO KNOWN AS: Sail strap

DESCRIPTION: Various design straps and cords with different end fittings for locking together.

TYPES:

Bungee or shock cord: Elasticized, jacketed cord sometimes called a *tie-down,* often with metal hooks at each end. Sold in varying lengths with different kinds of end fittings, including plastic ball and loop, wooden peg and loop, plastic clasp devices, or plastic snap hooks.

Nylon strap: Nylon webbing 1" diameter with plastic snap-shut buckle arrangement at ends. Sold in 3'–7' lengths.

USE: To lash sails to the boom, or to the deck or rail in the case of a jib or genoa.

USE TIPS: Also useful for tying off slapping halyards to reduce chafe—and noise.

BUYING TIPS: Sold four to a package, probably enough for one sail. Be sure to have several lengths on hand to accommodate bulky sails.

ABOUT SAILS

A boat's sails are usually custom-made to fit that particular model, and as such are not sold in marine supply stores. However, certain accessory sail types are generic.

Anchor-Riding Sail

DESCRIPTION: Small (15 sq. ft.: 75" leech × 58" luff × 73" foot) triangular sail hanked to the backstay or attached to the boom and hoisted with the main halyard. Made of 4.5-oz. Dacron with reinforced corners and brass grommets.

USE: To keep your boat headed into the wind while at anchor and help keep it from pitching. Not intended to be used while under way or for propulsion.

USE TIPS: Do not count on this sail to get you through a squall while under way in open water. It is not a storm jib. If you are really in trouble, though, the anchor-riding sail may be effective when used with a sea anchor or drogue. Better yet, be thoroughly familiar with distress- and emergency-signal procedures.

BUYING TIPS: Sized for boats over 26'.

Rig Pig™

DESCRIPTION: Kit that includes double-bolt rope, harness, draw string, five 18" × 6½" terrycloth pads with nylon borders and grommeted holes, various clips and fasteners, a 12-oz. needle-nose plastic bottle, and a can of silicone wax. Kit, which includes a roll-up nylon case with many pouches, comes in two sizes—Type I for all-around slides and bolt ropes from 5/16" to ½"; and Type II for flat internal slides in two sizes, ¾" and ⅞".

USE: Attach pad to bolt ropes and harness; wet pad with water, cleaner, or wax; insert in sail track; and work up and down with the boat's halyard to clean and smooth the track. Compression of the pad against the track is the key to successful cleaning.

USE TIPS: Lighter fluid or windshield-wiper fluid are the recommended cleaners—never acetone or one of the ketone solvents (or you'll be creating your own Saint Elmo's fire). Miniversion also works on furling gear tracks.

BUYING TIPS: Probably best suited for fully battened sails whose slides are often difficult to raise up the track. Otherwise this seems an elaborate and expensive, if clever, solution to a fairly simple problem. Your mast should come down regularly for inspection and cleaning anyway, and if you encounter a problem during the sailing season, try spraying some silicone spray onto your sail slides.

WINCHES AND ACCESSORIES

WINCH

DESCRIPTION: A stainless-steel, aluminum, or bronze drum housing gears that allow the drum to rotate, always in a clockwise direction, with a line wrapped around it. Several different types are made as noted below. Some winches operate manually by means of a handle that fits across the head of the winch and engages its internal gears, while others—generally only very large models—may be electric or (rarely) pneumatic. Winches are mounted on decks or on spars and are made in a large range of sizes (2"–7" drum diameter) to fit a wide range of tasks and boats. Manufacturers vary in their definition of size. Most refer to both the drum diameter and the power ratio; the latter is used to give a size, such as "No. 8,." which would indicate an 8:1 power ratio. (Windlasses are for anchors, noted in Chapter Four.)

TYPES:

Self-tailing winch: Any winch with a cam mechanism (generally a disk on top of the winch that has a small arm hanging down an inch or so on one side) that holds the line in place so that it will not slip, eliminating the need for a second crewmember to pull ("tail") the line as it is winched in, hence the name. Generally manufactured as such, but also available as after-market accessory (see page 98).

self-tailing arm

Single-speed winch (also known as *direct-drive* or *direct-action winch*): Winch with a gear ratio of 1:1. Most common on smaller boats.

Two-speed winch: Common on medium to large boats; the second speed, a very low gear, is engaged by cranking the handle in a counterclockwise motion for the final trim of the sail. Three-speed models are also available and have a switching mechanism for engagement of the third speed.

USE: This mechanical device, more sophisticated than block and tackle, makes it easier to haul in sheets or raise sails.

Self-tailing winch: Winching is a one-person operation because there is no need for a second person to tail the line off the winch and no need to cleat the line once the sail is trimmed.

Single-speed winch: Smaller models only. Used for trimming sheets on very small boats or for halyards on larger ones. Line must be cleated.

Two-speed winch: Most common model, useful on all sizes of boats except the smallest.

USE TIPS: Winches concentrate in one spot a considerable amount of force exerted by sails, sheets, halyards, or anchor lines. Before installing one in a new location on your boat, contact the boatbuilder for specific recommendations in order to see if the deck can take such stress. Unless it is equipped with a self-tailing mechanism, one person needs to tail the line as it comes off the winch while another cranks. When cranking most single-speed winches, you can ratchet (push and pull the handle back and forth) to tighten the line if you don't have enough strength to crank it 360°.

BUYING TIPS: Winches are probably the most expensive deck gear on your boat. This is one item where it pays to buy the best you can afford. Aluminum winches, preferred by racers because of their light weight, cannot be used with wire rope. Chrome-plated and polished bronze are heavy but durable and are suitable for use with wire. Some racing winches offer the best of both worlds—lightweight aluminum drums with stainless-steel sleeves for durability.

Self-tailing winches can be as much as five times the price of plain winches, but are worth the price for those who race, cruise alone, or when there's a limited crew (prices start at several hundred dollars and go quickly up to one thousand). Electric winches usually are made only for very large boats, are a drain on your electrical system, and are very expensive, but then again, if you have a very large boat, this may not be a problem for you. (Smaller, less expensive electric winches are now being introduced for boats 30' and under, primarily for the benefit of older sailors.)

Check the power ratio to determine the amount of pulling power on the line for every pound of pressure you exert on the handle. A winch with a 10:1 power ratio gives an estimated 100 lbs. of pull on the line for every 10 lbs of pressure exerted. The higher the ratio, the longer it takes to crank in the line. Be aware, however, that all ratios are estimates at best. Friction from lines, lead blocks, and the winch gears themselves reduces effectiveness. Check the manufacturer's literature for general guidelines in regard to the size of winch needed for your particular sail or boat size.

WINCH GREASE

ALSO KNOWN AS: White Teflon™ lubricant

DESCRIPTION: Calcium sulphanate-based or Teflon lubricant, water and heat resistant, sold in small plastic tubes.

USE: To lubricate winches, windlasses, trailer bearings and other marine equipment where extreme friction, heat, and exposure to salt and water are factors.

USE TIPS: Winches disassemble easily (but do this in the cabin or at home, because many small parts are spring-loaded and could fly overboard) and should be regreased at least once a year—more often for black anodized aluminum models. Follow manufacturer's instructions for maintenance.

BUYING TIPS: Winch grease has many applications and is relatively cheap. Definitely worth having in the toolbox. But don't just buy any kind of grease—get the kind that does not attract dirt or grit.

WINCH COVER

DESCRIPTION: Cloth "bonnet" with shock-cord openings. Usually blue.

USE: To cover winch—or compass—when not in use to protect from sun and salt spray.

USE TIPS: After use, winches should be rinsed in fresh water and covered.

BUYING TIPS: If you have leftover canvas scraps from awnings or sailcovers, you might want to make these yourself.

WINCH PAD

ALSO KNOWN AS: Winch wedge

DESCRIPTION: Beveled solid teak disk with top face at a slight angle to bottom. Sizes range from 2½" to 6" in diameter; bevel compensates for angle of deck.

USE: To provide a base for winches. Slight angle on face provides a better lead angle for operating winch.

USE TIPS: Available in round or oval, square, or wedge shapes. Rounder kinds provide a more finished look.

BUYING TIPS: Check winch dimensions for proper fit.

WINCH CONVERTER

DESCRIPTION: After-market rubber double-ring device fits tightly onto the top flange of any regular winch. Various sizes available. Sold in pairs.

USE: Snub rope into ribbed groove for self-tailing effect.

USE TIPS: Measure winch-drum diameter. Sold for specific makes and models, they will not work if they slip on the drum.

BUYING TIPS: Good for halyard winches but hardly a substitute for a self-tailing sheet winch.

WINCH HANDLE

ALSO KNOWN AS: Crank

DESCRIPTION: Anodized aluminum, stainless-steel, pressed-steel, or fiber-reinforced nylon arm, usually 8" or 10" long, with rotating hand grip. Opposite end has spring mechanism, sometimes with push-button release, which locks into winch head. *Standard handles* are used on primary- to medium-duty winches. *Lock-in handles* have a positive lock to keep them engaged with the winch. Lightweight glass-reinforced nylon *floating handles* also have lock-in devices. *Double grip handles* allow two-fisted winching for more cranking power.

USE: To engage the winch's internal gears for cranking.

USE TIPS: At a typical cost of $50 each (and a lot more for big ones), handles are pricey. Guests should be aware that tradition dictates that they pay immediately for any handle they drop overboard. Skippers should advise guests to immediately return handles to winch holders when not in use.

BUYING TIPS: Always keep a spare winch handle! Longer handles yield more leverage and thus more winching power. Sometimes you can avoid buying a new and larger winch simply by getting a longer handle.

WINCH-HANDLE POCKET

ALSO KNOWN AS: Winch-handle holder

DESCRIPTION: Foot-long rectangular PVC pocket with drainage hole and predrilled mounting holes.

USE: To store winch handles when not in use.

USE TIPS: Mount in an out-of-the-way spot—avoid high-traffic areas where you are bound to bruise your arms or legs.

BUYING TIPS: Good insurance against loss of expensive handles.

BLOCKS

ABOUT BLOCKS

The simple, effective mechanical advantage of blocks, or pulleys, as they're known on land, is a well-known basic of physics. On a boat the entire pulley assembly is called a block, but by definition the block is the wooden or metal case that houses the wheel, or sheave, over which rope is threaded, or reeved. Sides of the block are called cages or cheeks; where the line is fed in is called the throat. The exit end is aptly called the arse.

Blocks are used on boats to make it easier to control the running rigging (the halyards and sheets) as well as for hoisting flags or for raising or lowering dinghies on davits. Blocks often have more than one sheave when multiple pieces of rigging are controlled from the same point.

When choosing blocks, refer to the manufacturer's "working load" figure, which is the block's optimum working capacity. It is about 50% of the block's "tensile strength," the load at which the block will break. Select blocks that have stainless steel ball bearings and polished surfaces to prevent chafe. If lighter weight is a consideration, consider makes that contain Delrin™ or Torlon™ hard plastic ball bearings. Don't use blocks with aluminum sheaves for controlling wire-rope halyards. Yearly maintenance should include inspection of the running rigging for signs of wear from blocks.

ABOUT BLOCK COMPONENTS

Certain blocks are sold with some common components, such as:

Slide: Shallow, wide metal channel with spring-loaded pin for locking in place. Channel slips into or onto a track on the deck. Blocks attached to slides can be moved easily along tracks for fine-tuning sheets.

Becket: An eye made of rope (traditional on wooden blocks), metal or plastic, attached to a block and used to secure the block or to tie off or "dead-end" a line on the block. Usually found on fiddle blocks and multipart block systems.

becket

Spring mount: Fixed circular deck plate or slide-mounted base with flexible spring mechanism that holds block upright while still allowing it to tilt as it is used.

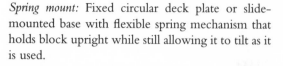

universal (loop) swivel head

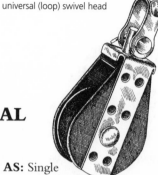

SINGLE BLOCK WITH UNIVERSAL HEAD

ALSO KNOWN AS: Single block with swivel loop top

DESCRIPTION: Basic block with one sheave (also made in double and triple models) available in a wide range of sizes for a wide range of purposes; a shackle or other fittings can be attached to the U-shaped swivel.

USE: Depending on size, to rig boom vangs (see page 116), cunninghams, outhauls, and travelers.

USE TIPS: Make sure you buy the right size for your application.

REEFING BLOCK

ALSO KNOWN AS: Jiffy reefing block, mainsail reefing block

DESCRIPTION: Block with slide attached to its cheek (side) that fits onto track installed along the length of the boom. Thumbscrew makes it possible to position block securely anywhere along the track. Sold according to track size.

USE: Key component of a simple slab reefing system used to shorten the sail area in heavy wind and weather conditions by tying the foot of the sail down to the boom.

USE TIPS: Periodically check the position of the block and adjust as conditions warrant, or the sail changes shape with age.

BUYING TIPS: Mainly for use on boats up to 35' long.

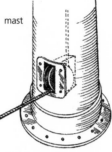

mast

Exit Block

ALSO KNOWN AS: Halyard exit block, sheave

DESCRIPTION: Block fits vertically into an opening at the lower end of the mast with mounting flanges that extend on either side of opening.

USE: To lead halyards or other lines out of mast, boom, or spinnaker pole.

USE TIPS: Rarely used lines, i.e., spinnaker halyards on a cruising boat, can simply be led through a mast-mounted pad eye.

BUYING TIPS: Useful on aluminum masts, but consult with boatbuilder before doing any cutting.

Cheek Block

DESCRIPTION: One side of block has a predrilled flange parallel with the sheave. A variation is the *multiline cheek block* with two or more sheaves mounted in line within a thin metal sleeve. Mounting flanges come curved (for masts) or flat (for decks, etc.).

USE: Designed for mounting on a curved spar or flat surface and used for turning sheets, halyards, and control lines, such as reefing lines, to provide a more efficient way of leading lines aft. The *multiline cheek block* is also known as a *deck* or *line organizer*. As its name implies, this block is useful for bringing some semblance of order to the myriad lines on deck.

USE TIPS: Mount only on surfaces that can support a load.

BUYING TIPS: Look for stainless steel ball bearings and polished surfaces to prevent chafe.

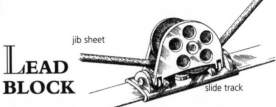

jib sheet

slide track

Lead Block

ALSO KNOWN AS: Swivel fairlead block, fairlead block

DESCRIPTION: Block is held perpendicular to its mounting flange by a heavy-duty spring. On large boats fairlead blocks are attached to a slide that fits onto a track, but they may also have a fixed mount.

USE: For halyards or in applications where line angle varies, such as genoa sheets.

USE TIPS: In combination with a *turning block*, a fairlead block is commonly used for genoa sheets.

BUYING TIPS: Very helpful item for those who sail shorthanded but want that jib up.

Snatch Block

DESCRIPTION: Combination item consisting of a block and a large snap shackle (see page 105), both of which can separately and easily snap open. They are joined together with a swivel.

USE: To temporarily install anything such as genoa sheets (as a genoa lead or temporary block), spinnaker foreguys, vangs, preventers, and cunninghams to a deck pad eye (see page 112), stanchion base, track, toe rail, or toe rail track. Key attribute is that it snaps open for instant removal of line at any point (no need to feed a line through).

USE TIPS: Be extremely careful not to accidentally pull a pin or open the block latch; better yet, fasten with a circular split ring pin (see page 130). Keep away from other lines and nonobservant crew members. Also ensure that block cage and shackle are fully latched prior to loading. Can be used for almost any purpose except as a genoa turning block, which would exceed its load capacity.

BUYING TIPS: One of the most versatile and practical pieces of gear made. Keep a spare pair on hand, despite the hefty price tag.

TURNING BLOCK

ALSO KNOWN AS: Foot block

DESCRIPTION: Block stands perpendicular to its fixed mounting flange. May be double-sheaved, in which case wheels are side by side on single-pin axle.

USE: Usually attached to base of mast or along the coaming to direct sheets aft.

USE TIPS: Check the lead angles before securing in place.

BUYING TIPS: An integral part of leading controls aft to the cockpit.

FIDDLE BLOCK

DESCRIPTION: Double-sheaved block with wheels in line with each other and one wheel smaller than the other. May have fixed or swivel head.

USE: For multipart systems, such as mainsheet and boom vang.

USE TIPS: Attaching by snap shackle permits easy removal. Even on small boats a cam cleat or Hexaratchet® block (see page 103) to secure the line is a welcome relief.

BUYING TIPS: Available with or without cam cleat, snap shackle (see page 105), or Hexaratchet® (see page 103).

BULLET BLOCK®

ALSO KNOWN AS: Utility block

DESCRIPTION: Multipurpose block with single, double, or triple sheave of stainless or anodized aluminum sheave, with diameters ranging from 1⅛" to 1½". Regular-size bullet block handles line from 3⁄16" to 5⁄16" and have a working load of about 300 lbs.; *big bullet blocks* accommodate line up to 3⁄8" and have working load of 300 lbs.; *wire/rope bullet blocks* handle rope up to 5⁄16" and wire up to 5⁄32" and have a working load of 500 lbs. Commonly available in simple *loop-top* style so that it can be simply lashed to a boom or other part. The loop-top may be called a *lashing eye* or *lash eye*.

USE: To provide light-duty leading of various control lines, including vangs, outhauls, and cunninghams, especially on dinghies. Big bullet blocks are used on bigger boats, where larger-diameter rope is used. Wire/rope bullet blocks have anodized aluminum sheaves and are for handling heavier loads or wire-rope.

USE TIPS: Do not attempt to use blocks with wire rope unless they have metal sheaves; all others will fail almost immediately.

BUYING TIPS: Primarily for dinghy sailors and racers where the reduced length of the block is a benefit.

Mini V-Jam Block

slot for jamming line

DESCRIPTION: Block made of either stainless steel or Delrin/resin with V-shaped slot in housing for holding line.

USE: General-purpose control on sailing dinghies or other light-load applications.

USE TIPS: Using the V-jam is safer than holding a line in your teeth.

BUYING TIPS: Stainless steel housing is stronger but heavier than Delrin/resin combination.

Hexaratchet®

ALSO KNOWN AS: Hexacat®

DESCRIPTION: Patented block from Harken whose eight-sided aluminum sheave grips a line passing over it. Measure 2¼" or 3" and handle line from up to ⅜" or ⁷⁄₁₆" with working strengths of 500 and 750 lbs.

USE: To add gripping power, depending on size, of 10:1 or 15:1, while permitting easing of line.

USE TIPS: Excellent means of "tying off" a sheet without actually cleating it.

BUYING TIPS: Great for sailing dinghies and other small boats.

SNAPS AND HOOKS

Snap

ALSO KNOWN AS: Snap hook, boat snap

DESCRIPTION: A strong, hook-shaped fitting a few inches long that has a spring-action tongue or other device of various designs, which closes to create a secure, oblong ring. May be made of stainless, forged, or stamped steel, or bronze. Ranges in design from simple two-part item to more complex model with swivels and eyes. Sized by both the inside diameter of the eye and the hook as well as the overall length. Smaller models are sometimes called *baby*

snaps. Do not confuse this item with the *snap fastener* (see page 213), a totally different item.

TYPES:

Fast eye spring snap (also known as *fast eye boat snap* or *forged snap*): Basic strong snap, with a lightweight, spring-loaded tongue and an eye which is part of the forged hook.

Swivel eye spring snap (also known as *swivel eye boat snap*): Common design with strong tongue and an eye that swivels around a joint in the middle of the snap.

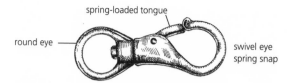

round eye — spring-loaded tongue

swivel eye
spring snap

Swivel eye piston snap (also known as swivel eye bolt snap): Generally lightweight design with a small hook and small eye, and with a small spring-loaded bar that slides back along the neck of the snap to open it up.

Swivel eye trigger snap: Shorter snap, with a round hook area opened by pulling back a spring-loaded trigger that opens the jaws of the hook.

Scissor hook: Quite different from other snaps, made of two plates that scissor back and forth to close or open. Higher safe working load due to flat design.

Spring-loaded snap hook (also known as *carabiner, safety snap,* or *safety snap hook*): Plain design of what appears to be a thick wire hook with one jaw that is spring-loaded; offered with or without *ringed eye* insert in small end. Also made in an extrastrong asymmetrical model for mountain climbers and harness users.

Canvas snap: Lightweight snap with flat oversized, oblong eye.

USE: Generally used only where quick and repeated connecting and disconnecting are important, such as connecting sections of rigging on small boats (like sail clews) and for items such as covers, flags, and dinghies.

USE TIPS: Snaps with swivels should be used when connecting to fittings on deck. Use snaps without swivels, such as scissor hooks or plain fast eye snaps only when there is no twist factor, such as on topping lifts or backstay boom pennants. Always keep in mind that spring-loaded tongues can be opened accidentally when in use, so use them with caution.

BUYING TIPS: Working load increases as the size of the snap increases (larger snaps can handle loads

up to 3,500 lbs.). For greatest strength choose forged stainless steel and be sure that snap pins are of the same material so that they last as long as the rest of the fitting. Don't underestimate the working load of the application.

Shackle

DESCRIPTION: A strong U-shaped fitting with a pin that can be inserted through a hole in one arm and screwed (*screw pin shackle* or *screw shackle*) or inserted into the other arm to complete the link. Generally made of stainless steel, but some are even made of nylon. Available in many different designs and strengths, and with pin diameters from $5/32"$ to $13/32"$, or a tensile strength from 1,765 lbs. to 12,300 lbs. Sizes are also noted by length of pin exposed and interior clearance from pin to curve. Pins on some models are designed to be *captive* (often called *double-threaded pins*) and will not fall out when unscrewed, as a *loose pin* would. Some pins are designed to be screwed in and out, while others use a *slot/key* system, sometimes called a *keypin,* which has a simple self-locking mechanism on the end of the pin that allows the pin to be removed or attached very quickly and easily.

TYPES:

Standard D shackle: Plain U-shaped, standard model.

Stamped D shackle: Lighter-weight model made from flat band of steel instead of rod.

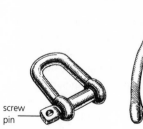

screw
pin

standard D shackle   twisted D shackle   bow shackle

Wide D shackle: Simply larger than the standard model.

Twisted D shackle: Twisted so that the top is at 90° to the bottom.

Long D shackle: Longer than the standard model. A long D sometimes has a bar across the top third to keep the shackle from falling out of the eye of the rope.

Halyard and headboard shackle: Usually the heaviest-duty model, often with a flared eye designed not to chafe the halyard; eye may be created by a second pin near the top. Models for use with rope as well as wire. Used to hoist sails.

Bow shackle: Distinguished from a standard model by its eye, which opens up slightly (for something of an Omega shape) to accommodate larger-diameter line or objects.

Double swivel shackle: Two small shackles attached to each other at their heads with a swivel.

USE: Like snaps, shackles connect a piece of rigging to another rigging system or to fittings on deck. They are often placed more or less permanently on blocks as well as at the ends of halyards.

USE TIPS: Most commonly found at the sail clew and head, for attaching sheets and halyards. Twisted shackles are especially useful where there is a lot of sideways movement on the line, compared with the relative stability of the sail itself.

BUYING TIPS: Unlike snaps, the shackle's pin bears the load, so don't use in applications that exceed 40% of the shackle's tensile strength (the point where the fitting will actually break). Sold according to various size determinations, such as inner eye height and exposed pin length. Larger ones are easier to handle. Because pins have to be screwed and unscrewed, attaching and unattaching shackles of this sort takes a little time and care. Snap shackles (see this page) are a quicker and easier but less substantial alternative.

SHACKLE KEY

DESCRIPTION: 4½"-long stamped metal tool that resembles a can opener (and in fact it also serves as one) with several holes and slots in it.

USE: To twist open small shackle pins with the added leverage of a tool.

USE TIPS: Can be used as a wrench on other small and recalcitrant items.

BUYING TIPS: Handy and inexpensive item that can be a godsend on a cold, wet sail when your fingers can't grab a small pin effectively. Sold separately or as one blade of a rigging knife.

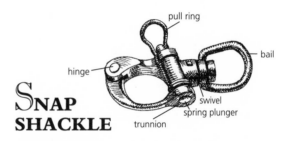

SNAP SHACKLE

DESCRIPTION: As its name implies, this is a combination of two devices, the snap (see page 103) and the shackle (see page 104). Snap shackles have two parts separated by a bar and swivel: the large half (the snap) is sort of D-shaped oblong with a hinge and the small half (the shackle) has either a small bail (ring) or a shackle. The middle bar is made of a small cylinder that contains a spring-loaded releasing pin that opens the (hinged) large part. The releasing pin usually has a small split ring (see page 130) in one end for easy grabbing (the spring is heavy-duty and resists pulling). When the pin is pulled slightly, the large half springs open. The whole thing swivels; *trunnion snap shackles* rotate as well. The small bail or shackle is usually permanently attached to another fitting or to the end of a line. Stainless steel.

TYPES:

Spinnaker bail snap shackle: Round, large bail.

D-Bail snap shackle: D-shaped, smaller bail.

Tack snap shackle: Small, square shackle.

USE: To create quick-release fittings that can be released under load, such as on spinnaker and genoa halyards and sheets.

USE TIPS: Remember that under some conditions the pin might be pulled open accidentally.

BUYING TIPS: Expensive but common and useful item in the right place. Experiment and consult with experts before using these heavy items. Manufacturers have a variety of sizes and shapes available, for example, one with a bail large enough to attach two lines.

S-HOOK

DESCRIPTION: Tapered stainless steel hook of several designs, one an actual S, the other more of a U-shaped hook with eye on one arm.

USE: To temporarily attach shackles (see page 104) or other fittings. With the closed-eye type, fasten eye to a fixed fitting or line, and hook shackle over open end for a more positive connection.

USE TIPS: Working load 500 lbs. Can be used as a quick connection between lines, such as those used to hold down a tarp.

BUYING TIPS: Lots of jury-rig uses: A few extra S-hooks in the toolbox never hurts.

TACK HOOK

ALSO KNOWN AS: Lash eye, lashing hook, sail tack

DESCRIPTION: Polished stainless steel hook with ¼" bolt hole in one arm. Available V- or

J-shaped or as a spiral, in various diameters (strengths). The spiral hook is also called a *mainsail hook.*

USE: To temporarily (and rapidly) secure sail tack (lower front corner) to deck (chainplate or gooseneck).

USE TIPS: Can also be used on mast, boom, and other locations to tie off lines.

BUYING TIPS: Bigger ones tend to be more useful because they hold more and hold more securely. But a shackle is even more secure.

CUNNINGHAM HOOK

DESCRIPTION: Stainless steel connector, similar to an S-hook with a closed eye, but with more of a V-shape than an S. A similar item with a hook at a right angle to the eye is a *reefing hook.*

USE: To connect control line to a cringle (eye) in the lower part of the luff of a mainsail (and sometimes headsail) that permits tensioning of the sail with a cunningham device.

USE TIPS: Helpful sailing close-hauled, especially in a brisk wind.

BUYING TIPS: Primarily used by racers on smaller boats.

JIB HANK

ALSO KNOWN AS: Snap hook, jib hook, jib snap, jibsnap, sail snap, jib snap hank

DESCRIPTION: Snap hook of stainless steel, bronze, brass alloy, or plastic (usually nylon) with a piston or spring-loaded tongue snap at one end and either a closed eye, pin, or hook (on forged models only) that slips through a grommet on the jib luff and is tapped or squeezed tight. Ranges in size from 1½" to 4" with a breaking strength from 550–3,100 lbs. for stainless steel type and 325–630 lbs. for bronze.

USE: Securing (hanking) the luff (leading edge) of a jib to the headstay; the hanks slip up the headstay as the halyard is pulled. Serves same purpose as sail slide on the mainsail (see page 95). Meant to be mounted on the jib permanently and designed for quick attachment and removal from the forestay.

USE TIPS: Hanks are prone to corrosion and generally getting gummed up; clean and lubricate regularly, especially before and after winter layup.

BUYING TIPS: Stainless steel and brass alloy hanks with the closed eyes are stronger and provide a more secure fastening to the jib luff.

SWIVEL-BASE MOUNT

ALSO KNOWN AS: Ball-and-socket mount

DESCRIPTION: Round permanent base about 2" diameter with ball-and-socket base that accepts blocks with ⅜" swivel posts.

USE: Mounting blocks for handling small-boat mainsheets. The swivel base gives a fair lead—in other words, guides the sheet in the desired direction—under load so that sheets don't foul. Also keeps blocks upright so that they don't hit the deck. Use only on light applications.

USE TIPS: Check the maximum working load to be sure it meets your needs. Some base mounts can handle only up to 400 lbs.; others are considerably higher.

BUYING TIPS: Buy a ready-made fairlead block with a high overall working load instead of trying to make do with the swivel-base mount.

STANCHION-MOUNT BASE

DESCRIPTION: Stainless steel fitting with shackle above a post that pins into bow pulpit or lifeline stanchions.

USE: Fitted into a lifeline stanchion, the mount creates a handy lead for lines going aft. Mount swivels so that lines don't foul.

USE TIPS: Use only on light load applications, such as furling lines or flag halyards, or light air sheets.

BUYING TIPS: Space these fairly closely on the stanchions for a neat appearance. Otherwise lines will droop.

NAB SHACKLE

ALSO KNOWN AS: Colored snap shackle

DESCRIPTION: Light-weight, color-coded (red and green) snap shackles with fixed eyes. Noncorrosive plastic, sold in pairs.

USE: Can handle sheets on small sailboats or light-weather spinnaker sheets on larger boats up to one ton.

USE TIPS: For line up to ⁵⁄₁₆" maximum, but not for heavy-duty use.

BUYING TIPS: Working load of 350 lbs.

SISTER CLIPS

ALSO KNOWN AS: Brummel hooks®, sister hooks

DESCRIPTION: Oval metal rings with two eyes, the larger one of which has a beveled slot in the side; sold in pairs. The two hook together by matching slots at a 90° angle. Wire or rope may be attached to the smaller eye. Made of stainless steel, magnesium-aluminum alloy, or manganese bronze, and in different sizes for different loads up to 3,000 lbs. (the lightest-weight models tend to be made of stainless).

USE: Instant connecting and disconnecting of lines without moving parts or shapes that can catch on something.

USE TIPS: Some of the load must be released in order to disconnect. Handy on clew of jib for quick sail changes, as well as hiking equipment and flag halyards.

BUYING TIPS: A decent alternative to snap hooks.

CLEATS AND CHOCKS

CLEAT

ALSO KNOWN AS: Horn cleat

DESCRIPTION: Traditional cleats have two arms, or horns, around which lines are wrapped and secured (belayed) and are mounted (always through-bolted) to the deck or other secure surface by two or four fasteners. They may be made of stainless steel, aluminum, Marinium® (a magnesium-aluminum-titanium-beryllium alloy), or bronze, as well as wood or plastic, which are less common. Fasteners, sold separately, should be of the same metal as the cleat. Cleats commonly have two legs to support the horns ("open base") but smaller models have a single leg ("closed base").

TYPES:

Traditional design: Can range from prosaic 5" *galvanized iron* cleat for utilitarian purposes, such as securing anchor lines, to the more elegant, all-purpose *Herreshoff* cleat, which comes in stainless or bronze.

Pop-up cleat: Fits flush into the deck in a recess when it is not in use. A molded plastic cup holds the cleat and keeps water from running below deck.

Quick-cleat: Raised oval device made of plastic, with center bolt holes and four slots that line up diagonally across from each other. It is supposed to simplify the already-simple process of belaying a line to a cleat.

Two-hole jam cleat: This is a hybrid of the traditional cleat and the jam cleat. One mounting base extends under one (usually the front) cleat arm with a tapering slot.

USE: To temporarily secure or *belay* mooring lines, halyards, sheets, and other lines to cleats by means of a figure-eight hitch or bight. The two-hole jam cleat requires fewer turns to secure the halyard or sheet. One simply "jams" the rope into the narrow slot, which makes for a quick release. Use adjacent to a winch for securing lines.

USE TIPS: Do not overload cleats or mounting surfaces. Install and choose size carefully. Make sure all your guests know how to secure a line to a cleat properly. When experienced sailors use cleats, they may wrap them so fast and effortlessly that less knowledgeable folks might think there is nothing to it. Always be sure your cleated lines are secure before leaving the boat.

BUYING TIPS: Tests show that two-hole cleats are stronger than the four-hole type. Cleats for heavy-load applications must be through-bolted, with backing plates. Stainless steel is the strongest material, but marinium comes in a close second, although it is more expensive. The chief advantage of marinium is its high strength-to-weight ratio, a factor for racers who are trying to keep everything as light as possible. Aluminum cleats are prone to corrosion, especially if they are installed with fasteners of a dissimilar metal (see discussion of electrolysis in section on zincs, page 162). Think carefully before you clutter your deck with gadgets like the quick-cleat. One cleat variation—a true improvement—is the 6" or 8" *pop-up* type.

USE: Very popular on mainsheets. A boon to racers, where quick cleating and release are a must. Provides a very secure grip.

USE TIPS: Be sure to use the proper size rope, as that is essential to its function. Also maintain, checking tension of screws that hold down arms.

BUYING TIPS: Nylon cam cleats hold ropes as small as ⅛" diameter, while aluminum ones hold ¼"- to ½"-diameter ropes. Rope size is specified on cleat or packaging.

Jam Cleat

ALSO KNOWN AS: Jammer, Clamcleat®, jamming cleat

DESCRIPTION: Small rectangle of aluminum or nylon with a large slot down the middle with teeth on either side. Also refers to a hybrid model of horn cleat with a jamming slot on one side called a two-hole jam cleat (see page 108).

USE: Extremely rapid fixing of a sheet where extremely rapid unfixing is required. One actually "jams" the line down into the teeth by pulling it through and stopping under tension. Line is released by pulling a bit more through and up.

USE TIPS: For temporary and supervised sheet cleating only.

BUYING TIPS: Available in a wide variety of shapes and sizes. Extremely common and popular item for jib sheets.

Cam Cleat

ALSO KNOWN AS: Cam

DESCRIPTION: Two flipperlike arms or jaws with teeth grab a line that is pulled down between them. Made of heavy-duty nylon or aluminum. When a rope is pressed into the slot, the tension jams the rope into the teeth, where it is held; a slight tug releases the line. An evolution in rope securing.

Midship cleat

ALSO KNOWN AS: Mobile cleat

slide

thumbscrew

DESCRIPTION: Traditionally configured aluminum cleat mounted on slide for 1" or 1¼" track. Has a thumbscrew for locking in place.

USE: To mount on a track in order to create a mobile cleat, for genoa sheets, for example.

USE TIPS: These are light-duty items with nowhere near the working loads of a standard, through-bolted cleat.

BUYING TIPS: A well-thought-out boat should have sufficient permanent cleats to handle all needs.

Shroud cleat

ALSO KNOWN AS:

Backstay cleat

DESCRIPTION: Cleat attaches by means of a set screw to wire shroud or rod up to ⅜" in diameter.

USE: For flag, radar, or navigation signal halyards—lightweight items only.

USE TIPS: Manufacturers say these devices won't damage shrouds, but it's a good idea to check from time to time for any signs of fraying.

BUYING TIPS: This is one way to fly a flag, but why compromise your standing rigging with set screws? Best left in the store.

Halyard organizer

halyards

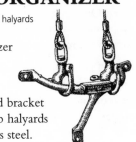

ALSO KNOWN AS:

Mast step/halyard organizer

DESCRIPTION: Combination mast step with nonskid footpad and bracket for attaching main and jib halyards when not in use. Stainless steel.

USE: Useful for attaching a safety tether when working on deck.

USE TIPS: Better used as a halyard organizer than a mast step. A more practical alternative is the eye strap (see page 113).

BUYING TIPS: Useful adjunct to cleats at the bottom of the mast for securing various halyards.

Rail and stanchion cleat

DESCRIPTION: Anodized aluminum cleat with stainless steel bracket and clamp that attaches to rails or stanchions up to 1⅜" diameter.

USE: As the name suggests, makes it possible to install a cleat just about anywhere there is a steel rod. For lightweight use, such as tying a flag halyard.

USE TIPS: Good for fenders or flag halyards.

BUYING TIPS: Inexpensive. Don't rely on this for heavy-duty applications.

Mainsheet cam unit

DESCRIPTION: All-in-one swiveling mainsheet block and cam cleat (see page 104). Sheet retaining loop (or *bail*) makes cleating fast and easy.

USE: To mount to boom end for compact, easy-to-use system for handling the mainsheet on smaller boats.

USE TIPS: Mount securely, as there's a lot of stress on this crucial point. Cam jaws should be tight enough to hold the sheet under any conditions but free enough for you to pop the sheet in and out with relative ease.

BUYING TIPS: Good on small racing boats where space is limited.

Backing plate

ALSO KNOWN AS: Under-deck pad, backing pad

DESCRIPTION: Rectangular or oval stainless steel, aluminum, or hardwood plate or pad. Typically 12" long × 2" wide × ⅛" thick, but higher stress loads may require thicker and larger pads.

USE: To mount high-load fittings such as cleats, winches, and windlasses with proper reinforcement on decks.

USE TIPS: Plate should be installed below the fitting, sized so that it is slightly larger than the fitting's base. Belowdecks a larger pad should be installed. On cleats, for instance, the pad should be twice the length of the cleat and one-half cleat length across. Heavy-load fittings should be through-bolted, with bolt holes bedded with compound to prevent leaks. (Checking the tightness of the through-bolt nuts should be a regular maintenance chore.) Don't install on balsa-core surfaces. If you have questions, contact the boat manufacturer.

BUYING TIPS: Inexpensive and much easier than making a metal one yourself.

Rope clutch

ALSO KNOWN AS: Sheet stopper, line stopper, jammer

DESCRIPTION: Lightweight composite aluminum body slightly larger than a standard desk stapler. Toothed bar closes over sheets and halyards fed through the stopper to hold them in place. Some models have separate controls for handling up to three lines (from 3/16" to ½" in diameter) at once. Working load of up to 1,500 lbs.

USE: To prevent accidental tangles in lines leading back to winches. Lines run easily in one direction, permitting you to sheet in, but clutch locking mechanisms prevent backsliding.

USE TIPS: To protect both lines and your clutch, only "fire under load" (unlock the clutch without easing tension on the sheet) when necessary—or when you are racing. These don't replace cleats completely. Unless a crew member is at the controls, cleat your lines to be absolutely sure they'll stay put. Also, the type of line you use makes a difference, with slippery Spectra® (see page 354) the best for smooth operation.

BUYING TIPS: Check manufacturer's boat-size and working-load recommendations before buying.

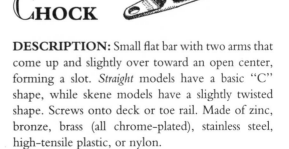

Chock

DESCRIPTION: Small flat bar with two arms that come up and slightly over toward an open center, forming a slot. *Straight* models have a basic "C" shape, while skene models have a slightly twisted shape. Screws onto deck or toe rail. Made of zinc, bronze, brass (all chrome-plated), stainless steel, high-tensile plastic, or nylon.

USE: Holds a mooring, anchor, or dock line in place where it crosses the toe rail to prevent chafe and to keep it in place.

USE TIPS: Mount as close to cleats as possible to reduce line stretch and chafe. Use stainless steel where mooring or anchor chains are in use. Use chafing gear on your lines (see page 72).

BUYING TIPS: Choose the better-quality brands and you'll have an item that outlasts the boat; also get the largest possible size for your particular application to reduce chafe on the lines. Avoid nylon for all but the lightest uses. Skene-type models hold dock lines better by keeping them from "popping" out when the boat is lower than the dock or piling.

── BLOCK AND LEAD ACCESSORIES ──

Rings

DESCRIPTION: Stainless steel O- and D-rings, ¾"–2½" ID. Sold individually.

USE: Make your own tie-down and lifting straps by attaching cloth tape, rope, or chain.

USE TIPS: For more or less permanent connections, as at the end of harness webbing, etc.

BUYING TIPS: Check workload capacities before relying upon these for heavy lifting—ring strength listed is usually the breaking strength.

Lifting Ring with Strap

ALSO KNOWN AS: Ring strap

DESCRIPTION: Predrilled mounting plate holds 1⅜" ring in place. Made of stainless steel. Attaches with four #10 fasteners (not included).

USE: With a working load of 5,000 lbs., this could be attached to a dinghy carried on davits or for other rigging purposes.

USE TIPS: Like other heavy-load fittings, attach to deck with backing plate.

BUYING TIPS: A folding pad eye (see next item) provides similar working loads but with a more finished look.

Pad Eye

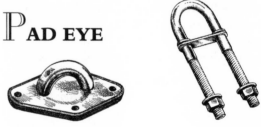

pad eye with standard mount   U-bolt pad eye

DESCRIPTION: Any of a number of stainless steel devices that attach a ring or eye to the deck or other permanent location. Some are *U-bolts* fitted with a plate that mounts flush on the deck, with the bolt in an upside-down U position. Others are one-piece fittings with predrilled holes in the mounts. Generally the eye or ring section stands perpendicular to the base, but the *folding pad eye* lies flat when not in use. *Toe rail pad eyes* have clamps that fit over the rail and attach with a large set screw to distribute the load and prevent dents. *Mast pad eyes* have a curved base to conform to the contour of a mast (check manufacturer's sizing specifications).

USE: To lift heavy objects or as a lead for a rope.

USE TIPS: Be sure the ring gives enough clearance to the rope that's passing through so that there's no chafe or bind.

BUYING TIPS: Folding pad eyes are useful for foredeck applications, where they can be folded down and out of the way when not in use, and as lifting rings on trailerable boats.

Mast ring

DESCRIPTION: Anodized aluminum or stainless steel ring permanently mounted on a predrilled flat or curved base.

USE: Attaches to any shape mast for a whisker pole or to tie off halyards.

USE TIPS: Helpful for keeping halyards organized at the mast base. Also help keep halyards close to the mast, thereby reducing slapping around.

BUYING TIPS: If they are to be permanently installed, you may as well go for the stainless.

Eye strap

ALSO KNOWN AS: Flange eye

DESCRIPTION: Stainless steel fasteners (resembling drawer handles) that range in size from 1½" to 3" long with many variations in between. Depending on size, accommodate line from ¼" to ¾" diameter and web strap up to 1¼". Predrilled holes on flanges at either end for fastening. Also available, in limited sizes, in bronze and chrome-plated zinc.

USE: Many uses, including attachment to mast to control halyards and provide fastening point for shackles.

USE TIPS: Can double as pad eye, but for light duty only.

BUYING TIPS: More practical and less unsightly alternative to mast step/halyard organizer (see page 110).

Shackle and block lanyard

ALSO KNOWN AS: Shackle leash

DESCRIPTION: Braided Dacron rope or leather thong with adjustable loops.

USE: As pull cord for shackles, blocks, spinnaker poles, sail covers, and bags.

USE TIPS: Use where you want a stronger or longer-lasting connection than shock cord or a simple knotted line would provide.

BUYING TIPS: Inexpensive. Sold in packages of two or three. Making a rope lanyard yourself would be an easy marlinspike (see page 92) project.

Rigging tape

ALSO KNOWN AS: Chafe tape, self-welding tape, chafing tape

DESCRIPTION: Self-bonding tape that adheres to itself to make an elastic, UV- and water-resistant covering of hardware.

USE: For chafe protection of sails, electrical repairs, and rope whipping. Rigging tape will make a serviceable hose repair in an emergency.

USE TIPS: Another version, *self-welding tape,* can be used underwater.

BUYING TIPS: A definite must for the toolbox.

JIB, GENOA, SPINNAKER, AND
MAINSAIL ACCESSORIES

ABOUT WHISKER POLES

Whisker poles are spars used to hold the clew (or aft bottom corner) of the jib or genoa out to one side when the boat is sailing downwind. Most often the mainsail will extend to the other side. This is called sailing wing-and-wing. In the old days whisker poles were of wood, which made them quite heavy and hard to control (imagine adjusting a 12', 2"-diameter wooden pole when all you can hold on to is the foot-long inboard section). The name *whisker pole* derives from sailing-ship terminology: whiskers are short horizontal crosspieces perpendicular to the bowsprit that spread the lines supporting the jib boom, which on sailing ships was an extension of the bowsprit.

HISKER POLE

ALSO KNOWN AS: Jib stick

DESCRIPTION: Adjustable-length anodized aluminum pole with a variety of snap-shacklelike fittings (*piston, trigger, easy latch* snap shackles or a plain *spike*) at the outer end. Some poles have *lock button* mechanisms to control length, usually in increments of 8"–12", while others have *twist-lock* controls. Sailors on larger boats may find it more convenient to use whisker poles with *line controls* that allow the operator easily to adjust the length from the inboard

end. Most have a bridle line of covered wire, which opens the snap at the clew.

USE: To hold the clew of the headsail (jib or genoa) away from the boat while sailing downwind, eliminating the need for constant small sheet adjustments.

USE TIPS: Follow manufacturer's recommendations for length of pole-to-boat size ratio. Overloading—skimping on the proper size—may cause the pole to compress and bend.

BUYING TIPS: This is an item where quality is proportionate to cost. Go for a good one. Racers need the fancier snap fittings; small boats can do with less.

ABOUT SPINNAKER POLES

Also known as a spinnaker boom, this pole is a long, light spar used to extend one of the bottom corners of a spinnaker or balloon sail. With some rigs the spinnaker may not be supported by anything, and if the sail collapses when the wind dies, the pole will fall. However, sailors can also get spinnaker poles with a variety of *single, double,* or *retractable bridles.* The lines that attach these bridles are called *guys.*

Spinnaker-pole length is determined by the J-measurement, which is the distance from the front of the mast to the headstay, measured at deck level. If you're not sure, ask the boatbuilder for the exact dimensions.

SPINNAKER-POLE
CHOCK

ALSO KNOWN AS: Pole chock

DESCRIPTION: Various designed clamps sized to accept spinnaker poles from 2" to 3½" in diameter.

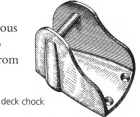

deck chock

TYPES:

Deck chock: Anodized aluminum frame with a horizontal pin for retaining spinnaker-pole hook.

Mast chock: C-shaped urethane chock with curved mount fastens to forward side of mast for vertical storage of pole.

Stanchion-mount chock: C-shaped urethane grip that clamps to 1"-diameter stanchion; sold individually, although two are needed to secure pole horizontally off the deck.

USE: To secure spinnaker pole when stored on deck.

USE TIPS: Check out your deck layout for the chock style that will best secure your pole but keep it handy for quick deployment.

BUYING TIPS: Most useful for racers or dedicated downwind spinnaker users.

SHACKLE GUARD

DESCRIPTION: 2¼"-diameter polyethylene "doughnut" fits around the spinnaker-pole guy adjacent to the shackle.

USE: To serve as a shield to prevent chafe.

USE TIPS: Can also be attached to lifelines to skirt the jib, thus preventing wear and tear.

BUYING TIPS: Available with ⅜" or ½" center holes.

LAZY JACK

DESCRIPTION: Adjustable harness extending from the mast to two points on either side of the boom to form an inverted Y. Lazy-jack kit includes vinyl-coated cable with swage fittings (a thick metal sleeve that is crimped with a special tool to fit tightly around the cable), ball bearing blocks, eyestraps (metal fitting with screw holes at either end and a hump in the middle), a cleat, and a fastener. Sold in small, medium, and large models.

USE: The cable/harness arrangement keeps the lowered sail relatively orderly and can be retracted against the mast when the sail is raised and the boat is under way. Not to be confused with a *lazy guy,* which serves roughly the same function for the boom, in terms of keeping it from swinging around when the boat is rolling.

USE TIPS: Invaluable for the single-hander (and older cruisers), as it eliminates the job of gathering the mainsail when the halyard is released.

BUYING TIPS: Despite its name, a lazy jack is actually a helpful system to have rigged on your mast when you're reefing or furling the mainsail, especially during heavy weather conditions. Available for boom lengths from 8' to 12'.

BATTEN TRAVELER SYSTEM

ALSO KNOWN AS: Battcars™

DESCRIPTION: Mainsail hoisting system of several designs that replaces conventional sail slugs and luff shackles. The most popular, by Harken Yacht Fittings, consists of special sail-track sections that snap over most existing sail tracks, a series of stainless-steel or hard plastic ball-bearing "Battslides" that fit into the track and attach, via a U-joint, to an aluminum car that is fastened to the sail luff. There is one car at each batten (smaller "luff slides" are installed at intermediate points) and a special over-sized headboard car at the top corner of the sail. Systems are available for boats from 30' to 80', and slides are sized for both flat and round bottoms. Each aluminum track section is 80¾" long and may be cut to size. Boats usually require five to ten sections, depending on the size of the sail luff.

USE: To ease raising of full-battened mainsail by distributing compression and friction loading at the points where the full battens press against the mast.

USE TIPS: Works well with a lazy-jack system, as the U-joint makes for easy "flaking" of the main.

BUYING TIPS: If you have a fully battened main, you are going to want a Battcar™ system eventually, and it will probably be cheaper and easier to have it installed when you order your sail.

ABOUT BOOM VANGS

A boom vang may look like just a simple block-and-tackle system, but it is an essential bit of rigging that virtually no sailboat should be without. Not only does the vang increase sail efficiency, it also helps prevent jibes, increases speed, smoothes out the ride in choppy seas, and cuts down on sail wear and tear.

The vang, sometimes known as a *kicking strap,* is attached to the boom with a movable nylon strap or a permanently mounted stainless-steel bail or claw. It makes a 45° angle with the boom and "dead–ends" with a block at the leeward rail (at the chainplates is best) on boats with long booms or at the base of the mast on boats with short booms.

The movable strap allows you to adjust the vang's position according to the point of sail (beating, reaching, or running). Permanently mounted bails or claws should be placed about one-quarter of the boom's length from the mast.

By holding the boom down, the vang helps to keep the leech of the sail straight for greater overall sail efficiency, especially when beating to windward. On downwind tacks the vang serves as a preventer, keeping the main from jibing.

BOOM VANG KIT

ALSO KNOWN AS: Kicking strap

DESCRIPTION: Two fiddle blocks with snap shackles rigged with ¼"–½" line. Blocks may include cam cleats or V-jam cleats found on light-duty systems. Working loads range from about 660 lbs. for boats up to 18' to 2,645 lbs. for boats up to 40'.

USE: Rigged between boom and rail or mast, a vang improves sail efficiency and overall performance, as well as prevents jibes.

USE TIPS: Experiment with tensioning the vang to achieve the most effective sail shape in various wind conditions.

BUYING TIPS: Vang kits for larger boats can be expensive. Try pricing out the individual components to rig the kit yourself—not a complicated task.

BOOM-VANG ATTACHMENT

DESCRIPTION: Nylon strap with hooked stainless steel plates that fit into the boom groove on aluminum spars. Not made for wooden booms. An eye is threaded through the strap and offers a convenient place to attach a block for rigging a boom vang.

USE: To make it possible to adjust the position of the vang on the boom according to your point of sail. Farther aft improves performance when beating, or sailing into the wind, nearer center when reaching with the wind on your beam, and farther forward helps when running ahead of the wind.

USE TIPS: Use only on boats under 35'.

BUYING TIPS: Tensile strength is 2,300 lbs.; the safe working load is half that much.

ROLLER-FURLING SYSTEMS

ABOUT FURLING SYSTEMS

Headsail furling systems have made sailing much easier and safer for the cruising sailor. Furling gear permits the jib to roll up on its luff like a window shade and eliminates the need for the crew to leave the cockpit to raise or douse sail. (Mainsail furling is newer and less common. The best units, such as Hood Yacht Systems' Stoway®, furl the main inside the mast and require a specially cut mainsail as well as a special mast.) New headsail systems have worked out some of the early bugs—halyard wraps, sloppy reefs, and bulging furls. Except for ocean racers, who often outfit with two or three separate furling systems, racers prefer the old-fashioned hanked-on headsail.

HEADSAIL FURLING SYSTEM

ALSO KNOWN AS: Roller furling

DESCRIPTION: Aluminum and stainless steel rodlike extrusion about 2" in diameter, often called

a foil, with a single or double groove or track along the aft edge for inserting jib luff. Sold in various sizes, matching the length of the average sailboat forestay—from about 38' to 60'; also sized according to headstay diameter—$\frac{5}{32}$" to $\frac{3}{8}$". Some models are free-standing, but most fit over the existing forestay. A rope-driven drum, or reel, at the base rotates the foil with the aid of a swivel joint at the top. Both drum and swivel joint operate on stainless steel or Torlon® ball bearings.

USE: Rolls up the jib by remote control via the furling line, which leads back from the drum to the cockpit. Unfurls by hauling on jib sheet.

USE TIPS: Unless you have a much flatter-cut headsail than usual, roller-furled sails lack tension on the luff and thus are too full to perform well under reef, especially in a breeze. You might consider a custom jib that is also fitted with Acrylon or similar ultraviolet-resistant cloth on the leech to prevent damage when the sail is furled.

BUYING TIPS: Sloop owners might want a double-groove extrusion that permits a second jib to be set; the alternative is a free-standing system, such as ProFurl, that permits the hanking of a storm jib, for example, on the original headstay. Other choices concern open drum, which permits easy inspection or untangling; or sealed drum, which better protects the ball bearings. Club racers will want a split drum, which quickly unfastens to permit tacking the jib to the deck. Excellent purchase for solo skippers, or those who need to limit their physical exertion.

FURLING-SYSTEM ACCESSORIES

FURLING LEAD BLOCK

DESCRIPTION: Stainless steel or plastic block with stainless cheeks that clamps to pulpit and stanchions from ⅞" to 1½" in diameter, with sheave (wheel) capable of handling line up to ⅜" or ½", depending on model. Working loads from 650 lbs. to 1,000 lbs.

USE: To lead headsail furling line aft to cockpit along outboard edge of boat, reducing deck clutter.

USE TIPS: Especially useful where a large cabin top interferes with lines leading straight back along foredeck.

BUYING TIPS: Sold in kits of one pulpit and three stanchion blocks.

FURLING FAIRLEAD

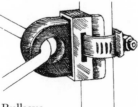

ALSO KNOWN AS: Bullseye

DESCRIPTION: Nylon or plastic circle ring (similar to pad eye) with clamp for attaching to stanchions of ⅞" to 1½" in diameter. Some have stainless steel inserts in the bulls-eye that can accommodate line up to ⅜".

USE: To lead furling line aft on outboard side without aid of blocks.

USE TIPS: More likely to snag than furling lead block (see above).

BUYING TIPS: Intended only for smaller boats.

HEADSAIL PREFEEDER

DESCRIPTION: Small stainless-steel or black rubber open-cornered triangle about 1¼" each side with welded bail (arch) on the far side.

USE: Attaches near furling drum to guide jib luff into foil groove of headsail furling systems for hoisting. Shock cord can be fastened to bail to further tension and steady the fitting.

USE TIPS: Helpful for shorthanded sailors who do not have a second person to manually guide the sail into the track (a little Teflon® spray helps too).

BUYING TIPS: Not a necessity, unless you race and make frequent headsail changes.

TRAVELER SYSTEMS

ABOUT TRAVELER SYSTEMS

A traveler is a sail-control device that permits you to alter the angle of the boom and mainsail to the wind without affecting sail shape. Once used almost exclusively by dinghy sailors and racers, travelers have gained wide acceptance among cruising sailors. While sailing to windward in heavy air the traveler can be used to adjust the boom to leeward to spill wind, reducing heel and weather helm (the tendency of a boat to round up). Conversely the traveler can haul the boom slightly to windward in light-to-moderate air to narrow the angle of attack and improve pointing. Off the wind the traveler can be used to center the boom and maintain pressure on it to preserve sail shape.

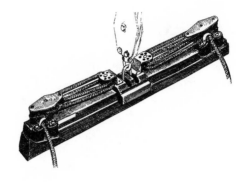

Mainsail Traveler

ALSO KNOWN AS: Traveler

DESCRIPTION: A hollow I-beam-shaped *track,* similar to a genoa lead track, along which slides an adjustable *car* (usually on ball bearings), which is connected to the mainsheet via a block-and-tackle arrangement. The traveler runs athwartships (side-to-side) and is set up on the cabin top, cockpit sole, or transom, under the boom.

Tracks for boats 20'–45' long are generally 1⅛"–1½" in width and 30"–40" in length. They are made of anodized aluminum or a high-grade alloy, such as 6061-T6 aluminum, sometimes with a Teflon coating to reduce friction. Drilled holes at close intervals (4" for example) permit securing to hull or deck with #10 fasteners or equivalent and also accept an *adjustable track stop* (see page 120), a U-shaped clamp with a screw-down stainless steel spring pin. The car, or *slide,* with four or six ball bearings (wheels), is made of aluminum and averages about 4" in length. The cars are fitted with one or more of a variety of controls, including sheaves (see page 99) for ¼" line, dead-end bails (tangs) for controlling lines, cam cleats, or stainless-steel channels with a pin for attaching a block.

USE TIPS: When adjusting the traveler, make comparable adjustments in the athwartships jib lead, moving it forward or back to keep jib angle in line with the main.

BUYING TIPS: Many production boats come *sans* traveler. When in doubt about unit size, consult your boatbuilder, class association, or traveler manufacturer.

TRAVELER ACCESSORIES

CONTROL END UNIT

ALSO KNOWN AS: End stop

DESCRIPTION: U-shaped neoprene and stainless steel fitting that encapsulates track end; fitted with single or double control sheaves (see page 99) and (often) a cam cleat (see page 109). Made in port and starboard versions, some with a pivoting cam cleat that allows the lead angle to be altered.

USE: To add anywhere from 2:1 to 4:1 purchase (mechanical advantage).

USE TIPS: Although they shorten the track, control units make it much easier to control the system.

BUYING TIPS: All but dedicated dinghy racers will want a cam cleat for tying off the mainsheet.

ADJUSTABLE TRACK STOP

DESCRIPTION: Small (2-oz.) aluminum clamp that fits over top side of I-beam track; stainless steel spring-loaded pin snaps down into one of track's predrilled holes.

USE: As a brake or block for the traveler car when control lines are uncleated.

USE TIPS: Check that screw is tightened before engaging the traveler.

BUYING TIPS: Get a few extras—they can serve as backups for both the traveler and genoa tracks.

TRACK END CAP

ALSO KNOWN AS: Track end stop

DESCRIPTION: Rubber or plastic cap that fits over end of traveler track.

USE: To cover rough ends of aluminum track while serving as final brake to car.

USE TIPS: Also imparts a finished look.

BUYING TIPS: Not needed when using end control units.

WINDWARD SHEETING CAR

DESCRIPTION: Patented Harken Yacht Equipment device, either a complete car or adaptor for conventional Harken car, with a stainless steel mechanical linkage between each of its two control cam cleats and the mainsheet block mounted between them. The linkage automatically opens jaws of the leeward cleat under pressure from the leeward-leaning mainsheet. Adapter version slips over existing car and is fastened with mounting cap screws (provided).

USE: To permit helmsman to sheet car to windward without loosening leeward control lines or moving out of position.

USE TIPS: Because the device may loosen control line at mooring, allowing the boom to slosh around, fix an extra line to control end cleats.

BUYING TIPS: Primarily for the racer who cannot afford to lose any ground to the competition. At $160–$300-plus, this is a luxury for the cruising sailor.

CHAPTER SIX

STANDING RIGGING

ABOUT STANDING RIGGING

Standing rigging consists of those components—shrouds, stays, tangs, chainplates, and other fittings—that hold up a sailboat mast against the forces of nature. Headstay (forestay) and backstay hold the mast fore and aft, respectively, while a series of upper and lower shrouds (extending to the masthead or close by and those reaching to the spreaders) keep it in place horizontally. Needless to say, these are critical parts of a sailboat that are subject to tremendous stresses. To keep the rigging standing, check fittings at least once each season for signs of corrosion, stress, or loosening, and inspect shrouds carefully for sign of wear (usually in the form of "meathooks," tiny but sharp wire ends) and distortion. Immediately replace any part of the standing rigging that is less than 100%.

STANDING RIGGING WIRE

ALSO KNOWN AS: Wire rope, shroud wire, wire cable

DESCRIPTION: Stainless steel 1 × 19 wire cable (that's one strand consisting of 19 wires) ranging in diameter from ³⁄₃₂" to ⅜" and in breaking strength from 1,200 to 17,500 lbs. Sold by the foot.

USE: Headstay, backstay, and upper and lower shrouds are used to hold the mast up and in position. Also used to "tune" (adjust) the fore and aft and side-to-side "rake" (inclination) of the mast.

USE TIPS: Many stock boats come with undersized wire. Check with the boatbuilder or a rigger to see if you can go up one size without changing chainplate size.

BUYING TIPS: A vital part of a sailboat. Buy only the highest quality U.S.-made stainless steel. Unless you are an experienced rigger and have the proper tools, have your supplier install the end fittings by which the shroud will be attached to mast and deck.

——— STANDING RIGGING HARDWARE ———

TURNBUCKLE

ALSO KNOWN AS: Bottlescrew (infrequently used), rigging screw

DESCRIPTION: Internally threaded fitting that accepts a screw at either end. One end is threaded in opposite direction to the other, so that twisting in one direction will release both screws and twisting in the opposite direction will tighten them. Sleeves may be *tubular barrel* with *check nut locks* or *open barrel* types. Stainless steel or chrome-plated bronze.

open barrel

USE: To adjust the tension of standing rigging. Located on the stays or shrouds close to the deck, adjacent to the chainplates. Toggle fittings at one or both ends allow free movement.

USE TIPS: Tape ends to keep water out, but check shroud tension regularly, as well as the bend of the mast, and adjust turnbuckles accordingly.

BUYING TIPS: Consult with boatbuilder for safe workload. Some turnbuckles are rated for as low as a 480 lb. workload, while others max out at 3,280 lbs. Keep a variety of port and starboard (left-hand and right-hand) extras on board.

TANG

DESCRIPTION: Stainless-steel strip with holes punched in either end for fasteners, 3"–14" long, ½"–1½" wide, usually straight but sometimes with bent ends.

USE: Bolted or riveted at one end to mast, boom, pulpit, or similar sturdy base for attachment of a stay or such things as mainsheet block and tackle.

USE TIPS: A couple of tangs at the end of the boom will handle the topping lift as well as the mainsheet controls.

BUYING TIPS: Tangs carry heavy loads, so buy only the best stainless steel and keep at least one extra on hand.

SWAGE STUD

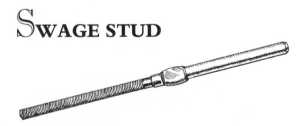

ALSO KNOWN AS: Swage, swage end

DESCRIPTION: Stainless steel rod threaded along half its 3"–4¼" length and ranging in diameter from about ¼"–⅝". Different sizes fit wire rigging measuring from 1/16" to ⅜" in diameter. *Marine eyes* and *marine forks,* which connect wire with clevis pins to mast fittings or double-jawed toggles (see page 124), are large versions that must be swaged by machine by a professional.

USE: Fastens to stay or shroud so that the rigging may attach to a turnbuckle.

USE TIPS: Only those with experience in rigging matters should attempt swaging; otherwise, let a professional do it.

BUYING TIPS: A stud comes with two dimensions—the wire end and the "deck" end. Be sure to match a stud with both your stay and turnbuckle dimensions. Requires a swage tool (see below).

SWAGE TOOL

ALSO KNOWN AS: Swaging tool, hand swage, oval sleeve tool

DESCRIPTION: Pliers-like crimping tool specifically designed for compressing swage studs and swage eyes.

USE: To mechanically affix swage studs or eyes to wire rope.

USE TIPS: Studs with oval sleeves require an oval sleeve swage tool.

BUYING TIPS: You can't swage without a swage tool.

RIGGING TERMINAL

ALSO KNOWN AS: Standing rigging terminal, mechanical terminal, stay connector, swageless terminal

DESCRIPTION: 316 stainless steel (occasionally bronze) multipart, self-locking fitting, about 2½"–7" in length (extra-long sizes are available) with a sleeve at one end to accommodate various sizes of

1 × 19 wire rope (³⁄₁₆"–³⁄₈"); deck-end configurations include eye, fork with clevis pin, and stud. Often called by brand name, such as *Norseman* or *Sta-Lok*.

USE: Do-it-yourself end fitting for connecting a shroud or cable to a deck fitting or stanchion.

USE TIPS: Some riggers swear by mechanical fittings, while others maintain swage fittings (see page 123) are more reliable. Boats with swage fittings can carry rigging terminals as emergency connectors. Be sure to follow the manufacturer's instructions exactly.

BUYING TIPS: Rigging shops often include terminals with stays and shrouds; however, you can request that a specific type be used.

TOGGLE

ALSO KNOWN AS: Toggle jaws, turnbuckle toggle

DESCRIPTION: U-shaped ("double-jawed") metal link, often bronze or chromed bronze, with a clevis pin that attaches to a chainplate (see below) or similar deck fitting. Some toggles are U-plates that come attached to a T-fitting on certain models of turnbuckles. Ranges in length from 1½"–1⅝" and in pin diameter from ¼"–⅝".

USE: To attach turnbuckle or shroud end fitting to chainplate; acts as a universal joint, swiveling to align standing rigging with fittings and reducing stress on shrouds.

USE TIPS: Wherever there is a turnbuckle there should also be a toggle, including on lifelines.

BUYING TIPS: Toggles that come as part of a turnbuckle are the most convenient; because they are under heavy loads, they should be kept lubricated for easy turning.

CHAINPLATE

ALSO KNOWN AS: Chain plate, chain strap

DESCRIPTION: Metal fitting, usually stainless steel, usually a plate or strip of stainless steel, 10" or longer, perforated with evenly spaced holes but also of other designs, including a square plate with a pad eye or similar arrangement for attachment of a toggle or turnbuckle. Often part of the hull, either bolted or fiberglassed in, but available as an aftermarket item as well.

USE: At-the-hull fitting to which all other components of standing rigging connect.

USE TIPS: If your hull shows signs of distortion under load, you may want to increase the size of your chainplate or switch from a horizontal plate to a vertical strap that bolts to the side or down the bow of the hull.

BUYING TIPS: A chainplate should be sturdy, with about a third more the breaking strength of the shroud it holds, and because it is at deck level and subject to saltwater spray, corrosion-resistant.

QUICK-RELEASE FORESTAY LEVER

ALSO KNOWN AS: Headstay lever

DESCRIPTION: Locking device attached at one end to the forestay and at the other to the bow or bowsprit with clevis pins (see page 129) that are included with the lever or with quick-release pins. Letting up on the locking lever releases tension on

the forestay, making it possible to detach the stay from the bow.

USE: To make it easier to step and unstep masts on smaller boats that are trailered.

USE TIPS: Because the last stay you want to lose under sail is the forestay, use a clevis pin fastened with a ring pin to secure the lever.

BUYING TIPS: Check the forestay loads before installing a lever; safe working load is about 1,400 lbs.

Backstay Adjuster

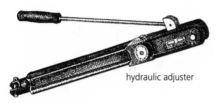

hydraulic adjuster

ALSO KNOWN AS: Backstay tensioner

DESCRIPTION: Device that attaches to the backstay in place of a turnbuckle.

TYPES:

Hydraulic adjuster. Oil-filled aluminum cylinder with stainless steel piston and attached handle; aluminum jaws attach the cylinder to the backstay and deck. Ranges in size depending on make, but generally from 22"–25" (closed), 29"–33" (open). Adjusters are fitted with a gauge that shows force in psi—which ranges from maximums of 4,600 psi to 8,600 psi. Remote hydraulic gauges (for hard-to-reach or split backstays) consist of a gauge panel and handle that is cockpit-mounted and connected to the hydraulic cylinder via high-pressure Kevlar® (or similar material) hose.

Mechanical adjuster: Stainless steel turnbuckle-like fitting that is hand-adjustable via a small wheel; typi-

cally measures about 14" closed and 20" open and permits play of about 6¾". A removable smaller version, called a *babystay adjuster,* is made for inner forestays with storm staysails or the like.

USE: Tensioning the backstay (and thereby the forestay) to alter mast bend and sail shape for maximum performance.

USE TIPS: Tensioning the forestay in a breeze flattens the headsail and permits a boat to point higher; it also flattens the main to reduce power somewhat when the wind pipes up. Smaller boats can get by with a mechanical adjuster; boats 28' and longer should consider the hydraulic version, which is self-contained and does not require a pre-existing hydraulic system.

BUYING TIPS: Not just for racers anymore, but cruisers who want a simple, effective way of controlling backstay tension. Because hose lines for remote hydraulic are fitted with swages at the factory, the length required for your boat should be carefully measured beforehand.

Wire Rope Clamp

ALSO KNOWN AS: Cable clamp

DESCRIPTION: Drop-forged high-quality Type-316 stainless steel U-bolt threads through twin-peaked mounting base. The base clamps down on the wire rope or cable as the nuts on the U-bolt are tightened.

USE: To secure high-tension cables, such as on standing rigging.

USE TIPS: Best used as a temporary, jury-rig connection for rigging on all but the smallest boats. May be used to connect cables in steering systems.

BUYING TIPS: Sold by wire-size capacity, ¼–⅜" (6–10mm) diameter.

Detent Pin

spring-loaded ball

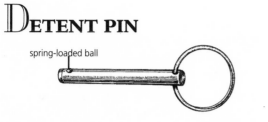

DESCRIPTION: Similar in appearance to clevis pin but operates with a spring-release mechanism that pushes out two tiny balls or knobs at one end.

May have hole at opposite end for split ring or cotter pin. Deluxe pins have wide push button. Made of stainless steel, ³⁄₁₆"–³⁄₈" diameter and as long as 1½".

USE: To allow for one-handed insertion or release—just shove it in or yank it out!

USE TIPS: Deluxe pins have push button in recess for syringelike action.

BUYING TIPS: More expensive than clevis pins. Sold singly.

— STANDING-RIGGING ACCESSORIES —

Bosun's Chair

ALSO KNOWN AS: Rigging chair

DESCRIPTION: Swing seat that attaches to a halyard. Originally little more than a simple wooden seat (sometimes a curved barrel stave was used for more comfort), bosun's chairs are now quite sophisticated arrangements with adjustable padded seats, safety harnesses, side pockets for tools, and D-rings at top and bottom.

USE: To hoist a crew member up the mast to make repairs to sails, rigging, and the mast.

USE TIPS: Some bosun's chairs have rings attached to the bottom of the seat to keep the seat from swinging as the boat rolls. Best used on (very) calm days at the dock.

BUYING TIPS: Look for water-repellent and mildew-resistant fabric, as well as stainless steel rings and hardware for greater durability. Check for comfort—preferably by trying out various models—an essential feature if you're going to be aloft for any length of time.

Cable Cutter

ALSO KNOWN AS: Wire cutter

DESCRIPTION: Plierslike tool with sharp pincers, often of heat-treated steel, capable of cutting metal.

USE: To cut standing rigging (or wire-rope running rigging), especially in an emergency, as when the mast has fallen and is threatening to dash in the hull.

USE TIPS: Useful for cutting any thick line, rope, or wire aboard the boat.

BUYING TIPS: A must on cruising and racing sailboats of any size. Smaller models will cut up to ³⁄₁₆" cable; those with thicker shrouds will need a bigger, long-handled version.

Spreader Roller

DESCRIPTION: High-impact UV-resistant Delrin™ doughnut that attaches to shroud above or below spreaders. Fits ³⁄₁₆"–³⁄₈" wire.

USE: To protect genoa jib from chafing against spreaders.

USE TIPS: Can be installed with rigging in place.

BUYING TIPS: Sold in pairs. Chafe protection is essential on the spreaders, considering the cost of repairing or replacing sails. However, you may not need the rollers if you have spreader boots (see next item).

SPREADER BOOT

DESCRIPTION: Flexible white rubber shallow T up to 8" long, with openings for shrouds and spreader ends.

USE: To reduce sail chafe around spreaders. Also prevents water from getting into spreader ends.

USE TIPS: More durable and effective than simply taping the spreader ends—but you should tape the boots securely and check annually for signs of cracking or wear.

BUYING TIPS: Sold in pairs, sized according to length of boat.

SHROUD ROLLER

ALSO KNOWN AS: Split shroud roller

DESCRIPTION: Hollow white plastic split tube, 5' long, 1" in diameter, with plastic grommets at ends or self-locking filled tubes that fits ³⁄₁₆"–³⁄₈" shrouds.

USE: To prevent fouling of jib clew and sheet while tacking.

USE TIPS: Also provides chafe protection for sails, sheets, and rigging.

BUYING TIPS: Sold in pairs. Essential to prevent wear.

MAST BOOT

ALSO KNOWN AS: Mast coat

DESCRIPTION: A waterproof covering of cloth or vinyl that fits around the mast where it goes through the deck. Secures by internal cord or external stainless steel *mast boot clamp,* an extra-large hose clamp.

USE: To prevent leaks into the cabin.

USE TIPS: *Wrap-around* cloth mast boot secures with cords in an internal skirt and fits masts with 24"–28" circumferences. *Molded* mast boots wrap around oval or round masts 17"–30" in circumference and are held in place by stainless steel *mast boot clamps.* Adhesive included with mast boot glues vinyl ends.

BUYING TIPS: Oversized stainless steel hose clamps for fastening are sold separately. Either mast-boot type will be more watertight if it is wrapped with mast-boot tape.

MAST-BOOT TAPE

DESCRIPTION: Elastic waterproof rubber tape, resistant to sun, salt, and fresh water.

USE: To make a waterproof seal where mast goes through the deck.

USE TIPS: Can be used alone or in conjunction with a cloth or molded mast boot.

BUYING TIPS: A good product that actually works. Sold in 40' roll.

DECK FITTINGS

ABOUT HARDWARE AND TEAK DECK FITTINGS

Boat owners have a wide variety of hardware, fitting, and components to choose from that improve the performance, comfort, safety, and convenience of operations and activities on deck. It is important to be mindful of the rigors of the marine environment—salt, sun, and water, as well as temperature extremes—when selecting materials. On board a boat, corrosion, rot, and rust will quickly render useless much of the hardware that is perfectly suitable around your house. Choose parts made of stainless, bronze, anodized aluminum, chrome-plated, teak, or oak for longevity. The application often determines which is the best material to use.

SPRING CLAMPS

ALSO KNOWN AS: Spring clips

DESCRIPTION: Familiar clamps with squiggled arms that extend from flat mount.

USE: The arms' shape gives a natural spring action that holds round objects such as boat hooks, rods, poles, and hoses in place.

USE TIPS: Handy down below. Choose stainless steel to resist corrosion.

BUYING TIPS: Sold in pairs.

MAST STEP

folding mast step

DESCRIPTION: Chrome-plated cast bronze 4⅛" wide × 2¼" deep step held in place by spring. *Folding mast step* folds flat when not in use. Other models include a simple V-shaped aluminum step that bolts to the mast or a *removable mast step* that slips into two predrilled holes in the mast and can be removed easily when not needed.

USE: Mount these on the transom, mast, or other places where a ladder is not often needed.

USE TIPS: On the transom, folding steps could provide a handy emergency ladder. If you are concerned about cluttering up your boat with a lot of odds and ends, consider using removable mast steps (or a bosun's chair).

BUYING TIPS: For best footing choose mast step with largest step.

DECK STEP PAD

ALSO KNOWN AS: Step plate

DESCRIPTION: Vinyl, plastic, rubber, teak, or aluminum and teak rectangles that mount with adhesive strips or screws.

USE: To install in high-traffic areas, such as at boarding gates, to prevent scratches in the gel coat.

USE TIPS: Can provide extra traction in areas that are frequently wet and slippery.

BUYING TIPS: Choose the screw-mounted type if at all possible. Step pads mounted with adhesives will eventually lift. The gummy adhesive residue is unsightly and difficult to remove.

——— FASTENERS AND ACCESSORIES ———

WOOD PLUG

ALSO KNOWN AS: Bung

DESCRIPTION: Cylindrical pieces of oak, teak, and mahogany ¼"–1" diameter × approximately ½" high. Other sizes and types of wood are also available, typically ⅜", 5⁄16", ½", and ⅝".

USE: To fill screw holes in wooden decks, moldings, or other woodwork.

USE TIPS: For even wear and a more professional finish, place plugs with their grain running in the same direction as the wood they're filling.

BUYING TIPS: Plugs are sold in small bags of twenty pieces but are also available in large quantities for much less cost. You can make your own if you have a drill press and plug cutter. Figure on using hundreds, if not thousands, of plugs when installing a new teak deck, cabin floor, or if you are refastening the planks of a wooden boat.

WELL NUT

DESCRIPTION: Threaded stainless steel sleeve with flange.

USE: Insert well nut with flange end on inside of work surface. Thread bolt through sleeve when mounting hardware on a wooden surface, for example.

USE TIPS: Prevents wear on the mounting surface, particularly if hardware "works."

BUYING TIPS: For specialized use; sold in packs of three.

CLEVIS PIN

ALSO KNOWN AS: Toggle pin, rigging pin

DESCRIPTION: Short stainless steel rod with wide, flat head at one end and small hole drilled through the other.

USE: To lock shackles or turnbuckles closed. Pin slides through open holes in arms and is held in place by inserting a cotter pin or a split ring through its hole.

USE TIPS: Use only stainless steel cotter pins or rings with stainless clevis pins to avoid corrosion.

BUYING TIPS: Assortments of clevis and cotter pins are sold in lidded storage boxes. Essential toolbox item.

COTTER PIN

ALSO KNOWN AS: Split pin (chiefly British)

DESCRIPTION: A half-round stainless steel, plain-steel, or brass strip bent into a pin shape with an eye at one end. Available in sizes from 1" × 1⁄16" to 1½" × ⅛".

USE: Secure shackle pins by inserting a cotter pin through the small hole in the shackle pin. Then bend or flare the cotter pin ends back on themselves.

USE TIPS: Use only stainless steel or brass on boats.

BUYING TIPS: An assortment is essential for the onboard toolbox.

SPLIT RING

ALSO KNOWN AS: Ring
pin, fastpin, cotter ring

DESCRIPTION: Open stainless steel ring, ⅜" to 1⅛" in diameter, with overlapping ends, similar to a keyring, only of lighter-gauge wire.

USE: To slip through holes in clevis pins to lock them in place.

USE TIPS: Safer to use on turnbuckles, where splayed cotter-pin wings can cause nasty cuts.

BUYING TIPS: Sold in assortment packs. Another toolbox necessity.

PLASTIC SNAP CAP

ALSO KNOWN AS: Screw cap

DESCRIPTION: Small plastic cover fits over screw or bolt head.

USE: To provide a finished look and to prevent leaks, vibration, and corrosion around fasteners.

USE TIPS: Also handy for preventing scrapes against sharp fastener heads.

BUYING TIPS: Sold in different sizes and lots of 20 or more. Available in several colors: teak, off-white, silver-gray, black.

BARREL NUT

DESCRIPTION: Chrome-plated ½"-long nickel mushroomlike sleeve with internal threads, has a

Phillips head. Sleeve inserts into the work piece to receive through bolt. Commonly available for #10 or ¼" bolts.

USE: Rather than having an unsightly nut-and-bolt end exposed on ports or other deck hardware, use a barrel nut to receive the bolt end.

USE TIPS: You will need to predrill a hole to fit barrel nut OD. Measure carefully; nut must fit snugly and may need to be hammered—gently—into place.

BUYING TIPS: Sold in packs of twenty-five, fairly expensive.

THREAD LOCK

ALSO KNOWN AS: Loctite™

DESCRIPTION: Liquid plastic compound in various formulas, e.g., methacrylate, that forms a watertight skin when applied to metal parts.

USE: To keep various fasteners, such as a nut and bolt at the masthead, from coming loose because of vibration and to protect them from corrosion.

USE TIPS: Tape over the connection for added protection. Light-duty thread lock can be broken with ordinary hand tools; heavy-duty seal may have to be heated to break the bond. Some brands contain suspected carcinogens, so handle with care and wash your hands after using.

BUYING TIPS: Reliable product that provides extra security for the racer and offshore sailor.

── WIND AND SAIL INSTRUMENTS ──

WIND VANE

DESCRIPTION: A lightweight plastic, aluminum device 10"–20" long, mounted on the masthead on a pivoting upright pole.

USE: To indicate wind direction relative to boat. Trim sails efficiently and maximize performance by keeping an eye on the wind vane for direction changes. Because the wind vane is mounted at the top of the mast, it is not affected by downdrafts or other air currents from the sails.

USE TIPS: Some units have red and green markings for port and starboard, and may be made of reflective material for nighttime use.

BUYING TIPS: Anodized aluminum vanes last longer, whereas plastic ones tend to get brittle and break easily. Look for stainless steel hardware that will not corrode.

TELLTALE

ALSO KNOWN AS: Tell-tale

DESCRIPTION: A short length of string, plastic, or cloth attached near the luff of a sail or to a shroud.

USE: Like a wind vane, a telltale mounted on a shroud indicates the direction of the wind relative to the boat. Those attached to the luff of the sail let you know when to trim the sail—they flow straight out in the same plane as the sail when trimmed properly, and flutter about when it is not.

USE TIPS: Some telltales come with adhesive patches or locator disks for on-sail mounting. Others

have grommets that slip easily onto stays or shrouds and rotate freely.

BUYING TIPS: Inexpensive and very useful.

OFFSET MASTHEAD MOUNT

DESCRIPTION: Aluminum L-shaped arm or boom (13" long) with mounting bracket at mast end and socket for windvane at opposite end. Mounting hardware included.

USE: The offset masthead mount keeps windvanes clear of antennas, anemometer rotors, or other hardware on the masthead. It can be adjusted to remain level even when mounted on a 20° incline.

USE TIPS: Arm can be cut to fit to the clearance you require.

BUYING TIPS: Before you buy one and add to the masthead clutter, be sure an offset is really needed.

HANDHELD WIND METER

ALSO KNOWN AS: Anemometer

DESCRIPTION: Any of a number of wind-speed measuring devices that are small and simple enough to be held in the hand. Readings may be given on a scale, analog dial, or digitally. Digital units require batteries; analog versions operate directly from windspeed. Some have expanded scales for more accurate readings of winds less than 20 mph.

USE: Typically, handheld wind meters have turbine devices that, when they're held into the wind, will give a fairly accurate reading of wind velocity. Racing sailors require anemometers for efficient sail use, but owners of larger boats will probably want more sophisticated electronic anemometers mounted to their mastheads.

USE TIPS: Also helpful to determine exact wind direction.

BUYING TIPS: This is an item where price reflects accuracy.

CLINOMETER

ALSO KNOWN AS: Level gauge inclinometer

DESCRIPTION: Protractorlike device with 0° at the scale's center, extending to up to 60° on either side. Nonmagnetic ball in glass race indicates angle. Dual-scale model includes an extra-sensitive 6° scale. Scales are in high-contrast colors, such as black and chartreuse, and fairly large size, 6" wide, for easy reading under way.

USE: Mounted athwartships on a sailboat, a clinometer shows the angle of heel.

USE TIPS: Knowing the exact heel or trim angle allows the skipper to make sail trim adjustments to maximize boat performance.

BUYING TIPS: Cheaper versions have self-adhesive backings. When accuracy is important, choose the more expensive, permanently mounted type.

WIND-SPEED/POINT INDICATOR

ALSO KNOWN AS: Wind module, wind detector

DESCRIPTION: Instrument that provides analog display of apparent wind and/or true wind speed and direction. Calibrated 360° and, depending on model, can measure wind speed from 0 to 99 knots. Most come with masthead transducer and wind vane and approximately 80' of connecting cable.

USE: To display wind speed and either/or true or apparent (define) wind direction.

USE TIPS: Compare readouts for trimming sail to maximum efficiency.

BUYING TIPS: Expensive item that is more useful for racers than cruisers.

TILLERS, RUDDERS, AND ACCESSORIES

TILLER LOCK

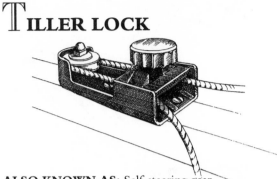

ALSO KNOWN AS: Self-steering gear

DESCRIPTION: System consisting of lightweight line and palm-sized tiller attachment (usually plastic) with a wheel through which line passes.

USE: To free up your hands from steering so that you can handle sheets or furl sails. Also ends need to lash tiller when moored. Tiller attachment is screwed onto tiller (may be a permanent or quick-release mount). Line that passes through attachment is tied off at either side of the cockpit and holds the tiller in place so that boat maintains its heading, or keeps its course.

USE TIPS: Much simpler to use and less expensive than sophisticated autopilots. Not reliable enough for single-handed sailors on offshore cruises.

BUYING TIPS: Not all boats will be able to hold a course, at least not on all points of sail—check with your manufacturer or class association. If you buy, look for stainless-steel hardware. It may be necessary to install cleats at strategic points to tie off control lines. Cam cleats (see page 109) work well.

TILLER EXTENSION

ALSO KNOWN AS: Walking stick, hiking stick

DESCRIPTION: Fixed or telescoping arm up to 4' long, with a handle similar to those found on shovels, a cushioned nonslip grip with a knob handle, or a plain handle. Opposite end has swiveling locking pin, or sometimes a universal joint, for attachment to tiller.

USE: An extra length of tiller allows the person steering to lean out over the side (called hiking) to help balance the boat. Especially useful on small sailboats. Modern versions are easier to use and install than the original version, which was often no more than a length of dowel lashed or tied to the tiller.

USE TIPS: A tiller extension can make it possible for the steerer to sit in a more comfortable position, particularly when the boat is heeling a lot or the cockpit is crowded.

BUYING TIPS: Look for universal joint at point of attachment with tiller.

REPLACEMENT TILLER

ALSO KNOWN AS: Wooden replacement tiller

DESCRIPTION: Graceful shallow S-curve of alternating layers of laminated wood, such as mahogany and ash, with protective coatings of marine varnish. One end is finished square to fit into the rudder stock (the upright extension to which the rudder itself is attached) and the other end is usually finished with a slight knob for a handhold.

USE: To replace original tiller.

USE TIPS: Also helpful as a backup in the event your tiller breaks.

BUYING TIPS: Sizes and models are available to fit most popular sailboats. Or if a backup is what you want, get a comparable-size stick of wood from the lumberyard and round off the edges with sandpaper—much cheaper.

TILLER COVER

DESCRIPTION: Mildew-resistant cloth sleeve that fits over tiller.

USE: To protect varnished wooden tiller from UV rays, salt, and dirt when boat is not in use.

USE TIPS: Most tillers can stand up to weather during the sailing season, but a cover is a good idea if you don't remove your tiller during offseason outside storage.

BUYING TIPS: This is one item that can be made from remnants of other canvas projects in and around your boat.

PINTLES AND GUDGEONS

DESCRIPTION: Separate but complementary stainless steel rudder fittings: The pintle is inserted into the gudgeon. A gudgeon takes the form of a strap with eye that attaches to the boat's transom or a U-shaped strap with eye that attaches to the rudder (a *rudder gudgeon*). The pintle is a corresponding fitting with a long pin, which is inserted into the gudgeon's eye. Made for rudders measuring ½"–1½" thick in both light- and heavy-duty models; a *transom pintle* is made for transom mounting. Pintle or gudgeon straps vary in length from about 3"–7" and pintles from 1¼"–3" in pin length.

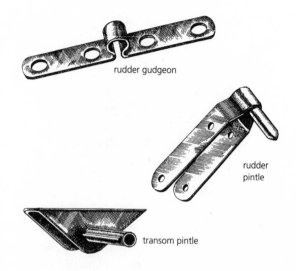

rudder gudgeon

rudder pintle

transom pintle

USE: On smaller boats with over-the-transom rudders these two items form a hinge upon which the rudder can pivot; they also keep the rudder attached to the boat.

USE TIPS: Pintles and gudgeons can be used for other installations where dismantling may be required occasionally—shelves, bunk boards, companionway stairs, and so on.

BUYING TIPS: Most applications require two or more sets of pintles and gudgeons; buy pintles with different lengths (but identical in other dimensions) to make slipping them into gudgeons possible without having to line the rudder up perfectly—an impossible task on a moving boat!

RETAINING CLIP

DESCRIPTION: Nearly enclosed ⅝"-diameter stainless steel ring-hook with small eye.

USE: To secure the rudder on small boats so you won't lose it if you capsize.

USE TIPS: For a more secure connection, use a cotter pin.

BUYING TIPS: Inexpensive item. Keep several spares handy.

Rudder stop

DESCRIPTION: L-shaped stainless steel fitting measuring ¾" × 1¼" with two predrilled holes for #10 fasteners. Some models have a spring-loaded tongue.

USE: Attaches to transom or rudder to prevent rudder from popping loose.

USE TIPS: Spring-loaded rudder stop enables removal of the rudder without unscrewing the stop—just depress the tongue.

BUYING TIPS: For those who expect fairly permanent installation of their rudders; otherwise, use the spring-loaded version or use a retaining clip (see page 134) or clevis pin (see page 129) through a predrilled hole in the pintle.

CHAPTER SEVEN

MOTORS, CONTROLS, AND ACCESSORIES

— STEERING AND CONTROL SYSTEMS —

ABOUT STEERING SYSTEMS

Steering systems on boats fall into two categories. The simplest and most direct is found on many sailboats where the skipper controls the direction of the boat by means of a tiller attached directly to the rudder post. Small outboard runabouts also have direct steering systems because the skipper can control direction by means of the tiller/throttle-handle combo attached to the outboard. A slightly more complex system employs a steering wheel and a simple arrangement of pulleys and control cables connected to the rudder. Usually the wheel is located close to the rudder because the steering cables need a fairly straight run with a minimum of bends, much less tight curves or kinks.

Remote steering systems, found most often on powerboats, are more complex because they rely on flexible mechanical and hydraulic cables that run from one or more helm stations in the boat to the rudder or to the outboard or I/O.

Mechanical cables contain a solid-wire core that slides easily within the cable housing. Throttle and steering controls at the helm move the core wire, which in turn relays movement to the rudder or engines. The main components of a hydraulic steering system are a pump mounted at the helm station that feeds a cylinder with hydraulic fluid. The cylinder in turn exerts pressure on the cable core.

Installation of remote steering requires careful measurement from the center of the wheel location, along the gunwale, to the center of the transom. Engines mounted directly on the transom or in splash wells require somewhat shorter cables than those used with engines on hinge pins or with tilt-tubes. Hydraulic cables are more flexible and therefore more forgiving of tight bends in installation.

PEDESTAL FRICTION BRAKE

ALSO KNOWN AS: Friction brake

DESCRIPTION: Bronze and stainless steel system mounts inside steering pedestal, with ABS plastic control handle that extends outside steering pedestal.

USE: Not exactly the nautical equivalent of cruise control, and definitely not an autopilot, a friction brake dampens or controls the swing of the steering wheel, which makes steering less tiring, and can be used as a temporary "lock" so that the skipper can leave the helm for short periods of time. The brake can be overridden easily if necessary.

USE TIPS: Brake can be used to lock the wheel at anchor or mooring to reduce wear and tear on the rudder and steering system.

BUYING TIPS: Easy to install.

PEDESTAL GUARD

DESCRIPTION: Long-legged hoop of polished stainless steel tube 45" long × 10 ½" wide.

USE: Mounted just forward of steering wheel, compass, and pedestal, the guard protects steering system from damage from mainsheet block on traveler or falling crew members. Also serves as a hand-hold.

USE TIPS: Good place to mount drink holders. Pedestal guard kit includes black plastic socket feet for mounting to cockpit floor.

BUYING TIPS: Sold in kit or alone as replacement part.

Steering Wheel

ALSO KNOWN AS: Helm, wheel

DESCRIPTION: Wood, plastic, galvanized, or stainless steel circle with spokes radiating from central hub, usually with a slot for steering control gear. Traditional varnished wooden design features a multitude of spokes, ending with shaped wooden knobs that extend beyond wheel's rim. Destroyer style is a streamlined circle of stainless steel with no protruding handles, while plastic versions resemble a sports-car steering wheel. Can range from as small as 13" diameter up to several feet across.

USE: Installed at the helm station for controlling the boat's direction.

USE TIPS: Wooden wheels require considerable care, in terms of varnishing or oiling, to maintain a shipshape appearance. Although attractive, the protruding spokes can cause injuries if you fall against the wheel in rough seas. Stainless steel wheels can get cold and numb the hands on long stints; be sure to use gloves or get a wheel cover.

The carlike plastic wheels are seen only on small runabouts and are not at all nautical in design.

BUYING TIPS: Available in a wide variety of price ranges. Inexpensive wooden wheels may not be glued well enough to stand up to anything more than decorative use. Steering-system kits may include a matching steering wheel.

Engine Control

ALSO KNOWN AS: Throttle

DESCRIPTION: Boxlike device roughly 6" long × 6" high × 4" wide with one or two knobbed handles and internal mechanical devices for connecting to engine throttle and shift-control cables. Designed for top mounting, on console surface, or side mounting.

USE: To control throttle and shifting action on single- and twin-engine boats from the helm station.

USE TIPS: Boat safety laws require that outboard motors and marine engines used in I/0 installations must not start in gear. Some outboards have built-in start-in-gear protection, but those sold with remote engine-control units from the engine manufacturer already contain start-in-gear protection, also called a neutral safety switch.

BUYING TIPS: Aftermarket engine controls are required to contain neutral safety switches, but check labeling to be sure. Control handles often have spherical black plastic knob handles, but you can customize your helm station with ridged or plain egg-shaped anodized aluminum knobs that come in silver or gold finish.

Steering Cable

DESCRIPTION: Flexible solid control wire encased in equally flexible jacket about ⅜" diameter. Eye fitting at one end and bare cable extension at the other, controlled by a thumbscrew fitting attached to jacket. Common lengths run from 8' to 20' long, although shorter and longer ones are available.

USE: To run from steering controls at helm to steering control on outboard motor or outdrive unit.

USE TIPS: Replace both cables at the same time in a dual-control steering system.

BUYING TIPS: Follow manufacturer's recommendations for your type of motor. For new installations, figure length by measuring the distance from the center of the wheel to the transom and from the center of the transom to the gunwale; deduct 6" from the total for transom- and splash well–mounted motors and add 6" for hinge pin/tilt tube installations. Or, you can measure the distance from the motor to the clutch and throttle connection, adding 8" for bend (and 3' for outboards).

Helm Pump

DESCRIPTION: Hydraulic pump run from the battery or off the engine. Roughly 4" diameter × 6" long, fits in 3"-diameter hole at helm station. Screw cap makes it easy to add extra hydraulic fluid. Standard ¼" NPF (National Pipe Fitting) fittings accommodate hydraulic hose lines.

USE: To convert manually operated hydraulic steering to "power steering."

USE TIPS: Easy to install, if you are handy, at one or more helm stations. Designed for use on boats up to 40' long with outboards, I/Os, or inboard engines. Works with autopilot.

BUYING TIPS: Complete "power steering" package includes cylinder kit for inboard or outboard engines (see below), back-mount installation kit, and outboard hose (14' to 18" long) kit with swaged fittings.

Hydraulic Cylinder Kits

ALSO KNOWN AS: Remote-steering kits

DESCRIPTION: Steering ram about 20"–24" with central control units that attach to a boat's hydraulic hoses.

TYPES:

Outboard cylinder kit: Front-mount kits attach directly onto the front of an outboard motor, producing hydraulic steering for most outboards up to 300 hp, except those with power steering, and may be used with a hydraulic autopilot. Where front mounts won't fit, side-mount cylinders can be used, but not in conjunction with autopilots because of the unequal number of turns between amidship and hard over. Models for single and dual engines.

Inboard cylinder kit: Stainless steel hydraulic cylinder about 20" long with stainless-steel ball joints and two-axis articulation. For boats with single engines.

Stern drive cylinder kit: Similar in size, appearance, and function to the inboard cylinder kit. Attaches directly to the stern drive steering arm inside the engine compartment.

USE: To connect engines and motors to the boat's hydraulic system.

USE TIPS: Make sure all fittings are tight and periodically check the fluid reservoir.

BUYING TIPS: Many engine makes come with their own brand of accessories, but aftermarket kits are avaiable as well. If your engine is under warranty, make sure using another brand will not void it.

Telescopic Tiller

ALSO KNOWN AS: Walking stick, outboard motor tiller extension

DESCRIPTION: Anodized-aluminum device 32" long with foam grip at one end and a socket that fits over outboard tiller/throttle control at the other end. Socket is kept in place with hose clamp included with tiller. Midpoint twist-lock telescope feature extends tiller to 50" long, universal joint near tiller socket lets you rotate throttle control, as well as have complete freedom of movement for steering port or starboard. Universal joint can be locked in straight position.

USE: Used on outboards without remote steering-control systems, the telescoping tiller lets the skipper steer from positions well forward of the transom. This is especially useful in rough sea conditions, when the boat might handle better with passenger weight placed closer to midships.

USE TIPS: Make sure tiller extension does not block access to kill switch.

BUYING TIPS: Useful item for those who go out alone, because it permits you to reach items stowed forward that you otherwise would not be able to reach.

ABOUT TRIM TABS

Trim tabs are two matching rectangular plates installed on the transom of most powerboats. They are similar in form and function to the elevator flaps on an airplane's tail and can be moved up and down together or independently of each other. By adjusting the tabs you can not only turn the boat while it is under way but also tilt the bow up or down to control the boat's attitude level in the water. This smooths the ride and improves handling, fuel economy, and performance by preventing or decreasing "porpoising" action under way and by keeping the stern from "squatting" in the water.

The tabs are attached to the transom by mounting bases that hinge along the rectangle's long sides. Controls at the helm station operate one tab at a time or both simultaneously utilizing hydraulic fluid or water to

deliver the proper pressure to actuating cylinders affixed to the transom and the top faces of both tabs.

Trim tabs are sized according to boat size and weight: larger, heavier, and slower boats require larger tabs. As the trailing edge of the tab is angled or deflected down into the water, the stern rises, and in turn the bow lowers. Steering into turns is aided by lowering the tab on the opposite transom corner from the direction in which you want to turn. In other words, to turn to starboard, lowering the port tab raises the port stern and lowers the starboard bow. The reverse maneuver in heavy seas will make the boat less likely to "dig in" on the same turn. Careful practice will take the mystery out of trim tabs, making them useful and practical boat handling tools.

HYDRAULIC TRIM TABS

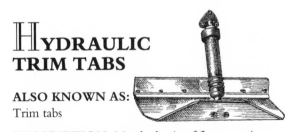

ALSO KNOWN AS: Trim tabs

DESCRIPTION: Matched pair of flat, sometimes curved, stainless steel rectangles, ranging in size from 12" long × 9" wide to as large as 42" long × 12" wide, with length of predrilled hinge along one long edge and slight upturned lip along other long edge. Connection points for usually one, sometimes two, hydraulic actuating cylinders (which usually use automobile automatic transmission fluid, or ATF) are found on top faces of both tabs. Complete trim-tab system includes tabs, actuating cylinders, hydraulic hoses leading to hydraulic power unit (5" long × 4" wide × 7" high), and angle indicators at the helm station, all controlled by "joy stick" or push-button controls. System uses 12-volt DC.

USE: To control bow angle and boat performance (see "About Trim Tabs," above).

USE TIPS: Trim-tab manufacturers have charts showing the proper size for your boat size, displacement, speed, and hull configuration. Size is determined by the width of your boat's transom. Measure the width of the transom from the centerline to the chine. Keeping in mind that outboard motors and outdrive units require at least 8" clearance (12" on larger displacement and semidisplacement hulls) at the transom's center, measure to within 3" or 4" of the outboard edge of the transom and choose the longest tabs that will fit in this space. When drilling through the transom to install tabs, be sure to use a marine-grade bedding compound to prevent leaks through bolt holes.

Maintenance includes monitoring of proper ATF levels and installation of trim-tab zincs (see page 163) on both flaps.

BUYING TIPS: Tabs are sold in matched pairs.

Planing Fin

ALSO KNOWN AS: Hydrofoil, auxiliary planing surface, lift plate

DESCRIPTION: Pair of plastic or metal (usually aluminum) wing-shaped plates that attach to the anticavitation plate (horizontal surfaces located above the propeller) on motors and outdrive units. Some planing fins have down-angled flaps on their trailing edge. Others extend laterally from the sides of the anticavitation plate. They can measure as much as 186 sq. in., although about half that size is more typical.

USE: Manufacturers say planing-fin systems increase lift in the stern and lessen the time it takes to

get the boat on plane, thus increasing speed, improving high-speed handling and reducing or eliminating cavitation. There is little evidence to prove that this is the case.

USE TIPS: Boat owners who are experiencing performance problems would be wise to look for the root cause—perhaps a wrong-size or damaged prop, a hull defect, an undersized engine, etc.—rather than take a Band-Aid approach that might mask a serious problem.

Installation of most models is straightforward. You simply clamp the predrilled wings in place on the cavitation plate, drill holes in the plate, and then bolt the wings in place with the stainless steel bolts and nuts supplied with the device.

BUYING TIPS: Models cost well under $100—not *too* expensive if you want to experiment with your boat's performance. But if your engine is still covered by the manufacturer's warranty, check beforehand to see whether installing a planing fin will void your coverage.

Power Trim Hose

ALSO KNOWN AS: Tilt hose

DESCRIPTION: Braided stainless steel-jacketed hydraulic hose about 1' long with swaged pressure fittings at either end.

USE: Outdrive units and some outboard motors can be trimmed to achieve nearly the same effect as separately installed trim tabs. Internal trim systems sometimes fail at the trim hose, hence the need for an easily replaced part.

USE TIPS: Engine manufacturers make specific parts to be used with their models, but aftermarket brands are also available. Just make sure you choose the one that matches your engine. Also, for best results use the hydraulic fluid recommended by the manufacturer.

BUYING TIPS: Aftermarket brands are cheaper, but hoses that fail on new engines may be covered by warranty, so check with your dealer or the engine manufacturer first.

Auto Tab Retractor

DESCRIPTION: 2"-sq. command module wires to ignition and trim-tab controls at helm station.

USE: To retract trim tabs automatically when ignition is off. By relieving pressure on trim tabs when they are not in use, the retractor helps prevent damage during trailering or storage and keeps barnacles and other marine growth from fouling actuating cylinders when boat is at the dock or on a mooring.

USE TIPS: Installs behind instrument panel or helm station.

BUYING TIPS: Inexpensive item that works with major brands of trim tabs.

Braided Flax Packing

ALSO KNOWN AS: Stuffing box packing, gland packing

DESCRIPTION: Continuous 2'-long braid, ⅛"–⅜" (larger sizes usually not available in stores catering to recreational boats), square in profile, made of flax fibers saturated with paraffin and tallow. Newer "dripless" packing made of carbon fiber impregnated with Teflon™ is also available.

USE: Through-hull fittings installed where propeller shafts or rudder posts enter the hull below the waterline are called *stuffing boxes* or sometimes *packing glands*. These shafts must turn smoothly without binding and rely on a small amount of seawater for lubrication. Flax packing is wrapped tightly around the shaft to serve both as a cushion for the shaft and as a means of keeping water out. Even so, it is not unusual for a few drops of water to slip past the packing and accumulate in the adjacent bilge.

USE TIPS: Stuffing box packing should be inspected at least once each year, although the prudent skipper always checks the bilge for any unusual amounts of water.

The stuffing box can be repacked while the boat is in the water. Consult your owner's manual before you begin, and be prepared for a hot, dirty, nasty job in an almost-inaccessible part of your boat.

BUYING TIPS: If traditional flax does not seem to work, you may want to try the new dripless packing or invest in a shaft seal (see page 144).

Cutless Bearing

ALSO KNOWN AS: Cutlass bearing (incorrect), shaft bearing

DESCRIPTION: Brass or bronze tube 3"–8" in length with inner diameter ranging from ¾"–2" that is often lined with grooved nitrile rubber or similar material. Installed in housing in the stern tube leading into the boat at the propeller shaft and held in place by set screws.

USE: Supports the propeller shaft where it extends through the hull. The grooved liner admits water for lubrication and cooling.

USE TIPS: Check periodically for excessive play; if there is, replacement is the only course of action.

BUYING TIPS: Replace with similar kind and size; look for fine machining—a sign of quality that also makes installation easier.

SHAFT SEAL

DESCRIPTION: A modern update of the traditional stuffing box features adjustable flanges at inboard and outboard ends and, in between, a neoprene and several friction rings. Installs with doubled stainless steel hose clamps at either end. Water injection vent protrudes from side.

USE: Replaces stuffing box as entryway for propeller shafts. Water still acts as a lubricant, but you control how much is introduced into the system.

USE TIPS: Can be used on both power and sail boats.

BUYING TIPS: Different sizes available for shafts from ⅞" to 1½" diameter, but selection is also based on boat speed, as well as stern tube or shaft-alley diameter.

ABOUT AUTOPILOTS

Skippers planning long passages through relatively open waterways can use autopilots instead of a crew member at the helm to control the boat's direction. Electric or hydraulic motors maintain a preset course and can make adjustments for small errors, changing sea conditions, boat performance, and speed. Precursors of today's high-tech gear were simple devices where ropes secured the tiller or wheel in one position. Today autopilot motors are guided by compass and read through a microelectric computer circuit. Manual override is a critical feature, so the person on watch can make sudden changes in heading in case of surprise obstacles or accidents.

The three main elements of an autopilot system are the sensor unit, which aligns itself with a magnetic course; the computer control unit, which analyzes information about sea and other operating conditions; and the multigear power unit, which makes adjustments "recommended" by the control unit.

Interfacing autopilots with electronic navigation equipment such as loran or GPS satellite navigation receivers makes it possible to correct for magnetic changes affecting compasses.

An autopilot's main drawback is that it does not think. While the crew and skipper may have their hands freed from the helm by using an autopilot, a thinking body must be on deck to serve as a lookout. It goes without saying that autopilots should never be used in crowded harbors. And extreme care should be taken when operating under autopilot during storms, in areas where there are heavy currents, strong seas, and heavy winds, or near shore.

autopilot for tiller-steered boat

AUTOPILOT

ALSO KNOWN AS: Self-steering device, automatic pilot, automatic steering device

DESCRIPTION: System consisting of handheld or console-mounted control touchpad, compass (usually fluxgate type, see page 27), wind vanes, sea-condition sensor(s), and a drive motor. Runs on 12-volt DC, requires 5-amp fuse. Visual and audio status indicators, plus off-course alarm, are included in control unit. Motor drive for tiller-steered boats mounts directly onto the tiller. Wheel-driven boats have the drive unit installed on the steering pedestal, with a belt-driven gear attached to the wheel hub.

USE: For robotic steering. After determining a safe course for your power or sail boat, by switching the steering system over to autopilot mode, you are free to leave the tiller or wheel to eat, make repairs, adjust rigging or sails, etc.

USE TIPS: Never use in crowded harbors. Autopilot navigation still requires a careful watch on deck, regardless of how "smart" the sensor-control equipment is. Capable of interfacing with other electronic navigation equipment (see "About Autopilots" page 144).

BUYING TIPS: Expensive, but absolutely necessary gear if you are sailing long distances alone or with a small crew.

AUTOPILOT ACCESSORIES

DESCRIPTION: Variety of devices designed to work with older autopilot systems, including:

TYPES:

Loran/autopilot interface: A palm-sized connection box for console mount, with sockets and inlets for connecting autopilot to loran and other electronic gear. By interfacing your autopilot it is possible to improve the accuracy of the system's sensor and control units.

Wind vane: Similar in appearance to mast-top wind-direction indicator (see page 131), connected to wire that plugs into autopilot control unit. Audio signal beeps every 30 seconds and LED readout pulses for two seconds. Feeds apparent wind-angle information to autopilot control unit.

wind vane

Handheld remote control keypad: Attached to 20'-long wire, adjusts and overrides autopilot course. Allows skipper to make course adjustments away from the helm station. Since the keypad is attached by wire to the control panel, "remote" may be a misnomer.

Tiller bracket: Clamps autopilot drive motor onto all sizes of tillers. Available in sizes from 1" to 5", the bracket adapts to all tiller-steered autopilot systems.

Pedestal: Provides mounting place for motor-drive-unit tiller-steered autopilot systems. When motor pedestals are not feasible, the motor may be mounted on a *cantilever mount* installed on the cockpit coaming or seat back.

Drive belts: Replacements for use with with all wheel-steering autopilots (see "Autopilots," page 144).

Push-rod extensions: Reach from the drive motor to the tiller, for use with tiller-steering autopilots.

USE: Upgrade, repair, and replacement parts for autopilots.

USE TIPS: Autopilots, for all their usefulness, are prone to breakdowns; keep spare parts on hand.

BUYING TIPS: Individual accessories are fairly expensive but make it possible to continue using older but still adequate equipment.

POWER INSTRUMENTS

RUDDER-ANGLE INDICATOR

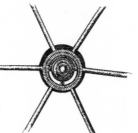

ALSO KNOWN AS:
Rudder reference, rudder position indicator

DESCRIPTION: Instrument that stands alone or in some models ties into autopilot (with rudder-angle transducer) and gives readout from 0° to 40° port and starboard.

USE: To prevent unpleasant surprises by giving you your exact rudder position before you engage your engine transmission.

USE TIPS: Especially helpful in close quarters or when docking.

BUYING TIPS: Helpful for shorthanded sailors with larger boats, who cannot always be in position to check the rudder angle.

TRIM GAUGE

ALSO KNOWN AS: Trim indicator.

DESCRIPTION: Instrument, usually electronic, that tells you the trim, or angle, of either a boat's trim tabs or an outboard or stern drive.

TYPES:

Outboard trim gauge: Electronic monitor that is connected via a sender to a sensor on an outboard or I/O that provides reading on angle of the motor in the water—from vertical to full tilt.

Trim-tab gauge: Either a mechanical or an electronic instrument (connected to engine either with a sender or a cable) that informs you of the position of either the port or the starboard trim tab—the

plates at the stern of the boat that keep it level at low speeds. Both LCD and LED readouts. Sold in pairs.

USE: To provide information that enables you to keep your stern up and the boat level and to move through the water at maximum efficiency, especially at lower speeds or when carrying a load.

USE TIPS: Each boat has its own handling characteristics. The appropriate trim indicator will help you determine the best configuration for your tabs or engine(s) at various speeds.

BUYING TIPS: A natural complement to a boat with either trim tabs or larger outboard.

DUAL-ENGINE SYNCHRONIZER

DESCRIPTION: Electronic instrument that provides readout on rpms of dual engines; works with most inboard diesel and gasoline engines, I/Os, and outboards.

USE: Lets you know if your engines are in synch and to adjust throttles accordingly.

USE TIPS: If throttles are even but rpms are out of synch, this could be an indication of engine problems.

BUYING TIPS: Good idea for anyone with dual engines.

WATER-RESISTANT INSTRUMENT COVER

ALSO KNOWN AS: Instrument bag

DESCRIPTION: Clear acrylic bag, basically, with drawstring on bottom for snug fit. Sized from 5¼"

× 2¼" × 7⅜" to about 10" × 7" × 3⅜" to accommodate smaller electronics, such as VHF radio.

USE: To protect electronic gear from dirt, spray, and moisture.

USE TIPS: Good for transporting electronics safely.

BUYING TIPS: Most electronics gear is pretty hardy to begin with and should not require extra protection while in place.

Rigid Instrument Cover

ALSO KNOWN AS: Instrument cover

DESCRIPTION: Plastic snap-on cover of various shapes and sizes, with diameters from 5" to 7⅝" and depths from 3⅛" to 5". Some come with predrilled holes for attachment with screws. Also available in very shallow, lidlike version for snapping over flush-mount instrument panels.

USE: To protect cockpit or other exposed instruments from spray, moisture, and dirt.

USE TIPS: Instruments exposed to the elements should be covered.

BUYING TIPS: Snap-on kind is the most convenient.

Electronics Box

DESCRIPTION: Molded plastic box with lift-up smoked plastic front panel, which is gasketed and held shut with built-in chrome lock. Measures 16½" × 32" × 11¼" to hold small- to moderate-sized electronics gear.

USE: To provide moisture, spray, and dirt protection for electronics.

USE TIPS: Good on-board protection for instruments you often remove for safekeeping.

BUYING TIPS: Especially helpful where electronics are exposed to the elements, such as in an open cockpit or flying bridge.

— OUTBOARD-MOTOR ACCESSORIES —

Outboard-Motor Lock

DESCRIPTION: 1"-sq. case-hardened steel tube, 10" long with weather-resistant vinyl coating. One side of tube has a slot that runs nearly the entire length. Comes with brass-pin tumbler padlock whose shackle fits into two holes at one end of the tube.

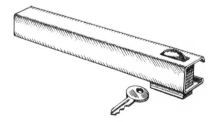

USE: For use with most outboard motors up to 40 hp that secure to transom with clamp screws. Remove padlock and, with slotted side against transom, slide motor lock bar across clamps, then replace padlock at open end. Prevents outboard from being stolen. Steel case resists prying, sawing, and cutting. Some versions come with a foam insert to deaden sound and vibration.

USE TIPS: Keep outboard motor lock in place while under way to keep motor from vibrating loose. A piece of waterproof tape over padlock opening will keep water from corroding the lock. It is a good idea to lubricate this and any other lock used on your boat with lightweight machine oil (not graphite) once in a while.

BUYING TIPS: Inexpensive security against theft. Comes with two brass keys.

Outboard-Motor Bracket

DESCRIPTION: Pair of stainless-steel plates with flanges predrilled for attachment to boat transom, extend to a 1½"- to 2"-thick plywood mounting board, usually about 8" sq. Extensions from transom may be stationary or adjustable in four positions ranging from perpendicular to transom to nearly upright against it.

USE: To provide secure mount for outboard motor up to 20 hp weighing as much as 115 lbs. Adjustable outboard-motor bracket works well on sharply angled (up to 28°) sailboat transoms, and torsion spring extensions for mounting board allow you to lift motor out of the water while under sail. Stationary bracket is made for fixed-height auxiliary or trolling motor up to 15 hp.

USE TIPS: Motor mounts for heavier outboards are available from engine manufacturers.

BUYING TIPS: Replacement mounting boards made of polycarbonate are available when the plywood originals inevitably rot or delaminate.

Outboard-Motor Carrier

ALSO KNOWN AS: Dolly, hand truck

DESCRIPTION: Upright, nearly 3 ft. tall, dolly made of reinforced 1"-diameter aluminum tubing, has mounting board located near handles. Semipneumatic rubber tires.

USE: To make it easy to move your outboard from the boat to a storage area. Motor secures to mounting board with clamps, same as on transom mounting bracket.

USE TIPS: Because the motor is in an upright position, this is a perfect stand for long-term storage or maintenance.

BUYING TIPS: Various models available for motors up to 30 hp weighing as much as 130 lbs.

Marine Spark Plug

DESCRIPTION: The marine version of the well-known automotive item, made of ceramic and metal that resists corrosion common on boats. Screws into engine's combustion chamber.

USE: To ignite fuel in engine cylinders.

USE TIPS: Refer to your engine manual for specifics on plug selection and gap settings. There are hundreds of plugs of various types and heat ranges, as well as vast differences between the needs of racing engines, for example, and engines that are subjected to less stressful uses. *Surface gap plugs* should be used only on engines with capacitor discharge ignition systems. Never use automotive spark plugs on a boat engine.

BUYING TIPS: Changing the spark plugs on your engine is a relatively simple, inexpensive task, but use a socket wrench designed for this job, otherwise you are bound to break the plug. Inexpensive gauges are available for setting the correct spark-plug gap. Any one of a number of excellent engine repair and maintenance manuals would also be helpful.

Motor HOIST

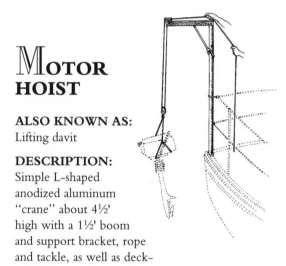

ALSO KNOWN AS:
Lifting davit

DESCRIPTION:
Simple L-shaped anodized aluminum "crane" about 4½' high with a 1½' boom and support bracket, rope and tackle, as well as deck- and rail-mounting equipment. 100-lb. lifting capacity. Dismounts easily and folds down to a narrow package less than a yard long.

USE: Removable lift attaches to deck and lifeline rails. Arm extends overboard, makes it easy to lift outboard motors and other heavy gear from the dock or dinghy.

USE TIPS: Most useful in areas where there are extreme tidal changes or on boats doing extended cruising.

BUYING TIPS: Sailboat owners can rig a block-and-tackle arrangement off their booms to achieve the same results.

Quick-Connect Motor Flusher

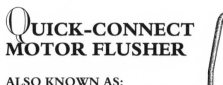

ALSO KNOWN AS:
Ear muffs, flush kit

DESCRIPTION: Resembles oversized metal tongs with rubber cups. Designed to fit tightly over water-intake openings on outboard or outdrive gear housing, the "tongs" are actually a hollow tube with a threaded attachment for freshwater hose (even your garden hose will work with these).

USE: To flush salt, silt, dirt, and minerals from outboard motor or outdrive raw water cooling system. Preventive maintenance to avoid overheating and/or corrosion caused by buildup of foreign materials.

USE TIPS: Flushing is easy and takes about 5 minutes to complete once boat is out of the water. Refer to engine manufacturer's recommendations before proceeding, however.

Because the engine must be run while it is being flushed, remove the propeller to avoid possible injury.

BUYING TIPS: Dual-intake flushers are recommended for higher-horsepower outboard engines and outdrives.

Portable Gas Tank

DESCRIPTION: 3-, 6- and 8½-gal.-capacity tanks made of polyethylene or galvanized steel. Red is the standard color for gas tanks. Some tanks are designed to fit in specific areas of the boat, such as the bow. Equipped with threaded outlets for tank fittings (usually not included with tank, see page 155). Built-in fuel gauge as well as dipstick for accurate metering of 50:1 or 100:1 fuel-oil mixture.

USE: To store and carry gasoline, as well as supply fuel to outboard motor when tank is equipped with fuel line and primer bulb.

USE TIPS: Store fuel tank in a well-ventilated area, securing it against unnecessary movement and exposure to rain or salt spray. Avoid chafing and friction, since any spark can cause fire or explosion (see tank protector, below). Wooden blocks fastened to the hull or floorboards prevent sideways or endways movement, and straps will hold the tank in place. Check at least once each season for signs of dents, rust, corrosion, or leaks.

Whenever possible, fill portable fuel tanks onshore, although it may not be practical to do this with larger tanks. It goes without saying that there must be no smoking when taking on fuel. If you have an outboard, each time you fill up, remember to add the proper oil mix.

Never use any container, whether plastic, glass, or metal for storing fuel unless it is expressly made for this purpose.

BUYING TIPS: Portable fuel tanks are inexpensive enough (and the potential for an explosion is great enough) that they should be replaced, rather than repaired if there are any signs of dents, rust, corrosion, or leaks. Choose only fuel tanks intended for marine use, preferably ones with the words *gasoline* or *fuel* clearly marked. Not much difference in price between metal and polyethylene tanks, although the latter may have a slight edge, since they will not corrode.

PORTABLE-TANK DECK PROTECTOR

ALSO KNOWN AS: Tank edging, tank guard

DESCRIPTION: White vinyl strip with U-shaped cross-section, 54" long.

USE: Channel fits over protruding bottom edge of most 6-gal.-capacity metal fuel tanks.

USE TIPS: Keeps tank from rattling and sliding, also prevents rust stains on decks and protects tank's seams.

BUYING TIPS: If you don't have a guard or the one you have is stripping away, get one.

INBOARD-MOTOR ACCESSORIES

FUEL-WATER SEPARATOR

ALSO KNOWN AS: Fuel filter/water separator, filter/separator

DESCRIPTION: Metal or metal-and-glass canister arrangement about the size of a quart oil can with internal baffles and pleated or spooled paper and cloth (both sometimes chemically treated) or woven metal-mesh elements. Has inlet and outlet for at-tachment to fuel lines and/or carburetor so that fuel can pass through filter "on its way to work."

USE: To remove water and other contaminants, such as rust, dirt, and products of corrosion, from gasoline and diesel before fuel enters engine.

USE TIPS: Diesel fuel filters with glass collection cups make it easy to tell when it is time to drain the filter and possibly replace the filter elements. Filters for gasoline engines are required to be made of metal.

One way to avoid water in the fuel tank is to keep the tank topped off at all times. Another way is to use fuel additives for this purpose, but check the engine manufacturer's recommendations before using any additive (see page 160).

BUYING TIPS: Refer to filter or engine manufacturers' charts when choosing a filter and/or replacement cartridge (see below). Use only filters intended for marine applications and be sure to pick the right one for the type of fuel you are using. Spare fuel filters and replacement cartridges should be kept onboard at all times. It is sometimes necessary to purchase fittings for fuel lines separately, since they do not always come with the filter.

Diesel engines require a more thorough water-separation system.

REPLACEMENT CARTRIDGES

ALSO KNOWN AS: Replacement filter elements

DESCRIPTION: Cylinder, usually with thin, perforated metal jacket, containing filter material, fits inside metal or glass filter housing.

USE: Replace clogged, dirty fuel-filter elements.

USE TIPS: Plan on replacing filter elements frequently.

BUYING TIPS: Inexpensive insurance against engine damage. Always keep a selection handy for fuel and oil filters.

FUEL-AIR SEPARATOR

DESCRIPTION: Glass canister slightly larger than a can of spray paint with fittings, for in-line installation on fuel-tank vent hose. Canister holds small amount of fuel but lets fuel vapors escape.

USE: To hold fuel that backs into fuel-tank vent line due to thermal expansion or air displacement while tank is being filled. Allows fuel to drain back into tank instead of overflowing from vent into the water or down the side of the boat.

USE TIPS: Not to be confused with a flame arrestor or backfire trap, which is an air filter fitted onto the carburetor of inboard marine gas engines to smother the flame from a carburetor backfire.

BUYING TIPS: Suitable for both diesel and gas engines.

EXHAUST HOSE

ALSO KNOWN AS: Steam hose

DESCRIPTION: Flexible helical wire-reinforced hose resistant to gasoline, oil, saltwater, and acids. Will not collapse under vacuum pressure. Effective in temperatures from −40° to over 240°F. Common hose sizes are 1½" to 4", although larger and smaller sizes are available. Should bear manufacturer's label specifying it is suitable for exhaust applications.

USE: To lead engine exhaust gases from manifold or riser to exhaust port above waterline. Must be supported along the way by stainless steel hose clamps (see page 157).

USE TIPS: Tremendous back pressure (a vacuum in the exhaust system) develops when engines are shut down suddenly. Weak spots that become leaks can develop where hoses collapse and crease.

Install all exhaust-system components so that they are not touching flammable materials, such as wood or fiberglass. Periodic checks for hose and other exhaust-gas leaks are in order, since carbon monoxide is highly dangerous.

BUYING TIPS: Sold by the foot in up to 12½' lengths.

Exhaust-pipe cover

ALSO KNOWN AS: Flapper valve, check valve

DESCRIPTION: Rubber ring with adjustable stainless steel hose clamp, hinged to flat black rubber cover. 3" and 4". Covers adjust up to 3½" diameter.

USE: Fits onto outboard end of exhaust port to prevent following seas from backing into port while boat is idling, stopping, or backing down.

USE TIPS: Does not take the place of an exhaust riser.

BUYING TIPS: Cheap insurance against a common problem.

Muffler silencer

ALSO KNOWN AS: Water silencer, water lift muffler

DESCRIPTION: Rubber or hard plastic device. One version that mounts on outboard end of exhaust port looks like a cover for two soft-drink cans; another is about the size of a gallon can of paint, with mounting flange.

USE: To trap exhaust noises and fumes in a baffled chamber, where they mix with water and are then discharged.

USE TIPS: External mount version can be used for engines from 40 hp to 275 hp (gas), from 15 hp to 125 hp (diesel).

BUYING TIPS: Follow manufacturer's guidelines for your engine size; bushings may be needed to adapt the silencer to your existing exhaust system.

OIL ACCESSORIES

Oil-flow pump

DESCRIPTION: Any of a number of different pumps with pickup tubes that extend into the engine dipstick tube or crankcase. Working parts are made of materials resistant to gasoline, oil, and solvents. May be a *hand pump* model that looks and operates like a bicycle pump or contains its own DC electric motor, as in the *12-volt DC oil changer.* Models set up to work with an electric drill, called *drill pumps,* should never be used for pumping gasoline because of the possibility that electrical sparks will cause an explosion.

USE: Invaluable for changing the oil on a marine engine, since there is rarely enough clearance below the oil pan to use the plug in the bottom of the crankcase, as is usually done with cars. The pickup tube extends into the dipstick and sucks out oil.

USE TIPS: It is easier to remove the oil if it has been heated up, so run your engine first. Be sure of course that the engine is not running when the oil is being drained.

Dispose of used oil, as well as any other petroleum product or harmful material, properly. Never dump oil overboard, on the ground, or down storm sewers or drains. Besides its being a major source of pollution, you also run the risk of hefty fines in most areas. Ask your marina or local gas dock if they collect used oil, since it can be recycled.

Your yacht club may want to start a recycling program. Otherwise most counties and cities have hazardous-waste disposal programs. Call for information.

BUYING TIPS: Essential if you plan to do your own oil changes.

OIL FILTER

DESCRIPTION: Sealed metal canister about the size of a quart can of oil, containing filtering elements.

USE: To remove solid contaminants from oil without removing valuable detergent additives.

USE TIPS: Follow engine manufacturer's instructions for proper selection.

BUYING TIPS: Always keep spares on hand.

ENGINE-OIL ANALYSIS KIT

DESCRIPTION: Plastic syringe with 30" plastic tube, sample collection vial, engine data sheet, instructions, and mailing envelope.

USE: Mail oil sample back to kit manufacturer for analysis of engine oil, which is a good bellwether for engine problems before they get out of hand. Once the sample has been sent to the lab, it is tested for unburned fuels, antifreeze, water, dirt, carbon, chromium, copper, and iron. The written analysis report will give tips for adjustments and engine maintenance, as well as hidden problems.

USE TIPS: Report takes 2 weeks to complete.

BUYING TIPS: Price of kit includes lab fees.

BILGE SPONGE

ALSO KNOWN AS: Oil brick

DESCRIPTION: Absorbent spongelike material, usually in a mesh bag. May be the shape and size of a large car-wash sponge or a 15"-long cylinder similar to a boat fender. Another version is the *engine drip pad* 28" long × 18" wide. Manufacturers claim the sponge absorbs as much as seven times its weight, and the pad model up to twenty-five times its weight.

USE: To absorb materials such as oil, transmission fluid, gasoline, diesel fuel, and antifreeze found in the bilge. Makes disposal easier.

USE TIPS: Most of these devices have tie-down straps so that they don't interfere with bilge pumps and drains.

BUYING TIPS: Bricks can be wrung out and used again, a messy job! At a cost of less than $10, it would be worthwhile just to buy a new one. Dispose of properly.

OIL-DISCHARGE STICKER

DESCRIPTION: Placard that must measure at least 5" × 8" by law and that must state, "Discharge of Oil Prohibited," and cite the appropriate section from the federal Water Pollution Control Act of 1972.

USE: Must be placed in or near the engine room of boats longer than 26' to warn guests and presumably remind owners that the government prohibits the discharge of oil or oily waste in all inland and coastal waters.

USE TIPS: If you do accidentally release a discharge that causes a noticeable sheen and fail to report it to the appropriate federal agency, you are subject to a fine of up to $5,000. In many harbors the Coast Guard and state environmental agencies rigorously seek out the source of oil slicks.

BUYING TIPS: A readily available and inexpensive way to comply with the law.

ADJUSTABLE OIL FILTER WRENCH

ALSO KNOWN AS: Oil filter wrench

DESCRIPTION: Swiveling wrench handle with hose-clamp-like attachment.

USE: "Hose clamp" tightens around filter and may be screwed into or out of position.

USE TIPS: Swivel handle makes it possible to reach out-of-the-way filters.

BUYING TIPS: Another inexpensive piece of essential equipment for do-it-yourself maintenance.

OIL DRAIN PAN

DESCRIPTION: Deep-dish triangular tray made of polypropylene, with a 7½-qt. capacity.

USE: To catch used oil during an oil change. Triangular shape allows you to push one corner under hard-to-reach oil drain plugs.

USE TIPS: As with all petroleum products, dispose of used engine oil responsibly: Bring to a gas station or your engine mechanic for recycling. Never dump oil on the ground, in the water, or down storm sewers. Retaining and proper disposal of used oil is the law, no longer an option.

BUYING TIPS: Inexpensive item available at auto or marine stores. Handy device for those who change their own oil.

LONG-NOSE FUNNEL

DESCRIPTION: Similar in shape and size (12"–15" long) to an old-fashioned foghorn, made of plastic. Some funnels have flexible nozzles that look like large bendable straws; others have removable bells and threaded nozzles so that the nozzle itself can be attached directly to a plastic bottle, such as a 1-qt. bottle of oil.

USE: Long nozzle reaches hard-to-get spots, allows you to add oil without risking a spill.

USE TIPS: Never use the same funnel for both fuel and water. Funnels that thread onto oil bottles speed up and simplify oil changes.

BUYING TIPS: Have an assortment of funnels, such as ½-pt., 1-pt. and 2-qt. capacity, in your tool chest onboard.

FUELING ACCESSORIES

PERMANENT FUEL TANK

ALSO KNOWN AS: Nonintegral marine fuel tank, gas tank, diesel tank

DESCRIPTION: Tank made of hot-dipped galvanized sheet steel, aluminized steel, aluminum, copper and certain copper alloys, or polyethylene (all corrosion-resistant materials) fitted with electrical sending unit for hookup to fuel gauge, outlets for 1½" diameter fuel fill hose and ¼" NPT fuel-line fitting, as well as ⅝" ID tank vent hose. Fittings and hoses usually sold separately. Internal stiffeners and baffles add strength and prevent fuel from sloshing or surging while the boat is moving. Capacity ranges from 11 gal. to 50 gal. Polyethylene tanks are formed with two bandlike indentations to make tying down easier. Adaptable for diesel use with conversion kit sold separately (see page 169).

USE: New or replacement fuel tank for fixed installation below deck, with deck fill arrangement (see page 156).

USE TIPS: Before installing a permanent fuel tank, review all applicable U.S. Coast Guard standards for gasoline engines. Sending unit must be grounded to prevent the possibility of sparks, which could cause fire or explosion. All venting must be to the outside of the boat to prevent buildup of dangerous fumes.

If you want to install a tank in a new location, check with the boat manufacturer or a competent marine mechanic for advice.

BUYING TIPS: Only buy a fuel tank that bears the statement "This tank has been tested under 33 CFR 183.510(a)-1988," which means that the tank meets tests for pressure, fire resistance, slosh-testing, and shock resistance for gas tanks intended for marine use. The tank should also be clearly marked with the manufacturer's name and address, the model, fuel type, capacity in gallons, date of man-

ufacture, material and minimum wall thickness, and maximum test pressure.

TANK HOLD-DOWN SYSTEM

ALSO KNOWN AS: Tank hold-down assembly, tank hold-down kit

DESCRIPTION: One version, to be used with polyethylene tanks, consists of four upright L-shaped brackets with slight lips on the upper arms and comes with stainless steel screws and aluminum mounting flanges for attaching horizontally to hull or internal frames. Metal fuel-tank model consists of a pair of predrilled metal flanges that screw down to the hull or frames.

USE: To mount permanent fuel tank to prevent any movement.

USE TIPS: Follow manufacturer's instructions carefully, especially tips about grounding and isolating tank from contact with unlike metals, since this can cause corrosion. Install belowdecks in an area where salt spray will not hit the tank and where it will be above any water in the bilge.

BUYING TIPS: Try to buy the hold-down system made by the tank manufacturer.

FUEL-HOSE BARB

ALSO KNOWN AS: Fuel barb, hose barb, adapter

DESCRIPTION: Aluminum or brass cylindrical fitting with ¼" NPT pipe threads on one end and a long nipple with barbs (a series of tapering rings) on the other. For ¼" ID or ⁵⁄₁₆" ID fuel hose. Less than 2" long.

USE: Screw threaded end into fuel tank withdrawal outlet and insert barbed end into fuel line to hose to engine.

USE TIPS: Use two hose clamps (double clamp) to attach the fuel line to the barbed end.

BUYING TIPS: There's little difference in price—go with the brass barbs.

Deck Fill

ALSO KNOWN AS: Gas fill, diesel fill, water fill, waste fitting, through-deck fitting

DESCRIPTION: Through-deck fitting with screwed-on or key-locked cap. Top flange fits flush with deck and has barb that extends through the deck and inserts into 1½" or 2" hose. Available in stainless steel, chrome-plated zinc, or nylon.

USE: To provide secure fill point for fuel and water (or discharge outlet, in the case of waste fittings).

USE TIPS: Double hose clamps are required on fuel-fill hoses and recommended on all other hose connections. Deck flange should be properly bedded to prevent leaks below decks or into tanks. To avoid confusion, install fill fittings that have permanently marked gas, diesel, water or waste markings. Or use the following color codes: blue—water, red—gas or diesel, black—waste. In any case always supervise fuel and water fill-ups to prevent accidents. It's not unheard of for inexperienced dockhands to mistake fishing-rod holders for fuel fills, to say nothing of switching diesel for gasoline.

BUYING TIPS: Look for fittings with caps attached by tethers so that they don't get lost overboard.

Gas Guard

DESCRIPTION: Hinged device, half of which is installed under fuel fill deck fitting flange. The other half folds over the fitting and secures with a padlock or can be swung back when loading fuel.

USE: To prevent theft or tampering with fuel supply.

USE TIPS: Padlock isn't included; choose one meant for marine use.

BUYING TIPS: Instead of a guard you can replace your deck fill cap with a locking version; just be sure to get the right size.

Deck Plate Retaining Cable

ALSO KNOWN AS: Tether, retainer chain

DESCRIPTION: Stainless steel cable or bead chain, approximately 7" with eye at one end and ring at the other.

USE: To tether cap to fill fitting and prevent the inevitable loss overboard.

USE TIPS: Helpful for tethering other items, such as tools, that are prone to take a dive.

BUYING TIPS: Even if you have retaining cables in place, keep a spare fill cap onboard for emergencies.

Deck Plate Key

ALSO KNOWN AS: Spanner, spanner wrench, cap wrench

DESCRIPTION: Key with two projections that fit into corresponding holes in fill fitting caps. The simplest is the *zinc* deck plate key with or without handle. Other types include a stainless steel key with a number of combinations and a palm-sized adjustable *hinged* deck plate key.

USE: To screw open and close deck fill fittings.

USE TIPS: All types of keys will fit any number of lugs, slots, and spaced holes and may be useful for opening shackles.

BUYING TIPS: Keep at least one spare, as these are easy to lose overboard—or use a retaining cable.

UNIVERSAL IN-LINE FUEL FILTER

ALSO KNOWN AS: Secondary gas filter

DESCRIPTION: Small aluminum canister about the size of a spool of thread, with barb (tapered rings) at either end. Replaceable filter element inside is made of bronze beads that have been sintered, in other words heated just short of melting, to the point where they adhere to each other. They trap particles as small as 40 microns.

USE: Secondary gas filter, to be inserted in the fuel line.

USE TIPS: Install with double hose clamps on either barb. Do not rely on this inexpensive device as your sole fuel filter, as it will not separate water.

Coast Guard standards require all filters to be supported, so use clamps or brackets rather than just hanging the filter from the fuel line.

BUYING TIPS: A must to keep your fuel system free of contaminents; keep a spare filter/gasket replacement kit on hand as well.

MARINE-QUALITY STAINLESS STEEL HOSE CLAMP

DESCRIPTION: Adjustable stainless steel strap, usually about ½" wide, with transverse slots, held in a ring by slotted stainless steel screw device. Many circumferences are available, the most common being ¼"–⅝", ¹¹⁄₁₆"–1¼", 1¹⁄₁₆"–2", and 1½"–2¾". A *hand-tightened* version, with a knob instead of a screw, is also available.

stainless steel hose clamp

hand-tightened hose clamp

USE: To hold all variety of hoses to metal and plastic fittings, such as fuel barbs, through-hull fittings (see page 270), and water lines.

USE TIPS: Never use automotive hose clamps with spring-action tightening devices. They will not last in the marine environment. Check hose clamps a few times each season and replace when in doubt. They are inexpensive.

Clamp should not cut into the relatively springy surface of the hose, unless it is overtightened. Always install clamps so that the screw is easy to reach, for future adjustments.

BUYING TIPS: Hose clamps for automotive uses may be a lot cheaper, but they are often not made of all-stainless steel components and will rust in no time. Hand-tightened model is excellent for temporary repairs.

TYPE-A FUEL HOSE

ALSO KNOWN AS: Fuel line

DESCRIPTION: Alcohol–resistant hose reinforced with two radial plies and helix (spiraling) wires. Flexible and kink-proof, this hose will not collapse when there is an internal vacuum. Marked "J1527 Type A1" fuel hose, with manufacturer's name and date. Sold by the foot in lengths up to 50' and in diameters of ¼" to ⅝".

USE: To run between fuel shut-off valve on gas tank and engine. Should be used only where the entire length is visible for inspection and when it can be protected from damage.

USE TIPS: The hose must be supported along its entire length to keep it from vibrating off the tank fitting or the engine. Inspection of the fuel line for damage or deterioration is an important part of regular maintenance. As with all hoses, double-clamp where hose attaches to fittings.

BUYING TIPS: Do not use hose without the "J1527 Type A1" marking. It probably will not be resistant to degradation by alcohol-based additives in today's gasoline blends. Fuel hose that is damaged by alcohol gets soft and gummy and ultimately becomes porous.

TYPE-A FUEL FILL HOSE

DESCRIPTION: Two-ply reinforcement with wire helix construction. Outer skin is resistant to heat, fire, alcohol, and all fuels and petroleum products. Flexible. Marked "SAE J1527–USCG Type A2 Standard." 1½" ID is standard. Sold by the foot, up to 12½' lengths.

USE: To connect the fuel fill spud or barb on the deck plate fitting with the fuel fill opening on the tank.

USE TIPS: Hose must be completely tight fitting (double-clamp at both ends!), so that no fuel spills inside the boat, where it poses a very real threat of fire or explosion. In addition, fuel fill pipe should extend into the tank almost to the bottom to avoid spills. Refer to Coast Guard requirements for permanent fuel systems for proper installation and use.

BUYING TIPS: Because of the changes in gasoline formulations since the mid–1980s you must use fuel hose made to the proper specifications. Purchase only hose with the above-referenced marking.

OUTBOARD FUEL-LINE ASSEMBLIES

DESCRIPTION: 7½' or 12'⅜" braided fuel line with fittings at either end. A goose egg–sized rubber squeeze-bulb is located midway along hose for use as a primer pump. Comes with barb fittings that thread into fuel tanks at either end. Female fittings on either end of hose fit over barb fittings threaded into tanks.

USE: To attach external or portable (nonpermanent) fuel tank to integral fuel tank on outboard motor.

USE TIPS: Primer bulb begins suction action that draws fuel from portable tank into tank on engine. Use double clamps at all connections.

BUYING TIPS: Primer bulbs can be replaced. Fuel-line assembly models available for different makes of outboards.

JERRY JUG

ALSO KNOWN AS: Jerry can, portable gas can, portable fuel can.

DESCRIPTION: Polyethylene tank with integral handle. Long, angled screw-on spout with snap-on cover. Threaded vent cap. Molded-in labels for gas, diesel, kerosene, and water.

USE: To carry small quantities of fuel and water from the pump to your boat.

USE TIPS: For storage and temporary carrying purposes only. Not to be used as an auxiliary fuel tank for outboards or for any permanent or semi-permanent fuel supply.

BUYING TIPS: Available in 1–5-gal. capacities for gasoline, 6-gal. for diesel, 5¼-gal. for kerosene, and 5-gal. for water, as well as other sizes.

SHUT-OFF VALVE

DESCRIPTION: Brass valve installed on the fuel line leading to the engine, can be manual or electric and operated remotely at the helmsman's station. ¼" or ⅝" NPT threads, for male-female or male-male outlets. Three-way valves are connected to twin tanks and can be adjusted to close off only one tank at a time.

USE: To allow for quick emergency shut-off of fuel to engine. Remote-controlled electric valve is wired into the ignition line and opens only when the ignition switch is on. It should have a manual override in case of electrical failure.

USE TIPS: Also serves as an antisyphon device.

BUYING TIPS: Shut-off valves are not required, but they give an added measure of safety in case of a fuel-hose leak.

GAS TANK VENT

DESCRIPTION: Stainless steel or chrome-plated zinc fitting projects through opening in hull above the waterline, held in place with a large lock nut. Hooded vent opening on external end, usually includes wire-mesh screen, which acts as a filter and flame arrester. Inboard end of fitting has hose barbs. May be straight or 90° elbow.

USE: To allow air into and out of the tank as fuel is being added (air needs to escape to make room for the fuel that displaces it) or is being withdrawn for use by the engine (if air doesn't replace the fuel as it is drawn, the resulting vacuum will cause the tank to collapse).

USE TIPS: Fuel system must vent overboard rather than into the bilge to minimize the danger of fire or explosion. Fuel may sometimes slosh into the vent and run down the side of the boat and damage detail striping tape found there. Some skippers combat this by hanging a plastic bag below the fuel tank vent while gassing up—a homely remedy, but it works.

Vents should always have a shield or splash guard to prevent rain and spray from backing into the tank. If you are having a problem with water in your fuel, do not overlook the tank vent as a possible source.

BUYING TIPS: Because vents vary widely in quality and style, you might want to upgrade the one that comes with your stock boat.

FILTER FUNNEL

DESCRIPTION: Funnel with relatively short nozzle and 1-qt. capacity tulip-shaped bell with wire-mesh screen.

USE: To keep large pieces of dirt and foreign matter from entering the fuel tank or whatever else you are filling.

USE TIPS: Don't rely upon this as your only filter.

BUYING TIPS: Filter funnels are especially important for diesel engines; get the flexible nozzle type for the most versatile use.

WATER ABSORBER

ALSO KNOWN AS: Fuel stabilizer, fuel conditioner

DESCRIPTION: Nonpressurized methyl-alcohol mixture harmless to fuel lines, gaskets, filters, or pollution-control devices.

USE: To evenly disperse water found in gasoline so that it will burn away.

USE TIPS: Useful for handling water that may be present in poor-quality gas or that enters the tank through the vent system. Treat gasoline with water absorber when storing your boat, since water will form due to condensation. Check engine manufacturer for specific recommendations.

BUYING TIPS: One 16-oz. plastic bottle will treat 250 gal. of gasoline.

GASOLINE ADDITIVE AND LEAD SUBSTITUTE

DESCRIPTION: Liquid petroleum mixture, sometimes including phosphorus, contains no methanol or alcohol.

USE: To provide the valve seat protection, fuel economy, and lubricating qualities once found in leaded gasoline but no longer available, since lead was banned from fuel in the mid-1980s.

USE TIPS: Should be added to fuel tank prior to fill-up; adding the fuel agitates the mixture in the tank for even distribution. Use a funnel to avoid spills on the deck. Some engine manufacturers frown on lead additives. Check before using, particularly on new engines still under warranty.

BUYING TIPS: 8-oz. bottle treats 80 gal. of gas.

—— PROPELLERS AND ACCESSORIES ——

PROPELLER

ALSO KNOWN AS: Marine propeller, prop, wheel

DESCRIPTION: Bronze, stainless steel, aluminum, or plastic device with a central hub and polished, evenly spaced cupped or flat blades (two, three, or four are most common on pleasure boats), in a spiral pattern. Center of hub may have a keyway or slot, or may have a whole series of evenly spaced slots so that propeller can be fitted to the propeller shaft. Some are made with inner hubs that permit the prop to spin freely of the shaft when an accident such as a grounding occurs.

Props are measured according to their diameter (the measurement from the center of the hub out to the tip of the blade, multiplied by 2) and pitch (the theoretical distance a propeller would move forward in one revolution—picture a screw going through wood—as a result of the angle of the blades).

Propellers are either right- or left-hand rotation, matching the rotation of the engine. When the prop stands vertically, the blades on a right-handed wheel slope up from the left; on a left-handed prop they slope down from the left.

Types of propellers include *adjustable pitch, folding* (used on sailboats, with blades that fold in line to reduce drag when the boat is under sail), and *weedless* to shed fouling plant growth. Engine manufacturers make special models for specific boating applications, such as trolling.

USE: The primary connection between the engine and the water, the propeller moves a boat forward or backward.

USE TIPS: Always keep a spare prop onboard. Using a badly damaged one can cause serious engine problems. Recondition the prop when it gets "dinged" if you run aground (see "Marine Shear Pin," below). Usually this is a less expensive alternative to a complete replacement. Even slight nicks will cause a significant loss in performance and speed.

BUYING TIPS: Prop selection is determined by boating activity (skiing, trolling, racing, for example) and sea conditions. Refer to the engine manufacturer's recommendations as to size, pitch, number of blades, and propeller material.

Props made of stainless steel cost the most but are highly corrosion-resistant and are least likely to sustain the minor nicks and bends that can reduce performance. Aluminum props, which cost less, are lightweight, and are easy to repair, are the most popular. Plastic props weigh even less and will not corrode, but are usually found only on electric and low-horsepower outboard motors.

Marine Shear Pin

ALSO KNOWN AS: Shear pin

DESCRIPTION: Stainless steel or brass cylinder as small as ⅛" diameter or as large as over ¼" and up to 1½" long.

USE: Inserted in the hub of the propeller as a link with the shaft, the shear pin is weak enough to break first, before serious damage is done to the drive shaft or the propeller as the result of a grounding or other underwater strike.

USE TIPS: Check your owner's manual to determine whether a shear pin is called for on your model motor. Check your shear pin regularly during the season; replace it immediately if there is any sign of wear or distortion or if there has been any grounding incident.

BUYING TIPS: Inexpensive insurance against engine damage. Have several spares on hand. Check manufacturer's recommendations for proper size for your motor. Supplied with cotter pin, normally.

Prop Nut Wrench

ALSO KNOWN AS: Prop wrench, lock tab removal tool

DESCRIPTION: Flat device about 9½" long made of chrome-plated steel, with hex wrench at one end and prying hook at the other.

USE: Some outdrives rely on nuts clipped on with two lock tabs to prevent a propeller from unscrewing, instead of a conventional screw-on nut; this tool removes both the nut and pries loose the two tabs.

USE TIPS: Primarily for use on MerCruiser and OMC Cobra stern drives, from 80 hp to 350 hp.

BUYING TIPS: Makes a not-too difficult job foolproof.

Prop Nut and Washer Kit

DESCRIPTION: Matched sets of prop nuts, cotter pins, and spacer washers or, simply, tab washers, according to engine manufacturer's specifications.

USE: Prop nuts and tab washers hold propellers in place on the drive shaft.

USE TIPS: Keep your old usable parts on hand as spares when replacing. Check your owner's manual for the parts you need—and make sure you have the requisite tools on board.

BUYING TIPS: Handy insurance for powerboaters who roam far from home.

Prop Lock

DESCRIPTION: Two-piece brass-and-aluminum locking system with key. Similar in appearance to lug nut on car tire.

USE: Locked onto the end of the drive shaft, this does double duty by keeping the prop from falling into the water or into the hands of thieves.

USE TIPS: Be sure to remove the detachable portion before launching. Especially useful on trailerable boats parked in public places.

BUYING TIPS: Select specific model for your engine.

ABOUT ZINCS

On boats corrosion is the nemesis of most metal hardware, fittings, engines, propellers, and myriad other parts. For items above the waterline, corrosion may simply create an unsightly cosmetic problem, such as pitting, which is caused by high humidity, salt spray, and exposure to pollutants in the air.

Below the waterline, however, corrosion is a different animal indeed, thanks to an electrochemical reaction called galvanic corrosion (sometimes incorrectly called electrolysis), which occurs when dissimilar metals that are either touching or connected electrically are placed in water. The water acts as an electrolyte because it is capable of transmitting an electrical charge. (Pure, distilled water has no current-carrying capacity, but seawater, a mulligatawny soup of salts and pollutants, is highly conductive.)

To understand galvanic action, think of how a car battery works. A series of anodes and cathodes are suspended in an electrolyte bath, in this case sulfuric acid, rather than seawater. Anodes and cathodes have different potentials for corrosion: the more active anode (with its positive charge) gives off electrons, which are gained by the negatively charged cathode. This flow creates an electric current, and in the process the anode is eventually eaten away.

Below the waterline on your boat dissimilar metal objects, such as your aluminum outdrive and a nearby bronze through-hull fitting for the cockpit drain, have the same anode-cathode relationship. The resulting corrosion weakens the aluminum-alloy outdrive housing, causing catastrophic failure of structural parts.

A "galvanic series" chart of metals places platinum, stainless steel, nickel, and bronze at the "noble" (cathodic or passive) end of the scale, least likely to corrode; while metals such as magnesium, zinc, aluminum, and wrought iron are placed at the "least noble" (anodic or active) end of the scale, most likely to corrode.

Unless all the underwater hardware on your boat is made of the same metal or metals that are close to each other in the galvanic series, it is virtually impossible to stop galvanic corrosion from occurring. But you can exercise some damage control by installing specially designed anodes made of pure zinc at key points, such as the propeller shaft, the rudder, and the outdrive, below the waterline.

Inexpensive zinc is very low on the noble scale and is more likely to corrode before your expensive aluminum outdrive does. Thus the lowly "sacrificial zinc" is on the front line, giving its all to protect other hard-to-replace objects. In fact, newer aluminum "zincs," which displace more electrical current, are replacing traditional zincs. In fresh water, even more efficient magnesium zincs are preferred.

Made in a variety of designs, sizes, and styles, zincs are easy to install and inexpensive to replace when they get worn down. Replace zincs at least once a year or when they are down to half their original size, but to be on the safe side, check them several times during the boating season, especially if your boat is moored in a swift-moving current.

ZINC

ALSO KNOWN AS: Sacrificial zinc, sacrificial anode, anode

DESCRIPTION: Objects made of pure zinc, aluminum, or magnesium. Oval *shaft zincs*, *barrel zincs*,

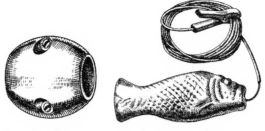

donut zinc collar   zinc guppy

and *donut zinc collars* split in half to fit around prop shafts from ⅞" diameter to 2" or more in diameter. Some engine manufacturers make specially designed *prop zincs* for outdrives. Pairs of round *rudder zincs* (2"–5" diameter) are through-bolted to either side of the rudder. *Engine water jacket zincs* (sometimes called *pencils*) ⁵⁄₁₆" diameter × 1¾" long to ¾" diameter × 3⅝" long) are threaded directly into the cooling water system. Both *teardrop* and *plate zincs* are through-bolted directly to the hull. Finlike *trim-tab zincs* bolt onto cavitation plates on outdrives and outboard motors. Fish-shaped *zinc guppy* or *zinc grouper* is attached to a free-hanging, nylon-covered stainless steel line, usually about 15' long, with an alligator clip on the inboard end.

Another type of anode is the cone-shaped *deicer zinc* made to protect "bubbler" systems from corrosion.

USE: To prevent or control galvanic corrosion on underwater hardware. Particularly necessary in saltwater. The *zinc guppy* is hung over the side when the boat is at rest, with the alligator clip attached to the boat's grounding system. *Water jacket zincs* protect the engine block itself from corrosion.

USE TIPS: Never paint anodes, as this will destroy their sacrificial characteristics! To prevent leaks, be sure to bed or caulk zincs that are attached with bolts through the hull. Zincs that bolt to cavitation plates enhance the plates' function by expanding surface area.

BUYING TIPS: Buy only anodes that are made of high-quality alloy. It is not worth making your own from "junkyard zinc"; they will not have nearly the same anodic capacity.

DEGREASER

ALSO KNOWN AS: Engine degreaser

DESCRIPTION: Aerosol mixture of solvents, typically includes xylene and ethyel benzene.

USE: All-purpose degreaser cleans electric equipment, removes dirt and oil from the surface of engines, tools, and other equipment. Material specifically intended for engine degreasing is sprayed directly onto the hot surface of an engine that has already been warmed up (but is no longer running).

USE TIPS: Besides being unsuitable for use on electronic equipment such as VCRs or tape decks, most degreasers contain chemicals that pose a health hazard. Avoid prolonged exposure, especially in enclosed spaces.

Manufacturer's instructions say to remove the air cleaner and cover the carburetor before applying engine degreaser to warmed-up motor. Clouds of white smoke or steam will arise, but do not be alarmed. Foamy material can be hosed off after 10 minutes. You may need to leave it on longer or reapply to remove heavy grease and oil buildup.

BUYING TIPS: All-purpose degreaser sold in 19-oz. can, engine degreaser comes in 12-oz. can.

ENGINE PROTECTOR

DESCRIPTION: Pressurized mix of lubricants.

USE: To lubricate internal moving surfaces of engine prior to long-term storage and to prevent rust and excess engine wear, particularly at start-up.

USE TIPS: Spray through the carburetor jets while the engine is running. Check with engine manufacturer for specific recommendations.

BUYING TIPS: Available for both two-cycle and four-cycle engines, sold in 12-oz. aerosol can.

CRANKCASE OIL STABILIZER

DESCRIPTION: Nonpressurized mix of petroleum oils.

USE: To leave a lasting film of lubricant on cylinder walls, crankshaft, and connecting rods.

USE TIPS: Important engine treatment prior to long-term storage, since normal lubricants drain off these parts, leaving exposed metal vulnerable to rust and corrosion. Check with engine manufacturer for specific recommendations.

BUYING TIPS: One 8-oz. bottle treats 5 qts. of engine oil.

ADDITIVE/STABILIZER

ALSO KNOWN AS: Gasoline stabilizer, diesel stabilizer

DESCRIPTION: Liquid petroleum distillate naphtha, a solvent or dilutant that contains no methanol or alcohol, for use with gasoline engines. Petroleum distillate formula made for diesel engines doesn't contain naphtha. Highly flammable and highly toxic to breathe or ingest.

USE: Prevents buildups of gums and resins that clog carburetors, intake systems, and tanks in gasoline engine, as well as sludge and deposits that form in diesel distribution lines, injectors, and strainers.

USE TIPS: Important addition to gas or diesel fuel tanks, especially prior to winter layup, when fuel tends to break down over time. Be sure to use the right type of additive for your fuel system. Stabilizers do not affect octane and cetane ratings. Check with engine manufacturer for specific recommendations.

Pour into fuel tank and run engine for 10 minutes to distribute throughout fuel system.

BUYING TIPS: A little goes a long way: 1 oz. of gas stabilizer treats 5 gal. of fuel; 1 oz. of diesel stabilizer treats 12 gal. of fuel.

LIQUID GASKET

DESCRIPTION: Silicon material of semiliquid consistency similar to toothpaste. Comes in squeeze tube with screw-on conical applicator tip.

USE: Do-it-yourself gaskets formed in place directly by applying a bead of silicon directly onto surfaces of water outlets, timing and valve covers, and water pumps.

USE TIPS: Unsuitable where working temperature exceeds 600°F or when exposed to fuel, exhaust, or on cylinder heads. Normal cure time is 24 hours; may be longer in cold weather.

BUYING TIPS: A 2.8-oz. tube will make many gaskets.

MARINE INSTANT GALVANIZE

DESCRIPTION: Aerosol-spray galvanizing material contains zinc dust, xylene, propane, epoxy resin, and a number of other highly toxic materials. Matte-gray color.

USE: To protect bare metal and touch up scratches to prevent rust and corrosion.

USE TIPS: Prepare metal surface carefully by removing scale, rust, grease, and dirt before applying. Spray works best when used in temperatures over 60° F. For overcoating, be sure paint is compatible with galvanized material, and prepare surface appropriately.

BUYING TIPS: Sold in 13-oz. can with extension tube or "straw."

ANTI-CORROSION SPRAY

ALSO KNOWN AS: Corrosion block

DESCRIPTION: Nonaerosol pump-spray liquid-petroleum lubricant.

USE: To prevent rust and corrosion by displacing moisture; lubricates, penetrates, and loosens seized parts, such as hinges. Suitable for most metals, but might have adverse effects on copper or silver components.

USE TIPS: Spray directly on metal or apply with soft cloth.

BUYING TIPS: 4-oz. can will last a long time. A must for the toolbox.

LUBRICANTS

BELT DRESSING

DESCRIPTION: Aerosol lubricant.

USE: To keep rubber drive belt supple and prevent slips and squeaks.

USE TIPS: Apply to inner working surface of belt while engine is running; allow to work in.

BUYING TIPS: Sold in 5-oz. can.

ANTISEIZE LUBRICANT

DESCRIPTION: Aerosol lubricant.

USE: To prevent working engine parts from seizing due to high temperatures or corrosion. Cannot be displaced by fresh or salt water.

USE TIPS: Effective in working temperatures up to 1,200°F.

BUYING TIPS: Sold in 12-oz. can.

FOUR-CYCLE ENGINE OIL

ALSO KNOWN AS: Four-stroke cycle oil

DESCRIPTION: SAE 30-weight oil for gasoline or diesel engines that are air- or water-cooled.

USE: Besides lubricating moving engine parts and reducing engine wear, this oil also protects against oxidation and reduces oil consumption.

USE TIPS: Follow manufacturer's recommendations for oil changes. Generally this should be done at least once each boating season, but it is wise to check the oil level every time you use your boat.

BUYING TIPS: Sold individually in plastic quart bottles with spouts. If you do your own maintenance, it is cheaper to buy motor oil by the case from your marine supply store, Always keep a few quarts onboard for emergencies.

COMBUSTION CHAMBER AND CARBURETOR CLEANER

ALSO KNOWN AS: Carb spray

DESCRIPTION: Aerosol mix of petroleum products, ethanol, naphtha, and liquefied gas.

USE: To clean buildups of gum, carbon, and varnish from carburetors and combustion chambers.

USE TIPS: Besides reducing the function of the carburetor, buildups on internal engine parts can lead to piston-ring failures and scoring of cylinder walls.

BUYING TIPS: Use one 12-oz. can for each cleaning. Should be used every 50 hours, at the same time you change the oil.

GAUGES AND METERS

ABOUT GAUGES AND METERS

Although some boat's helmsman's consoles or instrument panels resemble automobile dashboards, with "idiot lights" to indicate engine operation, most bear a wide variety of gauges or meters for accurate assessment of engine performance. Low-voltage electricity from the battery feeds most of these gauges, but some, such as engine and transmission oil pressure gauges, work mechanically, without electricity. All gauges have sensor devices, as well as sending units, for relaying information from the sensor to the gauge.

There are a number of aftermarket makes of gauges and meters available in addition to those models made by engine manufacturers. Some have lights for reading at night. For a professional, neat look on the instrument panel, try to stick with one make of gauge. Also, before replacing an old gauge, check to see whether the new one will fit in the existing cutout. Few things look worse than a patchwork of oversized holes and fillers. Choose gauges with nonglare surfaces and faces, as well as high-contrast numbers and needles.

Check gauge and meter accuracy by calibrating with an instrument whose fidelity is known. Although minute adjustments may be made, never adjust meters beyond their capacity. Besides causing errors and possible gauge burnout, doing so could also create a safety hazard.

ENGINE GAUGES

ALSO KNOWN AS: Performance gauges, instrument panels

DESCRIPTION: Various instrumentation, consisting of a remote sensor and an instrument panel, with 2"-or-larger dial and needle, under raised convex lenses (usually coated glass) and contained in a waterproof plastic or nylon housing. Modern gauges are electronic as opposed to mechanical and are connected to the engine block via a sending unit, which transmits the appropriate signal. Most gauges have dampeners to keep down needle vibration, and most have illumination. Some models offer dual standard/metric readouts. Average power draw of $\frac{1}{3}$ amp at 12 volts.

TYPES:

Water-temperature gauge: Measures temperature of engine cooling water, from either 0° to 250° or 100°

to 250°. Instrument only—the sender comes separately.

Oil-pressure gauge: Measures to 80 psi (pounds per square inch); sender comes separate.

Speedometer: Instrument that gives speed readouts of from 0 mph to 50 mph, 60 mph, or 65 mph. *Speedometer kit* includes approximately 20' of vinyl tubing to connect engine and speedometer's impact tube and transom-mounting hardware.

Tachometer: One of larger instruments (about 3¾"-diameter face). One version measures from 0 rpm to 6,000 rpm for 4-, 6-, and 8-cylinder gasoline inboards, inboard-outboards (I/Os), or outboards with 12-pole alternator. Second version for standard outboards measures 0–8,000 rpm.

Fuel gauge: Instrument panel that operates with fuel-level sender to indicate fuel supply from empty to full.

Fuel-flow meter: More sophisticated fuel-supply monitor that electronically measures fuel flow at the engine for gallons-per-hour readout. "Totalizer" keeps track of fuel consumed and displays it in LCD readout. Measuring capacity up to 9,999.9 gal. Gauge is 3¼". Several versions, for single and twin engines, with top speeds below 150 hp and above 150 hp.

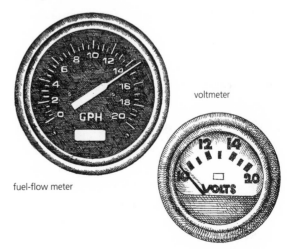

voltmeter

fuel-flow meter

Hour meter: Engine-hour meter keeps track of elapsed running time up to 10,000 hours in display similar to automobile odometer. Usually unlighted.

Voltmeter: Monitors voltage, anywhere from 8 to 18 volts, from various points in the circuit, although a display at the instrument panel is not very helpful in pinpointing a specific break in the circuit. Comes with ⅛" sending unit.

USE: To monitor various engine function and relay information via analog or digital display to instrument panel.

USE TIPS: Gauges and dials vary in size, color, and method of conveying information; choose those you will be comfortable with. Also, before installing, make sure you will be able to view each from the helm.

BUYING TIPS: Mostly for powerboaters; sailors would do better with instruments specifically relating to sail.

ENGINE ACCESSORIES

ENGINE-ROOM SOUNDPROOFING

ALSO KNOWN AS: Engine room insulation

DESCRIPTION: Fire-retardant ¼" foam encased in aluminized polyurethane. Comes in 4' long × 2' high sheets; can be cut with scissors and installs with steel hangers and insulation adhesive that sticks to metal, wood, and fiberglass.

USE: To dampen the roar of your engine compartment.

USE TIPS: Do not block vent ducts. Otherwise you may trap dangerous gas and exhaust fumes, as well as create dangerously hot engine-room temperatures.

BUYING TIPS: Soundproofing will cut down noise but has no effect on engine vibration.

ENGINE CABLE

ALSO KNOWN AS: Throttle cable, control cable

DESCRIPTION: Flexible, multistrand stainless steel cable in protective, insulating jacket, with stainless-steel and brass swage fittings at either end. Connects helmsman's-panel controls to gearshift lever and throttle at the engine. From 6' to 40' long.

USE: The push-pull action of the stainless steel cable in its jacket allows for remote-controlled gear shifting and adjustments to the throttle on outboard motors as well as on inboard-outboard (I/O) installations.

USE TIPS: Inspect cables frequently for kinks, chafe on the outer jacket, and misalignment, as well as corrosion of the swage fittings at either end. When in doubt, unhook the cable at both ends and move the stainless steel core manually. If it is stiff, follow the cable manufacturer's instructions for lubrication.

BUYING TIPS: Each engine manufacturer seems to have its own preference for end fittings, so special models are made for specific engines.

DIESEL CONVERSION KIT

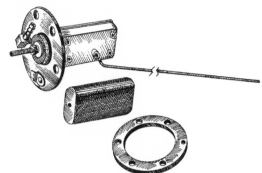

DESCRIPTION: A regular, permanent replacement sending unit that has a hose barb on the mounting plate to which you can attach a plastic fuel return line. Sized according to depth of tank.

USE: To convert a standard gasoline tank for diesel use by providing a return-fuel line from the engine.

USE TIPS: Unlike a gas engine, which uses all the fuel that is pumped to it, a diesel engine is fed an excess of fuel that helps to cool the injectors and injector pump before it returns to the tank. The conversion kit's clear plastic tube acts as the return line.

BUYING TIPS: Only works with certain makes of plastic fuel tanks.

MARINE IGNITION SWITCH

ALSO KNOWN AS: Starter switch

DESCRIPTION: Usually key-operated switch with multiple functions: off, ignition, start, and (sometimes) choke. Boats that have a separate starter button use a *battery ignition switch,* that has simple off-on functions. Corrosion-resistant construction, often brass or sealed plastic with a chrome-plated brass face, with brass inner workings and brass keys (two usually included). Different-length mounting stems from ¾" to 1¾" (for the thickest mounting panels).

USE: To begin the process of starting a motor by permitting current to flow through from the starter battery to the solenoid and starter motor.

USE TIPS: When installing an ignition, make sure your connections to the wire or screw terminals are secure, and follow up by waterproofing the connections.

BUYING TIPS: Pick an ignition whose maker warranties the anticorrosive finish for the duration of ownership. Snap-on caps are available to cover some ignition makes when not in use—a good means of prolonging the life of your switch.

SOLENOID

ALSO KNOWN AS: Starter solenoid

DESCRIPTION: Remote switch consisting of a plunger and an electromagnet and a set of contacts or points that open or close. When activated by the ignition switch, the magnet is energized, closing the circuit and allowing current to flow through to the starter motor.

USE: To start the starter motor that starts an engine. Because a starter motor draws heavy amperage, a solenoid is used as an intermediary so that heavy cable does not need to be used all the way to the ignition, which is usually some distance away.

BUYING TIPS: There are different types of starter motor and solenoid; follow the manufacturer's specifications.

CHAPTER EIGHT

CABIN, COCKPIT, AND DECK

The boat's cabin is a combination living area and operations center, separate functions that tend to be crammed into a relatively small space even with today's well-designed interiors. Aside from the navigation area, the electrical control panels, and various electronic instruments and gauges, most interiors are divided into several distinct areas—the galley or kitchen, the head or bathroom, berths for sleeping, and the main saloon, a combination living, dining, and sleeping section. Along with the standard equipment that comes with a boat, there are many items you can add to improve the functioning and your enjoyment of the cabin.

GALLEY

PROPANE STOVE

ALSO KNOWN AS: LPG stove

DESCRIPTION: Propane- or LPG-fueled stove intended for use inside cabin, with several designs.

TYPES:

Gimballed bulkhead mount: Model with a circular single burner with a drip pan fueled by a 6.4-oz. propane bottle. Flame adjuster and positive off switch are typical accessories. It holds a single pot up to 8" in diameter. Attached gimbal support slides into bracket mounted permanently into bulkhead.

Flush mount: Deluxe stainless steel range with two 5,000-Btu burners, measuring 2' long × 14" wide and extending below countertop by a little over 6". Male flare fitting attaches to permanently installed propane-feed line. Thermocouple feature on burners shuts them off completely if the flame is extinguished. On-off knobs are childproof.

Range and oven combination: Offers one 8,000-Btu burner and one or two 5,000-Btu burners, plus 1.3–1.5 cu. ft. oven with two-position black-glass-paneled door. Push-button spark ignition, built-in control-panel thermometer, infrared flame broiler with broiler pan. Requires 2 cu. ft. cutout.

USE: Gimballed stove is suitable for small boats with limited galley space. Gimbal arrangement keeps stove level, despite boat's heel or rough sea conditions.

Flush-mount style is an easy replacement for an alcohol stove, since it requires a standard-size counter cutout. Suitable for small to medium galleys.

A gimballed version of the range-oven keeps unit level during rough sea conditions or when boat is heeling.

USE TIPS: With gimballed model, since burner is fairly small, be sure your cooking containers fit.

BUYING TIPS: Small utensils, such as teakettles, are sold separately for single-burner stove. Cutting-board stove top is available for flush-mount model.

BUTANE STOVE TOP

ALSO KNOWN AS: Permanent-mount butane stove

DESCRIPTION: Single-burner stove drops into 12" long × 10" wide counter cutout, has glass top and enameled burner grate. Safety fuel shut-off, automatic ignition, and variable flame control. 3'-long fuel line extends beneath counter unit to bracket that holds disposable butane canister.

USE: Permanently mounted stove for use on boats where galley space is limited.

USE TIPS: Don't expect the same quick cooking you get from a propane stove.

BUYING TIPS: Butane canisters sold separately.

ALCOHOL STOVES

ALSO KNOWN AS: Nonpressurized alcohol stoves, pressurized alcohol stoves, camp stoves

DESCRIPTION: One- or two-burner stainless-steel cooking ranges fueled by denatured alcohol. In a *nonpressurized alcohol stove* the alcohol is poured into a moatlike "tank" below each burner and is absorbed into wick at burner's surface. A *pressurized alcohol stove* has a pump knob that forces alcohol fumes into the burner area. In either model, as fumes disperse, they can be ignited. A hybrid is the *alcohol/electric stove,* which can run strictly on alcohol or can switch over to electric power if you wish to run your generator or plug into shore power.

On all models temperature is controlled by a knob, located on front of stove, that regulates the amount of fuel admitted to burner. Flames are diffused in the familiar circular "daisy" pattern through evenly spaced holes around the perimeter of the burner. Pot grid approximately 10" long × 10" wide holds cooking container level over flame. Some stove models are flush-mounted with the countertop for a sleek appearance. These extend about 6" below the counter surface.

Some stoves are installed with gimbals to keep them level when the boat is heeling and some have sea rails and brackets for keeping pots in place. Stoves can be disassembled for easier cleaning.

USE: Onboard cooking. A clean, properly adjusted stove can bring 2 pts. of water to boil in about 8 minutes.

USE TIPS: Permanent, secure mounting systems should be provided for all stoves installed on boats. Be sure there is a metal drip pan beneath the stove. To avoid dangerous flare-ups, fires, and injuries, never add fuel while stove is lit! On a positive note, alcohol fires can be doused with water.

BUYING TIPS: Denatured alcohol is expensive, but it is safe to use and widely available in quart and gallon jugs. If space allows, buy a two-burner stove. Cooking a meal will be easier, faster, and will require less planning. Wooden cutting-board inserts are sometime sold with stoves or may be purchased separately.

BOAT-STOVE ALCOHOL

ALSO KNOWN AS: Denatured alcohol, ethyl alcohol

DESCRIPTION: Colorless, volatile, flammable liquid.

USE: Fuel for alcohol stoves. Burns cleanly, preventing clogging of stove parts with carbon buildup.

USE TIPS: The denaturing process renders boat-stove alcohol undrinkable, so do not try it! Use your radio to call the nearest poison-control center if someone onboard ingests denatured alcohol.

BUYING TIPS: Sold in plastic quart and gallon jugs.

FILTER FUNNEL

ALSO KNOWN AS: Funnel

DESCRIPTION: 1-qt. capacity tulip-shaped bowl with narrow neck across which a fine-mesh screen is placed. Often red in color to indicate its use with fuel. Plastic material floats if dropped overboard.

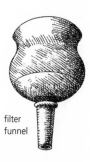

filter funnel

USE: An easy, efficient way to fill stove with fuel.

USE TIPS: Impossible to do without: imagine trying to pour alcohol from a gallon jug into a small fuel port on the stove, especially while your boat is pitching and tossing under way.

BUYING TIPS: Plastic funnels are inexpensive. You should have a separate one for each use to avoid contaminating water, for example, with gasoline or stove fuel.

ELECTRIC STOVE TOP

ALSO KNOWN AS: Electric range

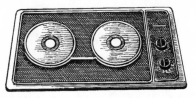

DESCRIPTION: One-, two- and sometimes three-burner cooking surfaces with enclosed electric heating coils flush or nearly flush with easy-to-clean enameled metal surface. Figure on approximately 10" wide × 10" long area per burner. Temperature-control knobs mounted adjacent to cooking surfaces. Operates on 120-volt AC from generator or shore power. Because cooking requires large amounts of heat, it is not feasible to use the boat's 12-volt DC system.

USE: Onboard cooking at dockside.

USE TIPS: Electricity is safe to use.

BUYING TIPS: Expensive, but "just like home" in terms of convenience and efficiency.

ELECTRIC RANGE

ALSO KNOWN AS: Electric stove

DESCRIPTION: Two- or three-burner cooking surface combined with front drop-door oven-broiler combo in single unit roughly 2 cu. ft. in size. Operates on 120-volt AC either off the generator or with shore power. Some deluxe models come with wooden cutting-board inserts for cook-top surface.

USE: Cook, bake, and broil to your heart's delight, as long as you have a supply of electricity.

USE TIPS: These are for those who must do some serious onboard cooking, as in feeding a crew. Measure your galley carefully to make sure there is sufficient room—and enough usable counter space left over.

BUYING TIPS: Electric ranges for boats are comparable in price to ones for home use. If you have room and if your budget allows, this is a great piece of equipment for the galley.

MARINE-GRADE MICROWAVE OVEN

ALSO KNOWN AS: Microwave

DESCRIPTION: Enclosed cooking system utilizing high-frequency electromagnetic waves similar to radio waves.

Marine-grade microwave ovens, operating on 120-volt AC from generator or shore power, are designed to withstand the vibrations from engine operation, as well as the movement of rough seas. They come equipped with hold-down brackets. Oven interiors, minuscule compared with home microwaves, are typically 0.4 cu. ft. to just under 1 cu. ft. Touch pad on face of oven includes cooking cycle, defrost, and timer controls.

USE: To cook and defrost foods in a matter of minutes.

USE TIPS: Microwaving has revolutionized cooking in the galley, as it has in the kitchen at home. You may never fire up the stove again. Works well with "retort" (reconstituted) foods that keep fresh for years and store easily.

BUYING TIPS: Considerably more expensive than home microwaves, but the marine model should not interfere with other electronic gear onboard. There is some word-of-mouth evidence that cheap analog-type microwaves designed for home use stand up better than the digital kind under the vicissitudes of a boat's electrical system.

ABOUT PROPANE

LPG—liquid petroleum gas, more often called simply propane—is a mix of propane, butane, butylene, and propylene, a highly flammable substance derived from crude petroleum and natural gas. On a boat it makes many creature comforts possible without the restricting umbilical cord of shore power or the expense of a marine generator. With LPG appliances you can cruise or anchor just about anywhere and still have hot water for showers, efficient heat in the cabin, and even a transom-mounted barbecue grill, all at a reasonable cost and with a limited investment of space. An added plus is that LPG is available just about anywhere you are likely to go cruising.

Propane gas is stored in its liquid state in aluminum or stainless steel *tanks* pressurized to about 125 psi. Disposable canisters are also available. When an appliance is turned

on or you open the valve at the top of the tank, the propane is released into a non-pressurized setting, at which point it becomes vapor, ready to be ignited. LPG systems are safe and easy to use, provided you follow a few precautions. For example, the system must contain a *remote shut-off control valve*, a *leak-test pressure gauge with automatic shut-off*, and a *pressure regulator*. A *vapor sensor* is also essential for detecting gas leaks near appliances or in the bilge. Boat owners should also install adequate fire extinguishers throughout the boat, particularly in the galley area (see page 342 for information about fire-protection equipment).

Propane gas is heavier than air, and if there is a leak, it will not dissipate into the atmosphere like other potentially dangerous gases, such as gasoline vapors or carbon monoxide. Propane gas that has found its way into the bilge will stay there. A stray electrical spark, a carelessly tossed match, or a cigarette lit belowdecks can trigger an explosion, but explosions can occur even without a spark if the gas is mixed with the right amount of air. It goes without saying that you should never use flame to test for leaks!

Key to safety with propane is proper containment, both in the tank and throughout the fuel lines feeding appliances. Tanks should be stored securely in specially designed abovedeck housings or in belowdecks compartments, called fuel lockers, that are completely sealed off from the cabin, engine compartment, and bilge. Inboard lockers must be equipped with venting systems at the bottom, and vent lines must exit overboard. Fuel lines must be one continuous run from the tank to the appliance being fed: remember, every joint or connection creates the potential for a leak. Wherever propane-fuel lines pass through bulkheads or decks, they must be completely protected against chafe, which can not only wear away hoses but create enough friction to cause heat and sparks.

The leak-test adapter (see page 179) found near the tank on most LPG systems gives you a quick and easy way to test for leaks before each use.

Problems can be kept to a minimum by carefully following LPG-system installation standards developed by the American Boat and Yacht Council (ABYC), a marine-industry advisory group. Copies of the LPG standard (Project A-1) may be obtained by writing to ABYC, 3069 Solomon's Island Rd., Edgewater, Md. 21037. Your marine insurance carrier may require that your boat

be equipped with an LPG sensor (see page 179) for detecting leaks.

LPG systems and appliances are quite different from those that utilize Compressed Natural Gas (CNG). Never try to use CNG in an LPG system or vice versa! Although some components of each system are interchangeable, others are not, so check caution labels carefully.

CNG is a fancy name for methane under pressure. Unlike propane, which is in a liquid state at relatively low pressure, CNG is always in the form of vapor and must therefore be stored at higher pressures to provide a comparable fuel supply. Also unlike propane, CNG is lighter than air and if released will rise and dissipate, so overhead ventilation is effective in clearing leaks. Because both LPG and CNG are odorless and colorless, they must be sold with odorants added to make it easier to detect leaks.

PROPANE-SYSTEM ACCESSORIES

MANUAL CONTROL SYSTEM

ALSO KNOWN AS: LPG control panel and solenoid

DESCRIPTION: Palm-sized electric-switch module with green on/off push-button light. Automatic shut-off in case of power loss. Switch module equipped with two ¼" NPT female pipe fittings. Draws ½ amp at 12 volts.

USE: To turn propane/CNG on and off. Green on/off switch lights up when gas is flowing, shuts off when switch is turned off. Manual control is overridden in the event of a power loss, when the unit automatically shuts the fuel system down.

USE TIPS: Install where signal light is readily seen.

BUYING TIPS: Buy only items specifically made for use with propane and/or CNG systems. These are bound to be expensive, but they have important safeguards built in to prevent leaks.

COMPLETE PROPANE-HOUSING SYSTEM

ALSO KNOWN AS:
Self-contained propane housing system

DESCRIPTION: Molded polyethylene tank housing with quick-release lid roughly 1 cu. ft. in size, containing a 1-gal. steel propane tank, vent kit including ports, hold-down brackets, in-line regulator, solenoid, leak-test gauge, and assorted flare fittings.

USE: Complete setup for propane system; lacks only the appliances and propane fuel with which to run them.

USE TIPS: Housing is for exterior storage (except inside a sailboat cockpit) and not to be confused with a propane locker (see page 178), designed for storage of one or more tanks in a cockpit or recess in a boat. Be thoroughly familiar with propane-system safety practices before attempting an installation on your boat.

BUYING TIPS: Consult installation instructions to see if additional switches are needed. Vents are located in bottom of housing, so be sure there is adequate clearance below housing, if it is mounted on deck, or run vent lines overboard.

Be thoroughly familiar with propane-system safety practices before attempting an installation on your boat. See "About Propane" (page 175) for additional information.

SOLENOID SHUT-OFF VALVE ASSEMBLY

ALSO KNOWN AS: High-pressure shut-off valve

DESCRIPTION: Electrical conductor installed between cylinder valve and regulator or leak tester. Consists of solid brass male and female pipe fittings and adapters. Draws ½-amp 12 volts.

USE: Serves as shut-off point between valves and regulators.

USE TIPS: For easy installation of a control valve without disassembling your fuel system.

BUYING TIPS: Quick-fix item that is not as useful as the manual control system with automatic shut-off.

LPG PIGTAIL-CONNECTOR REGULATOR

ALSO KNOWN AS: Remote single-stage regulator

DESCRIPTION: Flexible high-pressure thermoplastic LPG hose, 20" long, with male cylinder fitting and female receptacle.

USE: To connect cylinder to remote-mounted regulator or leak tester.

USE TIPS: Hose assembly is leak-tested by manufacturer.

BUYING TIPS: Don't try any substitutions or jury rigs here—use only the official connector.

PROPANE TANK

ALSO KNOWN AS: Vertical propane tank, LPG cylinder

DESCRIPTION: Polyurethane-coated steel or aluminum cylindrical tanks with raised ridge on base to keep bottom of tank from coming in contact with mounting surface. Female fitting on top of tank can be regulated by gate-style valve. Valve assembly is protected by circular vertical housing. Capacities from 6 to 100 lbs. of LPG fuel.

USE: To store LPG fuel under pressure.

USE TIPS: Aluminum tanks last longer and are less prone to deterioration in the marine environment than steel.

BUYING TIPS: Aluminum tanks are more expensive than steel, but added cost may be made up for because they last longer.

PROPANE-TANK STORAGE LOCKER

DESCRIPTION: High-density polyethylene locker shaped like a binocular case, only much larger, about 24" high × 24" wide. Cover has quick-release mechanism and is airtight, thanks to O-ring seal. Sump system collects leaking gas in lowest part of tank and vents it out of tank through attached hose pigtail.

USE: To store two same-size LPG tanks.

USE TIPS: Belowdecks use requires through-hull fitting and plumbing to vent overboard.

BUYING TIPS: Includes pressure gauge, but not mounting hardware and exhaust hose. Most common sizes hold twin tanks of from 6- to 20-lb. capacity, but other sizes and configurations are available.

MARINE LOW-PRESSURE REGULATOR

ALSO KNOWN AS: LPG regulator, pressure regulator

DESCRIPTION: Die-cast zinc housing encloses rubber diaphragm regulator and pressure-relief mechanism with male-inlet and female-outlet pipe fittings. *Two-stage* regulator has dual male inlets for connection to twin propane tanks. Many models include 300-psi leak-test adapters mounted on side, and all have drip-line vents to keep water out. Entire device is about the size of a hand.

Accessories include L-channel, predrilled zinc-plated steel mounting brackets, and *plastic regulator cover* that fits over virtually all regulators mounted in positions exposed to weather.

USE: To control flow of propane from cylinder to a constant 0.433 psi, which is much safer than the 125 psi under which propane gas is stored in the cylinder. Two-stage model switches to "full cylinder" setting when both cylinder valves are open and

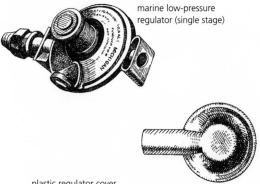

marine low-pressure regulator (single stage)

plastic regulator cover

shows an orange color in the indicator dome when one cylinder is empty. Two-stage regulator is used with pigtail hose connected to both LPG cylinders.

USE TIPS: For easy reading, mount at front of cylinder-storage area. For safe operation keep the regulator vent clear at all times. Never try to adjust the regulator!

BUYING TIPS: Spend a bit extra on a regulator that includes a leak-test adapter.

Connection Fittings for LPG Systems

DESCRIPTION: Solid brass male high-pressure and flare fittings with fine threads. Fittings with threads on either end have reverse threads.

USE: Leak-proof fittings for adding extra appliance feed lines or for connecting gauges or regulators to the propane system. Reverse threads on double-threaded fittings make it impossible to inadvertently loosen one end when you are trying to tighten or loosen the other.

LPG gauges, tanks, valves, and regulators have female fine-thread pipe fittings.

USE TIPS: For trouble-free LPG installations, follow safety regs to the letter (see "About Propane," page 175).

BUYING TIPS: Price is not relevant here, since these fittings, and no others, must be used.

Marine LPG Leak-Test Adapter with Gauge

ALSO KNOWN AS: Leak-test gauge

DESCRIPTION: Straight brass male tank fitting and female receptacle block with 300-psi gauge mounted in between.

USE: Test LPG system for leaks by installing this device on the high-pressure side of the regulator, between the tank and the regulator or pigtail hose.

To test system for leaks, turn off all propane-powered appliances, then open tank at the remote shut-off valve to charge the system. Check the reading, then close the tank valve and wait 5 or 10 minutes. If the needle falls, you have a leak.

USE TIPS: Intended only to test for leaks. This gauge does not indicate how much fuel there is in the cylinder.

BUYING TIPS: Only for those systems without a built-in pressure gauge.

Straight-Through Fitting

ALSO KNOWN AS: Liquid and vapor straight-through fitting

DESCRIPTION: Three-sectioned sleeve with locknut and sealing gland, made of saltwater-, fuel-, solvent-, and acid-resistant nylon. Withstands up to 70 psi. Fits over standard ¼" ID copper LPG supply lines.

USE: To guide and protect LPG hose from wear and chafing as it passes through bulkheads and decks up to ⅜" thick. Thanks to locknut and sealing gland, this sleeve fitting maintains water- and vapor-tightness.

USE TIPS: LPG hold must be chafe-protected where it passes through bulkheads and decks and must be supported every 2' to prevent kinks and sharp bends. Refer to "About Propane" (page 175) for how to obtain more information about marine propane installations.

BUYING TIPS: Absolutely essential for a safe LPG installation.

LPG FLEXIBLE CONNECTOR HOSE

DESCRIPTION: Supple thermoplastic hose with ¼" inside diameter and solid brass ⅜" female flare fittings on either end. Leakproof.

USE: To connect gimballed stoves, heaters, and outside barbecues to rigid copper feed line in permanent LPG systems.

USE TIPS: Can also be used with high-pressure solenoid shut-off valve assembly (see page 177) so that regulators (see page 178) can be mounted remote from cylinders.

BUYING TIPS: Sold in 5', 10', 15', 20' lengths, up to 40'. Measure carefully so you are sure to get the correct length.

PIGTAIL HOSE

DESCRIPTION: 15"- or 20"-long flexible thermoplastic hose; male tank fitting and ¼" male inverted flare fitting attached at ends.

USE: To attach LPG tanks to regulator (see page 178) in twin-cylinder setups.

USE TIPS: The kind with a built-in pressure gauge provides another degree of safety.

BUYING TIPS: A hose will be needed for each cylinder in your system.

STANCHION-MOUNT PROPANE STORAGE TUBE

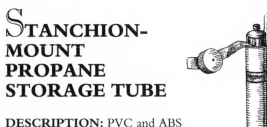

DESCRIPTION: PVC and ABS plastic tube mounts on stanchion and accommodates two 14.1-oz. propane cylinders stacked vertically.

USE: To store cylinders on stern rail or stanchion near stove.

USE TIPS: Won't hold 16-oz. cylinders.

BUYING TIPS: Good for those who do a lot of barbecuing; otherwise a propane locker is the better storage location.

PROPANE CYLINDER STORAGE DUFFEL

DESCRIPTION: Acrylic fabric satchel with three separate vertical compartments, has nylon webbing reinforcement and handles.

USE: To provide storage for three 1-lb. refillable or disposable propane cylinders; hangs from lifeline rail by straps fastened with D-rings.

USE TIPS: In case of rough conditions make sure duffel and its contents do not swing against anything on deck. Not intended for use with permanent LPG systems. Do not feed propane appliances from cylinders while they are stored in duffel.

BUYING TIPS: Handy storage when boat does not have built-in propane lockers.

GRILLS AND ACCESSORIES

PROPANE BARBECUE GRILL

ALSO KNOWN AS:
Gas grill

DESCRIPTION: 17" long × 11" or 14½"-diameter grill, stainless steel and aluminum, stands on 20" stanchion with deck- or rail-mount base or swing-arm mount for liferail. Lava-rock briquettes are heated by propane-powered flame. Safety-lock regulator adjusts temperatures. Uses 14.1-oz. or 16.4-oz. disposable propane tank. Usually has cover that serves as windshield.

USE: To barbecue food with natural-gas fuel. Cooking over lava rocks imparts charcoal flavor to food being cooked.

USE TIPS: Position grill over the side to avoid fires and messy drips on deck. Never place grill directly on deck.

BUYING TIPS: Accessories such as radiant screen (for dispersing heat), replacement grill and briquettes, burner assembly, and Venturi tube (for improved air circulation) are sold separately.

PROPANE AND CHARCOAL BARBECUE MOUNTS

DESCRIPTION: System of clamp-on or screw-down base into which support arm for barbecue grill is inserted. Clamp-on styles include *round-rail all-angle* for ⅞" to 1¼" rails and *square-rail mount,* which attaches to square or flat rail up to 2¼" horizontal or 1⅝" vertical. Screw-down models include *deck socket, fishing-rod holder* with pin-type rod holder, and four-footed stainless steel *floor stand.* These types may be used with either propane or charcoal grills.

Styles made specifically for propane grills include *square-rail mount* made of stainless steel and nylon and *rod-holder* mount, which inserts into installed rod holder and has flat bracket for grill, made of stainless steel and aluminum.

USE: There are as many ways to hold your barbecue grill as there are things to cook on it.

USE TIPS: Install near the stern where, with the bow heading into the wind at anchor or mooring, the smoke will blow off.

BUYING TIPS: Some propane grills are heavier than their charcoal-fired cousins and require the additional support given by propane-grill mounts.

BARBECUE GRILL

ALSO KNOWN AS: Charcoal grill

DESCRIPTION: 14½"-diameter grill with vented kettle cover, held on swivel arm attached to upright stanchion. Includes cooking grate that holds food over charcoal briquettes. Sealed ash compartment catches debris from charcoal.

USE: To grill food over charcoal briquettes.

USE TIPS: Swing grill over the side of the boat while in use to prevent fires and drips on deck. Never place lit grill directly on deck.

BUYING TIPS: Get a good-quality one with a secure mounting bracket, because nothing is more depressing than seeing your perfectly cooked dinner flip over into the water just as you finish cooking it.

WATERPROOF CHARCOAL BAG

DESCRIPTION: Black nylon bag opens square, has nylon webbing handles that extend down the sides and serve as reinforcement. May be labeled CHARCOAL.

USE: Holds up to 10 lbs. of charcoal briquettes, charcoal starter, and lighter fluid.

USE TIPS: Store away from the grill to prevent accidents with lighter fluid.

BUYING TIPS: For those who like to be organized—the rest can tote their charcoal in its own bag.

KETTLE BARBECUE COVER

DESCRIPTION: Fade-, mildew-, and moisture-resistant blue-domed acrylic cover.

USE: To cover 14" round barbecue grill.

USE TIPS: Be sure fire is out before replacing cover.

BUYING TIPS: A storage bag—a cover for the cover—is sold separately.

GALLEY ACCESSORIES

GALLEY SAFETY BELT

ALSO KNOWN AS:
Galley belt

DESCRIPTION:
Natural-color canvas belt with multicolor polypropylene adjustable straps, with brass snap hooks at ends.

USE: To snap yourself in while under way so both hands are free to cook dinner.

USE TIPS: Not necessary to use while boat is at anchor. Do not rely upon the galley safety belt as a safety harness for deck work.

BUYING TIPS: Do not joke about lashing the galley slave, or you'll find yourself cooking more often than usual.

STORAGE RACKS

ALSO KNOWN AS:
Racks, holders

DESCRIPTION: Plastic, wood (usually teak), and rubber-coated wire boxes, bins, shelves, racks, and holders of a wide variety of shapes, sizes, and designs, including the usual bathroom items for the head. Some collapse for easy storage when not in use; others are meant to be permanently mounted. Shelf-type racks, such as medicine cabinets, often have sea rails to prevent items from falling.

USE: To store, protect, and display utensils (dishes, glasses, flatware, tools), jars and bottles (wine, liquor, spices, condiments), and miscellaneous items (books, paper towels, dish towels, etc.). Some storage racks and holders are designed specifically to hold nesting items such as mugs and bowls, which are so common for picnic, camping, and boating uses.

USE TIPS: Look for gimballed drink holders for installation in the cockpit or at the helm station to prevent spills while under way.

BUYING TIPS: Teak items, while lending the most "finished" appearance to the boat interior, are sometimes chunky in design.

Sailing mug

ALSO KNOWN AS: Anchor mug, nonskid mug

DESCRIPTION: Ceramic, plastic, or insulated plastic 8- or 10-oz. mug with base that is about twice the diameter of the narrow mouth. Shoulders of mug slope diagonally outward to base. Some versions have a circle of nonskid textured rubber laminated to the bottom. Decoration often has a nautical theme, such as anchors, boats, seagulls, or fish.

USE: Broad base keeps mug's center of gravity low to prevent tip-overs; keeps contents from sloshing around when boat is under way; also supposed to keep in the heat. Nonskid pad on bottom prevents mug from sliding across a sloping deck or console.

USE TIPS: Perfect for that early-morning cup of coffee.

BUYING TIPS: Mugs are available in a wide variety of price ranges: ceramic and insulated ones cost a bit more.

Nautical wineglass

nonskid wineglass

ALSO KNOWN AS: Yachtsman's wineglass

DESCRIPTION: Unbreakable acrylic, Lexan™, and stainless steel, as well as breakable glass, tradi-

tionally shaped stemmed glasses, including 6-oz. champagne flute, 10-oz. red wine, and 14-oz. goblet. Often found in brilliant colors. Some models have stems that unscrew for easier storage. *Nonskid* glasses have rings of nonskid rubber on the base.

USE: To serve wine, champagne, and other beverages without worrying about shattered glass.

USE TIPS: Wine connoisseurs may find it close to sacrilege to serve a fine vintage in plastic or stainless steel, but it beats broken crystal down below.

BUYING TIPS: Sold singly, in pairs, or in sets of four or six.

Nonskid dish disks

DESCRIPTION: Rings made of gray, rubbery nonskid material ⅛" or ⅜" thick in diameters of 5", 3¾", 2½", and 1½". Peel-away backing reveals adhesive coating on one side. Adheres to ceramic, plastic, wood, and metal. Heat tolerant to 200° F; dishwasher-safe in cool temperatures.

USE: Apply disks to bottoms of plates, bowls, glasses, etc. to keep them from slipping while in use under way.

USE TIPS: Measure depth of indentation commonly found on the underside of plates and bowls and use disk of proper thickness.

BUYING TIPS: Made in a variety of sizes and sold in packs of sixteen.

Nonskid coasters, placemats, and rolls

DESCRIPTION: Gray woven polyester matting coated with vinyl in 12' long × 12" wide roll, 17" long × 13" wide ovals or 4"-diameter rounds. Will not fray when cut.

USE: To protect surfaces and keep the objects on them from sliding.

USE TIPS: Wash with soapy water.

BUYING TIPS: Oval placemats and round coasters are sold together in sets of four.

Peel-and-stick mini trash bags

DESCRIPTION: 7" wide × 10" high plastic bag has flap extension with adhesive strip covered by peel-away backing.

USE: Lets you put a trash receptacle wherever you need it. Could also be used to hold small snacks or for holding screws or small parts for a repair job on deck.

USE TIPS: Probably not essential, but a great discourager for tossing trash over the side. Large, bulky objects, such as aluminum drink cans, fill one of these up fast, so have several handy when there are large crews aboard.

BUYING TIPS: Sold often in inexpensive packages.

Dumping-law decals

ALSO KNOWN AS: Trash-discharge sticker, oil-discharge sticker

DESCRIPTION: Various stick-on labels outlining federal and regional trash- and oil-disposal prohibitions.

TYPES:

Save Our Seas sticker: Lists all at-sea garbage-disposal restrictions, as well as the universal ban on dumping of plastics. Must be displayed on all boats over 26' long.

Save the Great Lakes sticker: Lists all at-sea garbage-disposal regulations, as well as the universal ban on dumping plastics. Must be displayed on all boats over 26' long that operate in the Great Lakes.

USE: Boaters are required by law to post regulations that prohibit the dumping of trash, oil, and other polluting materials.

USE TIPS: Remember that it is mandatory not only to display the sticker but also to cooperate with the dumping prohibitions. Failure to do either can result in hefty fines.

BUYING TIPS: Inexpensive way to comply with the law.

─ DRINKING-WATER SYSTEMS ─

GALLEY HAND PUMP

ALSO KNOWN AS: Rocker pump

DESCRIPTION: Vertical brass or chrome-plated brass pipe with narrow gooseneck faucet spout (often with black plastic or rubber tip) and leverlike handle that moves up and down (double-stroke pump) or back and forth (rocker-action pump) from a single pivot point. Flange-and-locknut arrangement holds pump body securely upright through countertop cutout. Extends 6"–8" above counter, about 4" below. Portion below counter has barbs for insertion into water feed hose.

USE: To supply fresh water to galley or head sink by pumping handle up and down or back and forth.

USE TIPS: Forty-two to fifty-eight strokes of the pump handle produce 1 gal. of water.

BUYING TIPS: Self-priming and does not require electricity; however, pumping action will result in regular adjustments and repairs.

GALLEY FAUCET

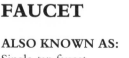

ALSO KNOWN AS: Single-tap faucet

DESCRIPTION: Stainless steel swing spout sits on white plastic base. Electric switch attaches to separate electric pump (see page 266) connected to water tank.

USE: Easy way to supply freshwater to the galley. Wires to boat's 12-volt DC system.

USE TIPS: Easier to use than a pump faucet; just remember that it's connected to a very limited supply source and not the municipal waterworks.

BUYING TIPS: Electric water pump sold separately.

WATER-PURIFICATION SYSTEM

ALSO KNOWN AS: Water purifiers

DESCRIPTION: Various types of filters installed at different points throughout freshwater tank and line system. Types include filter and hose hookup in feed line to water tank, chlorinator for tank, and countertop carbon-activated charcoal filter. Some incorporate more than one filtering point.

USE: Purifies water at various key points throughout freshwater line: Pretank filter reduces sediment and odors; in-tank chlorinator kills bacteria and germs in the water tank; and countertop carbon filter removes chlorine taste and odor, as well as kills bacteria.

USE TIPS: Follow manufacturer's recommendations for checking and replacing filters, which themselves can become a breeding ground for bacteria. To prolong the life of a filter, hook it up to where you will be purifying your drinking water, but not that which is used for showering. These systems are used to filter freshwater from your tank; they are not desalinators (see page 186), which create potable water from saltwater.

BUYING TIPS: Read manufacturer's description very carefully to be sure it will filter out the substance or bacteria you are most concerned about. Contaminated water is a major problem on boats, and you should be able to find a filter to fit your sink space and your needs.

WATER CONDITIONER

ALSO KNOWN AS: Water purifier, water-purification tablets

DESCRIPTION: Nontoxic powder or tablet designed for freshwater systems.

USE: To remove and eliminate algae, bacteria, fungus, molds, discoloration, tank scale, and odors (especially from fiberglass water tank). Tasteless, odorless, and harmless to stainless steel, rubber, or plastic.

USE TIPS: Small quantities treat large amounts of water. For example, 1 tsp. of powder treats 100 gal. of water.

BUYING TIPS: Water-conditioner kits include powder and tablets. Again, read manufacturer's claims carefully.

WATER-PRESSURE REDUCER AND FILTER

DESCRIPTION: Two-part device consisting of a foot-long rigid PVC tube containing a charcoal filter and baffles and a foot-long section of hose with hose fittings at either end. Fittings accommodate standard garden hose-style attachments.

USE: To eliminate odors and rubber taste from marina hose water, as well as sediment. Baffles prevent surges in pressure over 50 psi.

USE TIPS: Add water conditioner to filter element for best results. Attach filter tube section to marina water hose; connect flexible section of hose to onboard end of filter.

BUYING TIPS: Replacement filter sold separately.

DESALINATOR

ALSO KNOWN AS: Watermaker, reverse osmosis (RO) watermaker

DESCRIPTION: Hand and electrical pumps feed water into conversion tubular or boxlike device, and osmosis does the rest to remove contaminants and salt.

USE: To produce potable drinking water from salt, brackish, and contaminated water sources.

USE TIPS: For emergency as opposed to everyday use. These are not fast-acting. Manual models produce from 1 qt. to over 1 gal. per hour, while electric ones produce as much as 3 gal. per hour. Some electric models convert to manual in case of power outages.

BUYING TIPS: Essential safety equipment. Invaluable when traveling far from a ready source of supplies.

CABIN ACCESSORIES

BAROMETER

ALSO KNOWN AS:
Aneroid barometer, "the glass" (archaic, refers to mercury barometer)

DESCRIPTION: Main components are a capsule from which air is removed, a hair spring, and a rocker arm attached to a single pointer-hand on the surface of an analog dial measured out in millibars (one of which equals 0.03" of mercury; conversely 1" of mercury equals 33.86 millibars). Changing atmospheric pressure affects the airless capsule, which in turn activates the spring and point. Standard atmospheric pressure being 29.92", barometer dials usually range from 28.5" to 31.5".

USE: To tell you the atmospheric pressure at any given time.

USE TIPS: By periodically monitoring and tracking pressure, along with wind direction and cloud formations, you can do a fairly good job of predicting the weather. Generally when atmospheric pressure drops, you can expect weather to change for the worse.

BUYING TIPS: While a barometer adds a nice touch to the cabin interior, you are more likely to receive accurate weather information via radio. Price generally reflects the quality of what you are buying. Fancy mounting boards and decorative touches, such as steering-wheel spokes around the bezel of the barometer, add only to the cost.

WEATHER-STATION TIDEWATCH

ALSO KNOWN AS: Navigation device

DESCRIPTION: Wooden plaque, usually a tropical exotic wood such as bubinga, on which a ba-

rometer, quartz-movement battery-operated clock and thermometer/hygrometer are mounted, and sometimes a tide clock as well. Analog instruments have matching lacquered brass bezels in traditional designs or streamline white numbers on matte-black plastic faces. Instrument dials sometimes have nautical decorations, such as signal flags, instead of numbers. Thermometers may read in both centigrade and Fahrenheit to 120°. Tide clocks have a single hand that points to high or low tide, as well as indicating whether in-between tides are rising or falling.

USE: One source of information about the time, temperature, humidity, atmospheric pressure, and stages of the tide.

USE TIPS: A handsome gift that may not be super accurate.

BUYING TIPS: N battery for clock is sold separately.

CLOCK

DESCRIPTION: Analog dial divided equally into twelve sections for hours (sometimes with subdivisions for minutes, sometimes also marked for military "24-hour day"), with two or three hands to mark hours, minutes, and seconds. Available in windup or electronic versions. Gears, escapement, and clock housing are made of corrosion-resistant materials (brass and quartz movements) to withstand rigors of marine environment. Some marine clocks include chimes to coincide with the "bell" system of measuring nautical hours and "watches." Often have "nautical look" with polished brass casings.

Most ship's clocks are made to be hung from a bulkhead, but some battery-operated desk models are encased in protective wooden boxes 6" long × 6" wide × 4" high, often made of mahogany, with hinged lids. The 4½"-diameter clock rests in a snug recess inside.

USE: To measure time. Highly exact timepieces, called *chronometers,* are so exact that you can determine latitude by determining "local noon" with a sextant and comparing it with noon ("Greenwich time") at the Greenwich meridian, which is 0° longitude.

USE TIPS: Most boaters tell time by their wristwatch. Ship's clocks are as much decorative as functional, so get yourself a nice one and display it proudly.

BUYING TIPS: Instruments requiring a high degree of accuracy should be rated for marine use to be at all effective on your boat. In these days of affordable electronic navigation equipment, however, few mariners go to the trouble of finding their position by using a chronometer.

SMOKE BELL

DESCRIPTION: Wide, flat dome of polished brass, sometimes tin, suspended from its center by a horizontal arm attached to wall or bulkhead. Position of dome on arm is sometimes adjustable, via a thumbscrew.

USE: To hang over a candle or oil lamp to prevent burn marks and smoke stains on cabin ceiling (see page 53).

USE TIPS: Although a smoke bell imparts a certain nautical look, its function is primarily to prevent fires.

BUYING TIPS: Necessary item if you make use of a lantern that has a burning wick or candle.

NAUTICAL BEANBAG ASHTRAY

"deep dish" wind cover

ALSO KNOWN AS:
Nonskid ashtray, weighted ashtray

DESCRIPTION: Weighted cloth sack slightly larger than a teacup and decorated with nautical designs that holds "deep dish" *wind cover* stainless steel ashtray or shallow zigzag *cigarette rest* ashtray. Corrosion-resistant and nonmagnetic.

USE: To hold, snuff out, and store butts of cigarettes or cigars without having ashtray tip over when boat is pitching.

USE TIPS: Presumably, nonmagnetic ashtray will not cause interference with electronic gear if the skipper smokes while he or she is at the helm.

BUYING TIPS: Unnecessary if you do not smoke or do not allow smoking aboard your boat.

CABIN HOOKS

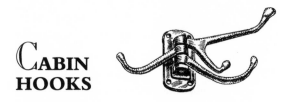

ALSO KNOWN AS: Coat hook, utility hook, hook

DESCRIPTION: Simple two-prong *utility hook* made of teak, roughly 7" high × 4" deep, or chrome-plated zinc, projects 1½" from predrilled mounting base. More stylish *folding coathook* is of solid brass and holds up to 4 curved, double-prong arms that swing sideways. Includes four brass mounting screws for predrilled bracket.

USE: Installed inside lockers, in head or inside cabin doors, hook provides a convenient place to hang coats, slickers, and other gear.

USE TIPS: Folding coathook is especially attractive and safer in the tossing confines of a cabin.

BUYING TIPS: Teak hook is more expensive than stainless steel or chrome-plated versions.

CURTAIN INSTALLATION SYSTEM

DESCRIPTION: Heavy-duty brown or white flexible plastic track. Slides with snap bases fit over track. Nylon snap tape has snap "caps" every 4". End caps secure on end of track.

USE: To provide a flexible curtain rod.

USE TIPS: Suitable for straight or curved window walls.

BUYING TIPS: Track comes in 3' lengths; tape is sold in 42½" lengths. Snap carriers come in ten-packs, while end caps are sold in pairs.

NYLON GEAR HAMMOCK

DESCRIPTION: 5'-long white nylon fishnet hammock with end loops.

USE: To store large, bulky items such as cushions, life jackets, sneakers, or anything else that does not damage easily.

USE TIPS: Not strong enough to use as a sleeping hammock, although children might like to try. Handy, traditional storage solution, but the resulting jumble might detract from the neatness of your cabin.

BUYING TIPS: Very inexpensive. Stainless steel hooks are sold separately.

SLEEP SYSTEM

DESCRIPTION: *Roll-out*-style rectangular navy-blue "polar fleece" sack with removable liner and sewn-in pillow cases. Nylon zippers run full length of both long sides of rectangle. Comes with polyester and cotton percale sheets and pillows with synthetic stuffing. Single and double/queen sizes available, as well as trapezoidal model sized for a V-berth, 80" long × 76" wide × 30" wide at tip. Set includes storage bag.

Another version is more like a *portable bed* than the sleeping bag–like roll-out. One side of the gray "sack" is a lightweight cover with synthetic stuffing for summer use, the reverse side is a heavier fill of synthetic stuffing for cold-weather sleeping. Polyester and cotton percale sheet/liner is kept in place by hook-and-loop fasteners. Replacement sheets and pillow shams are sold separately. Nylon zippers are on each of the long sides. Includes two pillowcases but no pillows. Available in twin, double/queen, and V-berth sizes. Rolls up for storage in plastic bag when not in use.

USE: An all-in-one sleeping bag designed for a boat bunk. Rolls up for easy storage when not in use.

USE TIPS: Completely machine washable; frequent airing and washing is a good idea.

BUYING TIPS: No need to buy a "system" if you already have a favorite sleeping bag.

SHEET SUSPENDERS

DESCRIPTION: Adjustable elastic straps with nylon clips at each end.

USE: To stretch straps diagonally from corner to corner of bedsheets underneath boat cushions to keep sheets in place.

USE TIPS: Useful at home as well.

BUYING TIPS: For those who like their sheets tucked in.

Stretch-Terry-Cloth Cushion Covers

ALSO KNOWN AS: Cushion covers

DESCRIPTION: Fitted beige or blue terry-cloth sheets with stretchable polyester backing to ensure snug fit. Designed for twin, double, V-berth, and quarter berth (70"–80" long × 24"–30" wide) cushions.

USE: To cover and protect boat cushions.

USE TIPS: Also makes them a shade more comfortable.

BUYING TIPS: Another cover for a cover.

Adjustable Bottom Sheets

DESCRIPTION: Polyester and cotton percale fitted sheet has adjustable bottom with cord running through hem and toggle at one corner. Pull cord tight through toggle to adjust fit on cushion. Single, double, and V-berth sizes available.

Another version is the *sleep sheet,* which is simply a sleeping bag made out of two flat light-blue polyester and cotton percale sheets, which can be used alone in summer weather or inside a sleeping bag when it gets colder. Available only in twin/single size.

USE: Bed linen.

USE TIPS: Custom sizes and colors of the *sleep sheet* can be made simply by sewing together two flat sheets along three sides. Adjustable bottom sheets can also be made at home, using favorite-color sheets or special sizes.

BUYING TIPS: For singlehanders.

Hammock

DESCRIPTION: White nylon fishnet with handles at either end. Double size has breaking strength of 2,000 lbs. and holds two adults or several children. Single size has breaking strength of 1,000 lbs. Overall length 20'.

USE: Good for lounging or relaxing, but it is unlikely two adults could get a good night's sleep in a hammock. Children are another story.

USE TIPS: Inexpensive and fun hung up on deck.

BUYING TIPS: Make sure you have at least 20' of space for stringing it up.

Laundry Bag

DESCRIPTION: Nylon-mesh bag comes in two sizes: 27" long × 22" wide with drawstring closure; or 36" long × 22" wide with built-in white plastic hangers.

USE: To carry laundry and store wet clothes and shoes.

USE TIPS: Good for hanging things up in a wet locker.

BUYING TIPS: A canvas bag won't drip and is less likely to tear.

Teak Cabin Fittings

ALSO KNOWN AS: Teak fittings, teak trim

DESCRIPTION: Any of various-shaped teak pieces that can be used to cover raw or sharp edges and corners (such as C-shaped *bulkhead molding*, curved *bulkhead corner*, straight and curved *edge molding*, and straight *L-molding*) or for filling inside corners, as with *quarter-round molding*. Teak is also shaped into two- to four-loop *handrails* as well as salty-looking straight and curved *pin rails* installed on shelves to prevent items from slipping off. Molding is generally sold in 5'–6' lengths, while handrails run from 1'–3½' long.

Louvered doors, louvered inserts, door/frame combinations, and *access panels/drawer fronts with frames* are available for cabin compartments and lockers.

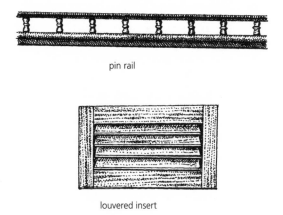

pin rail

louvered insert

Notched sections of teak *grating* are sold in 4' lengths for making custom floor grates and other items, such as hot plates.

Teak *wall plate covers* for switches, outlets, and ground fault mechanisms, as well as blank covers, complete the look.

USE: Teak lends a decorative finish to your cabin while being highly functional in a marine setting, since it is rot resistant and requires little upkeep, aside from occasional oiling (see page 289 for teak-care products). Handrails can be used inside or out.

USE TIPS: Use waterproof *resorcinal glue* for interior or exterior installations.

BUYING TIPS: Teak is expensive but beautiful wood. Teak harvesting is an environmentally touchy subject because of destructive harvesting techniques. If at all possible, try to buy teak products that come from recycled wood or that are certified as farm-grown.

Stainless Steel Handrail

ALSO KNOWN AS: Handrail

DESCRIPTION: Smooth tubes of stainless steel 1'–2' long with predrilled end bases. Stands nearly 2¾" off mounting surface.

USE: To provide a handhold anywhere, on surfaces of any thickness.

USE TIPS: May be mounted on deck (on the cabin top, for example) or down below. A little experience with your boat will let you know where rails are needed.

BUYING TIPS: Although aluminum rails are available, stainless steel is stronger.

Marine Decking

ALSO KNOWN AS: Nonskid flooring, nonskid decking

DESCRIPTION: *Interlocking* 1 ft.-sq. tiles of molded PVC or flexible PVC *rolled flooring* approximately ½" thick with an open grid pattern. Both

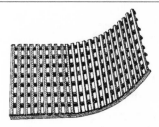

are resistant to oil, UV rays, saltwater, flame, and chemicals, as well as mildew and rot. Easy to cut, shape, and assemble. Common colors are white, royal blue, teal, and black, but custom colors are also available.

USE: To provide positive traction and a dry floor surface that is not slippery.

USE TIPS: Interlocking tiles can be put together easily in various patterns and colors and come with tapered edges and corners. Useful in mud rooms at home or in truck beds.

BUYING TIPS: Tiles are sold in packs of four, while edge pieces and corners are sold individually. *Rolled flooring* is 3' wide and comes in sections 4', 6', and 8' long.

PORT ACCESSORIES

Opening Port

ALSO KNOWN AS: Portlight

DESCRIPTION: Thick (¼") glass or high-impact glasslike plastic panel, with trim, hinged to flanged frame with O-ring seal or other gasket material. Cam or toggle closures keep panel shut. Drains in port frame keep water from accumulating. Ports measure from 10" long × 3" wide to as large as 14" long × 7" wide. Frames are made of plastic, stainless steel, bronze, or aluminum and are usually round, elliptical, or rectangular in shape, although other configurations can be had. Suitable for cabin sides up to 1¾" thick. A *deadlight* or *scuttle* is a nonopening port.

USE: To bring light and fresh air into the cabin. O-ring or gasket on window frame where glass panel seats seals out rain and spray when window is closed.

USE TIPS: Hinges on some ports are notched to automatically hold glass panel open. O-ring and gasket eventually crack or dry out due to exposure to sunlight, heat, cold, and salt spray and must be replaced regularly. Replacement may be available from port manufacturer.

Be sure outer part of frame does not extend far in high-traffic areas such as side decks, where crew members may skin their legs or sheets may get tangled.

BUYING TIPS: Price is a good reflection of quality. Think carefully of appearance when installing a port in a new spot on your boat. Proportion is everything. If the port is too big or too small, it just will not look right.

Sail Wind Scoop

DESCRIPTION: Canvas, ripstop nylon, or sailcloth funnel positioned with its large open "mouth" facing into the wind over a hatch or deck opening up to 4' wide. 4'7" wide × 5'9" high.

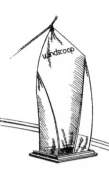

USE: To scoop air below to cabin using existing wind action.

USE TIPS: Cannot be used while under way.

BUYING TIPS: Inexpensive, effective ventilation.

Mosquito netting

DESCRIPTION: Fine-mesh, tough nylon netting 42" wide, steel gray in color.

USE: To screen hatches, ports, and other openings into the cabin to keep mosquitoes and other insects out.

USE TIPS: No guarantee this will work against no-see-ums.

BUYING TIPS: Sold by the foot or in a package of 2 yds.

Insect screen

DESCRIPTION: A variety of inserts and covers made of nylon or brass screening with vinyl, metal, or teak frames, made to fit deck vents, hatches, portlights, and companionways. A new hatch screen version is a complete hood of screening (similar to a plastic typewriter cover) with a length of chain to weight the hem down.

USE: To keep out flies, mosquitoes, and other annoying bugs, but may be ineffective against the ubiquitous no-see-ums that make boaters in southern waters miserable.

USE TIPS: Proper fit is essential. What may look like "just a small gap" to us humans is an open door to a hungry mosquito.

BUYING TIPS: Screens are essential when anchoring out overnight. The hatch-bonnet version is fairly simple to make—and inexpensive.

Cam-style replacement latch

DESCRIPTION: Lever resembling a policeman's whistle, with female threads at wide end.

USE: One-step closure mechanism for closing or opening port. Fits onto closure stud on some makes of opening ports.

USE TIPS: Only fits certain makes of port.

BUYING TIPS: Sold in pairs.

UV-resistant port hood

ALSO KNOWN AS: Spray shield

DESCRIPTION: Eyelidlike hood, 12"–17" wide, made of pliable white thermoplastic rubber; mounting flange is not predrilled.

USE: To mount on top of outside rim of opening port to keep out spray or rain.

USE TIPS: Can be trimmed to match the shape of port rim. Drill holes to match existing holes in rim.

BUYING TIPS: Sold in pairs.

CABIN HARDWARE

Hatch

DESCRIPTION: Hinged- or shoebox-type lid of fiberglass, wood, polypropylene, or clear, tinted, or smoked acrylic plastic, with frame of anodized aluminum, stainless steel, wood, or plastic. Built-in adjuster(s) on hinged models lock hatch closed or prop it open. Some hatches also have built-in dogs that screw down to lock hatch. Come in a variety of sizes from small (11" long × 7" wide to larger (24" sq.).

USE: To cover recessed locker or exit onto deck from cabin. Also forward-opening hinged hatch is a good wind scoop while boat is at anchor or under way.

USE TIPS: Choose a flanged hatch that has spigots for draining off accumulated water. Tinted acrylic gives privacy, but be careful what you clean it with, since many plastics can become abraded or cloudy due to cleaning.

BUYING TIPS: Ready- or custom-made screens (see "Insect Screen," page 193) are essential.

Hatch Adjuster

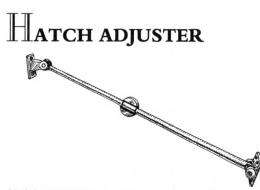

ALSO KNOWN AS: Pivoting hatch adjuster

DESCRIPTION: Telescoping stainless-steel rod adjusts from 12" to 22" long with thumbscrew midway along length. Mounts at both ends pivot 360°. Another style is heavy spring that folds on itself

when the hatch is closed and snaps straight when the hatch is opened. Mounting base attached to hatch coaming has slide mechanism so that you can preset the angle to which the hatch opens.

USE: To hold hatch (or windshield) open at any angle; those with pivoting mounts keep it moving smoothly.

USE TIPS: Springlike adjusters are sensitive and fold easily with only slight impact, causing the hatch to crash down. Be cautious when using these, especially with children onboard. Adjuster is not a secure locking mechanism. Use a hatch fastener (see below) for this purpose.

BUYING TIPS: Handy means of propping open your hatch from down below.

Hatch Fastener

ALSO KNOWN AS: Hatch latch

DESCRIPTION: Chrome-plated bronze or brass bar with threads and black plastic thumbscrew at one end, pivots at other end from predrilled base to which it is permanently attached. A second predrilled base has a corresponding slot with raised sides. Entire assembly is about 4" long × 2" wide. A similar device for windshields, called a *windshield keeper,* is sized somewhat smaller and, instead of the thumbscrew arrangement, has a straight handle.

USE: Attach base with pivot to cabin roof or side; attach corresponding base to hatch cover or a windshield. When pivoting bar is swung into place in base with slot and thumbscrew is tightened, this provides a positive closure for hatch cover (to "clog down" the hatch).

USE TIPS: Positioning is everything with hardware like this. Measure twice before drilling holes.

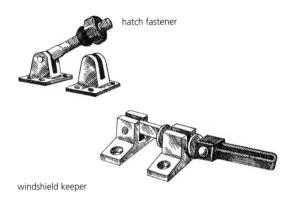

hatch fastener

windshield keeper

BUYING TIPS: A "must." Requires four #8 screws for fastening, not included. Available in models from utilitarian to fancy—just don't get a cheap one that won't survive a pounding.

Hatch Hinge

DESCRIPTION: One hinge bed (see "Hinges," below) has a raised plate that extends perpendicular to the barrel. Pin is usually removable, held in place with cotter pins. Chrome-plated brass or stainless steel.

USE: To keep hatch upright when open.

USE TIPS: Not as secure as a hatch holder. Hatch can be removed by pulling out two cotter pins.

BUYING TIPS: Stainless steel hinges cost slightly more than chrome-plated ones but are stronger and won't wear out.

Hinges

DESCRIPTION: Two flat, usually rectangular, predrilled plates (called "beds"), attached to each other by a central pin that extends through eyes, holes, or tubes (called the barrel) positioned along one edge of each bed. Materials commonly used for marine hinges are stainless steel, brass, and chrome-plated brass.

TYPES:

door hinge

Butt hinge: Cannot be taken apart, since the pin is captive between the beds and is held in place with two flat "heads" at either end. May be used for right- or left-hand opening doors.

Door or *take-apart hinge:* Has a pin that slides out, making it possible to remove the door from the frame. Because pin must be positioned so that it pulls up from the top—rather than falling out through the bottom—take-apart hinges are sold in right- and left-hand models.

Offset hinge: Has one bed larger than the other, and when the hinge is opened all the way, the beds are not flush with each other. This makes it possible to open the hinge wide without interference. Some offset hinges—also known as *flush door hinges* or hinges for inset doors—are arranged so that only the barrel shows when the door is closed.

Strap hinge: Long and narrow, with the beds extending out from the barrel, rather than lengthwise along it. Strap hinges are often installed at supports or frames on the door.

Piano hinge (also known as *continuous hinge*): Has beds totaling about 1½" wide with a continuous barrel its full length, which is usually 6'. Use where accurate fit and secure door or hatch support is needed.

USE: To hang a door so that it opens and closes.

USE TIPS: Hanging a door and installing hinges is a challenging project that requires more patience and careful measuring than technical expertise.

BUYING TIPS: Hinges come in a wide variety of prices, as well as styles.

Hatch Hood

DESCRIPTION: Square-shaped, forward-leaning nylon hood with brass grommets and internal framework.

USE: Sits upright over open hatch to keep rain out.

USE TIPS: Do not use while under way.

BUYING TIPS: Many sizes available.

Flush Handle

ALSO KNOWN AS: Flush lifting handle, lift handle, flush ring pull

DESCRIPTION: Round or rounded rectangular hinged handle falls flat into recessed base when not in use. Base usually has a fingertip-sized depression to make retrieval of the handle/pull easier. Predrilled countersunk holes on mounting base. The *spring-loaded flush pull* version features a handle that springs up for use when it is touched at the opposite end. Flush handles are available in stainless steel, chrome-plated zinc, or other corrosion-resistant material.

flush handle

spring-loaded flush pull

USE: For applications such as icebox, cupboard, hatch, or locker door where a projecting handle might snag clothing, gear, cause scrapes and cuts, or cause people to trip.

USE TIPS: Use #8 flathead screws to keep a low profile.

BUYING TIPS: Manual-lift handles are usually larger and squarer than spring-loaded type (2¼" × 2¾" compared to ¾" × 3¾") and less likely to break.

Sliding Window Handle

DESCRIPTION: S-curve of stainless steel 3" long has shallow curve for finger grip and narrow slot on other end.

USE: Slide narrow slot over glass or Lexan window panels that slide easily in tracks; push or pull window open or shut.

USE TIPS: For windows up to ¼" thick. Use care when compressing window slot for a snug grip.

BUYING TIPS: Worth a try if you have difficulty sliding your windows. But try one first to see if it interferes with window operation.

Sliding Window Stop

ALSO KNOWN AS: Security stop, antirattler, sliding window lock

DESCRIPTION: Predrilled mounting plate with hinged, plastic-coated tongue. Whole assembly, when extended, measures about 2½"; tongue is 1" wide.

USE: With sliding window closed, mount base outside window track below and just beyond the end of the inner window panel. When tongue is flipped up and over, it prevents the inner panel from sliding open.

USE TIPS: A deterrent to thieves.

BUYING TIPS: Sold singly.

ERTICAL WINDOW ANTIRATTLER

DESCRIPTION: Chrome-plated brass mounting base with two predrilled countersunk holes and an eye extension through which a plated brass or black plastic threaded stud passes. One end of stud has knurled thumbscrew knob or flat twist knob; other end is covered by a black rubber cap.

USE: Mount antirattler adjacent to window frame, then tighten thumbscrew so that black rubber cap presses against the window and prevents it from vibrating or rattling.

USE TIPS: Measure and position antirattler carefully before drilling any holes.

BUYING TIPS: Antirattler may be all you need, but too loose a window fit may mean you require a new frame; check with your dealer or manufacturer, who may have retrofits.

DOOR BUTTON

DESCRIPTION: Circular base 1¾" diam. in two separate predrilled pieces, one larger than the other. From center of larger base section a small black plastic crossbar pivots but is controlled by a spring mechanism so that it stays in position until moved.

USE: Mount large base section with bar on side of door opposite to the direction it opens. Smaller base

section is mounted on adjacent doorjamb so that pieces match perfectly when door is shut. Black plastic bar acts as a lock when it is positioned across the base on the doorjamb.

USE TIPS: This is not a secure locking mechanism. It is suitable for a privacy lock, if nothing else.

BUYING TIPS: Sold in spring-action and non-spring versions. Both require #6 fasteners, sold separately.

LUSH RING CATCH

DESCRIPTION: Two-part catch made of chrome-plated zinc. Ring pull lies flat in recess in mounting base; when it is lifted, bronze spring pulls latch back into mounting base. Corresponding latch plate installed on doorjamb has hole for latch when it is extended. Both parts installed with #6 fasteners.

USE: Low-profile hardware for keeping doors (cabin, head, locker, cabinet, etc.) shut.

USE TIPS: Not a security lock.

BUYING TIPS: Chrome plating adds to nautical look below.

FLUSH LATCH

DESCRIPTION: Chrome-plated zinc door-fastening mechanism, with or without black plastic escutcheon, in 2½" sq. or 2¼" long × 2" wide rectangular format. Half-circle or rectangular tab handle lies flat in recess when not in use. Lifting tab or lifting ring and twisting 90° withdraws latch into latch housing. Fit in doors up to 1⅛" thick; latch bars may adjust up from ⅜" to 3".

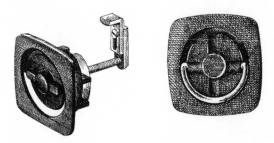

USE: To install on locker, cupboard, or cabin doors as a closing device.

USE TIPS: Although some models come with locks and keys, do not rely on these for external doors where security is a consideration.

BUYING TIPS: Just a latch, not a substitute for a lock.

Doorknob

ALSO KNOWN AS: Knob, drawer pull

DESCRIPTION: Brass, chrome-plated brass, wood, plastic, ceramic knob in many sizes, although 1" diameter is common, with threaded inner sleeve and separate stainless steel machine screw with round or oval head. May also come with permanent screw tip extending from knob.

USE: To open or close drawer or door to which it is through-bolted or screwed.

USE TIPS: Knobs can be strictly utilitarian or can add a touch of decoration.

BUYING TIPS: Generally inexpensive, but available in a wide variety of styles, colors, and sizes.

Doorstop

DESCRIPTION: Predrilled chrome-plated zinc escutcheon with protruding bumper made of black plastic, rubber, or other resilient material. Common size is 1¼" diameter, with bumper projecting about 1".

USE: Installed on a wall or other fixed surface against which door closes, a doorstop will prevent the door from banging against the wall, which could cause damage to the wall, the doorknob, or both.

USE TIPS: Measure carefully before installing and make sure bumper protrudes far enough to keep the doorknob from hitting.

BUYING TIPS: Fasteners are sold separately.

Sliding Bolt

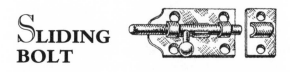

ALSO KNOWN AS: Barrel bolt, cupboard bolt, sliding latch

DESCRIPTION: Stainless steel, bronze, brass, plain steel, chrome-plated zinc, or brass bar, usually at least ¼" diameter with knoblike handle on the side. Bar is held captive on a predrilled mounting base with two or more raised straps through which it can slide freely, although the knob keeps it from sliding out completely. An accompanying mounting base is smaller, with a single raised strap. The whole system may be over 5" long. A lighter-weight version has a smaller base about 2" sq. and plastic bolt.

USE: To attach larger mounting plate and bolt to door, hatch cover, etc., and position smaller base to doorjamb or other solid frame.

USE TIPS: A sliding bolt is a secure lock—once you are on the inside of the door. Sliding bolts can also be used to secure lockers. The lighter-weight version is suitable for galley cupboards, where the idea is simply to keep the doors shut rather than intruders out.

BUYING TIPS: Sliding bolts provide one of the best means of securing something that may pop open.

Elbow Latch

ALSO KNOWN AS: Elbow catch

DESCRIPTION: L-shaped handle pivots with a tension spring on a predrilled base. One end of handle has a blunt hook. Separate predrilled base has a raised lip over which the hook snaps and locks when it is cocked back. Black plastic or chrome-plated brass.

USE: Mount each part of the elbow latch at corresponding points on sliding doors. Position hook over raised lip, then cock handle back. Tension spring keeps handle locked in place.

USE TIPS: Quick and easy means of latching and unlatching interior doors.

BUYING TIPS: Go with the metal for longer life.

Hook

ALSO KNOWN AS: Cabin door hook

DESCRIPTION: Metal hook with eye at one end permanently linked to predrilled eye base, accompanied by a second predrilled base, also with an eye.

USE: To hold doors shut; may also be used to keep open cabin doors from banging.

USE TIPS: Any latch that can pop open should have an extra fastener such as the door hook.

BUYING TIPS: Buy good-quality hardware that will stand up to onboard rigors.

Cupboard Catch

ALSO KNOWN AS: Icebox catch, antirattle door fastener

DESCRIPTION: Sleek chrome-plated device with contoured spring handle that, when lifted, slides a latch back into the handle housing. A second corresponding part consists of a predrilled base with a square, raised eye. Entire assembly is about 2" long × 1½" wide.

USE: To provide a secure way to close a cupboard door, borrowed from the obsolete household icebox.

USE TIPS: Some boats without marine generators may still have iceboxes, in which case you may see a cupboard catch keeping the icebox door shut tight.

BUYING TIPS: Good investment to keep cupboard doors securely closed; installation requires six #6 screws, sold separately.

Door Catch

DESCRIPTION: Two-part plastic knob and socket. Socket may have a vertical mount configuration, while knob may have horizontal mount. Some door catches rely upon simple magnetic attraction to keep both sections together.

USE: Install knob on cupboard or locker door, with socket in corresponding spot on cupboard or door frame. With knob snapped into socket door stays tightly shut. A slight pull releases the knob.

USE TIPS: Look for door catches with elongated screw holes for easier adjustments.

BUYING TIPS: Very inexpensive, sometimes sold in pairs.

HOLD-DOWN CLAMP

DESCRIPTION: Two-part device consisting of pivoting handle and ring on predrilled chrome-plated bronze or brass base, with a second predrilled base consisting simply of a raised hook.

USE: With handle lifted, ring extends outward from base and loops over hook on second base. By pressing the handle down, the ring is pulled back tightly.

USE TIPS: Careful positioning will ensure that this latch holds windows or hatches tight shut.

BUYING TIPS: Good investment if your hatches or ports rattle.

SAFETY HASP

ALSO KNOWN AS: Hinge hasp

DESCRIPTION: Two-part hingelike device. Larger half has predrilled plate attached by pin-and-barrel to somewhat longer, flat tongue with crosswise or lengthwise slot. For security reasons tongue folds over screwed-in bases, so fasteners cannot be removed by burglars. Second part of device consists of predrilled base with raised eye that can accommodate a padlock eye.

USE: Secure hatches, doors, or lockers with a safety hasp simply by threading a padlock through the eye once the slotted tongue is in place.

USE TIPS: Use a Grass padlock suitable for marine use.

BUYING TIPS: A must for doors and hatches you want to secure with a lock; you can enhance resistance by substituting bolts for standard #6 screw fasteners.

RAILS AND RAIL ACCESSORIES

ABOUT LIFELINES

Running from bow to stern, lifelines provide a secure attachment point for safety harnesses worn by sailors working on deck during rough weather. The typical lifeline system consists of vinyl-covered stainless steel cable strung along the sides of the boat between upright stainless steel or chrome-plated zamac posts called stanchions. Some boats have all-metal bow-and-stern pulpits with cable in between. Larger powerboats are most likely to have solid metal rails composed of stanchions, lengths of tube for rails, and various configurations of Ts, elbows, and sleeves connected with set screws. For a truly safe system, stanchions must be through-bolted with backing plates under the deck. Cables should be inspected carefully each year for signs of wear and stanchions tightened if necessary.

Sailors with small children onboard may want to install safety nets along lifelines. For an added measure of onboard safety all children should wear life jackets.

LIFELINE WIRE

ALSO KNOWN AS: Lifeline cable, cable stock

DESCRIPTION: White PVC-coated stainless 7 × 7 steel wire rope, which means the cable consists of seven bundles of seven twisted strands of wire.

USE: To string lifelines.

USE TIPS: ³⁄₁₆" OD cable has working load of 850 lbs.; ¼" OD cable, 1,850 lbs. Strength of the entire lifeline system depends on integrity and strength of cable, stanchions, and fittings.

BUYING TIPS: Can be obtained in custom-cut lengths (minimum 10'). When measuring, allow extra length for swage fittings.

TOGGLE JAW

DESCRIPTION: A swivel shackle fitting attached to the end of a lifeline, usually with a swage fitting.

USE: To connect the end of a lifeline to a stanchion for easy removal. The swiveling feature of this fitting makes it useful for lifeline gate or openings.

USE TIPS: Hand-swaged (see page 123) lifeline fittings are not strong enough to be used for standing rigging, which must handle much heavier workloads.

BUYING TIPS: To install swage fittings, you will need to buy or borrow a swaging tool, a crimping device specially made for the job. Cable cutters will also be necessary.

PELICAN HOOK

DESCRIPTION: Named after the bird whose "bill will hold more than his belican," the stainless steel pelican hook opens wide and locks tightly shut, usually with a ring that slips over the open end. The hook is attached by a swage fitting to a lifeline.

USE: To provide an easy-to-open but otherwise secure gate so that you don't have to straddle the lifeline when coming onboard.

USE TIPS: The pelican hook mates with a *single gate eye,* swaged onto the opposite side of the gate opening.

BUYING TIPS: Buy the forged rather than the stamped variety for better looks and strength.

INTERLOCK EYE

ALSO KNOWN AS: Interlocking gate eye, interlocking eye

DESCRIPTION: Two eye fittings permanently interlocked, are swaged on either end to the lifeline. Eyes are either fixed or swiveling.

USE: To provide a hinge where the gate opens.

USE TIPS: Eye on the standing part of the line also prevents whole line from going slack when the gate is opened.

BUYING TIPS: Swiveling eyes help avoid line twists.

ADJUSTER

ALSO KNOWN AS: Lifeline adjuster

DESCRIPTION: Similar in function to a turn-buckle, a lifeline adjuster has either a threaded rod for adjusting, which can be secured by clevis pin and a split ring, or a standard tubular barrel fitting. Another hand-swaged fitting. Adjustable either 1" or 1½".

USE: To ease or take up slack on a lifeline.

USE TIPS: Do not use this considerably cheaper item as a turnbuckle for standing rigging. It's not made to take heavy workloads.

BUYING TIPS: Barrel type is stronger and more in keeping with the looks of other lifeline parts.

CABLE COVER

DESCRIPTION: Split white plastic tube fits around ³⁄₃₂"–³⁄₈" cable.

USE: To snap over lifelines for temporary, inexpensive repairs to cracked cable cover.

USE TIPS: Can also be used to cover existing wire cable for those who do not want to replace it with cable stock.

BUYING TIPS: Sold in 6' lengths. Don't expect the longevity of ready-made covered cable.

LIFELINE COVER

ALSO KNOWN AS: Lifeline padding

DESCRIPTION: Padded foam tubes fit over lifeline cable.

USE: To make a fairly comfortable backrest out of lifelines. Particularly useful in the cockpit area.

USE TIPS: As with any covering of metal parts, check underneath periodically to make sure moisture hasn't seeped in.

BUYING TIPS: Sold in sets of four 3' sections.

T-FITTING

ALSO KNOWN AS:
Rail mount

DESCRIPTION: Stainless steel or zamac fitting that accommodates upright stanchion as well as two attachment points for horizontal rails. Cross may join upright at 60° or 90° angle.

USE: To connect vertical stanchion to horizontal rail.

USE TIPS: Try to match materials, either stainless or zamac, so that you have equal tolerances the length of your rails.

BUYING TIPS: Sold with the necessary #10 fitting you will need for installation and tightening.

BOW FORM

DESCRIPTION: Chrome-plated or stainless-steel 110° elbow that accepts either ⅞" or 1" OD tubing. Available in 110° and 125° versions.

USE: To lead from raised bow pulpit to handrail or lifeline.

USE TIPS: If your main concern is a lifeline, one can be attached directly to a bow pulpit without extending the rail.

BUYING TIPS: Sold with necessary stainless-steel set screws.

Handrail Fitting

ALSO KNOWN AS: Grab-rail fitting

DESCRIPTION: Predrilled base with upright 3"–4" topped by one of three types of caps: hollow, or forward or aft end sockets that fit ⅞" OD tube. Available in stainless steel or chrome-plated zamac. Set screws hold tube in place.

USE: Use *forward* and *aft* stanchions with a length of tube to create a handrail for side decks or cabin sides in the cockpit area.

USE TIPS: Like other heavy-load deck hardware, handrail fittings should be through-bolted with backing plates. Do not forget to use bedding compound at the bolt holes to prevent leaks.

BUYING TIPS: Add a sporty look to your handrail as well as provide extra support.

90° Elbow Fitting

DESCRIPTION: Stainless-steel or chrome-plated zamac L-shaped fitting with set screws on interiors of arms. Fits ⅞" or 1" tube.

USE: To make a neat, continuous corner for hand or grab rails, particularly across the transom.

USE TIPS: Because the 90° elbow isn't supported by a stanchion, it is necessary to install stanchions nearby for adequate support.

BUYING TIPS: Only necessary if you want a continuous rail.

90° Three-way Elbow

DESCRIPTION: Stainless steel or cast-zamac elbow with three arms, all at 90° angles to each other.

USE: Like the 90° elbow fitting, this elbow can be used with ⅞" OD tubing to make a continuous corner for hand or grab rails. Set screws in arms hold tubing in place.

USE TIPS: The "third arm" allows for the installation of a stanchion.

BUYING TIPS: This item provides the support required at the joint.

Round Tubing

ALSO KNOWN AS: Handrail tubing

DESCRIPTION: ⅞" or 1" OD 304 stainless steel tubing. Walls are ³⁄₆₄" thick.

USE: For handrails or grab rails.

USE TIPS: Essential component of a rail system that makes going forward or aft a lot safer. More secure than a lifeline system.

BUYING TIPS: Sold in 6' lengths.

Double Stanchion and Base

DESCRIPTION: Stainless steel 1"-diameter tube, 24" high, with predrilled perpendicular base at one end. Cross-holes drilled at two points along tube. Attaches with ¼" fasteners.

USE: Suitable for boats with upper and lower lifelines.

USE TIPS: Stanchion fitted with vinyl grommets that may be removed.

BUYING TIPS: Bases and stanchions are also sold separately.

Brace assembly

DESCRIPTION: Stainless steel 1"-diameter tube with angled base at one end and angled sleeve with set screw at the other.

USE: With the brace bolted through the deck and the sleeve slid over an upright lifeline stanchion, the brace will give extra support.

USE TIPS: Useful at gates.

BUYING TIPS: Check first to see whether your stanchion and rail system is rock steady or requires some extra support.

Safety net

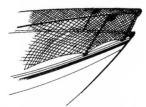

ALSO KNOWN AS: Lifeline netting

DESCRIPTION: White nylon netting usually in 1" sq. mesh; 2' wide sold in lengths of 5'–40'.

USE: Attached to top edge of lifeline and at each upright stanchion, the netting keeps kids, pets, sails, and gear from slipping overboard.

USE TIPS: Some families with small children place netting around entire boat or at least around the cockpit where children play. It can also be strung in high-risk areas, such as the bow. A must for offshore cruising. Also useful for keeping sails and miscellaneous objects on board.

BUYING TIPS: Much cheaper to buy at commercial fishing supply outlets.

COCKPIT ACCESSORIES

Cockpit table

ALSO KNOWN AS: Removable cockpit table, pedestal table, deck table

DESCRIPTION: Permanent- and semipermanent-mount tables, as well as portable tables made of plastic, teak, polyethylene, stainless steel, and aluminum, some with stainless-steel and/or aluminum mounting systems and hardware. Table surfaces range in size from "snack" size up to 4" long × 1½' wide.

Stainless-steel *table leg fasteners* and *table brackets* are sold separately for semipermanent mounting systems.

TYPES:

Folding deck tables: are designed to stand independently on deck on folding sawbucklike legs, trestles, or straight detachable legs.

Rail-mount tables: clamp onto rails or stanchions at a single attachment point, but *dual-mount* types provide for two attachment points, making them

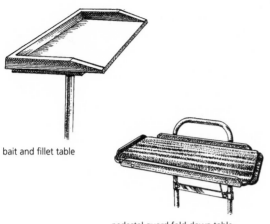

bait and fillet table

pedestal guard fold-down table

sturdier. Polyethylene or stainless steel *bait and fillet tables* are similarly mounted.

Pedestal guard fold-down table: a close relative to the rail-mount table that clamps onto the steering pedestal. Another type of mount fits into fishing-rod socket. Side and back guardrails to keep utensils and food from falling overboard. Some mounting systems provide for tandem mounting with barbecue grills.

USE: To serve drinks, snacks, and meals or to fillet fish on deck.

USE TIPS: Portable deck tables are probably not sturdy enough to use under way unless your boat is very large and very stable.

BUYING TIPS: If storage space is limited, select tables that fold flat when not in use. Be sure tables have a secure system for locking legs in position.

PEDESTAL GUARD BEVERAGE HOLDER

ALSO KNOWN AS: Drink holder

DESCRIPTION: Solid base and three- or four-hole ledge permanently spaced about 2" higher.

Predrilled stainless-steel bracket clamps onto steering pedestal guard (see page 138).

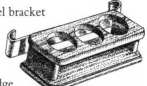

USE: Holes in top ledge are large enough to accommodate canned and bottled drinks and glasses. Provides a safe place to put drinks down on deck while boat is under way.

USE TIPS: Also a handy place to stick a flashlight on deck.

BUYING TIPS: While some may welcome it as a convenient means of storing a beer, singlehanders who can't leave the helm can use the holder to stash several bottles of water.

DECK SEAT AND CHAIR

DESCRIPTION: Permanently and semipermanently-installed seating, as well as portable chairs, benches, and seats made of durable materials intended for outdoor use. Upholstered with vinyl or treated canvas resistant to chemicals, UV rays, and saltwater. Hardware is stainless steel or aluminum.

TYPES:

Swingback seat: Does double duty with insulated, double-walled cooler or livewell (60- to 85-gal. capacity is typical) in seat base. Hinged cooler lid is chair seat. Padded back is supported by two upright arms that pivot from seat base so that you can sit facing either way.

Vinyl-covered *back-to-back, fold-down, sleeper-lounge* and *jumpseats:* resemble padded bucket seats in cars except that they have their own permanent bases that attach to the cockpit deck. Some designs allow seats to fold flat for sunbathing or sleeping.

Helmsman's armchair (also known as *helm chair, helmsman's chair,* or *flybridge helmseat*): Comfortably padded with separate seat, back, and arm rests to keep

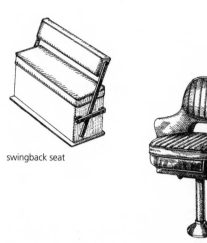

swingback seat

helmsman's armchair

water from collecting in corners. Designed for solid- or slide-mount on a pedestal base in at the control panel, so that skipper can sit while handling the boat. Seat unit is replaceable.

Fishing chair: Similar to helmsman's chair, but more streamlined to allow for quick and abrupt movement while fishing. Pedestal base allows seat to spin.

Director's chair: Made of a folding wooden frame and removable machine-washable canvas or mesh seat and back covers. Variations are the folding *lounge chair* with leg rest, the portable *stainless steel folding chair* with carrying case, and the *all-resin folding chair,* which is not particularly comfortable for long-term seating but suitable for meals around your cockpit table.

USE: To provide a comfortable seat on deck. All the seats described above are used on powerboats, with the exception of the *director's chair,* which could be used on a sailboat when it is not under way.

USE TIPS: Seating comfort is subjective; don't invest in seating until you have tried it out—preferably at length on someone else's boat.

BUYING TIPS: Seats come in a wide range of styles and prices. Let frequency of use and durability guide you in your selection. Protective covers are sold separately.

BOARDING LADDER

ALSO KNOWN AS: Swim ladder

DESCRIPTION: Two-, three-, and four-step ladders constructed of stainless steel or anodized aluminum tubing, may have 15" metal or plastic steps. Most are permanently mounted to the transom and gunwale. Other types are *portable ladders,* which simply hang over the side and are pulled in when not in use. Standoff arms with replaceable rubber tips (available separately, similar to cane tips) keep these ladders from scratching or denting the boat.

Some ladders, including *outboard ladders,* fold up at their halfway point, whereas *rigid ladders* pivot up from the top.

Owners of small runabouts and sailboats may want to use rope *emergency ladders* or *one-step swim stirrups,* which are essentially a loop of rope with a single step. It probably takes some coordination and strength to use stirrups. Emergency ladders are made with high-visibility orange treads.

USE: Boarding ladders make it easy to get off and on board, whether from a dinghy or when swimming or skiing. Anything bulky like a ladder will increase drag while under way.

USE TIPS: To make steps easier on bare feet and to increase traction, you can add *snap-on step treads* made of PVC, or *universal teak ladder steps.* Like fenders, removable ladders should never hang over the side while you are under way.

BUYING TIPS: A boarding ladder is essential for water skiers, divers, and swimmers.

SWIM PLATFORM

DESCRIPTION: Wide range of designs available, but the most popular are *teak* grates that span the full width of the transom; or *platform ladders,* combining ladders and small (15" × 18" to 15" × 22") teak landings in a permanent installation on the transom. Scissorlike *stretch ladders* extend away from the boat at an angle and fold for compact storage.

USE: To create a ledge or shelf for swimmers, skiers, or divers to slip in or out of the water easily.

USE TIPS: Integral swim platforms, long a standard feature on powerboats, are increasingly popular on sailboats with reverse transoms. They are also an excellent platform for working on an outboard motor or autopilot.

stretch ladder

BUYING TIPS: Permanently mounted ladders are the easiest to use but are suitable mainly for power boats. Choose a ladder that extends well into the water; it is extremely difficult to climb onto a ladder that is above water level. Even if your boat was not built with an attached swim platform, there are a variety of after-market ones to choose from.

Pontoon Ladder

DESCRIPTION: Three-step aluminum ladder 36" long × 24" wide. Uprights are 1" OD aluminum tubes; steps are oval in profile with nonskid surfaces. Folding stand-offs are perpendicular from uprights with rubber "crutch tips" to protect hull side. Hardware allows ladder to hinge horizontally against lifeline stanchion and vertically against side of boat.

USE: To serve as port or starboard side gate. Can also be hinged open or swung down to provide boarding ladder at gate.

USE TIPS: Designed for permanent installation on pontoon boats

BUYING TIPS: A must for the pontoon boat.

Folding Helmsman's Footrest

DESCRIPTION: Anodized aluminum frame with varnished oak tread, 15' wide × 8¼" deep.

USE: To provide a footrest at helm stations with high pedestal seats or at stand-up helm stations.

USE TIPS: Mounts to bulkhead.

BUYING TIPS: A footrest is good relief for the back—something saloon keepers have known for years.

Cushion

ALSO KNOWN AS: Deck cushion

DESCRIPTION: Closed-cell foam-filled cushion covered with UV-, salt-, and chemical-resistant fabric, will not absorb water, dries quickly. Contoured rectangular shapes fit flat on cockpit seats or snap onto lifeline rails.

USE: To provide softer seating in sailboat cockpit. May also be placed against the coaming for use as a backrest.

USE TIPS: Cushions also add to comfort when cockpit seating is wet from morning dew or rain showers.

BUYING TIPS: Look for foam that is dense and fairly thin—1"–2" thick—so it takes up less storage space.

Leaning Post

DESCRIPTION: Simple padded vinyl stool top fits on permanently mounted seat pedestal. May have rod holders and glove-compartmentlike storage.

USE: As an alternative to a helmsman's chair, some skippers like the support of a leaning post.

USE TIPS: Switch off between leaning post and armchair.

BUYING TIPS: Protective cover is sold separately.

SEAT PEDESTAL AND MOUNT

ALSO KNOWN AS: Seat base, seat spider, spider base, pedestal

DESCRIPTION: Upright tubular post with pre-drilled base and accommodation at upper end for bracket for attaching helmsman's chair, fishing chair, leaning post, or bass seat. Pedestal and seat base may be made of anodized aluminum, stainless steel, painted steel, or combination of different durable corrosion-resistant materials.

Some pedestal bases have telescoping height adjustment controlled by handscrew lock or power hydraulics. Seat bases may be stationary, swiveling, or spring-loaded for adjusting seat angle. Deck bases are permanent or allow entire pedestal and seat to be removed.

USE: Mounting system for helmsman's chair, fishing chair, or other seats on powerboat.

USE TIPS: Chairs that are mounted high, such as helmsman's seats and bass seats, are more comfortable if you mount a footrest attachment (sold separately) to the upright pedestal.

Fishing-rod gimbals can also be attached to the seat base so that gear is handy.

BUYING TIPS: It may be obvious, but it goes without saying that you should choose light colors when selecting upholstered furniture for on-deck use. Any vinyl will feel sticky and hot against bare skin, but dark colors absorb heat more than light colors.

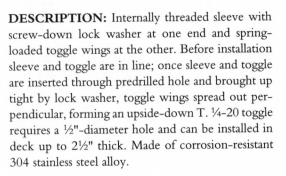

TOGGLE BOLT ANCHOR

DESCRIPTION: Internally threaded sleeve with screw-down lock washer at one end and spring-loaded toggle wings at the other. Before installation sleeve and toggle are in line; once sleeve and toggle are inserted through predrilled hole and brought up tight by lock washer, toggle wings spread out perpendicular, forming an upside-down T. ¼-20 toggle requires a ½"-diameter hole and can be installed in deck up to 2½" thick. Made of corrosion-resistant 304 stainless steel alloy.

USE: Once threaded sleeve is in place with toggle and lock washer, it serves as a secure attachment point for seat pedestal base, lifeline stanchion, and other deck hardware.

USE TIPS: Lock washer and toggle combination allow you to leave sleeve in place while installing or removing.

BUYING TIPS: Sold in pairs.

WEATHER-RESISTANT LOCK

ALSO KNOWN AS: Padlock

DESCRIPTION: Laminated steel padlock encased in thermoplastic cover, with ⁹⁄₃₂"-diameter stainless steel shackle and brass key.

USE: To secure cabin doors, motors, dock boxes, and other gear stored in places exposed to the elements.

USE TIPS: Keep a spare key in your car so that you don't get locked out.

BUYING TIPS: Only slightly more expensive than more common "unclad" padlock, offers an extra measure of longevity.

IPER MOTOR

ALSO KNOWN AS: Windshield-wiper assembly

DESCRIPTION: Hand-size rectangular electric motor and gear train, may have complete 11"-long windshield-wiper arm and blade attached, or simply a ⅜"–½"–diameter × 2½"–3½"–long shaft for mounting a wiper arm and blade. Typical blade sweep is 110°; may or may not be self-parking (in other words wiper arm returns to closed position when motor is turned off). *Deck-mount* motor comes with plate for through-deck installation (motor is located below deck). *Frame-mount* motor is encased in weatherproof housing of anodized aluminum, stainless steel, or enameled steel.

USE: Wiper motor is wired to boat's DC electrical system and powers windshield wipers.

USE TIPS: Measure sweep area carefully to gauge proper positioning of motor.

BUYING TIPS: Choose heavy-duty stainless steel and brass construction for longer life. ABS white plastic trim cover sold separately for some models.

WINDSHIELD-WIPER ARM AND BLADE

DESCRIPTION: Stainless steel arm, 16"–20" long, with socket that fits onto wiper-motor assembly. Black rubber blade, 11"–16" long, typically slides onto or into arm and is held snugly against the windshield by proper positioning of motor and arm. *Straight blade* is used on flat windshield. *Curved blade,* with bowlike arm, works on contoured windshields.

Hand-operated windshield wiper is simply a chrome-plated wiper arm with stainless-steel blade assembly. For flat or curved windshield. Attached to a small handle that mounts through the window frame or deck. Not attached to electric motor.

USE: To clear rainwater, seaspray, dirt, and mist from boat windshields.

USE TIPS: Serious boaters will want the motor-driven kind that comes standard on most powerboats.

BUYING TIPS: Replacement blades sold separately.

— TYING AND HOLDING MATERIALS —

HOOK AND LOOP FASTENERS

ALSO KNOWN AS: Velcro™

DESCRIPTION: Strips, squares, and rectangles of two-part black Velcro-like material (copy-cat material goes by the generic name hook-and-loop fastener). Loop part is fuzzy; its mate has bristly plastic hooks that stick to each other like burrs stick to a sweater. Sold in 1" × 1" squares, 2" long × 1" wide patches and 18"- or 24"-long strips, some with buckles for fastening ends together, as well as attached at the ends of foot-long nylon tape.

USE: Buckle a strip (usually the "loop" material) around radios, first-aid kits or other items you might need in a hurry. Attach the corresponding "hook" material to a bulkhead or storage area within easy reach. Small squares can be used for storing lightweight items, such as galley utensils, while larger patches are handy for keeping rugs in place or for storing heavier items. Long strips can be used to hang curtains.

USE TIPS: Who remembers life before Velcro? Incredibly handy.

BUYING TIPS: Although some hook-and-loop fasteners come with adhesive backings, you can also buy special adhesive for do-it-yourself projects.

JAM-CLASP CORD

DESCRIPTION: 24" length of shock cord attached to nylon fitting with V-shaped "jam" slot. Cord stretches up to 40".

USE: The jam fitting allows for precise, tight-fitting adjustments when bundling sails, sleeping bags, or other bulky gear.

USE TIPS: Use for any quick-tying purposes, including mainsail against the boom or jib on the foredeck.

BUYING TIPS: Sold in three-packs.

NONSKID TAPE

ALSO KNOWN AS: Grip tape

DESCRIPTION: Grainy-surfaced tape with pressure-sensitive backing, comes with peel-off paper strip to prevent roll from sticking to itself. Comes in white or clear, 1" or 2" wide. Weather- and water-resistant.

USE: Apply in slippery high-traffic areas around boarding points, in the galley, or in the head.

USE TIPS: Adheres well to most surfaces carefully cleaned of grease, dirt, oil, and moisture. Do not expect tape to adhere forever, some lifting is to be expected.

BUYING TIPS: Sold in 25' rolls.

BARRIER STRIPE TAPE

DESCRIPTION: Red-and-white diagonally striped weatherproof tape 2" wide with adhesive backing. May be reflective.

USE: To mark boarding ladders, dock ramps, flybridge ladders, dive platforms, and other places where there is a risk of accidents.

USE TIPS: Red and white stripes are a recognized "caution" symbol.

BUYING TIPS: Sold in rolls of 24".

COVERS AND ACCESSORIES

BIMINI TOP

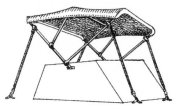

ALSO KNOWN AS: Awning

DESCRIPTION: A *bimini* is a canvas or nylon-and-vinyl fabric awning-type cover, usually blue or white, more or less flat, sometimes with slight downward lips for added shade protection. Held open by collapsible M-shaped ⅞" or 1" OD tubular aluminum frame anchored at three points on both sides of boat deck, flybridge, or gunwale. (A *dodger* is a collapsible, tight-fitting screen that often contains a windshield; the term also refers to the canvas covering over a bridge.)

A *T-top* is similar to a bimini, except that it is held up by two legs positioned in the middle of the awning sides. *Flying carpets* also shade the cockpit, but they are generally a square of canvas without frame, with the main or mizzen halyard attached to a grommet in the center. Ties at the corners are secured to cleats or lifelines on deck.

USE: *Biminis* shade flybridges and cockpits on powerboats. *Dodgers* shade doghouse cabins on larger sailboats. The tubular aluminum frame must be sturdy enough to withstand winds while underway.

USE TIPS: Get a *bimini top boot,* a canvas or nylon-backed vinyl cover for storing the bimini when it is collapsed and not in use.

BUYING TIPS: Most powerboats are sold with bimini tops or "canvas packages." You can also have biminis and dodgers custom made by a local canvas shop. Fit is important. Replacement nylon, stainless steel, and chrome-plated zinc fittings are sold separately (see this page).

BIMINI TOP REPLACEMENT HARDWARE

DESCRIPTION: Nylon, stainless steel, and chrome-plated zinc fittings that attach to deck or ends of tubular frames. Sized to fit ¾", ⅞", and 1" OD aluminum tubing. *Deck hinge* has flat, predrilled base and an upright slot with a bolt through the upper edges. *End socket* (frame tubing fits inside), *end eye* (fits inside frame tubing), and *tube slide* (can be positioned anywhere along length of tubing) are made for bolt on hinge to thread through.

Predrilled *side-mount deck hinge* with raised button that threads through eye sock or end mounts on vertical surfaces such as cabin gunwale sides. A variation on the deck hinge is the *slider kit*, which is simply a pair of deck hinges whose positions can be shifted along 36" lengths of aluminum track with nylon slides at either end.

USE: To provide attachment points for tubular bimini top and dodger frames.

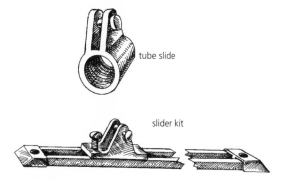

tube slide

slider kit

USE TIPS: Stainless steel fittings will cause aluminum frame to corrode. Stick with nylon or chrome-plated zinc.

BUYING TIPS: Nylon hinges cost a fraction of stainless steel versions, but are more prone to chafe; if you get stainless steel hinges, make sure they are of high quality—along with the fasteners you use.

TELESCOPING AWNING POLE

ALSO KNOWN AS: Awning pole

DESCRIPTION: Telescoping ⅞" and 1" aluminum poles extend from 45"–72" to 81"–144" and have protective rubber tips on both ends as well as grommets or eyes.

USE: Acts like a circus-tent center pole for a boat awning (flying carpet) or bimini cover.

USE TIPS: Be sure to tie pole down using eyes at ends, especially on longer extensions where the pole is likely to fall over.

BUYING TIPS: Less than $30.

GROMMET KIT

DESCRIPTION: Two-piece rings that form over each other to create a secure eye.

USE: Grommet kits, with a variety of different sizes available, are invaluable for creating eyes for installation of sail slides or repairing awnings, boat covers, or other heavy-duty cloth items.

USE TIPS: Practice on a scrap piece of cloth before taking hammer and die to one of your sails—and measure carefully before you begin punching.

BUYING TIPS: Buy kit that includes cloth-cutting tool, a base for holding one half of the grommet, and a die for hammering the second half into place.

RIVET GUN

ALSO KNOWN AS: Heavy-duty hand riveter

DESCRIPTION: Rivets are headed pins or spikes used to fasten two or more pieces of metal together. The hand riveter tool inserts the rivets and peens over (flattens by hammering) the plain end to create a second head so that the rivet doesn't pull through.

USE: For metal repairs in and around your boat, car, and home.

USE TIPS: For light-duty, nonessential fastening only; most things that require fastening on a boat need something stronger than a rivet.

BUYING TIPS: Riveter tool can handle 3/32", 1/8", 5/32", and 3/16" rivets. Usually sold with an assortment of rivets.

RIVET

ALSO KNOWN AS: Blind rivet

DESCRIPTION: Naillike fastener with elongated head, made of stainless steel and aluminum.

USE: Inserted through thin (see above) sheets of metal, canvas, or leather and compressed by a special tool, a rivet gun, so that the rivet forms a second head that will not pull out.

USE TIPS: Many small bass and jon boats are made of aluminum that is fastened by rivets.

BUYING TIPS: When making repairs on aluminum, be sure to use rivets made of aluminum, to prevent galvanic corrosion (see "About Zincs," page 162) caused when dissimilar metals are in contact with each other.

SNAP AND BUTTON KIT

ALSO KNOWN AS: Self-tapping snap fasteners, screw studs

DESCRIPTION: Female button and the stud (or male) half of a snap fastener; sometimes with a Phillips-head self-tapping screw. Similar to, but heavier than, snaps found on clothing.

snap and button kit   snap screw stud

USE: Affix self-tapping screw studs on decks or cabin roofs where you plan to attach boat covers or awnings. Operation requires use of a special base and die tool, sold separately.

USE TIPS: For proper fit, be sure stud placement corresponds exactly with snap-fastener locations on canvas. This is a painstaking process that must be done carefully. Measure!

BUYING TIPS: You might want to think twice before tapping 25 or so snaps into your gunwale. Most store-bought tarps come with grommets that permit nonintrusive fastening with rope. Kits contain both studs and snaps.

TURN-BUTTON FASTENER

DESCRIPTION: Flat upright button attached to deck or canvas inserts through corresponding slotted eye and twists 90° to lock both pieces together. Button may have a *screw stud base*, a predrilled *stud base*, or two prongs that pierce canvas and lock around a

small separate *plate* or escutcheon. Two-piece eyelet consists of *eye* with prongs that pierce canvas and clamp around a flat *washer*.

USE: To attach boat tops, awnings, and covers.

USE TIPS: Do not install turn-button studs in high-traffic areas. They will break if they are stepped on.

BUYING TIPS: Sold in kits with an assortment of stud types, as well as eyes and washers.

LIFT-THE-DOT FASTENER

DESCRIPTION: Similar in function to turn-button fastener. Small knobbed stud is inserted into socket that has spring mechanism to hold stud in place. Stud may have screw base or prongs and washer for installation in canvas. Two-part socket includes face with prongs that clamp around a plate.

USE: Another method for attaching canvas, tops, or awnings.

USE TIPS: Like turn-button fasteners, lift-the-dots should not be used in high-traffic areas. They will break if stepped on and will hurt bare feet.

BUYING TIPS: For light-duty uses; not as permanent as the snap and grommet kits (above), for example.

TARP SNAP

DESCRIPTION: Similar in function to old-fashioned stocking garters: the tarp is held fast to the raised button snap by means of a loop that slides over the button and tarp. The top loop has an eye that can be hooked to a bungee or shock cord.

USE: Handy for making temporary or additional attachment points on awnings or boat covers.

USE TIPS: Use in conjunction with a snap assembly tool.

BUYING TIPS: Sold in packs of four.

COMPANIONWAY BOARD BAG

DESCRIPTION: Cloth sack with narrow lateral pockets (usually four) and mounting grommets at open end.

USE: To store companionway or hatch boards when they're not in place.

USE TIPS: Especially helpful to prevent boards from banging around at sea.

BUYING TIPS: Measure hatch boards before buying, as bags come in various sizes.

BOAT UMBRELLA

DESCRIPTION: Acrylic-coated nylon multicolor umbrella has 6' diameter and stands on 5'-long fiberglass staff. Stainless steel and anodized-aluminum rail mount fits standards $\frac{7}{8}$" and 1" rails; can be adjusted to any angle. Comes with a carrying case.

USE: Position on deck where you want a spot of shade. An alternative to a flying carpet.

USE TIPS: Do not use umbrella while boat is under way.

BUYING TIPS: Sailboaters can construct their own umbrella (and sleeping canopy) with a piece of canvas strung over the boom.

CHAPTER NINE

ELECTRICAL SYSTEMS

ABOUT ELECTRICITY

Electricity brings many of the comforts of home aboard ship and, on all but the smallest daysailers, is necessary to power the running lights and light the compass. Electrical systems can range from a simple 6-volt battery to a boat wired for 12- and 24-volt DC power and AC current as well. Most boats fall somewhere in between with a 12-volt battery or two to start the engine and run the house "electrics." While electricity enhances safety and enjoyment afloat, it is the system most vulnerable to the harshness of the marine environment. For that reason all boat owners should have a working knowledge of their boat's electrical circuits, conduct regular maintenance checks, and be able to troubleshoot when problems arise.

MARINE BATTERIES AND ACCESSORIES

ABOUT MARINE BATTERIES

Marine batteries are used for two purposes: storing power to start an onboard engine or to operate a boat's electrical system. Ironically the two uses are contradictory. Starting an engine, especially an inboard diesel, requires the application of lots of amperage over a short period of time, usually 10 or so seconds, which is a typical job for an automotive battery. But powering a ship's electrical system while the engine is off creates the kind of deep discharging that damages an automotive-type starting battery. Marine batteries, on the other hand, are able to handle deep discharges and, while they recharge more slowly, are generally able to start engines, providing they produce sufficient *cold cranking amps*—the number of amperes a battery can deliver for 30 seconds at 0° F. Some boaters resolve the contradiction by using a conventional battery for starting the engine and reserving a separate bank for "house" use—powering the electronics, running lights, and so on. Another (and very common) solution is to install parallel banks of deep-cycle marine batteries, connected by a selector switch, and alternate their use between starting and operating functions.

To determine what size battery(ies) you need, add up the average daily amp hour use of your systems. Because marine batteries are operated between 50% and 85% of their charge—that is, at about 35% capacity—the rule of thumb is to install roughly three times the battery storage power of your average amp use. Once installed, batteries should be checked and monitored regularly and recharged frequently.

MARINE BATTERY

DESCRIPTION: Device consisting of (usually) six cells, each containing two lead electrodes, a positive and negative, immersed in an electrolyte, which are alternately charged and discharged with electrical current. 12 volts is standard.

TYPES:

Automotive-type starter battery: Standard 12-volt lead acid battery that delivers high amperage in short bursts; recharges quickly but is vulnerable to long-term drain.

Deep-cycling battery: Descendant of the golf cart battery, the typical marine deep-cycle battery has thicker lead plates able to withstand deeper discharges without damage. Premium deep-cycle batteries have excellent cycling ability and require less maintenance.

Gel-cell battery: Sealed deep-cycle battery with gel, or nonliquid, electrolyte; about twice as expensive as a wet-cell marine battery, but it won't spill, lasts longer without as much maintenance, and is more efficient.

USE: To store electrical power to start engine and run onboard electrics.

USE TIPS: On a boat electricity is like freshwater—to be used sparingly.

BUYING TIPS: Automotive or standard deep-cycle batteries are fine for just cranking the engine; a gel battery, although expensive, is the best bet for boats with multiple electrical needs.

BATTERY SWITCH

ALSO KNOWN AS: Isolator switch, selector switch

DESCRIPTION: Typically a round, hard polycarbonate casing (or square with round dial)

measuring about 5¼" diameter, 2⅝" deep, containing a mechanical device, installed in-line, with contacts that can be opened or closed by a dial or toggle. Usually comes with four predrilled holes for mounting.

TYPES:

battery selector switch

Battery selector switch: Four-position switch (Off, 1, 2, Both); standard version rated at 230 amps continuous, 345 amps intermittent, heavy-duty model rated at 360 or so amps continuous, 600 intermittent.

On-off battery switch: Similar to selector switch but contains simple circuit breaker with two positions, On and Off. Most rated at 230 amps continuous, 345 amps intermittent. Plastic casing with either click dial or toggle switch.

USE: Selector switch allows choice between two banks of batteries or both; Off position permits immediate shutdown during emergency and ensures all systems (except bilge pump) are off when boat is unattended. On-Off switch permits you to break or open a circuit and to isolate specific equipment, such as an air conditioner.

USE TIPS: Well-hidden switch can act as a "kill switch" to foil boat thieves.

BUYING TIPS: Any boat with high electricity use or high loads should be equipped with the heavy-duty switch.

AUTOMATIC BATTERY SWITCH

ALSO KNOWN AS: Circuit-breaker switch

DESCRIPTION: Circuit-breaker switch that trips at preset voltage level. Wires to positive terminal of battery. Reset button restores connection.

USE: To disconnect battery and thus avoid excessive drainage if electronics or running lights, for example, are inadvertently left on.

USE TIPS: Also works on automobiles. Low-drain emergency items, such as radios, can be wired separately.

BUYING TIPS: For the forgetful.

ABOUT BATTERY CHARGING

Batteries are recharged by connecting them to a charge whose current is a volt or two higher than that of the battery. Marine batteries are best recharged carefully and in phases. In the main, or *bulk,* recharging phase, you should charge at a rate of between 25% and 40% of the battery's amp capacity to a voltage of about 14.4 volts (but not more), restoring about 75% of the battery's capacity; in the second, or *absorption,* phase, voltage should be kept at 14.4 while amperage is decreased; in the final, *float,* phase, when the battery is charged virtually to capacity (about 85% in reality), amperage is minimal and voltage is reduced to about 13.3%. Solar panels are an excellent source for this float or trickle charge.

Most boat owners recharge by using an engine alternator, shore power, auxiliary generator, solar panel, wind generator, or some combination. Charging off an engine alternator is usually sufficient for small-to-medium boats. Chargers are required when shore power is the sole or main source of recharging current. Marine battery chargers contain several important features, including automatic shut-off when full charge is achieved, a "gate" to block shoreside AC power from the boat's DC system, and ignition protection to prevent sparks and also to avoid damage to the charger if the engine is started during charging. Other available features are variable line compensation, which balances fluctuations in shore power voltage, and amperage boost, which adds enough amps to start an engine when the battery is low.

BATTERY CHARGER

ALSO KNOWN AS: Dockside battery charger, battery converter, transformer

DESCRIPTION: Either of two types of electrical or electronic transformer device housed in a metal box, most often stainless steel or aluminum, and containing internal circuits capable of handling AC and DC current.

TYPES:

silicon-controlled rectifier

Silicon-controlled rectifier (SCR): Also known as a *switching charger,* this type varies its charge to keep a battery at a constant 13.4 volts. Ranges from 8 amps to 50 amps. Corrosion-resistant aluminum housing, measuring about 7" × 8¼" × 6⅓" and weighing from 4 to 10 lbs. Most efficient type of charger. Equipped with automatic shut-off.

Ferroresonant charger: Solid-state converter, often in steel housing, rated from 8 amps to 50 amps. Ranges in size from 7½" × 9½" × 6¼" (9 lbs.) to 7" × 9¾" × 16" (28 lbs.).

USE: To charge batteries by connecting to a regular electrical outlet. Converts AC current (either 110 volt or 220 volt) to DC current.

USE TIPS: For boats without great electrical demands that do charge at dockside, the newer, lighter SCR charger is best; it produces higher amperage for a longer time and features variable line compensation and automatic shut-off to prevent overcharging. For bigger boats, loaded up with electricity-devouring devices, a ferroresonant charger provides a continuous 12 volts and maintains a small maintenance charge to keep up with normal battery discharge.

BUYING TIPS: An SCR is the best deal for boats that require a charger rated at 25 amps or less. What size charger you require also depends on battery size (larger, more efficient batteries can be charged at lower amps).

DC VOLTMETER

DESCRIPTION: Instrument that detects and shows, with either digital or analog display, voltage (system pressure) at a given point in an electrical circuit. Information is conveyed in terms of volts, sometimes down to $\frac{1}{100}$ volt, or percentages (in which case, it is called a *percent meter*).

USE: To check battery or alternator voltage output; also gives a sense of which bank of batteries contains more charge.

USE TIPS: Because the difference between a fully charged and dead battery is less than 2 volts, a voltmeter is not accurate enough to give a true read on actual battery charge; this is really just a quick way to see if an alternator or charger is working.

BUYING TIPS: If you really want one, get the digital kind, which gives a closer read.

THREE-BATTERY VOLTMETER

DESCRIPTION: Voltmeter with switch connections to three or more points in a circuit (and monitors them similarly to the way a radio scanner works). 5¼" × 3¾" aluminum casing with dial giving readings in percentages. Some models require dashboard or instrument panel cutout.

USE: To measure voltage in one or more batteries or banks of batteries.

USE TIPS: Its primary use is to check which bank holds the larger charge.

BUYING TIPS: For boats with multiple batteries or battery banks.

LOW BATTERY ALARM

ALSO KNOWN AS: Battery alarm

DESCRIPTION: Essentially a small voltmeter with no dial, in a black styrene housing about 4½" by 2½", with an audible beeper that is triggered by a preset voltage level. Some have 30-second delay and/or shut-off button. Wire leads attach to battery terminals. Some versions permit two voltage-level settings—low and high.

USE: To warn of deep-cycling by beeping when battery voltage drops to a certain level (usually preset at 11.5 volts). Dual-purpose alarm (called *high-low* alarm) has second setting at 14.5 volts to warn of excess current.

USE TIPS: Handy but often sends out false alarm—when raising anchor or starting engine, for example, puts temporary strain on battery.

BUYING TIPS: Type with 30-second delay permits you to set warning level higher (12.2 volts), before the battery is seriously depleted.

DC AMMETER

ALSO KNOWN AS: Ampere meter

DESCRIPTION: Device of several designs—electrodynamic (responding to the magnetic field created by the flow of current) or digital—that detects minute increases and decreases in current flow and displays information in either analog or digital form. Small, measuring about 2¾" × 2¾" × 2⅛"; capable of measuring amps from 0 to 25, in whole numbers or fractions.

USE: To measure and display the rate of current flow (amps) to or from a battery.

USE TIPS: Install in-line, preferably in the common negative of the battery wires to tell whether battery is becoming more charged or more discharged. Alternative sites are at the alternator output and at the distribution panel.

BUYING TIPS: For greatest accuracy, get one that has at least 0.1 or, even better, 0.01 amp resolution.

DC AMP-HOUR METER

DESCRIPTION: Monitoring device that keeps track of energy added to or subtracted from a battery and displays this calculation in amp hours. Comes with 500-amp, 50-mV shunt (bypass) to minimize current loss. Four-digit LCD display. Amp-hour meter-plus model contains voltmeter and standard ammeter in 4½" × 3" × 1¾" water-resistant housing.

USE: To tell you how many amp hours you have used or restored to a battery, allowing you to know when to begin or cease recharging.

USE TIPS: Very useful when recharging because device lets you know when battery starts receiving only small amounts of current and thus is near full charge.

BUYING TIPS: Combination amp-hour meter, voltmeter, and ammeter is best choice for boats without separate voltmeters and ammeters.

MULTIMETER

DESCRIPTION: Combination device that measures volts, ohms, diode action, and (in some models) amperage. Basic accuracy range, depending on model, from 0.4% to 1.5%. Handheld, measuring 5½"–6½" × 2.8" × 1.35" and weighing under 2 lbs. Analog/digital display. Most models have a continuity beeper that sounds when a closed circuit is found. Powered by alkaline batteries. Some models come with batteries and test leads.

USE: To diagnose trouble spots in the electrical system.

USE TIPS: For the dedicated do-it-yourselfer.

BUYING TIPS: More a toolbox item for the professional electrician or repairman than the average boater.

BATTERY TERMINALS

DESCRIPTION: Metal fitting of various designs, either corrosion-resistant brass or lead, that fits over and tightens on battery post.

TYPES:

Standard battery terminal: Automotive-style lead fitting, sometimes called *wingnut terminal.* Omega-shaped (Ω) with bolt and nut for tightening at open end, lug and wingnut at closed end for attaching cables.

Noncorrosive terminal: Solid brass fitting that installs over existing battery terminal for good conduction and which has an opening for lubricating the existing terminal for corrosion protection. Up to five connection points for incoming wires. Fits ⅜" and ⁵⁄₁₆" post batteries.

Snap-on terminal: Quick-release stainless-steel cap with spring-loaded action; plastic cover protects against shock. Rated 500 amps continuous, and fits 6-volt and 12-volt battery studs without tools.

USE: To connect battery cables and wires to battery posts.

USE TIPS: Quick-release and noncorrosive terminals have their uses, but the standard type makes for a tighter connection. Check all terminals regularly for snug fit and signs of corrosion.

BUYING TIPS: Usually sold in pairs, for negative and positive posts.

QUICK-RELEASE BATTERY BOLTS

DESCRIPTION: Stainless steel terminal bolt with plastic positive-grip handle at right angle.

USE: To provide easy bolting/unbolting of terminal bolts.

USE TIPS: You can easily use a wrench instead.

BUYING TIPS: Kind of gimmicky.

BATTERY TERMINAL PROTECTOR

ALSO KNOWN AS: Terminal washer

DESCRIPTION: Felt washer, or doughnut, chemically treated and sized to fit over both ⅜" or ⁵⁄₁₆" battery post.

USE: To prevent corrosion by neutralizing any acid leaking from terminal posts.

USE TIPS: Good idea; cheaper than replacing battery terminals.

BUYING TIPS: Sold in twos, one red for positive pole, one green for negative.

BATTERY TERMINAL COVER

DESCRIPTION: Flexible plastic snap-on cap, with entry hole for either ½" or ⅝" wire cable; sold in one- or two-wire version.

USE: Snaps on over battery terminals to guard against corrosion and block short circuits.

USE TIPS: Goes on over existing terminals and cable.

BUYING TIPS: Sold as a pair, one red, one black.

BATTERY STUD AND TERMINAL TOOL

DESCRIPTION: Small, two-part steel brush—one part a short, stiff bristle (like a pipe cleaner), the other with a wire brush inside a thimblelike capsule, enclosed in a steel or plastic case that snaps together.

USE: Enclosed brush fits over and scours battery posts; regular brush cleans terminal of grime and corrosion.

USE TIPS: Use often while checking terminals for tightness.

BUYING TIPS: At under $5 a real bargain.

COPPER BATTERY CABLE

ALSO KNOWN AS: Battery cable

DESCRIPTION: PVC-insulated wire in 2, 4, and 6-gauges; sold in 25' lengths and color-coded black for negative, red for positive. Tinned- or uncoated-wire strand.

USE: To wire battery terminals to the boat's circuit and to connect parallel batteries.

USE TIPS: Keep cable leads as short as possible. Always parallel-wire multiple batteries in a 12-volt system; series wiring (positive to negative) can damage equipment.

BUYING TIPS: Tinned-copper strand is superior for resisting corrosion.

MARINE-GRADE BATTERY CABLE

DESCRIPTION: Precut battery cable with tinned copper to prevent corrosion; comes with attached connector lugs (⅜" eye) in lengths from 18" to 48" with PVC insulation and sealed lugs for waterproofness. Black or red covering.

USE: For standard battery installations and adding of additional batteries.

USE TIPS: Be consistent with color coding.

BUYING TIPS: Beats adding your own lugs.

HEAVY-DUTY LUG

ALSO KNOWN AS: Connector

DESCRIPTION: Tin-coated copper loop fitting, with ⅜" or ⁵⁄₁₆" stud; black or red and rated for either 2 or 4-gauge wire.

USE: To connect end of cable, by crimping or soldering, to battery terminal.

USE TIPS: Crimping provides the best connection.

BUYING TIPS: Sold in pairs.

BATTERY HYDROMETER

DESCRIPTION: Sealed, graduated tube containing a calibrated float and a rubber bulb at top end for sucking up a sample of the electrolyte fluid. Resembles an oven baster.

USE: To detect dead wet cells by measuring the specific gravity of their electrolyte (1,280 is fully charged, 1,100 is dead).

USE TIPS: For hot or cold lead/acid cell batteries. Be careful with the electrolyte—it's highly corrosive.

BUYING TIPS: Some come with storage tube.

ABOUT BATTERY INSTALLATION

How securely your boat's batteries have been installed will only be revealed when you strike heavy weather. It is at this point that your batteries become a vital part of your survival system—for powering your

VHF or single sideband radio, for starting your engine, and for running your electric bilge pumps. For this reason batteries must be firmly encased in their boxes, which must be secured to a shelf or tray, which, in turn, must be so strongly affixed that it is virtually a structural part of your boat. Batteries should be elevated so that they do not get submerged as a boat begins to take on water or corrode from ordinary bilge-water.

Battery Box

DESCRIPTION: Rigid or molded polypropylene (sometimes polyethylene) rectangular box with removable cover. Made in different sizes to accommodate different batteries. Dimensions range anywhere from 11" long × 9" wide × 9¾" high to 16" × 9" × 10¼". Some are vented and often come with a tie-down strap and mounting hardware and brackets.

USE: To enclose a battery and protect it from sun and saltwater.

USE TIPS: A battery box is a must, for anyone going offshore or into any kind of seaway. Batteries are heavy (50–60 lbs. and up) and filled with acid and can become dangerous objects if broken loose.

BUYING TIPS: Because of confusing specs, sometimes based on battery type, battery size, or box size, measure your battery before you buy.

Battery Box Strap

DESCRIPTION: Woven polypropylene or nylon strap, 1½" wide, sold in standard lengths of 38" or 42"; with buckle, two clamps, and four #8 screws for securing clamps.

USE: To secure battery box to battery tray (via clamps) and hold down battery box top.

USE TIPS: Always tighten the strap after opening the box.

BUYING TIPS: Most boxes come with a strap.

Battery Tray

DESCRIPTION: Rectangular, lipped noncorrosive plastic tray, with adjustable overhead crossbar and two retaining bolts; predrilled to take four or eight #10 screws (not included). Sized for standard and extra-large batteries.

USE: To secure battery box to boat.

USE TIPS: Make sure of the structural integrity of the shelf or other surface to which you fasten the tray. Use bolts instead of screws to secure.

BUYING TIPS: Low-tech item—any heavy-duty hard plastic tray will do.

Battery Mat

DESCRIPTION: Polypropylene felt pad, 8" × 12".

USE: To absorb and neutralize acid leaks, prevent corrosion.

USE TIPS: Place between battery and battery tray.

BUYING TIPS: Won't provide complete coverage for oversized batteries.

GROUND-FAULT CIRCUIT INTERRUPTER

ALSO KNOWN AS: GFI, residual-current circuit breaker

DESCRIPTION: Duplex outlet with device that senses minute (4–6 milliamps) imbalances in an AC circuit—ground faults—and instantly shuts off the power.

USE: To prevent electrocution.

USE TIPS: GFICs should be installed in place of regular dual outlets in the galley, head, on deck, or anywhere dampness or standing water can be a problem.

BUYING TIPS: Definitely a worthwhile purchase.

LOCKING POLARITY TESTER

ALSO KNOWN AS: Outlet circuit tester

DESCRIPTION: Essentially a voltmeter with light display that plugs into a 125-volt, two-pole, three-wire outlet.

USE: To detect reversed polarity and other wiring mistakes. Lights correspond to symbols to pinpoint problem (green means okay, red a problem; on red-light-only meters, no light means okay).

USE TIPS: Use to test marina outlets as well as your own wiring.

BUYING TIPS: Different makes vary widely in price, but do the same basic job.

GENERATOR

portable generator

ALSO KNOWN AS: Genset, generator set

DESCRIPTION: Self-contained gasoline or diesel engine/alternator unit with built-in fuel tank. Gasoline models are most common.

TYPES:

Portable generator: Compact, usually gasoline-powered unit. Ranges in size from about 17" × 8" × 12" (46 lbs.) for smaller models to 18" × 24" × 25" (150 lbs.) for larger units. Varies in horsepower from 1.6 to 5 hp, with fuel tanks sized from 0.5 to 5 gal. for operating range of 4–8 hours at half-load. Four-stroke, air-cooled motor. Models vary widely in efficiency, noise and vibration suppression, and optional features, such as low-oil shutdown and tool kits.

Permanent generator: Much larger, more powerful units, sized up to 23" × 21" × 31" (385 lbs.) for gasoline-powered, or 21¾" × 26¾" × 48" (1,025 lbs.) for diesel. Four-stroke engine is water-cooled. Requires professional installation.

USE: To produce both AC and DC electrical power. Used as a supplementary source of power and as an emergency backup system.

USE TIPS: Do not run a portable generator below-decks (or in a confined space) because of exhaust fumes.

BUYING TIPS: Only long-distance voyagers or owners of really big, power-hungry boats require a permanent generator. Other boat owners can usually find another power source for their electrical needs, unless shore power is not available.

12-VOLT POWER PACK

ALSO KNOWN AS: Portable battery

DESCRIPTION: Portable, sealed, rechargeable 12-volt lead acid battery that provides 6.5 amp hours of DC power. Measures 7" × 3" × 10", and weighs 8 lbs.; comes with an adjustable shoulder strap.

USE: To provide portable 12-volt DC power; emergency backup.

USE TIPS: Good for light duty, such as powering a spotlight, handheld radio, or cellular phone.

BUYING TIPS: Power pack will recharge off car or boat battery, but you can buy an optional 110-volt AC wall charger.

MARINE INVERTER

ALSO KNOWN AS: Marine power inverter, DC/AC inverter

DESCRIPTION: An electronic transformer that steps up DC power to AC power by creating AC wave forms. Ranges in capacity from about 600 watts continuous power output to about 2,000 watts, and from 1,200 watts surge capacity to 8,000-plus watts. A midrange inverter is a "black box" that might have an aluminum casing and measure 12" × 10" × 7" and weigh about 35 lbs. Some models have built-in battery chargers to restore 12-volt power to a boat's batteries when plugged into an AC power source. Inverters with MSW (modified sine wave) are more efficient than those with square waves.

USE: To convert 12-volt DC power from a boat's battery(ies) to 110-volt AC power; some inverters, in the presence of shore power, will act as battery chargers. Permits the use of AC equipment without using a generator.

USE TIPS: An inverter is useful for supplying power for smaller-drain items, such as tools or a stereo, and higher-drain but short-duration appliances, such as vacuums or coffeemakers; turn on the generator for such intensive uses as hot-water heaters or microwaves and concentrate their use, if possible, during a one- or two-hour period.

BUYING TIPS: To decide what size inverter a boat requires, you must calculate both your DC and AC daily needs in watts. And be sure to take into account *surge loads,* the brief but intense drain heavy appliances require upon start-up.

PORTABLE INVERTER

DESCRIPTION: Smaller and less powerful inverters that operate from a cigarette-lighter-style outlet. Measures as small as 4½" × 4½" × 1½" with a continuous power output, depending on size, from about 100 watts to 200 watts with surge capacity from about 250 watts to 500 watts. Most have automatic shut-offs or alarms when battery power runs low.

USE: Converting DC power to AC power for low-drain items, such as tools, hair dryer, and portable computer.

USE TIPS: Although you can power such things as a stereo with a portable inverter for a time, it is actually intended for small drains for short periods.

BUYING TIPS: Beware inferior brands that come cheap but do not have precise voltage regulation (which can harm voltage-sensitive items) or low-power cutoffs.

MARINE ALTERNATOR

DESCRIPTION: A generator that produces alternating (standard) current. A generator is a device that

converts mechanical energy into electricity. An alternator is belt-driven by a boat's engine and consists
of a magnetized *rotor* that turns within a *stator* (series
of coils) to produce AC current; a bank of diodes
that permit the current to flow in one direction only,
effectively making it DC (direct current); and a regulator that balances alternator output with voltage
loads and a battery's level of discharge. A good marine alternator can produce up to 200 amps.

USE: To recharge a boat's batteries. Most boaters
do most of their recharging with an engine alternator.

USE TIPS: While many boaters rely on automotive
alternators and regulators (and many inboard engines
come with these as stock equipment), marine alternators deliver maximum amps in the shortest period
of time without damaging marine batteries; marine
regulators ensure the charge is done in separate
stages, much like a high-quality battery charger (see
page 218).

BUYING TIPS: Alternators are sold with internal
and external voltage regulators; most electrical experts recommend the external kind, which is more
easily adjusted. The rule of thumb for determining
the optimum-size alternator is that it should create
an output between 30% and 40% of your boat's batteries, and 50% in the case of gel batteries, which
accept charge more readily.

BATTERY ISOLATOR

DESCRIPTION: A
diode or complex of diodes
in aluminum housing that permits current to flow
into, but not between, batteries. Rated depending
on the model from 70 amps to 160 amps. Draws
almost a volt when in use.

USE: To split the output from a single alternator
into multiple "paths" so that more than one battery
or battery bank can be charged simultaneously; also
prevents overcharging of batteries and isolates them
so that one battery cannot discharge another.

USE TIPS: Because the isolator consumes almost a
volt while in use, it may undercharge your batteries
by a volt. Counteract this by attaching the sense wire
on your alternator's external regulator to the battery
side of the isolator, which in turn is connected to
your starter battery. Keep in mind, though, that the
isolator will conclude its job is done when the starter
battery is charged, which can lead to undercharging
of the house battery or battery bank. More even
charging is possible by using a battery switch to
charge the batteries in parallel, then isolate them
during discharge or with a battery combiner (see
next item) that automatically isolates batteries after
they have been charged together in parallel.

BUYING TIPS: The isolator is designed for alternators with an external regulator—internally regulated alternators require dismantling to get at the
sense wire. Better to go with an ordinary selector
switch (see page 217), providing you remember to
use it to isolate the batteries when charging is over.

BATTERY COMBINER

DESCRIPTION: A voltage-controlled relay
switch that closes (makes a connection) when it
senses that the voltage of either multiple batteries or
banks of batteries has risen above 13.2 volts, indicating they are being charged; the relay opens and
breaks the connection when voltage drops below
12.8 volts. Available in two-bank/70-amp, three-
bank/70-amp, and two-bank/130-amp versions.
Relay is contained in a plastic box with three or four

brass and/or stainless-steel terminals that attach directly to the boat's batteries with #8 wire. Dimensions are 4¼" high × 2¼" wide × 1¼" deep for the two-bank models and 6" × 2½" × 1¼" for the three-bank combiner. An LED light indicates when the switch is On.

USE: To parallel, or *combine,* batteries when they are being charged, but isolate them when charging is complete. Permits simultaneous charging of multiple batteries or banks with alternators, solar panels, or inverter-chargers.

USE TIPS: Unlike a battery isolator, the combiner works well with all types of alternators and does not cause a voltage drop. May also be used to parallel-charge batteries in a home alternative-energy system.

BUYING TIPS: If you have a third bank of 130-amp batteries (either a second starting or house bank of batteries), an optional adapter kit will handle all three via the two-bank 130-amp model.

ALTERNATOR PROTECTOR

DESCRIPTION: A diode—an electronic device that restricts current flow in one direction—activated when current through an alternator reaches 16 volts.

USE: To divert excess current that would damage an alternator if the main battery switch was turned off while the engine is running.

USE TIPS: Install the protector from the alternator output to the ground.

BUYING TIPS: This is especially needed if you use your battery selector switch to direct current between two or more batteries while under way. Alternatives are a special master switch that disconnects the field current within the alternator if tripped while the engine is running, or a prominent sign at

your switch that warns users to stop the engine before switching to Off.

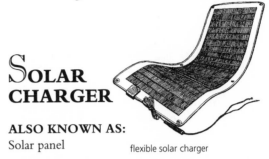

SOLAR CHARGER

ALSO KNOWN AS:
Solar panel

flexible solar charger

DESCRIPTION: Thin sheet of solar cells (semiconductors that convert sunlight into electrical power) that range in size anywhere from 13" × 7" to 50" × 15" and in power (watts) from 5 to 48. Cells are silicon alloy encapsulated in EVA rubber and other moisture barriers. Many include 12-volt battery hookup cables, and some come with diode blockers to prevent reverse flow of electricity at night or when batteries are fully charged.

TYPES:

Rigid solar charger: Panel with stiff (often aluminum) frame and protective tempered glass top. Most efficient of solar panels, producing about twice as much energy per area.

Flexible solar charger: Frameless panels, with cells mounted on thin sheet of stainless steel or other flexible material. Less efficient than rigid panels in power production, but easier to install because they can be mounted on curved or flexible surfaces.

USE: To provide a supplementary power source for such things as radios, lights, and batteries. It will not produce enough energy to crank an engine or power a heavy-duty item such as a refrigerator.

USE TIPS: Best mounted away from shadows—near the transom rather than on the deck.

BUYING TIPS: Calculate whether the size your boat can accommodate will really help your energy budget. These have a high up-front cost, but are quiet and ecologically sound.

SOLAR-CHARGE CONTROLLER

ALSO KNOWN AS: Charge controller

DESCRIPTION: Circuit closer with sensors in block of epoxy resin, measuring about 2" × 2", that regulates flow of charge to and from solar panels. Different models can handle inputs from 2 to 16 amps and consume less than 1 watt for largest version.

USE: To prevent overcharging (and gassing) of batteries by limiting voltage from panels; also acts as substitute for a blocking diode to prevent reverse flow of current from batteries when the sun goes down.

USE TIPS: Input capacity should approximate maximum output of solar panels—an 8-amp charge controller, for example, can accommodate three 3-amp panels.

BUYING TIPS: If you are serious about solar and have multiple panels, this safety device makes sense. Otherwise, a single low-power panel will not overwhelm your batteries.

GALVANIC ISOLATOR

DESCRIPTION: Diode or multiple diodes mounted in an aluminum housing, about 5" × 4".

USE: To prevent galvanic corrosion by blocking any stray current that may be flowing between the AC ground and the DC bonding system.

USE TIPS: The isolator only works if no piece of AC equipment is grounded to any bonding circuit or DC ground circuit. Installed on the incoming AC power connection, an isolator will protect against current leaks originating ashore or from other boats, but will not impede—and may aggravate—current leaks emanating from within the hull.

BUYING TIPS: The best protection against stray currents is a properly wired and bonded boat.

ELECTRICAL ACCESSORIES

ABOUT MARINE WIRE

Wire is what distributes electrical current from a power source to the various appliances and lights on a boat. The size and material of a wire determines the current it can safely carry. For marine purposes wire should be multistrand copper. Thickness of a wire is denoted by its American Wire Gauge (AWG) number: the smaller the number, the thicker the wire. Length also affects resistance and the tendency to build up heat to hazardous levels. As a general rule, thicker and shorter is best for boat wiring. Size also affects the performance of your equipment, with electronics and running lights being especially sensitive. Color coding helps professionals and amateurs keep things straight. American Boat and Yacht Council (ABYC) guidelines for DC systems less than 50 volts call for red wires for hot (positive) circuits, either black or white for the return (negative) circuit, and green for bonding circuits. There are other color-coding standards as well. The ABYC *Safety Standards for Small Craft* and the National Fire Protection Association *National Electric Code* are the two main sets of standards for wiring small boats. They should be consulted by anyone contemplating doing their own wiring work.

MARINE ELECTRICAL WIRE

ALSO KNOWN AS: Primary wire

DESCRIPTION: Single conductor multistrand 12-volt copper wire, preferably tin-plated, that is jacketed in various insulating materials, including most commonly PVC, as well as polyethylene, butyl rubber, nylon, or neoprene (see Appendix A). Rated by AWG gauge numbers 8–16, which covers most marine 12-volt uses. Sold by the foot, in 8'–25' mini-spools, or 100' spools.

USE: To supply electricity from a power source (distribution panel, junction box, etc.) to lights or electrical equipment and back via the ground wire from the equipment.

USE TIPS: Follow manufacturer's advice or consult an AWG chart to determine the gauge of wire you require for the equipment in question, the amount of power being carried, and the distance of the wire run required (you must account for a round trip when measuring distance). The goal is to choose wire that will keep voltage drop within 3%.

BUYING TIPS: Premium wire pays for itself in performance and safety. Buy only UL-approved marine-grade, fully-tinned Type III (Class K) strand, which is corrosion-resistant and flexible (much of this information should be printed on the outer jacket). Also be sure the wire is properly colored for the job at hand.

MARINE DUPLEX WIRE

ALSO KNOWN AS: Two-conductor wire

DESCRIPTION: Essentially two primary wires separately insulated but joined in a single exterior sheath for added insulation and protection from oil, grease, etc. Same specs as for primary wire.

USE: Since equipment requires two wires—one positive and one negative—this is a convenient means of running both in a single jacket.

USE TIPS: Preferable means of wiring when long wire runs are involved. For wiring in the vicinity of sensitive devices, such as compasses, ABYC recommends *shielded twisted pair wire,* which is insulated with copper for minimal interference.

BUYING TIPS: This looks like household appliance wiring, but it is not. Be sure it meets marine specifications.

TRIPLEX WIRE

ALSO KNOWN AS: Three-conductor wire

DESCRIPTION: Unlike DC circuits, which require a positive and negative wire for each piece of equipment to be powered, AC circuits require a third grounding conductor or ground wire. Sold in 100' spools or by the foot.

USE: To power AC appliances either from shore-power or a boat's alternator.

USE TIPS: AC wiring has its own color coding: *green* for the grounding conductor or ground wire, *white* for the neutral wire or grounded conductor, and (this can be confusing) either *black* or *red* for the ungrounded conductor or hot wire. ABYC standards insist that an AC system be polarized—one in which the hot and neutral wires are connected in the same way for all devices in a circuit. AC receptacles will generally indicate the proper terminal for each wire by indicating, for example, G for the green wire, W for the white.

BUYING TIPS: Get only the best marine-grade, tin-coated multistrand wire.

Wire Markers

ALSO KNOWN AS: Wire labels

DESCRIPTION: Adhesive-backed letters and numbers that come in sheets or a "book."

USE: To identify the various wire runs in a boat, which can easily total 1,000' in a boat 30' or longer. Use them to identify use, whether a wire is negative or positive, and the voltage that it is carrying. Peel markers off and wrap them around a wire near the terminal and at several stages along the way.

USE TIPS: For easy reading, wrap them around once and stick the ends together—just as manufacturers do on various appliances you buy. For further identification keep a diagram and written record of the various circuits on your boat, especially if you have transgressed the color-coding standards in some instances.

BUYING TIPS: If you do not find them in a marine store, try an electrical supply store.

Solderless Terminal

ALSO KNOWN AS: Connector, lug

DESCRIPTION: Tin-plated copper connector made in various shapes and sizes with a shank that can be crimped (usually double-crimped) onto the end of a wire.

TYPES:

spade terminal   ring terminal

disconnect

Spade terminal: U-shaped terminal with two projection arms, upcurved slightly at the ends in the case of a *flanged spade terminal.*

Ring terminal: Connector, often with a nylon-covered base, with an enclosed ring at one end.

Hook terminal: Connector with semicircular end that can be slipped around a retaining screw.

Disconnect (Also Known As *spade lug, multistack connector, braised seam disconnect, flat connector, solderless connector*): Male and female terminals that connect by inserting the male side (flat spade) into the female side (with flanges that have been bent around 180° to receive and hold the male part). Can be disconnected easily.

USE: To crimp onto a wire so that it may be connected to a terminal or junction block. The crimp is then insulated with shrink tubing or other weatherproofing material.

USE TIPS: Tight connections are critical. Match the terminal to the wire size and do not use over-sized terminals. And despite the *solderless* designation, many electricians solder over the crimp for added strength.

BUYING TIPS: Spade and hook lugs make for quicker installation, but a ring terminal by far provides the most secure connection in the bouncing marine environment. Although steel lugs (from the automotive industry) are prevalent, they will not work in the marine environment—use "marine grade" tin-plated copper terminals.

CRIMPACE TOOL

ALSO KNOWN AS: Crimper, crimping tool

DESCRIPTION: Plierslike pressing tool with different-sized notches in jaws to receive various diameter wire. Steel with chrome or black powder finish.

USE: To strip insulation from wire or compress a connection, such as a lug, onto a wire in what is called a solderless connection. A solid, voidless crimp permits easy flowing of current and resists corrosion.

USE TIPS: Do not solder over a crimped connection.

BUYING TIPS: If you want good connections, get a quality crimping tool.

SHRINK TUBING

ALSO KNOWN AS: Heat shrink tubing

DESCRIPTION: Short lengths of tubing made of nylon or similar water-resistant material and lined with a heat-activated adhesive. Commonly sold in 3" lengths (although 12" lengths are available) with diameters of ⅛" to 1" that will shrink to fit most commonly used wire gauges.

USE: Inserted on a wire end before a terminal is crimped on, then slipped over shank and bare wire and heated (you can use a match or cigarette lighter) to provide waterproof insulation for the connection.

USE TIPS: Cut your tubing about 50% longer than the area to be covered to allow for shrinkage. Also useful for exposed connections, such as those on boat trailers.

BUYING TIPS: Shrink tubing lasts longer than electrical or similar insulating tape, which eventually will peel loose.

LIQUID ELECTRICAL TAPE

DESCRIPTION: Fast-drying liquid vinyl polymer that is nonconductive and adheres to metal, plastic, vinyl, rubber, and composite surfaces. Often sold in 4-oz. can with applicator brush. Available as clear liquid or in colors that can be coordinated with the wire it is used on.

USE: To paint over electrical connections to form a waterproof seal.

USE TIPS: Liquid tape was developed for the marine industry and is especially useful in wet areas for such things as bilge pump connections that are exposed to moisture. Also helpful around the home for outdoor or underground wiring connections.

BUYING TIPS: Not as effective as shrink tubing for creating a seal, but better than regular electrical tape, which will unwrap eventually, or the varnish used in earlier days.

Spiral wrap

DESCRIPTION: Black polyethylene tape with UV inhibitors that comes in a coil or spiral. Ranges in size from ¼" to 1" diameter; sold in 5' and 10' rolls.

USE: To bundle up wires for easier routing and to generally keep things neater. Also provides abrasion protection.

USE TIPS: Spiral allows it to be gapped (in a barber-pole pattern) to permit leadouts of terminals where necessary. Leaving gaps also permits you to identify the various wires at different stages along the length of the run.

BUYING TIPS: For the naturally neat; for others the occasional plastic cable tie will do.

Cable tie

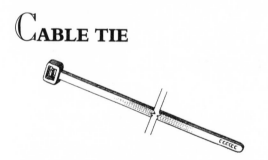

DESCRIPTION: White or black nylon strip 3"–14" in length with locking mechanism similar to a belt buckle at one end. Some have a mounting hole (if not, you can buy an optional cable tie mount (see next item) for affixing the tie to a bulkhead with a #8 fastener. Material is resistant to fuel, acids, and UV rays. Sold in packages of 5 to 100.

USE: To bundle up wires or secure them to a bulkhead or other surface.

USE TIPS: Quickest and easiest way to organize wire runs.

BUYING TIPS: Buy a pack of at least twenty-five—you will always find uses for ties aboard a boat.

Cable tie mount

DESCRIPTION: Square plastic device about ½" square with two raised loops and central screw hole.

USE: To provide secure mount for cable tie. Fasten mount to bulkhead or other surface with a screw, then thread cable or wire tie through the loops. Proceed as usual with cable tie.

USE TIPS: Install every 2' to minimize sagging and vibration.

BUYING TIPS: Sold in twenty-five-piece packs.

Cable clamp

ALSO KNOWN AS: Cable clip, line support clip

DESCRIPTION: Nylon or rubber and aluminum clip with holes punched at the two open ends for mounting. A clamp may range in diameter from ⅛" to 1½" and is sold in multiples of six to one hundred.

USE: To hold and support electrical cables or wire bundles. Some experts recommend mounting a support to a rigid surface every 18" along a wire run. Helpful for securing wires leading to a distribution panel; install a cable clamp (to a bulkhead) several inches from the end of the wire to ensure that tugging or jostling does not pull the connection loose.

USE TIPS: Excellent means of supporting and bundling (without obscuring) single or multiple wires.

BUYING TIPS: Provides more secure mounting than a cable tie. The rubber-lined clamps are for especially sensitive wire or locations where vibration or flexing may be a problem.

WIRING GROMMET

DESCRIPTION: Small rubber or vinyl grommet (eyelet or collar) that ranges in hole diameter from ¼" to ⅞". Sold in packets of five or ten.

USE: Inserted in a panel hole to protect wires passing through it from abrasion.

USE TIPS: Good idea in the turbulent marine environment.

BUYING TIPS: Check your panel and wire dimensions to be sure you get the proper size grommets.

ABOUT CONTROL PANELS

A control/distribution panel provides a safe central mounting location for the various equipment—switches, circuit breakers, use lights—that control the distribution of electricity throughout the boat. The panel should be conveniently located, easy to reach, preferably at eye level, but also out of the weather. It should not be located on a bulkhead fronting a fuel or engine compartment. Electrical systems have a way of growing on boats; if your control panel starts to become a jumble, it may be best to start all over and replace it with a larger central junction that can accommodate the new circuits.

DISTRIBUTION PANEL AND BREAKER

ALSO KNOWN AS: Control panel/circuit breaker, master panel

DESCRIPTION: Combination control panel and circuit breaker. A panel is wired to accept multiple circuits, which are led to switches via a *bus bar,* a brass plate with screws that is wired to the main power source. It also contains magnetic circuit breakers— one for each lead coming in— which open at a preset amperage level, usually slightly above the current for which a circuit is rated. Panels and breakers can handle AC or DC service or both and usually are set up for varying amp levels—5 amps, 10 amps, 15 amps, and so on. A panel cover is corrosion-resistant aluminum, often black anodized aluminum, and measures about 5¼" × 7½" × 2½" for a typical eight- or nine-switch panel. A distribution panel might have lights to show whether a various circuit is on and gauges that monitor various system functions, such as amps and volts. Most have space alongside each switch for a preprinted identifying label, which are often included or can be bought separately. This is also the location for your main battery switch, which controls the DC power (see page 217). All switches installed should be of the ignition-protected, nonsparking variety.

USE: To provide a convenient central location for the switches that control the flow of current for a boat's various circuits; the circuit breakers interrupt the flow of current in the event of overload or short circuit, preventing damage to equipment and possible fire.

USE TIPS: Even a smaller boat with a relatively simple, single 12-volt system is better off with a central distribution panel. The combination switch/circuit breaker panel also provides automatic overload protection for each circuit, which is what you want, and breakers, unlike fuses, do not need replacement.

BUYING TIPS: Better to buy a panel with room for a few extra circuits so that you or the boat's next owner have room to expand without adding another panel.

FUSE PANEL

ALSO KNOWN AS: Fuse holder panel/fuse block

DESCRIPTION: Molded plastic board measuring that is fitted with brass fuse clips. Ranges in size from 3" × 3⅓" for a two-fuse panel to 9" × 3" for a twelve-fuse panel. Rated for 20 amps at 12 volts; accepts ¼" × 1¼" fuses. Also available in modular blocks that can be snapped together to create a custom fuse panel.

USE: Similar to a circuit breaker panel, except that replaceable fuses instead of circuit breakers protect against current overload or short circuits.

USE TIPS: As with a household fuse box, you should not try to circumvent the system by installing higher-rated fuses than called for, especially if one has already blown. Replacement fuse holders are available if needed. Also fuse holders and fuse tips should be checked regularly for signs of corrosion.

BUYING TIPS: Fuse holders are cheaper than circuit breakers and may do the job for simple systems. Just be sure to buy extra fuses. Also, check the finish work for uniformity and precision—there are some inferior knockoffs on the market.

IN-LINE FUSE HOLDER

ALSO KNOWN AS: Fuse connector

DESCRIPTION: Molded plastic twist-together capsule that is sized to take a standard marine fuse. Rated for 20 or 30 amps that typically are fitted with 4½" wire leads of 12-gauge and 10-gauge respectively.

USE: Installed in-line to hold a fuse that will interrupt current flow to an appliance in the event of a circuit overload or short circuit.

USE TIPS: Remember that an in-line fuse only protects a single item of equipment and not any other that may be on the same circuit.

BUYING TIPS: Not necessary if you have a central circuit breaker or fuse panel; some manufacturers include in-line fuse holders with a piece of equipment, in which case you should check the connection for corrosion periodically and also keep spare fuses in reserve.

TERMINAL BLOCK

ALSO KNOWN AS: Hot feed terminal block, bus bar

DESCRIPTION: Junction center for a boat's electrical circuits consisting of an insulating base often made of plastic or Bakelite™, brass screws, and a brass plate known as a bus bar. A four-terminal block might measure 4" × ⅝".

USE: To connect leads along the hot, or positive, line of a typical two-wire marine electrical system. (The hot feed is the wire that carries the juice to lights and appliances; the second insulated wire leads to ground, usually from a negative bus bar in the distribution panel and thence to a common ground, such as the engine block.) Connecting a lead to the bus bar ties it in with the main power source.

USE TIPS: A terminal block can be a useful adjunct to a distribution panel by minimizing the number of wires being fed into a central point—multiple wires for running lights, for example, could be directed to the terminal block and a single wire run from there to the main panel. (Of course this arrangement means that everything on that circuit goes on when the switch at the main panel is tripped.)

BUYING TIPS: Combination terminal/fuse blocks are available and a good idea for those whose wiring needs are simple and do not require a master panel.

DC CONNECTOR

ALSO KNOWN AS: Molded round connector, flat connector

DESCRIPTION: Two- and four-pole connectors for 6-volt, 12-volt, and 24-volt circuits.

TYPES:

molded round connector

Molded round connector: Polarized two- and four-pole connector with insulated body (Bakelite™, plastic, or rubber) and brass contacts. Some have insulated copper wire leads, 6" long. Often waterproof.

Flat connector: Small, flat rectangular connectors with 2, 3, or 4 poles for 18-gauge wire.

USE: In-line connections—and disconnections—for 6-, 12-, and 24-volt systems. Flat connectors are often used for trailer power hookups and other low-amperage jobs.

USE TIPS: A connector/disconnector should be installed in the wire leading to each piece of 12-volt equipment. Disconnecting equipment during an electrical storm is the surest way to protect it in case of a strike.

BUYING TIPS: Flat connectors are a bit cheaper and fine for temporary duties such as supplying power to a boat trailer. So-called butt connectors and wire screws, although available to marine buyers, are not recommended for use on boats. And wires should never be twisted together and taped with electrical tape.

GROUNDING SHOE

ALSO KNOWN AS: Ground, bonding plate

DESCRIPTION: Bar-shaped plates of various makes and sizes that are usually made of a sintered porous bronze matrix (*sintered* means "formed into a shape by heating but not to the point of melting"). Size ranges from 6" × 2" × ½", which provides an area of 12 sq. ft. and is referred to as "standard," to 18" × 6" × ½" for an area of 100 sq. ft.

USE: To direct stray currents and (theoretically) lightning strikes away from a boat's electrical system and electronics into the ground (water), minimizing damage to equipment, hull, and people.

USE TIPS: Recent University of Florida studies have shown that a grounding system, contrary to folklore, does not encourage lightning strikes. At the same time, a properly grounded boat is less likely to sustain severe damage than an unprotected boat in the event of a strike.

BUYING TIPS: Follow manufacturer's recommendation as to the proper size ground for a given piece of equipment or function: for example, a minimum of 12 sq. ft. is recommended for lightning protection, 40 sq. ft. to ground a loran set. However, there is little evidence that a porous ground shoe is any more effective a ground than a simple copper grounding strap run fore and aft along the bottom of the hull.

GROUNDING STRAP

DESCRIPTION: Tin-plated copper strap 2" wide × 25' long sold in 10' and 25' lengths.

USE: To connect electronic gear to a grounding plate for increased performance and lightning protection.

USE TIPS: The strap does not provide enough area to serve as a ground in itself; it must be attached to a grounding plate or shoe.

BUYING TIPS: In lieu of a grounding strap, copper wire (at least #4 and not the smaller diameter #8 recommended by some authorities) may be used as the ground connector.

Switch

DESCRIPTION: Lever-type device that functions by interrupting—and reconnecting—electrical flow. Marine switches are made of corrosion-resistant materials, such as nylon, plastic, stainless steel, or combinations of same. The other crucial consideration is that marine switches be spark-free. Some switches have small lights to indicate a circuit is on. A switch may be rated for anywhere from 5 to 25 amps at 12 volts.

TYPES:

Toggle switch: Familar switch with a projecting lever that engages a toggle joint with a spring to open or close a circuit. May be two-way (on-off) or three-way. Often stainless steel body, but sometimes made of nylon.

Push-pull switch: Another common marine switch, this has a lever, usually with a knob at the end, that opens a circuit when it is pulled out. Often three-way.

Push-button switch: A simple on-off switch that opens a circuit when the button or knob is depressed.

Rocker switch: Switch with a broad lever that operates side-to-side and is usually housed in a nonmetallic—plastic or nylon—housing with brass innards. One model, a "lighted" rocker switch, has a built-in indicator light.

rocker switch

USE: To turn one or more electrical circuits on or off by making or breaking a connection.

USE TIPS: A waterproof switch, in which the switch mechanism is encased in thermoplastic plastic or rubber, is best for wet locations—cockpits, center consoles, etc. Just be certain the wire leads have been covered and waterproofed. Further protect them when not in use by covering them with waterproof rubber or plastic caps designed for toggle and push-button switches.

BUYING TIPS: Which switch is a matter of personal preference, as long as it is rated for marine use; three-way push-pull and toggles are popular because of their multiple functions. Be sure to locate them, especially the push-pull type, out of the way where they will not be bumped accidentally.

Momentary Push-Button Switch

ALSO KNOWN AS: On-off switch, push-button switch

DESCRIPTION: Depress button to activate electrical device.

USE: To make a brief or temporary signal via a horn or light.

USE TIPS: Helpful for switching on a masthead floodlight to illuminate your sail briefly for others to see at night.

BUYING TIPS: As with all electrical devices onboard your boat, make sure you buy only ignition-protected equipment, which means that the housing prevents sparks from entering the atmosphere, possibly igniting gas fumes that may be present.

— SHORE POWER AND ACCESSORIES —

ABOUT BUILDING A SHORE POWER SYSTEM

AC (alternating current) power onboard can come from three main sources—a generator, an inverter, or via a cord plugged into a shore power outlet. Generators, or gensets as they are often called, are bulky and usually found only on larger boats (their noise also makes them inconvenient for regular use at the dock). Inverters, which translate DC battery power to AC, take a toll on marine batteries. For many the outlet at the dock is the main provider of AC power. Most boats and marinas are wired for 30-amp, 125-volt current. Marinas also offer 15-, 20-, and even 50-amp power, but, to be safe, the average boater should use a 30-amp shore-power cord and inlet and add an adapter for other available amperages. Amperage and volts should be marked on dockside connections. Aside from plugs and adapters, there are a number of accessories that make tapping into landside power possible. Fortunately for compatibility the companies that make marine cords and plugs also make accessories. Bigger boats that require 250-volt power need 50-amp equipment. Just be sure all your components are UL listed and designed specifically for marine use.

CORDSET

ALSO KNOWN AS: Shore-power cord.

DESCRIPTION: 10-gauge, 3-wire conductor wire with molded vinyl covers (often yellow) and rated at 30 amps and 110, 115, or 125 volts. Fitted

with one male and one female plug. Sold in standard lengths of 12', 25', and 50'. Many come with 5-year warranty. Also available in 115-volt, 50-amp version.

USE: To connect boat's electrical system to shoreside power.

USE TIPS: Always turn off the breaker switch on your boat's main service panel before plugging in. Plug one end into boat's electrical receptacle first, then hook up to the dock outlet (flip that off first, too, if a switch is available). Give dockside end a clockwise twist to lock plug in for a secure connection.

BUYING TIPS: What will you do when the dock outlet is 25' 1" away? Bite the bullet and get the 50' cord.

BULK SHORE-POWER CABLE

DESCRIPTION: Yellow 3-wire cord (12-gauge for 20-amp use, 10-gauge for 30 amps) with oil-resistant PVC cover. Good for indoor/outdoor use.

USE: To customize your shore-power cable with respect to length or plug type.

USE TIPS: Remember that AC color coding differs from DC. Specifically the hot wire in AC coding is either red or black (black is the ground wire in a DC system).

BUYING TIPS: Sold by the foot. Get the 30-amp version.

Marine Extension Cord

DESCRIPTION: 15-amp, 125-volt three-wire (copper) 14-gauge cord with weather-resistant vinyl cover. Sold in 20' and 40' lengths.

USE: To serve various electrical uses in and around a boat.

USE TIPS: For safety's sake install a ground-fault circuit interrupter (see page 224) when working around water.

BUYING TIPS: There's always use for an extension cord, especially when hauled out.

Plugs

ALSO KNOWN AS: Connectors

DESCRIPTION: End piece on wire that either is inserted into an outlet (male) or serves as an outlet (female). Plugs are rated in amps. Male plugs come with two or three prongs, either straight (most two-bladed plugs) or locking, with one or more of the prongs having a flange at the end that can be turned (clockwise) in the appropriate female receptacle.

TYPES:

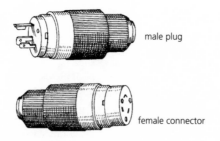

male plug

female connector

Male plug: Plug with two or three prongs.

Female connector: Plug with two or three slots or receptacles.

USE: Male plug inserts into receptacle (outlet) to obtain electrical power for whatever it is connected to. Female plug (receptacle) receives male plug to provide the power. Also used to combine two lengths of electrical cord.

USE TIPS: Try to match male and female plugs—two-prong to two-slots, or three to three (locking plugs will fit standard receptacles and vice versa).

BUYING TIPS: Use waterproof, marine-grade plugs and receptacles for any application around water. Locking plugs are best because of the added protection against coming loose.

One-Piece Cordset Adapter

ALSO KNOWN AS: Outlet adapter

DESCRIPTION: 5½" plug with male and female ends of different amp size—15 amp to 30 amp, 20 amp to 15 amp, etc. Comes in both straight-blade and locking-blade versions.

TYPES:

Standard adapter: Adapter that is not water-resistant and therefore of dubious use in a marine environment.

Water-resistant adapter: Same as above but has waterproof cover and sealing collar.

USE: To adapt your cordset to an outlet of different amperage.

USE TIPS: Can also be used to plug a power tool, such as a drill, directly into an outlet without pulling out the whole cordset.

BUYING TIPS: For those who visit many different marinas. If you need one, spend the few extra dollars and get a water-resistant adapter.

Pigtail Adapter

DESCRIPTION: Short cord (20") with different size male and female plugs.

USE: Same as cordset adapter, but cord gives more flexibility and length.

USE TIPS: Pigtail has cover and sealing collar so that it may be used in wet locations.

BUYING TIPS: Flexible cord makes it more useful than one-piece adapter.

Pigtail

ALSO KNOWN AS: Adapter blank

DESCRIPTION: 15-amp cord, about 20" long, with one blank end and one with either male or female 15-amp plug. Also available in 50-amp version. Both versions have sealing collar.

USE: To adapt 15-amp system to 20- or 30-amp system (or 50-amp to 30-amp), either boat-to-shore or vice versa.

USE TIPS: Two-way capability allows you to step up or down; 15 amps will allow you to run most power tools.

BUYING TIPS: Only necessary if a regular pigtail adapter will not do the job (or you have an extra plug around).

Y-Adapter

DESCRIPTION: Y-shaped cord with one male end and two female receptacles. Comes in both 30-amp, 125-volt and 50-amp, 125/250-volt versions. All have covers and sealing collars.

USE: To give you two boat connections from single shore outlet.

USE TIPS: You can only get the amount of amps the shore outlet is rated for.

BUYING TIPS: Most Y-adapters are rated for 50 amps—for bigger boats that require more power.

Reverse Y-Adapter

DESCRIPTION: Y-cord with special circuit at junction of stem and branches.

USE: To prevent reverse polarity by blocking current flow from outlet until both plugs are properly inserted into a boat's inlet; to prevent blades on an unconnected plug from becoming "hot."

USE TIPS: For use when drawing from two 30-amp shore outlets into 50-amp boat system.

BUYING TIPS: Expensive, but can save a life as well as your electrics.

Y-Adapter Blank

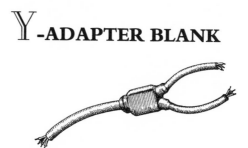

ALSO KNOWN AS: 50-amp Y-blank

DESCRIPTION: Y-shaped cord with three empty stripped ends. Main trunk 6-gauge with four conductor leads; two branches are 10-gauge with three conductor leads.

USE: To create a customized Y-adapter.

USE TIPS: Using a Y to draw from two shoreside outlets can cause dangerous current overload.

BUYING TIPS: Primarily for larger boats using 50-amp power.

Sealing Collar

sealing collar with ring

DESCRIPTION: Plastic collar with threaded Lexan™ ring for tightening.

USE: To create positive, moisture-proof connection between cordset and adapter or cordsets in series on 20-amp and 30-amp systems. Threaded ring alone is used with 50 amps.

USE TIPS: Excellent means of protecting temporary connections from dampness.

BUYING TIPS: Because the marine environment is inherently wet, you should have one for every connection.

Male Cover Without Ring

ALSO KNOWN AS: Watertight cover

DESCRIPTION: Yellow bullet-shaped ribbed vinyl casing, 5½" long, without a sealing ring. Sized for 20-amp/30-amp, or 50-amp connections.

USE: To slip over male plug and coverless female connector to seal against moisture.

USE TIPS: Should be used for all but the most temporary of connections.

BUYING TIPS: Keep a spare for nonadapter hookups.

Female Cover With Ring

ALSO KNOWN AS: Watertight cover

DESCRIPTION: Bullet-shaped ribbed yellow vinyl covering with a threaded ring of Lexan™ on wide end. Sized for 20-amp/30-amp or 50-amp systems.

USE: To slip over female connector to protect against moisture.

USE TIPS: Use in lieu of threaded ring on nonadapter connections.

BUYING TIPS: Keep a spare for nonadapter situations.

Hinged Cap Boat Inlet

ALSO KNOWN AS: Threaded boat inlet

DESCRIPTION: 30-amp, 125-volt, three-pronged outlet box (or receptacle), measuring about

3" × 3½". Made of either 316 stainless steel or Valox® polyester resin interior with steel trim. Square or round hinged snap-up cover and bezel holds incoming female connector (some steel inlets have polycarbonate cap insert). Certain models have screw-on cap for extra moisture protection when not in use. 50-amp, 125/250-volt inlets are made of

316 stainless steel. Mounts to hull with four screws or bolts (not included). Most have rear safety enclosure.

USE: To provide connection point on boat for threaded shore-power cordset.

USE TIPS: 50-amp, 250-volt connections needed only to power large appliances, such as clothes dryers or electric ranges.

BUYING TIPS: Polycarbonate cap insert solves thread-corrosion problem on stainless-steel inlets.

ELECTRICAL DECK ACCESSORIES

WATERPROOF DECK PLUG AND SOCKET

ALSO KNOWN AS:
Electrical connector

DESCRIPTION: Chrome-plated brass deck fitting consisting of base, two-pronged plug, and screw-on cap. Stands 2⅜" off the deck.

USE: To provide on-deck source of 12-volt power.

USE TIPS: Although the plug is watertight, keep the cap on when not in use for extra moisture protection.

BUYING TIPS: Handy source of power for where it is not possible or practical to plug into a cigarette lighter outlet.

USE: Gaining extra length from a 12-volt power source, such as a cigarette lighter outlet. Often used with spotlights.

USE TIPS: Also useful for such things as vacuuming your car.

BUYING TIPS: Coiled cord stores more compactly and is less likely to tangle.

DUAL OUTLET CORD

DESCRIPTION: Pigtail 12-volt cord about 10" long with one male plug and two female connections. Some versions include a 10-amp fuse.

USE: To provide two outlets from one 12-volt source, such as a cigarette lighter.

USE TIPS: Twice the outlets means twice the drain; be careful not to run down your battery.

BUYING TIPS: If you want one, get one with the built-in fuse to prevent overload.

12-VOLT CORD

ALSO KNOWN AS: Outlet cord, extension cord

DESCRIPTION: Two-conductor 16-gauge multistrand copper wire in a plastic or rubber insulating jacket. Sold in 6', 8', and 12' lengths, either straight or coiled.

CHAPTER TEN

REFRIGERATION, HEATING, COOLING, VENTILATION, AND PLUMBING SYSTEMS

REFRIGERATION AND
AIR-CONDITIONING

ABOUT REFRIGERATION AND COOLING

Boat refrigeration is one of those areas that is in flux because of changing environmental laws. The most common refrigerant, R–12, also known as Freon™, is a chlorofluorocarbon whose production will eventually be banned. Refrigeration units now cooled with Freon still should provide years of use, and it now appears that the existing systems can be recharged with HFC 134a, the most popular replacement refrigerant. (R–22, the refrigerant used in airconditioning, is an HFC and relatively "ozone-friendly," and should be around for some time.) The compressor that pressurizes the liquid refrigerant is either water-cooled or air-cooled. Water-cooled systems (seawater is the source) are twenty-five times or so more efficient than air systems but are more complicated and prone to breakdowns. Boaters in tropical climates should consider the water-cooled models, while those in cooler environments can make do with the simpler, and cheaper, air-cooled units.

Air-conditioning on boats is taking the path of the automobile world: Once considered a luxury, air conditioners now are becoming almost standard equipment on boats in tropical waters. While manufacturers have made it relatively easy to retrofit boats with air conditioners powerful enough to make life belowdecks bearable, installation still involves careful placement of the air-conditioning unit, the creation of a system of ducts and vents, which requires cutting holes in bulkheads, and the installing of through-hull fittings to serve as intake and discharge for water-cooled systems. Because all air conditioners run on AC current, they require either shore power or a generator with enough capacity to run the system. These considerations make it advisable to enlist the services of a professional if you decide to retrofit.

REFRIGERATOR/ FREEZER

ALSO KNOWN AS: Icebox

DESCRIPTION: Small refrigerators ranging in capacity from about 1.5 cu. ft. to over 6 cu. ft. and in size from 17" × 21" × 21" for smaller models to 23" × 52" × 23" for the largest. Many marine models switch automatically from AC to DC power when a shoreside connection is broken and vice versa. Some combination refrigerator/freezers offer little more than an ice tray, others genuine, if small, freezer compartments. The less freezing, the less power drain. Drain ranges from about 3.4 amps to 6 amps on DC, less on AC.

USE: To keep food and beverages cold.

USE TIPS: Refrigerators are a constant power drain, always a concern on a boat. Minimize drain by keeping your unit as small as you can and by minimizing freezer size. Most weekend boaters can carry extra ice in a cooler or other container.

BUYING TIPS: Aside from the AC/DC feature, refrigerators built specifically for the marine market are made of corrosion-resistant materials (such as marine-grade stainless steel) and are equipped with compressors that can take the pounding and heeling (up to 30°) of a boat at sea.

ICEBOX CONVERSION KIT

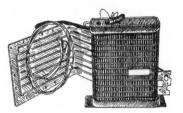

DESCRIPTION: Sealed compressor unit made of aluminum and copper with stainless-steel fasteners. Will switch automatically to AC or DC power. Some include wiring, refrigerant tubing (often in an L-shaped aluminum panel), and hardware. Some models must be hooked to a battery charger (see page 218) to operate, some not. Different kits for boxes up to 6 cu. ft. and 9 cu. ft. or more. Draws maximum of 2-plus amps while cycling, 5-plus while operating, and will create temperatures from 35° to 40° if the box is well insulated.

USE: To convert a nonrefrigerated icebox to a refrigerator.

USE TIPS: Do-it-yourselfers may want to read up on refrigeration first. Nigel Calder's *Refrigeration for Pleasure Boats* is one helpful source.

BUYING TIPS: Kit is for converting larger iceboxes to refrigerators. If you can get by with a smaller refrigerator, it is cheaper and easier to buy a marine refrigerator.

PORTABLE REFRIGERATOR

DESCRIPTION: Smaller totable refrigerator usually made of polyethylene and with AC/DC power capability; top-loading, with a sealed compressor. Size ranges from 24" X 13" X 12" to 25" X 18" X

14" with an average capacity of 1.4 cu. ft. Most consume a fair amount of energy for their size—from 3.5 to 5.5 amps DC. Some models have removable trays, and many include a power cord for shore power.

USE: Same as larger installed refrigerators, but capable of being carried to and from the boat.

USE TIPS: Portables are not designed for constant exposure to the marine environment, so do not leave them aboard for long periods.

BUYING TIPS: Get the smallest version you will require; it will consume less electricity and be easier to carry. Some larger models weigh close to 60 lbs. and can pack up to 75 lbs.—stretching the definition of "portable."

AUTOMATIC ICE MAKER

DESCRIPTION: Freezer box of various designs that, for the time being, uses pressurized Freon® 12 to create temperatures below the freezing point of water. A typical marine freezer has an insulated polyethylene case, about 2' X 1', sometimes with a stainless-steel front. Powered by 12-volt DC, 115-volt or 120-volt AC; some models are AC/DC. Sold both as freestanding and permanently installed units.

USE: To convert water to ice—anywhere from 22 to 30 lbs. per day.

USE TIPS: If you have the room, a built-in model will serve you best.

BUYING TIPS: Remember the Dudley Moore line to a nondrinker? "Oh, so you never have to worry about running out of ice." Only fishermen and larger yachts with dedicated cocktail drinkers really need an ice maker; others can pack ice in a cooler and get by.

THERMOELECTRIC COOLER/WARMER

DESCRIPTION: Combination cooler/warmer that chills air to 40° below ambient air temperature and can warm interior to 155°. Polyethylene case with ABS plastic lining measures approximately 21" × 16" × 15" and has interior capacity of 1.2 cu. ft. or 36 qts. Includes cigarette-lighter plug for DC power (drawing about 4 amps) and can be hooked to AC power with a converter. Some models can be used horizontally or stood upright like a mini-refrigerator.

USE: To keep food and beverages cool without packing ice, or to warm foods to some degree.

USE TIPS: Better for cooling than for warming; at 155° it would take some time (and lots of amps) for food to "cook."

BUYING TIPS: Useful for those who have a long drive to their boat from home—just plug into your vehicle's cigarette lighter and keep things cool as you drive to the shore. Others may find a traditional ice-packed cooler does the job just as well.

MARINE COOLER

ALSO KNOWN AS: Marine ice chest

DESCRIPTION: Insulated coolers of various makes and sizes from 25-qt. to about 160-qt. capacity, measuring from 11" × 20" × 13" to 19" × 44" × 21". UV-resistant polypropylene casing with seamless ABS plastic interior liner and foam insulation. Equipped with drains, locking latches, and removable food trays. One has a fish scale on the lid for fishermen to measure keepers.

USE: To keep small, medium, and fairly large quantities of food, fish, bait, and drink cool.

USE TIPS: You might want to install some cleats on your deck or wherever you keep the cooler and secure it with cord.

BUYING TIPS: Other than a fish scale, there is not much to distinguish a marine cooler from any quality coolers designed for outdoor use. Compare prices and shop accordingly.

SOFT-SIDED COOLER

DESCRIPTION: Nylon and vinyl case (similar in size and shape to camera cases) with adjustable carrying strap and zippered lid. Leakproof liners and, on some models, temperature "eye" that displays the inside temperature. Available in 5-qt. (enough room for a six-pack) and 20 qt. sizes.

USE: To keep cool small quantities of food and drink.

USE TIPS: Flexible shape makes a soft-sided cooler especially suited for small boats that do not have sufficient room for a rigid cooler.

BUYING TIPS: As with "marine" coolers, shop around for the best price.

COOLING

AIR CONDITIONER

DESCRIPTION: A refrigeration device that extracts heat from the air in one location and discharges it in another. A typical air conditioner consists of a liquid *refrigerant,* which absorbs heat when it is evaporated; a *compressor* pump, which compresses the refrigerant when it is a gas; an expansion device called a *capillary;* and a pair of heat exchangers, one to absorb heat, the second a *condenser* to transfer it to a cooling flow (usually seawater). Other features include a seawater intake, a filter, a pump to move the cooling seawater through the condenser, and a control to make the whole thing work.

Marine air conditioners range in rated capacity from about 5,000 Btus to just under 20,000 Btus; they range in size from about 12" × 12" × 14" to 20" × 12" × 11" and in weight from 50 to 85 lbs. They consume electricity anywhere from 8 amps to 16 amps AC. Some units double as air heaters, either with a separate electric heating element or by reversing function, a process called *reverse cycling.*

TYPES:

Self-contained air conditioner: The standard air conditioner on boats, a single-unit device with factory-sealed refrigerant. Because they produce heat, especially the type with a rotary as opposed to a piston compressor, they are not to be installed in an engine room.

Split-system air conditioner: Not nearly as common as self-contained units, a split-system air conditioner has a separate condenser, which can be located out of the way in the engine compartment. These units must be charged with Freon™ 22, a job that should only be done by a professional.

USE: To cool the ambient temperature of a cabin or cabins by removing heat from the air and discharging it, most often overboard.

USE TIPS: There are various ways to determine the size (in Btus) your boat will require. One way is to calculate the area to be cooled. Cabin area below deck = L × W × H (7' on average) × 14 Btus. Cabin area above deck = L × W × H (7') × 17 Btus. Add the two for total area. Each person in the area will add an average of 500 Btu/hour if sedentary, 800 Btu/hr if active. The more crowded, the more capacity you will require. As outside air and temperatures approach 90°, you may want to move up 2,000 Btus or so to the next size air conditioner.

Some manufacturers tout that their units can be installed either vertically or horizontally; units tend to work more efficiently with the condenser mounted horizontally. If you lay up for the winter, be sure the system, especially the condenser, is fully drained to avoid freezing. You may want to add nontoxic antifreeze as well.

BUYING TIPS: Different makes have different features, and manufacturers tend to make conflicting claims. Generally, industry experts recommend units with a piston rather than a rotary compressor, reverse-cycle rather than electrical heating (except when water temperature regulary goes below 40°), and digital as opposed to manual controls (although the old "knob" kind is suitable, especially for smaller units). Shop around and check with owners of various types for their impressions.

PORTABLE AIR CONDITIONER

ALSO KNOWN AS: Carry-on

DESCRIPTION: Smaller air conditioner designed to fit over 12" × 12" hatch. Measures 14" × 15" × 30" and weighs about 60 lbs. Rated at 5,000 Btus with power draw of 5–6 amps at 110-volt AC. Runs off shore power or an inverter.

USE: Portable air conditioner that fits over forward hatch (for example) and does not require permanent installation. Ideal for 20'–30' boats.

USE TIPS: Plugging into a shore outlet (you will need an AC extension cord) is the most efficient way to power one of these units. Even though the most common model has a rotary compressor, its location outside the hull dissipates any heat that is generated.

BUYING TIPS: A portable is a simple cooling alternative for boats in the 20'–30' range that do not require heavy-duty cooling. Although there are even smaller permanent models available, they require all the ductwork and through-hulls of larger units.

HEATING SYSTEMS

ABOUT HEATING

Unlike cooling, which requires electricity, heating can be achieved using a variety of fuels. Many boats that are used during the temperate months will not require any heating, except that created by the galley stove of a morning. (You should never, however, use your galley stove as a cabin heater.) From there you can go up in increments from small heating units to major systems, depending on your needs and your boat's capabilities.

PORTABLE HEATER

ALSO KNOWN AS:
Space heater, cabin heater

alcohol heater

DESCRIPTION: Smaller, nonpermanently mounted heater, either fueled or electric, that produces a maximum of between 5,000 and 9,000 Btus, depending on the fuel, available in a variety of designs.

TYPES:

Electric heater: Cleanest of the portables because it does not burn fuel and compact—about 12" × 12" × 6". May be cylindrical, square, or rectangular in shape and made of aluminum, plastic, or ceramic. Often rated in watts (1,500 watts equals about 5,000 Btus), an electric heater can draw as high as 15 amps at full power, which may be too much for some marinas. At least one marine model, designed differently from the type used in homes, has a low setting that prevents freezing in the bilge.

Alcohol heater: Alcohol "pots," as they are sometimes called, measure about 12" × 12" × 11" and can produce over 6,000 Btus. These operate on the same alcohol that fuels many galley stoves, which can get expensive for long-term heating. One popular model doubles as a small cooking stove when its dome top is removed.

Kerosene heater: A kerosene space heater produces much heat—between 6,000 and 9,000 Btus—fairly cheaply, but its large wick must be adjusted periodically for clean burning. Some models are top-heavy and are a hazard if burning while a boat is under way.

Catalytic heater: A form of propane heater, catalytic heaters produce heat by combining propane and oxygen in the presence of a catalytic agent, usually platinum. A catalytic heater typically produces about 7,000 Btus at the maximum setting, consuming most of the fuel, which reduces carbon monoxide concerns. Because they require attaching to a propane tank, catalytic models are not as "portable" as other portables.

USE: To warm small spaces in cold weather or, in milder climes, take the chill out of a larger space, such as the main cabin.

USE TIPS: Electric heater requires adequate onboard wiring, a circuit breaker, and a ground-fault circuit interrupter (see page 224) in the event of a short. They also require shore power. Fueled heaters should be properly vented, and catalytic heaters should also be equipped with an automatic shut-off in case there is a propane leak.

BUYING TIPS: Portables are an excellent source of heat for many boaters—all except those in the coldest zones or who live aboard their boats. Choice comes down to personal preference and what fuel you use for other purposes.

PERMANENT HEATER

ALSO KNOWN AS: Furnace, stove, cabin heater, radiant heater

DESCRIPTION: Larger fixed, nonelectric heater of various designs and shapes, often tied

diesel/kerosene heater

into a ventilation system. Commonly fueled by propane, kerosene, or diesel fuel and found in a variety of designs.

TYPES:

Propane heater: Available in wide variety of designs with a heat output of between 7,000 and 10,000

Btus. A propane heater is convenient for those whose galley stove is propane fired. Good for occasional use but expensive for constant heating. Propane is clean-burning, but the gas is explosive and can create carbon monoxide problems.

Diesel/kerosene heater: Diesel heaters come in many designs and are popular with sailors because many carry diesel auxiliaries and have a ready and cheap source of fuel, which can be fed to the heater via an electric fuel pump and then gravity-fed into the stove. Fuel is fed into a combustion "pot" with either a manual or a float-controlled valve, the latter of which will automatically shut down if the fire dies. Average output of 6,000–10,000 Btus, but some models produce as many as 15,000 or more. Kerosene heaters are often the choice of those whose stoves and lamps are fueled with kerosene. Most kerosene heaters are pressurized and require frequent pumping of a pressure tank.

Solid-fuel heater: Stainless-steel heater typically measuring 16" × 1" × 8" for a freestanding model (there are also flush-mount fireplace versions, which are less efficient) and fueled by either charcoal, wood, artificial logs, or other solid fuels. Produces up to 10,000 Btus, but also lots of smoke, so the on-deck stack, fed by a 3"-diameter flue, should be positioned accordingly.

USE: To keep a boat warm in cold-weather climates and for all-season heating for liveaboards.

USE TIPS: Permanent heaters require exhaust ventilators, which also serve to remove water vapor from the cabin—a major source of "chill" on a boat.

BUYING TIPS: Most boaters go with a fuel they already use, whether propane for the stove or diesel for the auxiliary engine. Diesel is the most economical, while propane ignites more easily. Of the solid fuels, charcoal burns most cleanly but can be difficult to get started.

HEATING ACCESSORIES

PRESSURIZED FUEL TANK

DESCRIPTION: 2-gal. cylindrical tank measuring 15" tall and 8" in diameter and made of welded steel that has been primed and painted for weatherproofing. Equipped with pressure gauge and connection for ¼" fuel line with female fittings.

USE: To store diesel, kerosene, or alcohol to fuel a cabin heater.

USE TIPS: Easily pressurized with a bicycle pump.

BUYING TIPS: Most useful with portable propane heaters, which consume much fuel. Diesel heaters are best fed from the engine fuel tank.

EXHAUST VENTILATOR

ALSO KNOWN AS: Charlie Noble, smokehead

DESCRIPTION: Stainless steel pipe-shaped vent with a square top; measures about 12" tall with a 3" diameter. Does not include a deck cap.

USE: To vent exhaust gases and stale air from cabin.

USE TIPS: Best used in mild breezes. Should be removed when the wind pipes up.

BUYING TIPS: When installing, you might want to match your Charlie Noble to a 3"-diameter stovepipe adapter.

STOVEPIPE

DESCRIPTION: Stainless steel piping measuring 3" diameter and sold in 2' lengths, either straight or with slight elbow.

USE: To vent hot air, gases, and water vapor from a cabin heater. Connects from heater to outside vent or pipe. Also for extending the height of the "chimney" on deck for better draft.

USE TIPS: Be sure to position a stovepipe so that the gases do not reenter the boat via a porthole or intake valve.

BUYING TIPS: Buy marine-grade stainless steel, never galvanized steel.

STOVEPIPE ADAPTER

ALSO KNOWN AS: Deck iron with ring.

DESCRIPTION: Stainless steel or chromed bronze tubing 3" in diameter with 7"-diameter flange on the bottom; stands 6½" high.

USE: To rout a heater stovepipe to on-deck smokestack, and also to insulate the deck from heat. The ring seals the exit hole.

USE TIPS: Ring should be bedded with sealant for waterproof fit; do not bend the ring to fit the deck contour while installing.

BUYING TIPS: Plastic deck rings are for regular air vents and *not* for insulating hot stove exhausts.

VENTILATION

ABOUT VENTILATION

"In with the good air, out with the bad" is a good maxim to keep in mind for both physical fitness and boat ventilation. But adequate ventilation of your boat's cabin has more benefits than just making life onboard more comfortable. A strong flow of air down below is the number-one weapon against rot, mold, and mildew, all of which thrive in warm, damp places that are not exposed to sunlight. In addition the combination of gasoline fumes and the natural funk of fiberglass is often enough to make boaters seasick.

Ventilation can be accomplished in a number of passive and active ways, the simplest of which is leaving portlights and hatches open, an option only when you are onboard. Then there is also the simple cowl-style vent resembling a hooded cobra extending its neck above the deck (see page 252). Cowl vents are sometimes mounted on dorade boxes containing baffles to keep water from going below.

Wind activates spinning turban vents set in place when boats are at anchor, while sunlight powers low-profile, highly effective solar vents. Bilge blowers and engine-compartment vents, as well as galley and head exhausts, are powered by the boat's 12-volt DC system for most reliable results, although simple louvered vents are effective when the boat is moving. Regardless of how the vent is powered, though, good vent designs include baffles, a cover, or some other means of keeping water out while letting air in.

The Coast Guard requires that engine compartments for gas-powered boats, as well as areas where gasoline fuel tanks and batteries are housed, be mechanically ventilated to the outside, with fresh air replacing compartment air to prevent the buildup of explosive fumes. To meet Coast Guard requirements, boatbuilders must install at least two scooplike vents for the engine compartment, but four vents, one exhaust and one intake per side, is more typical. Exhaust ducts are always mounted facing aft, astern of intake ducts, to prevent fumes from reentering the boat. Intake vents face forward. This safety regulation accomplishes a practical goal as well, since engines run better when compartment temperatures are reduced.

SOLAR VENT

ALSO KNOWN AS: Solar-powered vent, sun vent

DESCRIPTION: Low (less than 2" high) profile 7"-diameter vent with clear plastic dome top and frosted polycarbonate or stainless steel cover. Interchangeable plastic fan blades are turned by small solar motor run off of a rechargeable nicad battery. Requires a 3¾" cutout. Inboard sleeve has damper cover with handle.

USE: To install in cabin roof to improve cabin ventilation; blades can be changed for either exhaust or intake. When solar receptor is exposed to sunlight even on moderately cloudy days, the solar vent will spin, moving about 850 cu. ft. of air per hour at optimum operating levels. Rechargeable battery stores enough solar energy to run for about 48 hours without additional sunlight.

USE TIPS: This is a great product that really works, but solar vents are somewhat fragile and may break if tripped over or if a sheet gets fouled on them.

BUYING TIPS: Plastic version costs a few dollars less than its stainless steel counterpart.

Passive Ventilator

ALSO KNOWN AS: Mushroom ventilator

DESCRIPTION: Resembles miniature flying saucer, a resemblance more noticeable with the stainless steel version than with the white plastic style. Passive vents are 6"–8" diameter and have domed lids that spin or snap up, still parallel with the deck, to allow air through.

USE: Rely upon boat movement or natural wind movement for air to scoop into these vents. Lid can be pressed down when ventilation is not needed or if mosquitoes and other pests are coming in the cabin.

USE TIPS: Vents should be installed with matching trim rings to ensure a tight fit and keep water out.

BUYING TIPS: Passive or not, these vents can move 500–1,000 cu. ft. of air per hour in a breeze and make life below much more bearable.

Deck Plate

ALSO KNOWN AS: Twist-and-lock or screw-in deck plate, snap-in or pry-up deck plate, inspection port

DESCRIPTION: Sleeve with predrilled flange is 4"–10"-diameter ID, extends 1" deep. Comes with fitted cover. White or black polypropylene.

TYPES:

Snap-in deck plate: Cover pops into place with slight pressure, easy to pry out with a knife, screwdriver, or your fingers, thanks to pry notch cut into rim of sleeve.

snap-in deck plate

Screw-in deck plate: Cover has threads around portion extending into sleeve, which has corresponding threads. Lid surface has finger recesses or slots for deck plate key.

USE: Sleeves fit many plastic cowl-style vents (see below), so you can "move" ventilation where you want it to go. Plates also serve as inspection ports (lids may even be "clear") in decks adjacent to hard-to-reach engine equipment or fuel tanks.

USE TIPS: Cowl vents should be removed and deck plates inserted during winter layup and at the approach of a major storm. Plastic deck plates are not reliable for those uses.

BUYING TIPS: Very inexpensive.

Vent

ALSO KNOWN AS: Cowl vent, dorade (not technically correct)

DESCRIPTION: Upright hood or low-profile scoop on predrilled base for mounting flush or perpendicular to mounting surface. Upright vents usually require a deck cutout of 3" or 4" diameter. Made of plastic or PVC (usually treated to resist UV damage), bronze, or chrome-plated brass.

TYPES:

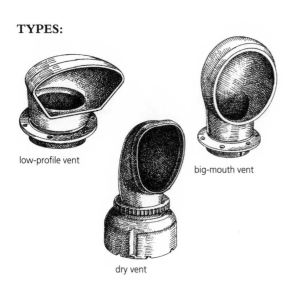

low-profile vent

big-mouth vent

dry vent

Low-profile vent: Curved rectangular hood on low arch base. Rises about 5" from deck surface. Similar in shape to surface-mounted vent (see this page) but raised above deck surface.

Big-mouth vent: Upright arched hood with 3"-diameter opening × 9" high, 3½"-diameter deck cutout.

Dry vent (Also Known As *water trap vent*): From the outside this looks like any other cowl-style vent. Inside, however, are two baffles to keep water from pouring in down below. Small drainage openings above lower baffle allow water to leak out.

USE: To flush out fumes and stale interior air and bring in fresh air from outside. Mount exhaust vents facing aft and intake vents facing forward.

USE TIPS: Position cowl-style vents so that they do not scoop up spray. These vents may be matched with deck plates (see page 252). Mount on dorade boxes (see page 255) to prevent spray from entering cabin (dry vents have their own dorade box in their bases).

BUYING TIPS: Great cheap ventilation for any boat. Some models include deck plate and have optional insect screen inserts.

CLAMSHELL VENT

ALSO KNOWN AS: Clamshell

DESCRIPTION: Flush-mounted, slightly raised scoop made of chrome-plated brass, stainless steel, or PVC. Vent does not have a sleeve that extends into deck opening. Sizes range from small metal (1½" long × 1⅝" wide × 7/16" high) to large plastic (7" long × 5½" wide × 3" high).

USE: To bring air into engine compartment, lazarette, or locker. Low profile keeps vent from interfering with lines. Usually installed over screened opening, but make sure hull or deck cutout is properly sealed. Mount exhaust vents facing aft and intake vents facing forward.

USE TIPS: Be sure to position so that you do not scoop up spray along with air. Do not install plastic vents on hull sides, since they are less durable than metal and are bound to be damaged by docks and pilings.

BUYING TIPS: Plastic vents cost less than metal ones.

SURFACE-MOUNT COWL VENT

ALSO KNOWN AS: Cowl vent

DESCRIPTION: Resemblance to clamshell vent is only skin deep. Although this vent has a low-profile scoop, it also has a sleeve extending down through the deck and can be fitted to ventilation hose (see page 257) to the engine compartment, for example. Chrome-plated die-cast zinc with black plastic base and sleeve.

USE: Face mounting aft on deck or over the hull side adjacent to engine compartment for exhaust, forward for clean-air intake.

USE TIPS: Follow boat-safety standards for installing engine-compartment ventilation. Vent hoses should be securely clamped onto the vent sleeve.

BUYING TIPS: Sold with three predrilled holes for mounting, but you supply the #8 fasteners.

LOUVERED VENT

DESCRIPTION: Rectangular panel of stainless steel sheet as large as 12" long × 4½" wide. Slots are cut and bent up from the sheet to form vent scoops and may be positioned so that they are vertical or horizontal on the vent plate. Mounting holes drilled around the perimeter. Lacks backing panel found on Venturi vent.

USE: Engine-compartment ventilation equipment, down-facing horizontal styles are usually installed inboard, where they will not catch spray, while vertical styles are sometimes mounted on the hull side, opening aft.

USE TIPS: Follow boat safety standards for installing engine-compartment ventilation. Vent hoses should be securely clamped onto the vent sleeve.

BUYING TIPS: Gives a lower-profile, sportier look (especially on powerboats) than the surface-mount cowl vent.

VENTURI VENT

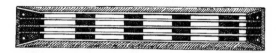

ALSO KNOWN AS: Louvered vent

DESCRIPTION: Outward appearance is similar to louvered vent, but there is a backing panel with small openings behind the vent fins. ABS plastic will accommodate 3" or 4" ventilation systems. Less than an inch high, 17" long × 2½" wide.

USE: Air rushing out through the small openings speeds up when it reaches "freedom" at the louvers. This triggers a vacuumlike chain reaction of augmented air flow, a real boon to ventilation in the engine compartment and other areas around the boat.

USE TIPS: Flexible plastic conforms well to highly contoured boats.

BUYING TIPS: Plastic Venturi or stainless louvered vent? It's as much a choice of aesthetics as performance.

VIEW VENT LOUVER KIT

DESCRIPTION: Exterior resembles stainless-steel louvered vent, but is made of clear, smoked, or tinted Plexiglas. Kit includes screen to be sandwiched between outer louvers, "teak look" interior trim, and installation template. Vent measures 15" long × 9" wide, projects out nearly 2", requires 14" long × 7" wide cutout.

USE: Besides allowing air to circulate in and out without allowing water to enter, the view vent also lets in a bit of light.

USE TIPS: Do not install in a location where the vent could get kicked or fouled in rigging. It will get broken.

BUYING TIPS: Good for sailboats, where lack of light and a view out can be a problem.

Dorade box

ALSO KNOWN AS: Dorade

DESCRIPTION: Sturdy teak box, like a shoebox in size and shape, that opens downward and has a series of internal baffles (see cutaway drawing).

USE: Mount open end of box over vent hole cut in cabin roof or deck, cut 3" or 4" circle at opposite end and side of box to mount a cowl-style vent (see

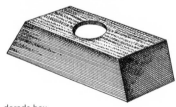

dorade box

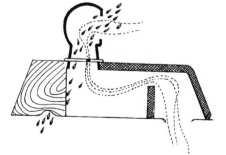

dorade box with vent (cutaway view)

page 252). Air can circulate through vent and through baffle passages, but water cannot.

USE TIPS: Sturdy, but do not use for mounting hardware such as cleats.

BUYING TIPS: A less expensive alternative to the dorade-box-and-vent combo would be to use a cowl vent with built-in baffles, but it looks good on traditional-design boats.

Cabin vent trim ring

DESCRIPTION: Predrilled white plastic 3" or 4" ID sleeve with flange. Also, flat teak ring about 1" wide with 3"- or 4"-diameter cutout. Trim rings may be fitted with insect screening.

USE: Use either plastic ring alone or in combination with teak ring to finish-trim deck plate entry holes in cabin.

USE TIPS: Provides the desired finished look to any cut-through.

BUYING TIPS: Neither component is particularly expensive.

Spacer ring

DESCRIPTION: Compressible white vinyl ring with 3" or 4" ID.

USE: To serve as padding between plastic deck plate ring and trim ring.

USE TIPS: Okay to drill through spacer ring when installing deck plate with sheet-metal screws. Glue spacer ring to underside of deck plate for a more watertight installation.

BUYING TIPS: Fairly expensive, considering what you are buying. The alternative, however, is a leak through the deck plate ring.

PROTECTIVE RING

DESCRIPTION: Pliable soft white nylon ring, with 3" or 4" ID.

USE: To give finished look to inboard edge of deck plate ring when installed on a hatch.

USE TIPS: Also "softens the blow" if you hit your head against the deck plate ring from down below.

BUYING TIPS: About the same price as the spacer ring (above).

FAN

ALSO KNOWN AS: Cabin fan, circulating fan

DESCRIPTION: Three to six blades radiate from a central 12-volt DC- or battery-run motor, usually installed inside 6"–7"-diameter plastic-coated wire cage or behind 7" long × 5" wide louvered plastic

folding cabin fan

panel, although some models have soft blades and do not need protective housings. Fans are mounted in stand-up swiveling brackets.

USE: To circulate as much as 100 cu. ft. of air per minute. May oscillate while running or can be locked in one position. For interior use only.

USE TIPS: Do not use in bilge or engine compartment; model may not be ignition-protected. Battery-operated version can be plugged into cigarette lighter.

BUYING TIPS: Don't expect air-conditioning with one of these little fans; the semblance of a breeze may be more cooling to your psyche than to your body.

THROUGH-DECK HOSE FITTING

DESCRIPTION: Flanged plastic or stainless steel sleeve mounts flush on deck or bulkhead surface, extends through surface several inches with fitting for 3" or 4" hose.

USE: To hold ventilation hose (see page 257) securely to deck or bulkhead and present a finished ring on exterior surface.

USE TIPS: Requires either a 3¾" or 4¾" cutout, so plan accordingly.

BUYING TIPS: As with wiring, if you run hose through a bulkhead or deck, there should be a rigid fitting to prevent chafe or twisting.

Ventilation Hose for Bilges

DESCRIPTION: Paper-thin fire-retardant plastic hose, white or black, 3" or 4" diameter, supported by internal wire spiral bonded to hose material. Extremely flexible, it does not collapse easily.

USE: Large diameter helps move large volumes of air into or out of the engine compartment, bilge, head, and galley areas. Be sure that hose extends below level of carburetor, but not so low that it extends into the area where bilgewater might accumulate.

USE TIPS: Only for ventilation use. Do not stretch when installing, as flexibility is a virtue.

BUYING TIPS: Inexpensive, sold by the foot.

Hose Adapter

DESCRIPTION: Sleeve extension that fits into mounting-plate end of upright- or surface-mount cowl vents.

USE: To convert vent into a vent hose receptor.

USE TIPS: Works on mounting surfaces only up to 1" thick.

BUYING TIPS: Allows for more precise ventilation, but certain adapters only work with certain brand vents; check before you buy.

Locker Vent

DESCRIPTION: Round, oval, rectangular, or square stainless steel or chrome-plated brass palm-sized plates with a regular pattern of slots cut through, but with no raised scoops, as with louvered vent.

USE: To ventilate lockers, cupboards, or closets in protected areas where rain and spray are not a problem.

USE TIPS: Predrilled holes make mount easy.

BUYING TIPS: Closets can get nasty fast in the damp, lightless environment down below. If you don't want to install a vent, at least drop in a reusable dehumidifier (see page 258) that contains a desiccant.

Bilge Blower

ALSO KNOWN AS: Bilge fan

DESCRIPTION: "Squirrel cage" fan run by 12-volt DC motor inside high-impact plastic housing. May have fixed flanged or flexible mount. Two 3" or 4" outlets extend on either side of blower motor for connection to ventilation hose.

USE: Mechanical means of ventilation for engine compartment, bilge, or fuel tank area. In compliance with Coast Guard safety regulations, blower motor, like all other electrical components in the engine area, must be ignition-protected so that no stray sparks leak outside housing to ignite gas fumes.

USE TIPS: To clear engine compartment of lingering fumes and to prevent their being ignited by sparks when the engine is started, run the bilge blower for 15 minutes prior to startup (less if you know your boat and there is no odor of gasoline). You can install a plastic placard at the helm station to remind you of this procedure.

BUYING TIPS: Not an option but rather a legal requirement and a lifesaver.

AIR QUALITY AND COOLING SYSTEMS

OZONE GENERATOR

ALSO KNOWN AS: Ozonator

DESCRIPTION: Small, boxed electronic fan and device that runs on 110 AC current (no 12-volt version available yet), so you must have access to shore power. Consumes about as much electricity as a 60-watt light bulb. Ionizer sparking device.

USE: Removing mildew and the musty smell that develops in a closed-up belowdecks. Run it for several hours before layup and again in the spring to get rid of winter odors and replace them with a "forest after a rainstorm" odor. However, too much "rain forest" and you probably should lower the setting, especially if you intend to remain onboard. Ozone, despite its cleansing properties, can irritate the respiratory system.

USE TIPS: Also effective for killing viruses and bacteria and useful at home as an air purifier.

BUYING TIPS: The machine, while very expensive (at least several hundred dollars), is more effective than other means (calcium chloride crystals, warming rods) at controlling mildew. Available in several sizes, but the smallest versions are sufficient for boat use.

WARMING ROD

ALSO KNOWN AS: Heating rod, thermoelectric dehumidifier

DESCRIPTION: Golden-colored aluminum rod with attached cord that plugs into 110-volt AC power. Sold in four sizes, 12", 18", 24", and 36" long, rated to heat to 110° and warm from 100 cu. ft. to 500 cu. ft. Plastic mounting brackets included.

USE: To retard mildew growth by warming the air.

USE TIPS: Not for heavy-duty warming. Must be mounted horizontally and indoors.

BUYING TIPS: Handy for owners of smaller boats without sophisticated electrical systems and who have access to shore power.

REUSABLE DEHUMIDIFIER

ALSO KNOWN AS: Desiccant dehumidifier

DESCRIPTION: Passive dehumidifier of several designs, including a plastic box filled with calcium chloride cystals and a two-part plastic bowl in which crystals are placed in the ventilated top half, which drains into the bottom half for emptying. Crystals are refillable.

USE: To control dampness by removing moisture from the air.

USE TIPS: Handy for small spaces such as compartments.

BUYING TIPS: Not terribly effective, but it is cheap and does not use electricity.

PLUMBING SYSTEMS

ABOUT MARINE SANITATION DEVICES

Growing awareness of the need to preserve the environment and protect water quality have led to federal, state, and local regulations addressing the discharge of all kinds of waste, including sewage. Although recreational vessels are not required to be equipped with toilet facilities—a head, in nautical parlance—if a head *is* installed, it must be equipped with an operable Marine Sanitation Device (MSD) that meets U.S. Coast Guard requirements that went into effect January 30, 1980. Discharge of raw sewage from a vessel in U.S. territorial waters (the 3-mile limit) is illegal.

MSDs treat sewage chemically so that it can either be discharged safely into the water or be stored in an onboard holding tank until a suitable pump-out station (sometimes called a reception facility) is located. Some busy harbors actually have floating pump-out barges. Pump-out facilities are few and far between in many parts of the country, so if you are cruising away from home, you might want to check cruising guides or boating almanacs for lists of stations.

There are three types of MSDs:

Type I devices treat sewage with disinfectant chemicals to achieve a safe level of bacteria content before waste is released. Waste must not show any visible floating solids, according to Coast Guard standards.

Type II devices are similar treat-and-discharge systems, but they must meet a higher level of sewage treatment. Type IIs are generally larger in size than Type Is and are therefore usually only found on larger recreational boats.

Type III MSDs are so-called "holding-tank systems" because they meet the Coast Guard's no-discharge standard. These devices treat waste with chemical disinfectants and deodorants before it is collected in the holding tank. Even so, disagreeable odors are a common problem. There are also Type III systems that involve recirculation of liquids collected or incineration of wastes. These latter methods are quite expensive to purchase and maintain, but probably give the best results in terms of aesthetics.

Although the Coast Guard regs do not stipulate what kind of MSD must be installed on your boat, all boaters must observe "No-Discharge Zone" restrictions in areas that have been declared to require greater environmental protection. These areas include freshwater lakes, reservoirs, and rivers not capable of interstate vessel traffic, as well as areas closed to discharge via cooperative agreements between state governments and the federal Environmental Protection Agency (EPA). The EPA has approved No-Discharge Zones in California, Connecticut, Massachusetts, Michigan, Minnesota, Mississippi, New Hampshire, New Mexico, New York, Texas, Vermont, and Wisconsin, and the list is growing. Eventually, more likely sooner than later, most coastal and inland waters will be declared no-discharge. It has been determined that even discharge of treated sewage could be harmful to these waters. Boating-law authorities in each state can advise boaters on discharge restrictions.

When operating in a No-Discharge Zone, Type I and Type II MSDs must be actively secured against discharge via padlock or wire tie on the seacock handle. The Coast Guard says that locking the door to the head is an acceptable alternative!

Manual AND ELECTRIC HEAD

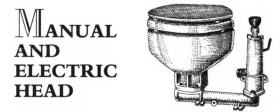

ALSO KNOWN AS: Toilet, marine toilet, head

DESCRIPTION: Toilet connected to waste-treatment system and/or sewage holding tank (see page 263). Fills and flushes with seawater by means of manual pump with level or push-pull handle or by 12-volt DC–powered pump. Vitreous china bowl has neoprene rubber seals and valves as well as stainless steel and bronze hardware.

Bowl may be smaller than that which is typically found in homes, but larger, more commodious versions are available. Pumping systems are usually on right-hand side, but some models can be adapted for left- or right-hand use.

USE: To provide an onboard toilet.

USE TIPS: Observe all U.S. Coast Guard, state, and federal requirements closely when it comes to disposing of sewage (and other) waste (see "About Marine Sanitation Devices," page 259).

If you own an old boat with a marine head that flushes sewage directly into the water, the responsible—and legal—thing to do is to convert to a modern treatment and/or holding tank setup.

Typically this involves a Y-valve, which diverts waste to a holding tank or to a through-hull fitting to the open water only after it has been disinfected and macerated. All hoses should be double-clamped. Marine heads are less forgiving of foreign matter and get clogged easily, so be careful what is flushed! Most manufacturers have repair kits containing all the parts most likely to need replacement. Repair is not necessarily difficult, but it may be messy.

An alternative to an installed head is a portable version.

BUYING TIPS: Manual versions cost about a third the price of electric ones, but an electric-head con-

version kit with a motorized base that installs under the bowl converts a manual-flush toilet to a self-priming electric one. A complete head installation includes a sewage-treatment and/or holding tank, which adds to the cost.

Waste TREATMENT SYSTEM

ALSO KNOWN AS: Marine sanitation device, flush-through marine sanitation device, MSD, macerator

DESCRIPTION: Sewage-treatment device runs on 12-volt DC and breaks down solid waste through maceration. Electrodes turn saltwater into hypochlorous acid that acts as a disinfectant. System treats up to 2½ gal. between discharges. Includes intake and discharge hoses, 16" long × 9" wide × 13" high treatment unit, 4" wide × 7" high × 3" deep control unit, and 9" wide × 6" high × 9" deep salt-treatment tank.

USE: To disinfect solid and liquid sewage.

USE TIPS: Meets current U.S. Coast Guard requirements for Type I marine sanitation devices.

BUYING TIPS: Handy for larger vessels and those going offshore, but if no-discharge becomes universal, your treated water, even though it meets or exceeds EPA standards, may not be disposed of overboard and you will have an expensive white elephant on your hands.

Portable HEAD

ALSO KNOWN AS: Porta Potti, camping toilet

DESCRIPTION: Boxlike toilet and waste tank (capacity 2½–6 gal.) combination slightly larger than 1 cu. ft. Some models include freshwater tank for manual pump flushing; others have electric pumps and flush mechanisms powered by 4 C batteries.

USE: To provide an onboard toilet.

USE TIPS: Suitable for small boats without separate head compartments or for when you are traveling in waters where discharge is prohibited. Limited holding-tank capacity makes portable heads unsuitable for extended cruising, unless onshore discharge facilities are available.

BUYING TIPS: Good value for small boats. Remember, if you don't have a marine head, you don't need a holding tank. Better yet, day sailors should make use of shoreside facilities before shipping out.

Head Chemicals

ALSO KNOWN AS: Deodorant, lubricant, disinfectant

DESCRIPTION: A variety of chemicals in liquid, powder, and granule form designed to keep marine heads operating smoothly and without offensive odors.

USE: To add to holding tank or treatment system or to flush directly through toilet, depending upon product and its function.

USE TIPS: Read manufacturers' labels carefully.

BUYING TIPS: Life onboard quickly becomes unbearable without these inexpensive treatments.

Marine-Grade Toilet Tissue

ALSO KNOWN AS: Toilet paper

DESCRIPTION: Familiar roll of two-ply tissue.

USE: Disintegrates quickly, won't clog discharge lines.

USE TIPS: Some Captain Blighs have been known to discourage clogging by refusing to issue marine toilet paper at all. They may be on to something.

BUYING TIPS: About twice the price of household toilet tissue, but worth it.

Marine Electric Hot-Water Heater

DESCRIPTION: Stainless steel or glass-lined 4- to 20-gal., pressure-resistant tank enclosed in fiberglass-lined stainless steel housing. Brass inlet with check valve, thermostat, and 110-volt AC 1,500-watt brass heating element (can be rewired for 220-volt AC). Some models have heat exchangers. Propane-fired models are also available.

USE: To heat fresh water for bathing, washing, and laundry.

USE TIPS: Larger boats may need more than one heater. Ideally the heater is located in a sealed compartment that does not vent into the head or any living area, but that is often not the case. Because of the danger of CO poisoning, any area containing the heater must be properly vented, and if possible, open a port as well.

BUYING TIPS: Choose a heater with controls and water connections all on one side for easier servicing and maintenance.

Shower

DESCRIPTION: Fixed or handheld hose-and-nozzle system for spraying freshwater. May be connected to boat's pressurized water system or to manually operated pump. *Hand shower* has adjustable nozzle on the end of a 40"-long flexible hose, with bracket for holding nozzle against shower stall or bulkhead. *Pressurized shower system* installs on transom or gunwale in a covered compartment and includes hot- and cold-water control knobs. A variation is the *power shower* combining a small 12-volt DC pump (plugs into cigarette lighter) and feed hose to freshwater source. An ingenious gravity-fed system consists of a 1- to 6-gal. heavy-gauge vinyl *shower bag* with hanger and discharge hose. Filled with freshwater and hung in the sun, the water quickly heats up to provide water as hot as 100° within a few hours on a 70° day. A popular accessory is a hanging vinyl enclosure for deck-top privacy.

USE: Bathing. *Shower bag* can also be used to hold drinking water.

USE TIPS: Large boats may have heads roomy enough for a shower enclosure, but showering on smaller boats could mean a setup on deck. Square nylon hanging shower encloser provides privacy on deck.

BUYING TIPS: Bathing onboard, particularly on a cruise or when you have been swimming, is both a luxury and a necessity. Shower systems that rely on the sun are very inexpensive and require a minimum of setup. More sophisticated systems command higher prices and fancier plumbing. Get whatever you can afford.

FLUSH-MOUNT SHOWER DRAIN

ALSO KNOWN AS: Shower drain

DESCRIPTION: Reinforced plastic fitting similar in appearance to through-hull fitting, with barbed end that accommodates 1½" ID hose. Screw-down locknut holds drain grid in place.

USE: Drain outlet for shower water. Install at lowest point of shower stall or shower pan; attach to drain hose.

USE TIPS: This is not strong enough to be used as a through-hull fitting (see page 270).

BUYING TIPS: Drain may be included in shower-stall setup.

PUMPS

FOOT PUMP

DESCRIPTION: Horizontal black synthetic rubber bellows with foot pad on top, mounted on white nylon base with inlet and outlet barbs, rated at about 45 gph, measures 5½" long × 4" wide × 3" high. Another version, with foot pedal extending from a vertical black rubber bellows, rated at about 180 gph, measures 8" long × 5" wide × 6" high.

Both pumps have ½" hosing fittings and are self-priming.

USE: Pumping water to galley and head sinks with foot power. Foot-pedal version is more efficient because it pumps on both the down and the up strokes.

USE TIPS: Both pumps have mounting bases for through-bolting to the cabin sole.

BUYING TIPS: Repair kits are available for both pumps.

Tank

ALSO KNOWN AS: Water tank, water jug, holding tank, waste tank

DESCRIPTION: Leak-proof container made of polyethylene, PVC, or similar material with capacity from 3 gal. up to 42 gal.

TYPES:

Rigid tank: Best bet for permanent installation because solid molded tanks won't leak, crack, or impart chemicals or noticeable taste to drinking water. Sold with ready-made fittings.

Flexible tank: PVC or Hypalon-type flexible bags range in size from about 14 to 37 gal. Lighter than polyethylene tanks, flexibles are suited for installation in small boats or boats that must be retrofitted. Installation can be tricky—you must install your own hardware. Better suited for drinking water than waste, PVC tanks still produce an unpleasant taste when new and should be thoroughly flushed with water and a baking-soda solution.

USE: To store drinking water or discharge from marine sanitation device (see page 260).

USE TIPS: Water left in tanks on boats used only on weekends can be a prime medium for bacterial growth. It is common practice to add 1 tsp.–1 tbsp. household chlorine bleach for each gallon of water in the tank. The water can be dechlorinated by boiling it for a short length of time—a minute or so—to evaporate out all the bleach or by running it through a charcoal filter (see page 185).

Leaving unattended waste in a hot environment is asking for trouble. However, the source of unpleasant odors may be the fitting and permeable soft hoses and not the tank itself. Because even the best hoses are permeable to some degree, manufacturers suggest installing rigid PVC sections in areas where odors are especially likely, attaching your regular hose with the appropriate fitting.

When installing any type of tank on your boat, be aware that when it is full, it will add a considerable amount of ballast to that part of the boat. For example, water weighs 8.3 lbs. per gal., so a full 25-gal. tank will weigh 200 lbs. One way to offset the ballast effect is to locate the tank opposite to where another heavy component—perhaps even another water tank—is located on the boat.

BUYING TIPS: Be sure to use water-tank fittings that will not corrode.

ABOUT BILGE PUMPS

All boats collect a certain amount of water and other liquids, including engine fluids, in the bilge as a result of spray, rain, and stuffing box or even hull leaks. On smaller boats, such as dinghies or inflatables, bilgewater can be handled with a scoop bailer—a gallon milk or water bottle with the bottom cut off is an efficient, flexible, inexpensive tool. Bailers are not a viable tool for larger boats, which should be equipped with at least one manual pump or an automatic one run off the boat's 12-volt DC system. A better idea is to have several pumps placed throughout the bilge to handle water buildups in specific areas or to serve as backup.

Most bilge pumps are activated automatically by adjustable, buoyant switch levers that float up when bilgewater levels rise and by manual switches located at the helm station or fuse panel. Inside the top of the plastic pump housing is a 12-volt DC motor, with a shaft-driven impeller for moving water in the lower section. Small intake ports keep most debris out. Some pumps use a diaphragm pump.

Whether you are away from your boat for a long time or just a few hours, be sure that the battery has a good charge so that the pump will operate when it is needed. If you have a "To Do" plaque mounted near the companionway (a good idea), make sure one item is to turn the bilge-pump switch on before leaving the boat. Know that when water in the bilge rises high enough to short out the battery, bilge pumps will no longer function (one reason to keep your batteries elevated).

All hose connections should be double-clamped for safety, and discharge hoses should have a supported raised loop (really an inverted U) to keep water outside of the boat from siphoning in.

Manufacturers rate their pumps in gallons-per-minute (gpm) or gallons-per-hour (gph), according to how much water they move. Take these ratings with a generous pinch of salt, however, because they are achieved under ideal conditions in the laboratory rather than in real-life situations, where the pump may have to fight gravity to lift water through an antisiphon loop or to a through-hull outlet well above the waterline.

Gravity is not the only factor working against pumps. The texture of the inner wall of the discharge hose (corrugated hoses create more friction), the ID of the through-hull fitting (often smaller than the hose ID), and the very real possibility that debris such as wood chips will further clog constricted passages all add to reduced capacity. The bottom line is that normal obstacles—known as static head or friction head—in the bilge discharge path can reduce pump effectiveness to as little as half the manufacturer's rating.

BILGE PUMP

DESCRIPTION: Pumping device consisting of hand plunger with diaphragm or sealed, ignition-protected 12-volt DC motor and impeller-driven or diaphragm suction chamber with male water intake and outlet fittings for ¾" ID hose. Can run dry without damage. Common types are:

TYPES:

Submersible bilge pump: Square or round plastic housing about the size of a quart can of paint. Flanged base for mounting directly in bilge. Impeller system. Advertised flow capacities of 360 to 8,000 gph (see "About Bilge Pumps," page 263).

Dry-mount bilge pump: Slightly larger than submersible, stands on flanged legs above bilgewater level. Diaphragm action. Advertised flow capacities of up to about 2,000 gph.

Manual bilge pump: Resembles large-bore bicycle pump connected to wire-reinforced corrugated discharge hose. Noncorrosive plastic, not meant for use with oil. Larger pumps required fewer strokes to move a gallon of water. For example, a 1¼"-diam-

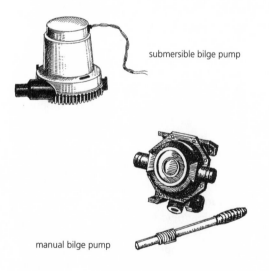

submersible bilge pump

manual bilge pump

eter × 18"-long pump requires ten strokes to lift a gallon of water, while a 1¾"-diameter × 36"-long pump requires only four strokes. It is a good idea to have the handle for at least one manual pump installed in the cockpit near the helm.

Bulkhead pump: Another manual version that features a lever handle attached to a black rubber bellows. Ports for 1" or 1½" ID hose are built into the pump's noncorrosive body, usually made of polypropylene. Can be mounted vertically or horizontally. Highly efficient, moves a great deal of water—as much as 22 gpm—without much effort—as little as 2.8 strokes per gal.

USE: To drain bilge of water in order to keep boat afloat and gear and passengers dry.

USE TIPS: If your bilge floods with gasoline, do not turn on your bilge pump. The risk of fire and explosion is enormous, to say nothing of the environmental impact of spilling gas into the water. The same holds true for pumping out oil. Enlist the services of an expert.

All bilge-hose connections must be double-clamped (see "Stainless Steel Hose Clamp," page 157). Use only hose made specifically for bilge discharge below the waterline. A raised antisiphon loop in the discharge hose prevents water from backing into the bilge from the outside. Mount pumps securely in the lowest part of the bilge.

Bilge-pump maintenance includes a periodic check of the impeller to see that it and the drive shaft move freely. If the pump is not working up to snuff, a clog of debris is the likely culprit. Otherwise malfunctions of the pump motor cannot be repaired, since it is sealed. Keep limber holes in bulkheads and frames clear so that water can drain from all parts of the bilge.

BUYING TIPS: Wide range of styles and prices, with cost usually reflecting quality—beware of cheap knockoffs. When considering pumps, look for one that has an easily removable top for quick cleaning of clogs.

BILGE FILTER

ALSO KNOWN AS: In-line water filter

DESCRIPTION: PVC cylinder, 13" diameter on ring base, has stainless steel lid with ¾" inlet and outlet ports for water. Contains replaceable filter element. Handles discharge water flow rate of from 12 to 60 gpm, depending on filter size, which ranges from 13" to 42" high. Stainless steel mounting bracket is attached.

USE: To remove petroleum products and hydrocarbons from bilgewater before it is discharged.

USE TIPS: Mount securely in the bilge, double-clamping all hose connections. Filter lasts for about a year with normal use. Although filter has obvious environmental benefits, it adds to pump's "head" resistance, cutting down on flow capacity.

BUYING TIPS: These filters do not come cheap, but do work and are the responsible thing to use if your boat is in a no-discharge area or if your engine is notorious for leaking oil.

BILGE PUMP SWITCH

ALSO KNOWN AS: Float switch

DESCRIPTION: 12-volt DC ignition-protected switch activated by a water-level sensor such as a buoyant foam lever. Some of these float-style switches can be wired to an audial and visual alarm device at the helm station. Another type of switch is a remote one located at the helm station, with a toggle switch for automatic and manual operation, as well as "off."

USE: Used in combination with a bilge pump and wired to the boat's 12-volt battery, the bilge pump switch monitors the level of water in the bilge, activating the pump when water reaches a prescribed level. Most switches can be adjusted for various depths of water. Can also be used with a high-bilgewater alert (see below), which lets you know before water reaches a dangerous level.

USE TIPS: To be effective, switch must be securely mounted in the bilge so that it does not float. Keep float levers free of debris.

BUYING TIPS: Remote switch that can be located near your other important switches is the best way to go.

HIGH-BILGEWATER ALERT

ALSO KNOWN AS: Bilge alarm

DESCRIPTION: Kit includes a small, enclosed, round 12-volt DC audial alarm device for helm station and float switch for installation in bilge.

USE: To sound alarm as water level rises.

USE TIPS: Accommodates any number of float switches. Wire alarm/monitor in-line between battery and float switch.

BUYING TIPS: May be easier to use float switch with a built-in alarm.

FRESHWATER PUMP

ALSO KNOWN AS: Galley pump, water pump

DESCRIPTION: Self-priming belt-driven or direct-drive pump with ignition-protected 12-volt DC motor and check valve, as well as ½" NPT male and female fittings. Most can be run dry without damaging pump. A few models can work with either fresh or salt water, and some are reversible. Flow capacity from about 1.5 to over 4 gpm.

USE: To supply water to sinks, galley fixtures, and head fixtures.

USE TIPS: Can be mounted vertically or horizontally on rubber-padded feet.

BUYING TIPS: Each water tank must have its own pump to maintain good pressure.

SHOWER SUMP SYSTEM

ALSO KNOWN AS: Sump pump

DESCRIPTION: 10" long × 7" wide × 5" high noncorrosive housing contains 12-volt DC motor and pump, has outlet fitting for ¾" ID hose and inlet fitting for 1½" ID hose. System includes strainer, hold-down strap and clamps, as well as screws.

USE: Installed in the sump or area where water collects below shower stall or tub drain, this pump moves water from a point below the waterline to the through-hull discharge opening above the waterline.

USE TIPS: Unpleasant odors, mold, and mildew are kept at bay by an efficient sump pump. Double-clamp all hose connections. Use only water hose intended for below-waterline installations. Some general-purpose pumps (see page 264) can be used instead of ones specifically called sump pumps.

BUYING TIPS: Useful for ridding boat of "gray water," but remember that this, too, has been banned in several locations, including Canada, and may become the next target of no-discharge regulations.

WASHDOWN KIT

ALSO KNOWN AS: Deck washdown

DESCRIPTION: Diaphragm pump runs on 12-volt DC and has built-in pressure switch activated or deactivated when spray nozzle is opened or closed. ¾" pipe fittings on pump comes with ⅝" hose adapter for standard garden or washdown hose. Can be run with salt or fresh water. Kit includes pistol-handle spray nozzle.

USE: To hose off your boat or your crew members, even when shore water supply is not available.

USE TIPS: Use with deck or utility hose (see page 282), not included in kit.

BUYING TIPS: Handy for those on extended cruises or who do not have access to dockside hoses.

Bait Tank Pump

ALSO KNOWN AS: General-purpose pump

DESCRIPTION: Self-priming, direct-drive pump operated by sealed, ignition-protected 12-volt DC motor, can be used with salt or fresh water. Flow capacity about 225 gph. Low-profile 9"-long non-corrosive cylindrical housing, ½" threaded inlet and outlet, as well as ½" hose adapter, in-line strainer to keep pump free of weeds and debris.

USE: To circulate water to bait and live wells; use for washdown and sump pump.

USE TIPS: A must for serious fishermen.

BUYING TIPS: Accompanying switch sold separately.

Emergency Safety Pump

ALSO KNOWN AS: ESP℠, emergency pump

DESCRIPTION: Lightweight aluminum pump driven directly by boat's driveshaft.

USE: Under normal, nonemergency conditions, pump draws clean air into engine compartment. Discharge hose can be connected to pump if engine compartment floods. Flow rate far exceeds normal bilge pumps—a whopping 50,000 gph, according to manufacturers.

USE TIPS: Will not harm engine or shaft.

BUYING TIPS: Available in sizes for shafts 1"–1⅞" diameter, 2"–2⅞" diameter, and for shafts over 3" diameter.

Accumulator Tank

ALSO KNOWN AS: Water-pressure regulator

DESCRIPTION: Cylindrical tank at least 9" long × 5" diameter contains diaphragm pump with water-pressure gauge. Some 12-volt DC models may not be ignition-protected and are therefore not suitable for marine use.

USE: To install in waterline between water feed (from dock or "city water") and electrical water pump onboard in order to protect pump from pressure surges.

USE TIPS: Reduces noise besides protecting the pump engine from constant on-off cycling.

BUYING TIPS: Choose an accumulator with a drain plug for easier winterization.

Intake Strainer

ALSO KNOWN AS: Water filter

DESCRIPTION: Filters of various designs including clear plastic bowl 9" high × 7" wide with mounting bracket and 1½" inlet and outlet ports for female pipe fittings. Can be taken apart for cleaning, including filter element.

USE: To strain debris, such as seaweed, trash, or tank residue, from water supply before it reaches your pump.

USE TIPS: Antifreeze suitable for drinking-water systems should not be used with strainer. Use only plastic pipe fittings, and double-clamp all hose connections.

BUYING TIPS: Filters vary in degrees of fineness—what they will strain from the water—so read the manufacturer's specs before buying.

RUBBER-LINED HOSE CLAMP

ALSO KNOWN AS: Insulated strap

DESCRIPTION: C-shaped stainless steel sleeve lined with black rubber, with two extending tabs with bolt holes. With tabs held together the "C" (now an "O"). Ranges in size from 3/16" diameter to 1⅛" diameter.

USE: To support hose, cable, or pipes, while rubber lining protects from chafe and acts as a shock absorber. Screw tabs to bulkhead or other secure surface.

USE TIPS: Space clamps to provide firm support the length of a run; hoses should be as secure as possible from vibration and, because of possible corrosion, should not just be run along the bottom of the bilge.

BUYING TIPS: Sold in boxes of ten of one size.

THROUGH-HULL FITTING LOCKNUT

DESCRIPTION: Familiar hexagonal nut shape has wide flange base. Bronze, most common sizes are for ¾", 1", 1¼", and 1½" fittings; larger and smaller sizes are available.

USE: To thread onto inboard portion of through-hull fitting (see page 270). Wide flange keeps nut from cutting into hull and distributes the stress load over a larger area.

USE TIPS: Use bronze locknut only with bronze through-hull fitting.

BUYING TIPS: Sold individually.

BILGE STRAINER

DESCRIPTION: Plastic strainer resembling a shower head. Male hose fitting inserts into 1" or 1½" ID hose or bilge pump intake port. Contains a non-return check valve.

USE: Placed in the bilge, it keeps large debris, such as wood chips, plastic, and trash, from being sucked into bilge pump while it is operating.

USE TIPS: Easy to clean simply by sweeping away debris (and disposing of it elsewhere).

BUYING TIPS: An extra line of defense if you find your pump getting clogged often—the most common cause of breakdown.

DRAIN ACCESSORIES

BAILER PLUG

ALSO KNOWN AS: Drain plug, bilge plug, garboard drain plug

DESCRIPTION: Plug resembling a bottle stopper with brass or plastic handle and neoprene rubber or plastic seal that is oil- and fuel-resistant. Seal has cam feature or internal expansion nut to maintain a snug fit once plug it in place. Another version is bronze, with a flange with female threads for ½" fitting. Accompanying bronze plug has raised ½ cu. in. head, sometimes with T-handle.

USE: Installed inside a small boat's hull, this device makes it easy to drain spray, rain, or washdown water from the bilge (once the boat is on dry land of course). Bottle-stopper styles are installed near the transom, while bronze flange and plug styles are installed farther forward near the keel. This style is called a garboard drain, referring to the planks or strakes laid closest to the keel on wooden boats.

USE TIPS: Floating bailer plugs can be retrieved if they go over the side, but you may not want to spend time "fishing" if water is coming in through the drain tube. It would be better to have several spare plugs within easy reach.

BUYING TIPS: This is fine for a (very) small boat, such as a sailing dinghy that can easily be retrieved; you really wouldn't want to lose your 30-footer because someone forgot to replace the plug. If you use them, keep some spares on hand.

SEACOCK

ALSO KNOWN AS: Full-flow seacock, ball-valve seacocks

DESCRIPTION: Bronze or plastic (actually reinforced nylon) valve with flanged base and threaded opening for male pipe fittings at both ends. Lever handle controls chrome-plated bronze ball valve with circular opening through it. Handle is in upright position when ball valve opening is in line with fitting orifices and perpendicular when ball valve is in closed position. Thread sizes from ¾" to 1½" meet the needs of most recreational boats, but larger sizes are available.

USE: Installed in the bilge, this valve controls the flow of seawater into the boat for engine cooling or head operation, for example. The valve can be closed quickly if a hose connected to it ruptures or, especially for sailboats under way, to prevent water from backing into the head when the boat is heeling.

A seacock is installed in conjunction with a through-hull fitting (see page 270) of corresponding size inserted through the hull from outside. Both fittings should be adequately bedded with the appropriate polysulfide or polyurethane caulk/sealant (see page 298). A length of noncorrosive pipe should be run up from the seacock to a level above the waterline for connection to a hose. Always double-clamp hose connections.

USE TIPS: Seacock maintenance involves annual inspection for corrosion and other damage, as well as periodic lubrication of the ball valve. Some boat owners swear by bronze seacocks because of their superior strength and longevity. Use reinforced plastic fitting only with a similar through-hull, since the stronger, more rigid bronze version can split the plastic one when they are being tightened. Better, don't use plastic for any through-hull equipment if you can help it.

Do not even think about using a household gate valve or sillcock in place of a marine seacock. Though far less expensive, the valve workings will corrode almost immediately and leave you holding a handle that has simply snapped off the valve.

Likewise do not use an in-line shut-off valve (see page 271) screwed down onto a through-hull in place of a flange-based seacock. Safe installation requires that seacocks be securely mounted to the hull.

BUYING TIPS: Plastic versions are cheaper but not as strong as marine-grade bronze or stainless steel and subject to failure (usually at the arm connecting the lever to the ball valve) within several years.

Through-Hull Fitting

ALSO KNOWN AS: Through-hull, thru-hull

DESCRIPTION: Bronze or reinforced plastic pipe fitting with flange and threaded extension. Sometimes sold with a matching through-hull locknut (see page 268). Pipe sizes range from ¾" OD to 1½" OD, on larger sizes pipe extension long enough to fit through-hulls up to 3" thick.

USE: To insert into bilge from exterior surface of hull to provide a secure attachment point for drains, like seacocks (see page 269). Held in place by locknut or seacock. For safety, through-hulls should connect directly to valves, not hoses, where they enter the hull.

USE TIPS: Use like materials when installing through-hulls to valves (refer to "Seacock, Use Tips" page 269).

BUYING TIPS: Buy only fittings made for marine use.

Emergency Through-Hull Plug

ALSO KNOWN AS: Bung

DESCRIPTION: Truncated cone of soft wood in a variety of sizes from ⁷⁄₁₆" × 1¼" minimum/max-imum diameters up to ⅞" × 1¾" minimum/max-imum diameters.

USE: Quick, temporary stopgap repair for broken hoses, through-hull fittings, and valves. Emergency plugs are required equipment on offshore racing boats.

USE TIPS: Drill a small hole at larger end of plug and attach by tether to through-hull fittings so that plug will always be on hand in an emergency.

BUYING TIPS: Sold individually and in packages of assorted sizes. Failed through-hull fittings and hoses are a major cause of sinkings. Get some plugs.

Scoop Strainer with Through-Hull

ALSO KNOWN AS: Scoop strainer

DESCRIPTION: A bronze or reinforced plastic through-hull fitting with slotted oval or round shield in place of normal flange. Shield measuring 4" long × 3" wide to 6" long × 4" wide resembles masks worn by fencers. Range in size from ¾" to 1½" NPT.

USE: Particularly useful for engine cooling water intake, where the strainer removes large debris such as plastic or seaweed.

USE TIPS: Use like materials when installing through-hulls to valves.

BUYING TIPS: Buy only fittings made for marine use.

PIPE-TO-HOSE ADAPTER

ALSO KNOWN AS: Hose barb

DESCRIPTION: Straight or 90° curved bronze or reinforced plastic fitting with pipe thread at one end and hose barb at the other. Fitting with larger pipe thread end than hose barb end is called a tailpiece.

USE: To provide a secure attachment point for hoses connected to seacock or other pipe fitting.

USE TIPS: Double-clamp all hose connections.

BUYING TIPS: Fitting makes for a stronger connection than just leading hose in.

WATER SYSTEMS ACCESSORIES

IN-LINE SHUT-OFF VALVE

DESCRIPTION: Same ball-valve configuration as bronze or reinforced plastic seacock (see page 269). Most have a flange located on the side of valve, instead of at the base as with a seacock, but some in-line valves have no flange at all. Female pipe threads at both ends range in size from ¾" to 1½".

USE: To provide a shut-off point for water fed to engines or head.

USE TIPS: Mount to a secure base, such as a bulkhead or frame when pipe-to-hose adapter is inserted at either end and hoses are connected.

BUYING TIPS: In-line valves without mounting flanges are less desirable and should be used only when they are in a rigid, hose-free installation where the pipe run is not particularly long.

SCUPPER VALVE ASSEMBLY

ALSO KNOWN AS: Scupper

DESCRIPTION: A deck-level drain with rubber-like one-way flapper or check valve connected to through-hull fitting. Predrilled drain flange, about 3" diameter, may be made of reinforced plastic.

USE: Mounts above the waterline in cockpit to clear away spray or rainwater. If used in below-waterline location, the drain hose must have an antisiphon loop to prevent water from backing up.

USE TIPS: Scuppers are a time-honored way of clearing the decks of water; today's boats tend to be contoured to steer water away from seats and the cockpit floor into one kind of drain or another. Even above the waterline, scuppers can draw water in a following sea, sometimes creating more problems than they solve.

BUYING TIPS: Think about installing one only if cockpit water is a recurring problem.

CLEAR PVC TUBING

DESCRIPTION: Heavy-walled fairly flexible tubing, ⅜" to 1" ID, sometimes reinforced for pressurized water systems up to 60 psi.

USE: PVC is safe for carrying drinking water, but this hose is not intended for connections below the waterline, such as engine water intake.

USE TIPS: Keep a spare length or two around (along with connectors and stainless clamps) for bilge-pump hose replacements or extensions.

BUYING TIPS: Sold by the foot, for a maximum continuous length of 50'.

ENGINE WATER INTAKE HOSE

ALSO KNOWN AS: Intake hose, drain hose, bilge hose

DESCRIPTION: Two-ply hose with helical wire reinforcement and heavy tube cover. Flexible, with good bend radius, this hose is resistant to collapse and degradation from ozone and heat. Sizes from ⅝" ID to 1½" ID.

USE: To carry water to or from the engine cooling system, as well as for all bilge, drain, holding-tank, and sanitation applications.

USE TIPS: Not suitable for drinking water.

BUYING TIPS: Sold by the foot, in lengths up to 12½'.

VENTED LOOP

ALSO KNOWN AS: Antisiphon valve, backflow eliminator.

DESCRIPTION: U-shaped bronze or reinforced plastic fitting with hose barbs at either end and, mid-way, an upright extension containing an air-intake valve. Made to fit ¾" ID to 1½" ID hose.

USE: Install in drain systems, for example, engine water cooling or head, to keep water outside the boat from siphoning back in. Air enters the line when it is not in use, and its pressure keeps water from flowing in. When the drain system is in use, however, the valve closes, preventing air from entering and water from exiting through it.

USE TIPS: Choose a vented loop with mounting flanges for a secure installation, and always double-clamp hose connections.

BUYING TIPS: Plastic loops are only slightly less expensive than bronze ones, but weigh much less, creating less of a strain on the drain system.

BILGE AND LIVE WELL HOSE

ALSO KNOWN AS: Sanitation hose, potable water fill

DESCRIPTION: Flexible black or white hose with corrugations on outside, smooth wall inside. ¾" ID to 1½" ID.

USE: Used for bilge, holding tank, and drain discharge, also suitable for potable water fill. Some types should not be connected to below-waterline fittings; check labeling.

USE TIPS: Some of this stuff is pretty light-duty. You will get better results from the solid-but-still-flexible kind.

BUYING TIPS: Sold by the foot in lengths up to 50'.

CORRUGATED POLY-ETHYLENE BILGE HOSE

ALSO KNOWN AS: Bilge hose

DESCRIPTION: Highly flexible hose with corrugations alternating with smooth cuffs every 12" on outside, smooth wall inside. Resistant to oil, acids, and seawater. Sizes from ¾" to 1½".

USE: To provide a conduit for bilge discharge and intake; can be used with below-waterline connections. Cuffs make this hose easy to clamp.

USE TIPS: Refer to "About Bilge Pumps" when selecting discharge hose. Its ID and inner texture can affect the efficiency of pumps. Cuffs are for easier clamping.

BUYING TIPS: Sold by the foot in lengths up to 50'.

Y-VALVE

ALSO KNOWN AS: Y-fitting

DESCRIPTION: Fitting is bronze, rubber, or reinforced plastic pipe shaped like a Y; may also be a ball valve that shuts off one port feeding two outlets (or vice versa, depending on how valve is installed).

USE: To divert waste from marine head either to a holding tank or for overboard discharge. When the simple, valveless Y-fitting is used (arms facing downward), in-line valves (see page 271) must be installed below the arms.

USE TIPS: Double-clamp all hose connections. Rubber Y-fittings should not be used with bilge pumps, since they are soft enough to collapse under pressure.

Review state and federal discharge regulations before pumping waste overboard (see "About Ma-

rine Sanitation Devices," page 259). Y-valves, because of their potential for abuse, have been banned in some states, a trend that is likely to spread.

BUYING TIPS: All-in-one Y-valve is much less expensive and easier to use than Y-fitting, with its requirement for two separate in-line valves.

IN-LINE CHECK VALVE

DESCRIPTION: Flexible black rubber or plastic, looks like two plumber's helpers joined at their bells. ½" ID, 1" ID, and 1½" ID hose extensions at either end may be barbed; check valve is inside bells.

USE: Install on freshwater and bilge drain system to prevent backflow and to help pumps keep their prime by keeping air out of the hose.

USE TIPS: Double-clamp hose connections.

BUYING TIPS: Not expensive.

REGULATOR WITH GAUGE

DESCRIPTION: Palm-sized plastic analog water-pressure gauge measures from 10 to 60 psi, connected to ¾" brass pipe hose fitting with male and female threads at either end. Adjustable pressure valve adjacent to gauge.

USE: For use with water-system feed line from dock or "city water." Protects onboard water system from pressure spikes. Valve is factory preset at 40 psi, but can be adjusted up or down.

USE TIPS: Should not be used when temperatures are below 38°.

BUYING TIPS: Unless it really turns you on, why spend money for a pressure gauge when you can buy an in-line pressure regulator (next item) for less or take matters into your own hands and . . . turn the faucet down.

Deck-Mount In-Line Regulator

ALSO KNOWN AS: Reducer/filter

DESCRIPTION: Flanged device contains check valve and pressure regulator set for 40 psi, its only setting. In white or chrome-finished plastic. In-line intake and outlet ports fit ½" hose and spin freely to make hose connection easier, external screw-on plug for when not in use.

USE: For use with water system feed line from dock or "city water." Protects onboard water system from pressure spikes.

USE TIPS: Regulators range from simple faucet screw-on devices to more complicated units containing charcoal filters to cut down on foreign tastes, etc. (although most municipal water systems are fairly trustworthy).

BUYING TIPS: If you feel you need protection from water "surges," buy one, although there have been few recorded cases of serious plumbing damage from sudden increases in water pressure from shoreside sources.

Raw-Water Washdown Faucet

DESCRIPTION: Brass hose faucet fits standard ⅝" hose connections. Has sillcock- or gate-style valve. Daisy handle spins clockwise to close, counterclockwise to open.

USE: To provide a connecting point for raw-water feed and vinyl washdown hose (see page 282); acts like garden-hose spigot.

USE TIPS: Under no circumstances should this faucet be used as a valve for a through-hull feed line. Secure enough valve only for washdown or similar purposes.

BUYING TIPS: Inexpensive.

Water Inlet and Outlet Fittings

DESCRIPTION: Chrome-plated bronze flanged fitting with female and male ports for ½" pipe fitting. Inlet version has swiveled female hose connector, and outlet version has male hose connector. Plastic watertight plug on bead chain is connected to both.

USE: To provide hose-connection points for water system.

USE TIPS: Male outlet fitting is for hooking up to the boat's water supply for a washdown, the female fitting for attaching to a shoreside source.

BUYING TIPS: Female version is more expensive because of swivel fitting, but probably more useful since you'll likely be using shoreside water more often than depleting your own precious water supply.

CHAPTER ELEVEN

GENERAL MAINTENANCE

CLEANING PRODUCTS AND
EQUIPMENT

SAIL CLEANER

ALSO KNOWN AS: Sail bath

DESCRIPTION: Various liquid products for cleaning, removing stains, and whitening sails. Sold in pint-size plastic bottles or ½-pt. plastic pump spray bottles.

USE: Sail cleaning products labeled as *baths* are mixed with water (1 pt. of cleaner to 10 gal. of water) and sails are given a long soaking (typically 10 hours) to remove most salt, dirt, grease, and oil stains. *Sail bleaches* are used to spot-remove stains that do not come out in the bath. *Foaming cleaners* are sprayed full-strength directly on stains and rubbed in with a cloth.

USE TIPS: Be prepared for a dripping mess when you remove a wet sail from the bathtub, if that is where you leave it to soak. Sails should be dried flat in the sun to prevent mildew and mold stains. Avoid overapplying bleaches because this may weaken or remove "body" from some types of sailcloth.

BUYING TIPS: Sail bath, bleach, and spray-on cleaners are sold individually or together in *sail maintenance kits.*

VACUUM

ALSO KNOWN AS: Wet-or-dry vacuum, portable vacuum

DESCRIPTION: Device consisting of cylinder containing an electric motor, filter, and usually a porous dust bag or other collecting chamber for both dry and wet debris, even liquids. Cylinder is attached directly to either an external nozzle or to a flexible hose about 3' long with nozzle at the end. Nozzles can be replaced, depending on the job. Motor drives a fan that pulls air out of the vacuum hose or nozzle and into the dust bag or chamber. Air, minus dust, exits through the opposite end of cylinder.

Portable vacuums are generally much smaller than household vacs—about the size of an electric drill or hand mixer. One-gallon capacity wet-or-dry vacuums are also available. Vacuums run on 12 volts, using a cigarette-lighter-type plug or 110-volt AC current with standard plug.

USE: Dust, wood chips, sand, and dirt can be collected efficiently and disposed of easily with all boat vacuum models.

USE TIPS: Only models designated for wet-or-dry use can be used for picking up liquids, but do not expect even these to substitute for a bilge pump when there is a significant leak or amount.

BUYING TIPS: Portable vacuums are fairly inexpensive and can be used at home or in the car as well.

CABIN DEODORIZER

ALSO KNOWN AS: Air freshener

DESCRIPTION: Plastic pump spray bottle containing 8 oz. of liquid deodorant, scented or unscented. Also available are pouches of deodorant or flat disks made of deodorant-laced wax, which are inserted in a wood-look plastic box the size of a butter dish. A small fan driven by two D batteries blows wafts of deodorizing fragrance (several different ones are available) through boat cabin.

USE: To overcome all types of unpleasant odors found in boat cabins.

USE TIPS: Persistent odors caused by mildew, fuel, and holding-tank leaks or spoiled food should be eliminated at their source for health and safety reasons.

BUYING TIPS: Some air fresheners smell unpleasant in a different way from the unpleasant odors you are trying to get rid of. These "scents" can be overpowering in a small cabin with little ventilation.

BIODEGRADABLE CLEANING AIDS

DESCRIPTION: Concentrated liquid soaps for bathing, dishes, and laundry that contain no caustics or phosphates. These biodegrade in water or if accidentally spilled on land. Pumice may be added to improve foaming action. Packaged in recycled plastic bottles.

USE: These soaps are formulated to foam in salt or fresh water, either hot or cold. Some contain aloe for its skin-soothing properties. If the product you are using is not intended for bathing or dishwashing purposes, it probably is a good idea to use rubber utility gloves to avoid rashes.

USE TIPS: Concentrated formulas mean that you do not need to use much to get results. Some makers of biodegradable products sell small containers of refill cleaner, which is even more highly concentrated. When you get home, pour this into the larger, original container you first purchased and add the amount of water recommended by the manufacturer.

BUYING TIPS: Try your local food co-op for the best prices and selection of "green" cleaning products.

HULL CLEANER

ALSO KNOWN AS: Cleaner wax

DESCRIPTION: Nonabrasive liquid cleanser can be applied by spray or sponge. Usual dilution is 2 or 3 capfuls per gal. of water, enough to clean a 24' boat. Oxalic acid is often a main ingredient.

USE: After a few minutes on stained fiberglass, hull cleaner will remove rust stains, oil and grease scum at waterline, fish blood, and very light marine-growth fouling. Brightens color of gel coat, but is not a substitute for periodic hull waxing.

USE TIPS: You may find that some products lose their cleaning "oomph" as time goes on. This could have something to do with the age of your boat, along with exposure to UV rays, chemical reactions in the gel coat, pollution levels in the water, and a number of other factors. Most boat owners try different products from time to time, usually with good results.

BUYING TIPS: Sold in quart and ½-gal. plastic jugs.

VINYL SHAMPOO

ALSO KNOWN AS: Vinyl cleaner, vinyl and rubber cleaner/sealer

DESCRIPTION: Spray-on cleaner in 16-oz. plastic bottle. Petroleum distillate.

USE: To clean and brighten vinyl-covered objects of all kinds: foul-weather gear, fenders, and for some brands, inflatable boats. Sprays on and then wipes off.

USE TIPS: Do not use vinyl cleaners on inflatable boats without checking the label or with the manufacturer first. Chemicals from some cleaners can destroy seams or penetrate inflatable skins, causing adhesion problems later on when you want to make patch repairs.

BUYING TIPS: Useful in the car as well as on the boat.

Waterless Hand Cleaner

DESCRIPTION: Hand cleanser with the consistency and appearance of vegetable shortening, sold in 16-oz. widemouth tub with screw-on lid. Often contains lanolin for skin conditioning; may also contain irritating chemicals, so look for brands specifying they do not contain alkalis, kerosene, or other skin-sensitizing materials.

USE: A tablespoon or two of cleanser rubbed on your hands will remove difficult stains from oil-based paints, as well as grease, oil, and grime. Works with or without water. Rinses off.

USE TIPS: These products often have a very unpleasant odor and you may want to wash your hands with regular soap afterward.

BUYING TIPS: Available at boating goods stores, as well as auto supply shops, hardware stores, and some groceries.

Surface Cleanser

ALSO KNOWN AS: Household cleaner

DESCRIPTION: Slightly abrasive, thick liquid cleanser, may contain bleach.

USE: To clean hard, nonporous surfaces such as head and galley fixtures. Can be used straight from the bottle, or diluted and applied with a wet sponge.

USE TIPS: May not be compatible for use on countertops or painted and varnished surfaces, so check label before using. Wear rubber work gloves to protect your hands. Look for cleansers that are biodegradable.

BUYING TIPS: Sold in plastic quart bottles.

Bilge Cleaner

DESCRIPTION: Biodegradable, phosphate-free liquid cleaner that contains a mildewcide ingredient.

USE: To break down oil, grease, and sludge in the bilge and treat surfaces so that mildew will not grow. Leaves fresh odor.

USE TIPS: Choose a bilge cleaner that will not harm fiberglass, metal, or plastic. One qt. will clean 25' of boat length.

BUYING TIPS: Sold in quart or gallon plastic jugs.

Rust-Stain Remover

ALSO KNOWN AS: Rust remover

DESCRIPTION: Liquid cleaner applied with a sponge. Comes in 8-oz. or larger plastic bottle. Oxalic acid is often a main ingredient.

USE: To clean fiberglass, metal, porcelain (for example cooktops), or similar hard-to-remove rust stains. Does not require scraping or wire brushing, which can scratch surfaces.

USE TIPS: Leaves metal surfaces etched enough to accept paint.

BUYING TIPS: Sells for about 50¢/oz. Try a bottle; if it doesn't work, ask around to see what works for others.

Metal Wax

ALSO KNOWN AS: Metal polish, marine polish, rubbing compound

DESCRIPTION: Stiff, nonabrasive, acid-free paste wax with cleansers and polishers. Another version uses natural cotton fiber impregnated with cleansers and polishers. Small amounts—less than ½ lb.—sold in tubes, tubs, or cans.

USE: To clean, polish, and bond to chrome, brass, aluminum, and stainless steel, sometimes even countertop surfaces, leaving behind a waterproof seal that protects against pitting, discoloration, and rust.

USE TIPS: Don't use silver polish or just any general-purpose metal wax because it may contain abrasives.

BUYING TIPS: Fairly inexpensive, since a little goes a long way.

COLOR RESTORER

ALSO KNOWN AS: Cleaner wax

DESCRIPTION: Thick liquid cleanser contains mild abrasives and silicone oil; comes in pt.-size plastic bottle.

USE: Smooth on with a cloth, allow to dry, then rub off. Removes dirt, chalky surface stains, and oxidation to let gel coat's color shine through. Silicone oil penetrates gel coat to protect it.

USE TIPS: Probably will not remove oxidation or discoloration caused by chemical reactions in the gel coat. Try a dab of the color restorer on an inconspicuous spot to see how it reacts. (You should contact the boat manufacturer if serious gel-coat discoloration develops, particularly on boats less than 5 years old.) Red and blue gel coats are most prone to turning chalky, while white gel coat sometimes turns yellow.

BUYING TIPS: Color restorer is only the first step in cleaning your boat's hull. Follow up with wax for a longer-lasting treatment.

MARINE WAX

ALSO KNOWN AS: Boat wax, hull wax

DESCRIPTION: Paste-wax compound often containing carnuba wax, Teflon, and other polishing agents. Sold as liquid or solid in plastic bottles or 1-pt. cans.

USE: To polish the gel coat above the waterline.

USE TIPS: Follow the directions for applying and removing—wax left on for hours in the hot sun or, worse, overnight may have to be cleaned off and reapplied.

BUYING TIPS: Similar compounds are available at half the price in auto discount or hardware stores. Check the ingredients list to be sure there are no abrasives.

CLEANER WAX

ALSO KNOWN AS: Fiberglass rubbing compound

DESCRIPTION: Wax contains cleansers and polishers, sold in quart plastic bottle.

USE: Purports to clean and polish your boat's hull in one process. Apply wax with soft cloth, allow to dry, then buff off. Frequency of waxing depends on your boat's exposure to sunlight, pollution levels of water, salt deposits, and personal preference.

USE TIPS: Use a clean cloth for buffing, otherwise dirt gets ground in.

BUYING TIPS: Despite manufacturer claims, don't expect to "clean and polish" your hull with a single multipurpose product. Before you apply any wax, the hull should receive an old-fashioned soap-and-water scrubbing.

Mildew-Stain Remover

ALSO KNOWN AS: Mold and mildew remover

DESCRIPTION: Spray-on liquid containing mildewcide and cleansers.

USE: Bleaches out mildew stains and protects against mildew growth (particularly effective on porous surfaces), but check label before applying. Otherwise you may end up with bleached-out areas.

USE TIPS: Use rubber work gloves, as mildew cleaner can cause skin irritation.

BUYING TIPS: Common household chlorine bleach diluted with water is very inexpensive and may work just as well. Likewise nonchlorine bleaches are safe and inexpensive on many surfaces.

Boat-Bottom Cleaner

ALSO KNOWN AS: Hull and bottom cleaner

DESCRIPTION: Liquid cleaner that contains nonabrasive cleaner and degreaser, as well as algicides and other antifouling chemicals. Rinses off with fresh or salt water.

USE: To remove algae, marine-growth, scum, oil, and grease buildups from boat bottoms without scraping or scrubbing. Apply, let stand, then rinse off.

USE TIPS: Not very effective when simply applied to hull heavily fouled with marine growth. It is necessary to first scrub off or use a pressure washer (see below).

BUYING TIPS: Sold in quart-size plastic jug.

High-Pressure Washer

ALSO KNOWN AS: Pressure cleaner

DESCRIPTION: Sprayer motor (runs on 120 volts AC) about the same size as an electric drill and a housing containing a reservoir for cleanser, degreaser, or wax, which is combined with water when sprayer is in use. Hose connection is for water, which is sprayed at 1,000 psi pressure. Nozzle extension is adjustable to four different spray-pattern settings. With its fairly heavy weight (14 lbs.) a shoulder strap is a necessity, not just a convenience.

USE: Aim high-pressure spray of water at fouled boat bottoms, storage-dirty decks, as well as cars and house siding to wash dirt away. Adding cleanser and degreaser to the water reservoir improves cleaning action. After hull surface is cleaned, use wax for the final coat.

USE TIPS: Powerful spray is painful on the skin and will cause eyes injuries, so remember that this is not a toy. Do not let unsupervised young people use this. Use safety goggles with this item, since dirt particles tend to fly off with considerable velocity. May remove loose paint.

BUYING TIPS: Expensive, but probably necessary if you store your boat at home and do not have access to a marina's sprayer. If you are hauled out at a boatyard with its own pressure sprayer, have it done there.

Handle

ALSO KNOWN AS: Mop handle, broom handle

DESCRIPTION: Solid or two-piece varnished or painted wood or plastic rod, at least 4' long × ¾" diameter, with threads cut in one end. Also two-section 4'–8'-long telescoping anodized aluminum handle with screw-locks and plastic threaded fitting at one end, plastic cap at the other. An interesting accessory is the low-profile plastic handle with two large suction cups attached.

USE: To provide a handle for a variety of implements, including brushes, mops, and cleaning pads with threaded sockets.

Suction-cup handle presses onto hull side, giving a firm handhold useful when scrubbing the boat's bottom and waterline from a dinghy while the boat is in the water. When properly attached, handle can hold up to 180 lbs., but should not be relied upon as a weight-bearing support, like a boarding step.

USE TIPS: Paint on wooden handles eventually chips off, at which point you will be plagued by bits of color left here and there on the deck.

Telescoping aluminum handles are versatile and can even be used to clean cobwebs from cathedral ceilings at home.

BUYING TIPS: Handles are often included as part of cleaning/maintenance kits with brushes, mops, and cleaning pads.

Canvas Boater's Bucket

DESCRIPTION: Cylindrical sack made of canvas, measuring 9" high × 9" wide, with canvas strap handle. Top and bottom edges are reinforced. Stiffness of canvas keeps bucket upright, but it can be crushed flat for storage.

USE: To carry water without scratching a deck. Provides a bucket that takes little storage space. Treated canvas is thick enough that bucket will hold

water for hours before it starts seeping out. Bucket has no hard edges to scratch varnish work and no metal parts to leave rust stains.

USE TIPS: Not suitable for carrying drinking water, since the canvas imparts an unpleasant taste and smell to the water. May also be used for carrying tools.

BUYING TIPS: Inexpensive and salty in appearance.

Cleaning Aids

ALSO KNOWN AS: Cleaning accessories

DESCRIPTION: Various bristled and/or textured implements.

TYPES:

Brushes: Square or oval with handle 6" to 8½" long to prevent scraped knuckles; rectangular, rounded, or hourglass shape without handles for tight areas; and with threaded sockets in bristle base so that a long handle can be attached. Scrubbers are bristled with coarse, crimped brass strands for scrubbing (do not use on painted and varnished surfaces) or with soft or firm polypropylene strands for general-purpose cleaning. *Boat wash brushes* come with rubber bumpers around the perimeter, to prevent dings and dents in bulkheads or rails.

Scrubbing or cleaning pads: Made of a tight mesh of synthetic fibers graded for light-, medium-, and heavy-duty cleaning purposes. May come with rectangular plastic base and low-profile handle or have a plastic base with threaded socket for accommodating a screw-in handle.

Mops (also known as *swabs*): Consist of long twisted strands of cotton at the end of a 4'-long handle.

Sponges: Usually of the synthetic cellulose variety, larger (6" long × 4" wide) than used at home. Some have a soft surface on one side and a scrubbing pad on the other, another variation is the sponge encased in a mildly abrasive nylon-mesh bag. Large *bailer sponges,* roughly 10" long × 4" wide × 3" thick, absorb as much as twenty times their weight in water, so they are a big help in wiping up spills, as well as bailing out a dinghy or inflatable.

Cleaning and polishing cloths: Your basic rag for washing and wiping may also be chenille-textured like an old bathrobe. Cotton is the most absorbent, although synthetic cloths are okay too.

USE: To clean surface dirt and grime, as well as hard-to-remove dirt and stains from all kinds of surfaces both on deck and below. Tenacity of dirt determines the stiffness of brush bristles (for example, use brass bristle brushes on fouled boat bottoms) or density of cleaning pads. May be used with plain salt or fresh water or with water and cleanser.

A swab swished over the side is used to sluice loose dirt and sand from the deck and cockpit. In addition, it is the traditional way to remove the morning's dew from the deck.

USE TIPS: Rinse brushes, cleaning pads, and mops frequently to avoid grinding in dirt.

BUYING TIPS: Scrubber and maintenance kits containing a variety of cleaning tools are available from both marine and nonmarine stores. Follow boat manufacturers' recommendations for which products to use and how to clean new boats.

Vinyl hose

ALSO KNOWN AS: Garden hose

DESCRIPTION: Vinyl hose 25' to 50' length with ⅝" fittings at both ends. Safe for drinking water. Hoses for boats are often white or white and blue; the garden variety is green. *Reinforced hose* has extra plies that make it stiff so that it will not kink when it is coiled. *Self-storing hose,* which is softer, comes

with its own dinner-plate-sized carrying case with handle and "collapses" when water is not coursing through it.

USE: To bring water from the tap to your boat.

USE TIPS: Make sure every opening is securely shut before you hose down your boat.

BUYING TIPS: Many marinas and boatyards supply hoses for use by customers. If you must buy your own, get the longest length of hose you can conveniently store.

Marine spray nozzles

ALSO KNOWN AS: Spray nozzle, hose sprayer

DESCRIPTION: Plastic or zinc tap with plastic stem and spring handle valve to release water. Perforated screen over "faucet" mouth creates spray pattern, ⅝" threaded female fitting for attachment to hose.

USE: To concentrate water pressure and disperse spray when attached to a hose.

USE TIPS: Works better than your thumb over the end of the hose.

BUYING TIPS: Plastic nozzles are very inexpensive, and zinc ones only slightly more. Large variety available at garden and hardware stores.

Protectant

ALSO KNOWN AS: Stain guard, sealer

DESCRIPTION: Spray-on liquid sold in pint- and quart-sized plastic bottles. Some formulations are environment-friendly.

USE: Sprayed and allowed to dry on cloth, sails, vinyl, wood, fiberglass, and plastics, protectant forms a waterproof coating that resists stains and keeps surfaces from cracking.

USE TIPS: Check a small patch for surface compatibility before applying over a large area. This product may cause blotchy discoloration or may pucker fabric. Wears off with time.

BUYING TIPS: Quart refills available.

PAINTS AND VARNISHES

ABOUT PAINT

The combination of intense sunlight and exposure to salt spray, rain, sand, and petroleum products, in addition to extremes in temperature, make the marine environment an extremely harsh one, especially for nondurable materials such as wood and cloth. Even products such as gel coat, the glasslike outer-shell finish on fiberglass boats, succumb in time to the elements. Steel and aluminum surfaces are subject to rust and corrosion.

In addition underwater hull and hardware surfaces are potential hosts for marine algae, grasses, and barnacles, not to mention the dread toredo worm, nemesis of wooden hulls. Underwater hardware needs proper care so that it does not become damaged by galvanic corrosion (see "About Zincs," page 162). Trailered and dry-stored boats also suffer damages from chafe against trailer bunks and storage racks.

A broad spectrum of paints, varnishes, finishes, and other durable coatings is available for marine use above and below the waterline. These products serve not only to beautify and enhance a boat's cosmetic appearance, but they also reduce or prevent deterioration. And by keeping hull bottoms clear of fouling you can improve boat speed, a plus for sailboat racers and high-speed powerboat skippers. Finishes are also available for touching up or marking boat-related equipment.

Most marine paints have a binder or resin of water-based latex (or acrylic/vinyl), oil-based alkyd, or epoxy to hold them together. While latex/vinyl paints are water-soluble; alkyds and epoxies require special chemical solvents and thinners. Marine paints come in liquid form in the familiar ½-pint, pint, quart, and gallon can with pry-off lid. A few kinds of paints come in 12-oz. aerosol spray cans. They can be brushed on, sprayed or applied with a roller. Most are intended for do-it-yourself painters. Review first-aid techniques before beginning a paint project. Paints and related products can irritate skin and cause damage to eyes, as well as emit noxious fumes.

In fact some finishes are restricted to professional application because they contain ingredients that are highly dangerous to health or the environment. They may also require special application training and careful handling. In addition, spray equipment might be beyond the scope of the average casual user, in terms of expense or difficulty of use.

Companions to paints and finishes are a myriad of thinners, solvents, primers, and undercoats. All finish products are labeled with specific handling, use, and safety instructions, in addition to recommendations for use on appropriate surfaces and environmental considerations. These instructions should be followed *to the letter* for best results, but if you have other questions, most paint manufacturers have technical hot lines you can call for assistance.

Solvents, toxins, and fumes—also known as volatile organic compounds, or VOCs—emitted from paint products contribute to depletion of the ozone layer in the atmosphere. Because of this, state and federal environmental and health agencies are restricting VOC emission levels of such products. Expect to see new paint formulations in stores over the next few years.

Always keep in mind that many paint products are highly flammable. Smoking, open flames, electrical sparks, and the like should be avoided at all costs.

For paint to properly adhere and dry, all dirt, dust, grease, and other materials should be removed from the surface being painted. Mix paints thoroughly before applying, but be gentle when it comes to stirring enamels and varnishes because they tend to form air bubbles that are hard to smooth out. Paint on a low-humidity day with temperatures between 50°–80° F for best results. Varnish tends to bubble and get cloudy when it is applied in hot weather in direct sunlight.

Be sure to protect skin, eyes, and clothing with gloves, goggles, dust masks, and overalls when using paints. Respirators are needed when paint is sprayed. Avoid spraying on a windy day, when overspray can damage nearby boats, cars, or buildings. Some marinas do not allow their customers to use spray equipment because of the overspray factor. Check before you begin working.

REFINISHING BUOY PAINT

ALSO KNOWN AS: Mooring paint

DESCRIPTION: Water-resistant paint that adheres to vinyl surfaces. Sold in 12-oz. aerosol spray cans in yellow and other high-visibility colors.

USE: To spray on buoys, markers, and other vinyl objects.

USE TIPS: Also compatible with some inflatable rafts. Keep in mind that mooring buoys (see page 71) are required to be painted white with a horizontal blue stripe.

BUYING TIPS: It is much cheaper to repaint your nonconforming mooring buoy than to buy a replacement.

STENCIL KIT

ALSO KNOWN AS: Lettering stencils

DESCRIPTION: Reusable alphabet and number cutouts made of durable vinyl or plastic, usually in a simple utilitarian lettering style without ornamentation. Kit includes primer for preparing surface and vinyl paint.

USE: To apply boat registration numbers to inflatable boats and dinghies; label dock boxes and ring and horseshoe floats; and letter boat names on utility craft. Stenciled letters are usually easy-to-read and not particularly attractive. The alternative is plastic rigid or stick-on letters and numbers (see next item).

USE TIPS: Registration numbers must be 3" tall, according to state regulations. Lay out guidelines before painting stencils.

BUYING TIPS: Art supply stores may have more extensive lettering styles if you want to be fancy— just be sure your harbor patrol can read the result.

REGISTRATION LETTERS AND NUMBERS

ALSO KNOWN AS: State boat registration numbers

DESCRIPTION: Rigid plastic, reflective adhesive material, or stencil kit 3"-high letters and numbers. Available in white or black, sometimes with beveled edge in contrasting color.

USE: To meet state requirements for display of assigned registration number, which is usually a combination of letters and numbers. Registration numbers must be permanently affixed to both sides of the bow.

USE TIPS: State registration requirements vary regarding letter color and position, in addition to the types of boats that must be registered. Check your state's regulations before applying your number.

Plastic letters are fairly brittle, so look for predrilled ones. They are installed with short (no more than ½" long) #4 screws. If you must drill them yourself, first clamp the letter to a block of wood and use a very small drill bit with a countersink.

Lay out guidelines on the hull before installing— nothing looks worse than uneven lettering, especially when the letters are the adhesive type or stenciled on.

BUYING TIPS: Stick-on letters may not last as long, but they don't require drilling into the gelcoat.

REGISTRATION PLATES

ALSO KNOWN AS: Name boards

DESCRIPTION: Pair of 24" long × 4" wide ABS rigid white plastic sheets, with predrilled holes in each corner.

USE: To provide a display mount for state registration numbers, used primarily on inflatable dinghies and other small boats. Plates may be glued directly to the bows, attached with suction cups, or hung by shock-cord loops strung through the corner holes.

USE TIPS: Some states require that registration numbers be permanently affixed to the hull to prevent theft. Check your state's regulations.

BUYING TIPS: An attachment kit, containing adhesive, suction cups, and shock cord, is sold separately.

ABOUT BOTTOM PAINT

Whether boats are used in fresh or salt water, they are likely to accumulate unwanted passengers on their bottoms, such as algae, marine grasses, and barnacles. Antifouling paints contain a number of different toxicants or biocides to prevent this accumulation, chief of which is cuprous oxide, Cu_2O. Until a federal ban was imposed on it a few years ago because of its harmful effect on marine life, tributyltin, or TBT, was the biocide of choice. Now TBT is banned from all but a few uses. In fact tin paints can be applied only by state-licensed applicators in settings where paint runoff is collected and disposed of properly.

Most boats need to be bottom-painted only once every year or two because toxicants are released slowly from the paint. In conventional antifouling paint, toxicants leach out, usually spending themselves by the end of the boating season. With ablative antifoulants a controlled amount of paint wears off as the boat moves through the water, so these paints tend to last for more than one season. In warm-water climates, some boat owners dive beneath their boats several times each summer to brush away surface scum and expose a fresh paint surface.

When deciding which bottom paint to use, consider the type of bottom paint already on the boat. Oil-based paint can be applied over water-based vinyl, but the opposite is not true. Vinyl paint will bubble and lift when applied over oil paint, so you will first have to remove all the old paint. Hull material is also a factor. Copper paints will cause galvanic corrosion if they are applied directly onto bare aluminum boats. Like steel hulls, aluminum ones require a barrier-coat primer before the final coat is painted on.

Sailboat racers and owners of high-speed powerboats take special precautions to keep bottoms free of growth to lessen drag on the hull. In addition paints that dry with a hard, smooth surface (see next item) give speeders an extra edge.

Finally, whether the boat is stored on land or in the water makes a difference when choosing a bottom paint. Since hard ablative paints release toxicants only when they are wetted, these are suitable for dry-stored boats. Leaching paints lose their effectiveness when they are allowed to dry out. If your boat is left at the dock for a long time, you may notice more marine growth on the side of the hull that is exposed to sunlight. Likewise, hulls will foul more heavily in areas where the current is minimal.

BOTTOM PAINT

ALSO KNOWN AS: Antifouling paint, antifouling bottom paint, ablative paint

DESCRIPTION: Vinyl-, rosin-, alkyd-, or epoxy-based paint containing toxicants or biocides, chiefly cuprous oxide (Cu_2O). May be applied with brush, roller, or sprayer to wood, fiberglass, primed metals, and previously painted surfaces. Sold in quart or gallon cans, although some kinds are available in 12-oz. aerosol spray cans. 1 gal. covers about 400 sq. ft., about enough for a 25' sail or power boat. Colors are limited to red, blue, green, brown, black, white, and gray. Custom-mixed colors are not available. Types of antifouling paints and products include:

TYPES:

Epoxy-based paints: Average around 50% Cu_2O. These are easy-to-use paints that require about 8 hours to dry before a second coat can be applied or the boat is launched. They produce a finish that is harder than conventional alkyd paints. Some epoxy paints can be applied up to 60 days before the boat is launched. Most require a special thinner specified by the paint manufacturer.

Ablative paints: Activate only when immersed in water and are dormant during haul-outs. They produce an extremely hard surface, so they are ideal for boats that are trailered or dry-stored. Cure time is over 12 hours. These paints must be used with a specific thinner.

Rosin-based paints: Used on slower-speed boats with top speeds of 18 knots or less. Applied with a roller or brush, they produce a soft finish that requires at least an overnight cure. This paint is not suitable for boats that are trailered or dry-stored.

Vinyl-based paints: Give a smooth finish, besides being easy to use and easy to clean up. Since they are water-based, they require no thinners. They can only be applied over previous vinyl-coated surfaces.

Some water-based paints are good for trailered boats. A soft finish is the main drawback, at least for racers.

Spray paint for aluminum outdrives and outboard motors: Two coats are usually applied, with a dry time of about 4 hours (oil-based). Because aluminum corrodes when coated with copper-based paints, the federal ban on TBT (see page 285) permits its limited use for engine applications. New paint formulations with greatly reduced amounts of tin are becoming available. Sold in 12-oz. aerosol cans.

Transducer paint: Water-based formula for depth-sounder transducers (see page 29) installed on the boat bottom. When depth sounders stop being accurate, a transducer fouled with barnacles and other growth is the usual culprit.

Biodegradable, nontoxic antifouling additive: Can be added at a rate of 1 gr. per gal. of paint to enhance bottom paint's effectiveness. Hot sauce and chili powder are folk antifoulants that some people swear by, while others scoff.

USE: To prevent or inhibit marine growth from forming on boat bottoms in fresh or salt water. By keeping bottoms clear, drag on the hull is kept to a minimum, so boat is free to perform at its best. Many of the hard bottom paints favored by racers contain a "slickening" agent such as Teflon® that is also supposed to improve performance. Hard paints are not only fine-sanded to improve slickness, but they can also be "burnished" or polished. Most paint manufacturers recommend two coats.

USE TIPS: Because of pigmentation, Cu_2O levels in blue paints are sometimes lower than other colors. Check labels to see which colors offer the best protection.

BUYING TIPS: Soft paints need to be applied every season, while harder paints will last for at least two seasons, possibly more. So, while hard paints usually cost at least 50% more, they pay for themselves over the long run.

Bottom wax

ALSO KNOWN AS: Drag-resistant coating racing wax

DESCRIPTION: Nontoxic liquid wax.

USE: Manufacturers claim these waxes make hulls so slick that barnacles and algae slide right off. Some bottom waxes contain materials that are touted as effective against zebra mussels. May also be applied to sails to make them more efficient.

USE TIPS: Apply to underwater hulls, water skis, and sailboards, allow to dry, then buff. For freshwater use only. 1 pt. coats a 24' boat. Since bottom wax contains no toxicants, it is an effective coating for trailered and dry-stored boats.

BUYING TIPS: Slightly less expensive than conventional bottom paint, and with no harmful side effects.

Polyurethane undercoater

ALSO KNOWN AS: Water-based primer

DESCRIPTION: Brushable white primer paint for all painted surfaces, including fiberglass and properly primed and sealed wood and metal. Water-based. 1 gal. covers about 350 sq. ft.

USE: To provide a stable substrate for finish paint. Also masks previous paint colors.

USE TIPS: Water base makes cleanup easy.

BUYING TIPS: Sold in quarts and gallons.

Topside coating

ALSO KNOWN AS: Finish paint, enamel, topside enamel, bootstripe paint

DESCRIPTION: Polyurethane and epoxy high-density one- and two-part paints dry to a glossy, hard finish that is resistant to water, UV, abrasion, and chemicals. Wide range of colors available. May be brushed, sprayed, or rolled on fiberglass, wood, and stainless steel or aluminum, although some surfaces may have to be sealed and/or primed.

USE: To provide durable finish for exterior surfaces above the waterline or at the waterline, in the case of bootstripe paint.

USE TIPS: Follow manufacturer's recommendations for surface preparation, thinners, and solvents, as well as drying times. Some topside paints require more than one coat. A qt. will cover about 125 sq. ft.

BUYING TIPS: Topside paints are available in quart and gallon cans, although bootstripe paint is usually available only in half-pints. This is a quick way to restore the shine to a hull that is badly oxidized or discolored.

Engine Enamel and Inboard/Outboard Lacquer

DESCRIPTION: Oil-based enamel and lacquer paint produce a hard, heat-resistant finish. Colors match engine manufacturers' original colors, such as Caterpillar yellow and Crusader red.

USE: To touch up inboard engines, outboard motors, and I/Os where rust, repairs, or corrosion have marred the surface.

USE TIPS: Read the label carefully—some enamels may require a primer undercoat.

BUYING TIPS: Sold in 12-oz. aerosol cans and pint and quart cans (larger sizes usually only for inboard-engine paints).

Exterior and Interior Polyurethane Varnish

ALSO KNOWN AS: Spar varnish

DESCRIPTION: Clear or amber-colored protective and decorative coating for wood, usually applied by brush or spray over unpainted or stained wood surface. Available in satin (matte or "rubbed effect"), gloss, or high-gloss finishes. Exterior varieties contain UV inhibitors and antioxidants to prevent clouding and may also contain phenolic resins, tung oil, and linseed oil. May be oil- or water-based.

USE: To produce a glossy protective coating on previously stained, painted, varnished, or unfinished wood surfaces. Surfaces coated with interior varnish will tolerate some standing water, but exposure over a long period of time will leave cloudy marks. Likewise, both interior and exterior varnishes can be marred by hot objects such as cooking pots or other utensils. Satin varnish works best on interior countertops and cabinets.

Many types of wood left untreated outdoors will develop unsightly black stains from rain and salt water, while heat and sunlight may cause wood to check and crack. Varnish seals wood from the elements, keeping it looking attractive as well as structurally sound. It is also chip- and abrasion-resistant.

USE TIPS: Water-based polyurethane varnish is easy to use since brushes can be washed with water. Oil-based varnishes require a thinner, usually one recommended by the paint manufacturer, so check the label.

Apply varnish when the weather is mild and humidity is low. And avoid working in hot, bright sunlight because this can cause varnish to bubble and cloud. Surfaces can be recoated after 3–6 hours, although some oil-based varnishes take a bit longer. Careful sanding between coats is a must. A high-quality (expensive) badger hair brush is the right tool for the job. Apply thin, even coats for best results. For the best "Bristol look," at least ten coats are recommended. Maintenance requires frequent wipe-downs with a damp rag and the occasional bath to remove dirt and salt spray crystals, which will pit the finish.

BUYING TIPS: Exterior varnish is sold in quart and gallon cans. Interior varnish is available in pints and quarts.

ABOUT TEAK CARE PRODUCTS

Teak, with its inherent good looks and naturally oily finish, has long been a favorite of boatbuilders. Teak protects itself well but still requires maintenance in the rough marine environment. While some boat owners with a minimum of teak trim prefer the "natural" look (the silvery-gray patina untreated teak takes on), most experts advise some form of finish for longer-lasting protection (even untreated wood must be scoured and bleached occasionally to restore its luster). Traditionalists prefer the look of varnish, multiple layers carefully applied, cleansed regularly, and sanded and renewed periodically.

Teak oils, or dressings, as they also are known, were once considered the low-rent version of varnish—cheap but transistory in effect. While it is true that some oils are little more than petroleum distillates with a little pigment thrown in, others are more sophisticated, sharing some of the same ingredients as varnish, including tung oil, which, often as not, now contains synthetic compounds. A good oil is faster to apply than spar varnish—a day or two as opposed to two weeks—and can hold more UV inhibitors than a varnish. The best also require less day-to-day maintenance (the worst,

however, will start to peel or blotch within weeks). Walking the docks to look and ask and just plain word of mouth are the best means of deciding what is right for your teak.

Some teak dressings are sold as part of a "system," requiring cleaner, sealer, and finisher, which can drive up the price considerably. Whether you are varnishing or oiling, all you really need is a clean surface (light sanding may be required, depending on the condition of the wood) that can be achieved by scrubbing with a solution of TSP (trisodium phosphate) and water or by rubbing with acetone. A thorough rinsing followed by sufficient time (at least a day) for drying and the wood is ready for coating. Follow manufacturer's recommendations, but remember that, as with painting, multiple thin coats produce a better effect than slopping oil or varnish on. If any pooling does occur, smooth the surface with a soft cloth, which also helps the finish penetrate the wood.

TEAK OIL

ALSO KNOWN AS: Teak dressing

DESCRIPTION: Mineral oil base with tung oil, linseed oil, UV inhibitors, and other wood-protecting agents. Amber color, resembles varnish in appearance but does not dry hard. Tung oil gives this material a pleasant odor.

USE: To provide a restorative and cosmetic: replenishes teak's natural oil and prevents it from checking and drying out, while at the same time bringing out the wood's natural golden color.

USE TIPS: To maintain bright color, oil teak several times each boating season. Simply apply with a brush or cloth and rub off excess. Badly soiled or stained teak should be cleaned first. Greasy residue may be left on fiberglass or metal surfaces that are accidentally coated.

BUYING TIPS: Experiment with several different formulations. Some teak oils are more effective than others and every skipper seems to have his own favorite.

TEAK BRIGHTENER

DESCRIPTION: Non-oil-base biodegradable liquid.

USE: To enhance color and restore grain of teak. Apply with a cloth and rub off excess.

USE TIPS: Teak should be cleaned before brightener is applied.

BUYING TIPS: Sold ready-to-use in quarts or triple-strength concentrate in half-pints (mix 3:1, water to concentrate).

TEAK CLEANER

DESCRIPTION: Foaming cleanser. May be biodegradable with no chlorine, acidic, or caustic ingredients.

USE: Scrub cleanser into wood grain, then rinse off.

USE TIPS: Will not damage or leave greasy residue on fiberglass or metal surfaces. Some cleaners may soften wood fillers or caulks, so use cautiously, especially when cleaning teak decks. Test first in a small, obscure area.

BUYING TIPS: Sold in quarts and gallons.

TEAK FINISH

DESCRIPTION: Glossy, brush-on finish with UV filters, dries to scratch-resistant surface.

USE: To protect teak, fiberglass, epoxy, and painted surfaces.

USE TIPS: Follow maker's recommendations, but don't feel compelled to buy a host of pretreatment products, especially if your teak is in good shape.

BUYING TIPS: Sold in quarts.

TEAK SEALER

DESCRIPTION: Clear, quick-drying liquid, clear or with reddish-brown tint or wood-darkening ingredients.

USE: To give teak a waterproof seal to keep it from drying out and checking.

USE TIPS: Can be overcoated with other teak maintenance products.

BUYING TIPS: Sold in pints, quarts, and gallons.

TEAK PREP

DESCRIPTION: Liquid contains drying agent and neutralizer.

USE: Apply before using teak oil to draw moisture (water, not oil) to surface of teak so that oiled wood does not streak or turn blotchy. May also neutralize teak-cleaner residue for better oil adhesion.

USE TIPS: Healthy teak does not require the "acid" (and subsequent neutralizing) treatment. Overuse of preps will raise and deplete natural oils, making sanding necessary.

BUYING TIPS: Sold in quarts.

TEAK-SHINING CLOTH

ALSO KNOWN AS: Polishing rag, chamois

DESCRIPTION: Rag made of cotton or other absorbent, textured natural or synthetic fabric or supple oil-dressed leather.

USE: To polish oiled or varnished surfaces, increasing shine. In the process, cloths absorb some of the oil they are polishing, so they are useful for touchups later on, between oilings.

USE TIPS: Store oily rags safely because they can be a fire hazard.

BUYING TIPS: Old sheets and towels from home can be recruited for all kinds of jobs on board, including oiling and polishing teak.

BLISTER PROTECTION

ABOUT BLISTERING

Osmotic blistering occurs when water migrates through the gel coat of a fiberglass hull's underwater surface and concentrates in specific areas. The resulting "blisters" can number in the dozens or the thousands and may range from pencil eraser–size to the size of a quarter or larger. Conservative estimates are that at least 50% of all new boats will blister between their third and seventh season on the water.

In most cases blisters are a cosmetic problem involving just the gel coat and the underlying "skin coat" of the hull. Left untended over 3 or 4 years, however, blister damages can cause delamination of the hull's fiberglass layers, at which point the hull loses its structural integrity.

Some manufacturers recommend that new boats be coated with a barrier coat prior to being launched. When this is done, the barrier coat can be applied directly over the gel coat and no sanding is necessary. Barrier coats should not be applied to unblistered hulls that have seen a few seasons of use until the hull's moisture content is measured, using a moisture meter (ask a competent marine repair facility for help). Otherwise you may cause more problems by trapping moisture in the hull.

The repair process becomes more complicated when boats have already blistered. Then it is necessary to open up the blistered areas using either a sandblaster or a sophisticated peeling machine that shaves off a measured layer from the hull surface. For best results avoid spot repairs of individual blisters, since new ones will surely develop in other areas later on. Dry-out is the next step and is crucial to the success of the job. It could take as long as 6–8 weeks, or somewhat less time if the boat is "tented" with dehumidifiers, fans, and heaters. Throughout the drying process, a moisture meter should be used.

Once the hull is dry, the next step is to smooth the hull surface with the fairing compound, which works like body putty but is made for below-the-waterline use (do not use body putty, because it absorbs water). Then several coats of barrier coat are applied, following the manufacturer's recommendations. Throughout the recoating process it is necessary to prepare the surface properly for good adhesion before applying a new coat. When the repair job is complete, you can paint on antifoulant if you wish. Properly done, blisters should not reappear.

Epoxy Barrier Coat

DESCRIPTION: Two-part system consisting of a fairing compound and a nearly waterproof finish-surface barrier coat. May be a straight epoxy-based formulation or may contain coal tar. Barrier coat is natural white in color.

USE: To prevent or repair damages caused by osmotic blistering of fiberglass hulls.

USE TIPS: When buying a new boat, check the manufacturer's warranty to see if blister damages are covered. In addition, if your boat is out of warranty but develops blisters when it is less than 5 years old, contact the manufacturer. Some boatbuilders have goodwill policies for helping out with repair costs. Blister repairs average $100 to $200 per ft. of boat length when the job is done completely by a boatyard. An alternative barrier coat consists of a layer of vinylester resin, laid just below the surface of the gel coat. Many newer boats now come with a vinylester barrier built-in.

BUYING TIPS: Some manufacturers offer guarantees on their blister-repair materials. Check before using.

Nonskid Additive

ALSO KNOWN AS: Nonskid, Awlgrip®

DESCRIPTION: Tiny spheres of polymer plastic grit dry or suspended in a latex liquid that is usually gray but can be tinted.

USE: Added to paint or applied in wet form, nonskid gives traction to otherwise slick surfaces, such as decks and docks. Made of fiberglass, wood, concrete, or metal. For indoor or outdoor use.

USE TIPS: When adding dry nonskid to paint, stir the pot frequently to keep particles suspended evenly. Some nonskid compounds are highly toxic and should be applied only by a professional.

BUYING TIPS: Inexpensive. Some people use sand for nonskid grit, but it is highly abrasive and wears through paint easily, in addition to being hard on bare feet. This additive is better.

Vinyl Coat

DESCRIPTION: 6-oz. aerosol can of paint in a limited number of basic colors. Aerosol contains no hydrocarbons, so it is easy on the ozone layer.

USE: Sprayed on leather, vinyl, ABS plastic, or PVC to change color, this paint bonds with the material for a finish that will not crack or flake. Can be used on upholstery, synthetic sails (to spray on numbers or class marks, for example), and tarps.

USE TIPS: Painted surfaces that see a lot of use may not hold up as well as others.

BUYING TIPS: One can covers 10 sq. ft.

THINNERS AND PAINT-PREPARATION PRODUCTS

MARINE-PAINT CONDITIONER

ALSO KNOWN AS: Paint conditioner, mineral spirits, brushing thinner, brushing liquid, special thinner

DESCRIPTION: Additive for oil-based paint and varnish.

USE: Adding a small amount of paint conditioner will help oil-based paint or varnish flow more smoothly so that overlapping brush marks are easier to avoid. Also helps remove sanding residue and useful for general cleanup.

USE TIPS: Add conditioner a small amount at a time (usually a capful per quart will do, check label for specific instructions) to the paint pot from which you are working. Be consistent, for consistent results. Never add to the entire can of paint—mix in a "working" can of a small amount. Conditioners are highly volatile and flammable.

BUYING TIPS: You should always have a container of conditioner available when painting.

PRIMEWASH

ALSO KNOWN AS: Metal etcher, etch primer

DESCRIPTION: Two-part system of a pint of prime-wash base and 4 oz. of reducer produces enough liquid to cover over 100 sq. ft.

USE: Applied to bare aluminum and steel surfaces, primewash formulations finely etch the surface so that finish-coat paint adheres properly. Primewash is applied to lead keels as a precursor for steel undercoat.

USE TIPS: Only one coat is needed. Comes with measuring cup for exact rationing of primewash to reducer.

BUYING TIPS: Make sure the paint you plan to apply is compatible with the primewash.

SOLVENT

DESCRIPTION: Clear liquid to be added to paints. Specific solvents are made for each type of paint, depending on the paint's base.

USE: To extend paint, making it easier to apply and feather in. Also useful as a dewaxer to prepare the bottom of a new boat for its first paint job by removing wax and other substances that may be left over from the building mold.

USE TIPS: Very handy for cleaning brushes and "erasing" painting mistakes. Follow manufacturer's direction regarding which solvent to use with paint. Usually only a capful is needed for a quart of paint, but read the label and be consistent. Also dispose of "oily" rags in designated receptacles; because they are highly flammable, you should not store them aboard your boat or keep them in your house or car.

BUYING TIPS: Sold in pint and quart cans with screw tops.

BRUSHING LIQUID

ALSO KNOWN AS: Thinner

DESCRIPTION: Slow-drying solvent sold in pints and quarts.

USE: To thin enamels and oil-based polyurethane for easier brushing and extend the drying time of both in hot weather. Also used alone to remove sanding dust from fiberglass and wood.

USE TIPS: Like all volatile products, use with care and ventilation.

BUYING TIPS: Experiment to see if you need this specialized product before relying on it.

SPRAYING THINNER

ALSO KNOWN AS: Paint thinner

DESCRIPTION: Liquid thinner sold in pints and quarts.

USE: Added to enamel and undercoat paints that are going to be sprayed, this thinner will make them flow more easily, so that spray equipment will not clog.

USE TIPS: Spraying thinner can also be used to clean brushes as well as sanding residue off the bottom.

BUYING TIPS: One can a season should do it—most paints require little thinning.

FIBERGLASS PAINT AND VARNISH REMOVER

ALSO KNOWN AS: Paint remover, paint stripper

DESCRIPTION: Formulations for removing the various types of topside and bottom paint (see page 286), as well as varnish applied to fiberglass surfaces.

USE: To strip paint effectively without etching or damaging the gel coat.

USE TIPS: Damaging the gel-coat surface can result in water incursion into the hull laminate, as well as blister damages (see page 291) below the waterline.

BUYING TIPS: Sold in rectangular quart and gallon cans with screw tops.

SOLVENT FOR SPRAY EQUIPMENT

ALSO KNOWN AS: Spray-equipment cleaner

DESCRIPTION: Formulation dissolves vinyl-based antifouling paint.

USE: Run solvent through spray equipment to completely clean out all paint residue.

USE TIPS: Can also be used to clean brushes.

BUYING TIPS: Sold in pints. Larger size containers may be available from paint manufacturer.

NO-SANDING PRIMER

ALSO KNOWN AS: Fiberglass primer, sandless primer

DESCRIPTION: Liquid that is brushed or rubbed on bare fiberglass.

USE: Alters chemical makeup of gel coat so that paint adheres more readily. This is a less-damaging alternative to sometimes-overvigorous sanding.

USE TIPS: May be used with both topside and bottom paints.

BUYING TIPS: 1 qt. covers 600 sq. ft.

METAL PRIMER

ALSO KNOWN AS: Zinc chromate primer, aluminum primer, steel primer

DESCRIPTION: Various liquids formulated for aluminum, steel, stainless steel, or lead surfaces.

USE: On bare metals, these primers improve paint adhesion. They also serve as sealants to prevent or inhibit corrosion on new metal and metal that may already have been damaged.

USE TIPS: Can be used above or below the waterline. Be sure primer is made for the metal you want to paint. Two or three coats are recommended.

12-oz. aerosol spray can be used to treat and coat already-rusted areas.

BUYING TIPS: 1 qt. covers about 100 sq. ft.

— MAINTENANCE SAFETY EQUIPMENT —

ABOUT MAINTENANCE SAFETY EQUIPMENT

During regular maintenance and fitting-out chores, a boat owner is subjected to numerous hazardous substances. Some of the most common—toluene, isocyanate, methyl ethyl ketone, xylene—read like the contents of a toxic-waste dump. Even brief exposure to these substances can make you ill if you do not exercise the proper precautions and wear suitable protective gear. Warnings on labels, which are required by law but often go unread, spell out the known and suspected hazards and advise you on how to avoid exposure. For more detailed information, you can request an MSDS (Material Safety Data Sheet) from dealers or manufacturers (most maintain information hot lines).

There is ample equipment out there to protect you from most of these hazards, although you may have difficulty locating it through a marine outlet. The following is a list of some of the basic items you should acquire for the most common boat-maintenance jobs. The rest is common sense—covering up head, eyes, and exposed skin, and properly laundering or discarding clothing worn while working with hazardous materials.

RESPIRATOR

ALSO KNOWN AS: Face mask, half-mask

DESCRIPTION: Face mask with single or dual prefilters and cartridges often containing activated charcoal. Straps over head and covers nose and mouth. Type of cartridge is specified by a number, such as TC-21C, which is not to be confused with the manufacturer's model number. Masks are rated by NIOSH/MSHA (National Institute for Occupational Safety and Health/Mine Safety and Health

Administration). Warnings on labels of solvents, paints, expoxies, etc., will specify which level respirator is required. Permanent masks with interchangeable cartridges are available (it is the cartridge, not the mask, that provides the protection); for occasional jobs 3M makes an excellent disposable respirator that is light, comfortable, and inexpensive.

USE: To protect your lungs against harmful particles and vapors.

USE TIPS: Proper fit is essential to obtain benefit from your respirator. Straps should be adjusted until an airtight seal is achieved (beards and 3-day growths hamper this); if in doubt, open a bottle of vanilla extract—you should detect no odor. Because masks restrict oxygen by as much as 20%, you should work at a reasonable pace and take a fresh-air break every 20–30 minutes.

BUYING TIPS: Dedicated do-it-yourselfers might want one of the permanent models that, with new prefilters and cartridges, should last for years. Occasional users will find the 3M disposable a great bargain.

Dust Mask

ALSO KNOWN AS: Comfort mask

DESCRIPTION: Light, comfortable paper half-mask that attaches to your head with an elastic cord. Adjustable to a certain extent by means of a flexible aluminum band over the bridge of your nose.

USE: To provide temporary protection against nuisance dusts.

USE TIPS: Although often sold in marine stores alongside the hazardous materials, a dust mask provides no protection against hazardous vapors or toxic dusts. Fit two masks together for extra insulation if you plan to raise plenty of dust, and check the inside frequently to see if dust has penetrated.

BUYING TIPS: Inexpensive; buy a bunch.

Safety Goggles

DESCRIPTION: Oversized goggles with plastic lenses, including side lenses, and ventilation holes to prevent fogging.

USE: To protect the eyes during grinding, sanding, sawing, and painting operations.

USE TIPS: Because they don't fog up, they work well with loose-fitting dust masks.

BUYING TIPS: Definitely worth it.

Gloves

ALSO KNOWN AS: Safety gloves

DESCRIPTION: Vinyl or latex gloves, either disposable or long-lasting.

USE: To protect the hands against various paints and chemicals.

USE TIPS: Solvents will dissolve thin surgical-type gloves while you watch, so wear heavy protective latex gloves if you can do the job at hand with them. Because bottom-paint sanding dust can be toxic (as well as hard to remove), wear a pair of light vinyl or latex gloves under cloth work gloves.

BUYING TIPS: Another inexpensive item that provides protection.

MAINTENANCE ACCESSORIES

WET/DRY SANDPAPER

ALSO KNOWN AS: Fine-grit sandpaper, wet-or-dry sandpaper

DESCRIPTION: 11" long × 9" wide paper coated on one side with various grits of sand or abrasive material. Grit, from very fine 220 to ultrafine 600, is marked on back. Wet/dry sandpaper is usually black or charcoal gray in color.

USE: May be used dry like conventional sandpaper to smooth wood or fiberglass surfaces. Finer sanding—to the point of polishing—is possible by wetting paper or sanding surface with water or a light oil. Water cuts quickly and smoothly and leaves behind no residue. It should not be used on shellacked surfaces. Oil takes longer to abrade, and the residue must be cleaned off with benzene or a similar solvent.

USE TIPS: Wet/dry sandpaper is used to burnish hard bottom paint on racing boats, as well as for finish sanding on high-quality varnish jobs. Use a sanding block for an even surface. Left alone, a wet-sanded surface will have an attractive satin finish.

Sandpaper grit numbers refer to the number of grains of sand per sq. in. Coarse is lower; finer is higher.

BUYING TIPS: Bulk packs of one hundred sheets are much cheaper than prices for five- or fifteen-sheet packs.

NAVAL AND ALUMINUM JELLIES

DESCRIPTION: Naval variety is a petroleum jelly with corrosion-resistant ingredients, while aluminum version contains polishes and cleaners.

USE: Apply a liberal glob of naval jelly to rusted areas, allow it to penetrate, and then use a brush to loosen. Besides cleaning, naval jelly also seals against further rust and can be followed by aluminum jelly to brighten and polish.

USE TIPS: Both jellies are thick, so they do not slide off vertical surfaces.

BUYING TIPS: Very inexpensive, an old-fashioned, effective metal-care product.

DETAIL TAPE

ALSO KNOWN AS: Detailing tape, pinstripe tape, decorative tape

DESCRIPTION: Mylar or vinyl weatherproof tape with adhesive backing sold in a variety of widths (from ¼" to 2") and colors, including metallic gold and silver. Some tapes are reflective.

USE: To add decorative detailing to boats on topsides and at bootstripe at waterline. For a traditional look, apply gold metallic tape as a cove stripe just below the gunwales.

USE TIPS: Lay out guidelines before applying tape. It is helpful to have a second person when laying down a straight, or properly curved, line. For best adhesion be sure underlying surface is completely clean of grease, oil, dirt, and scum. Reflective tapes are useful on small boats such as dinghies or inflatables that are hard to see at night.

BUYING TIPS: Tapes are inexpensive alternatives to a hand-painted stripe, but may not be as attractive or traditional-looking. Sold in 50' rolls.

CAULKS AND SEALANTS

ALSO KNOWN AS: Silicone rubber, adhesive/sealant

DESCRIPTION: Most commonly one-part substance with polysulfide/thiokol, polyurethane, or silicone base and gummy, peanut-butterlike consistency sold in 2.8-oz. or 3.0-oz. tube or 10-oz. to 10.6-oz. cartridge. Sealants remain effective in applications for about 20 years. All have shelf lives of over a year if properly stored.

TYPES:

Polysulfide sealant: The most versatile sealant, having excellent adhesion to most materials, although less so to plastics and vinyl. Suitable for use above and below waterline, since it is highly waterproof and resists gas, salt, weather, and chemicals. Some oily woods, such as teak or mahogany, may need to be primed. Slow cure rate makes this material easy to work, although some versions are fast-curing in cold weather. It dries more rigidly than other sealants. Black, white, mahogany, and teak colors.

Polyurethane sealant and adhesive: Not only seals but also grips to fiberglass, glass, metal, and wood. May be used above or below the waterline; resists sunlight and water. Cures flexible and may be sanded and painted. Cure time is slightly less than most polysulfides. Sometimes found in a highly flexible polyurethane-silicone mix. Black, white, tan, and mahogany colors.

Silicone sealant: Although the favorite of homeowners, should not be used below the waterline on boats because it tends to peel over long periods of immersion in water. Otherwise it stays strong and flexible, thanks to its rubber content, when used on most surfaces. Fast cure time. Black, white, or clear colors.

USE: To fill gaps and spaces between different materials, such as wood rails to fiberglass hulls, window glass to frames, through-hull fittings to fiberglass or wood hulls. Prevents leaks and keeps water from collecting, which rots wood components. Not intended for surface sealing, as with wood sealants.

USE TIPS: Primers required for oily woods with some sealers. Use what the sealant manufacturer recommends.

Both squeeze tubes and cartridges have long plastic nozzles. You will need a caulking gun, found at hardware stores and most marine supply stores, to utilize cartridges. When you are done using either the tubes or the cartridge, squeeze a little more sealant from the nozzle and let it harden in place to form an airtight seal so that the rest of the contents do not harden.

BUYING TIPS: Containers of all types of sealant cost less than $10 each. Check the directions so that you get the right sealant for the job.

BOAT CAULK

ALSO KNOWN AS: Caulking, caulking compound, seam compound

DESCRIPTION: Traditional caulking material is loosely woven rope made of hemp or raw cotton (including some seeds and stems), while more modern versions have synthetic bases: polysulfide, polyurethane, and silicone.

USE: To fill seams and gaps, particularly between wood planking below the waterline in the case of traditional cotton or hemp.

USE TIPS: Use a caulking iron with flat, screwdriverlike tip, but heavier, to apply rope caulk.

BUYING TIPS: Rope caulk is sold by the pound, synthetics by the tube or cartridge.

Sealer

DESCRIPTION: Clear resin-based liquid. 1 qt. covers about 150 sq. ft.

USE: Applied to bare wood, sealant penetrates the surface and provides a good substrate for paint or varnish to adhere to.

USE TIPS: Do not use on oily woods, such as teak or mahogany, before varnishing or painting since it may not adhere well.

BUYING TIPS: Usually available in quarts at the retail level, although you can also obtain gallons for really big jobs.

Vinyl and Rubber Cleaner/Sealer

DESCRIPTION: Liquid cleaner in pint plastic bottle.

USE: To remove dirt and stains and leave "wet look" finish on vinyl and rubber; temporarily eliminates dullness caused by oxidation. Rub on, allow to dry, wipe off.

USE TIPS: Do not use this product on inflatable boats. It can penetrate the skin, making repairs impossible since the surface may become too slick to accept adhesives.

BUYING TIPS: As with other specialized cleaners, try it and see how it works; then try something cheaper and see how that works.

Closed-Cell Foam Weatherseal Tape

ALSO KNOWN AS: Weatherstrip tape

DESCRIPTION: Off-white adhesive-foam tape ⅛" thick × ⅜" wide, made of PVC.

USE: To provide a seal around windows and doors or to eliminate rattle and vibration where metal components come in contact with each other.

USE TIPS: Not to be used as insulation for electrical components or underwater.

BUYING TIPS: Sold in 10' roll.

Hose Seal

DESCRIPTION: Rubberized, stretchable black strap comes in widths of ¾" and 1¼". Resistant to fuel, heat, and water, but not for prolonged periods of time.

USE: To wrap around split or leaking hoses as a temporary patch until they can be replaced.

USE TIPS: Should be used for no more than 8 hours on leaking fuel lines.

BUYING TIPS: Sold in lengths up to 24".

Emergency Repair Tape

ALSO KNOWN AS: Fiberglass tape

DESCRIPTION: Fiberglass cloth tape 3" wide impregnated with resin, comes in sealed plastic pouch. Bonds to metal, plastic, wood, or fiberglass and is not affected by oil, gasoline, water, or diesel. Fast-setting, above or below the waterline. Cure is activated by air and speeds up under water.

USE: To make an emergency repair; used wadded as a plug or wrapped several layers around an object such as a fuel line.

USE TIPS: Does not work on flat surfaces and will not cure in a single layer.

BUYING TIPS: Sold as a kit including instructions and gloves.

WATERPROOF EPOXY PUTTY

ALSO KNOWN AS: Underwater patching compound

DESCRIPTION: Claylike epoxy-based adhesive cures fast above or below waterline. Can be sanded, filed, sawn, tapped, or painted after it cures. Fast cure within ½ hour. Adheres to most surfaces, although some putties are formulated for use with aluminum.

USE: To make a quick repair when adhesion is needed fast. Suitable for making repairs to outboard engines and I/Os.

USE TIPS: Epoxy putty made for underwater use may be two-part.

BUYING TIPS: Good to have in the toolbox on board.

TWO-PART WATERPROOF GLUE

ALSO KNOWN AS: Waterproof glue, Resorcinol

DESCRIPTION: Two-part glue of tan powder and liquid resin, mixed approximately 3:1, powder to resin. Resistant to extremes in temperature, exposure to oil, gas, water, chemicals. Rigid when cured. Cure time is about 10 hours at 70° F, less at higher temperatures. Cures to translucent purple.

USE: Very strong glue for woods, eminently suitable for boatbuilding projects and underwater adhesion, although it will not cure in water.

USE TIPS: May be cleaned or wiped away with water before it hardens, but cannot be removed after it hardens. Mix only the amount you will use right away. Unmixed components keep indefinitely.

BUYING TIPS: Commonly sold in quantities enough to make a pint of glue, but larger quantities are available for big projects.

PLASTIC REPAIR KIT

ALSO KNOWN AS: Marine Tex®

DESCRIPTION: Plastic resin, catalyst, and use instructions. Resin contains metal dust for extra strength and bonding. Waterproof and heat-resistant up to 300° F, this material dries hard enough to be sawn, sanded, or drilled. White or gray.

USE: To repair leaking tanks, exhaust manifolds, cracked engine blocks, vent pipes, and the like. May be a only a temporary patch, depending on severity of damages. Can be primed and painted.

USE TIPS: Versatile product that's as useful at home as on a boat.

BUYING TIPS: Sold in 2-oz., ¾-lb., or 1-lb. kits.

EPOXY WATERPROOF SEALER

DESCRIPTION: Two-part formulation of resin and catalyst mixed in a ratio of about 8:1, resin to catalyst. Waterproof. Adheres to fiberglass, wood, metal. "Gives" when cured.

USE: Brushed on, sealer penetrates cracks and crevices on and under surfaces; also makes wood surfaces stronger.

USE TIPS: Although this makes a glossy coating over wood, it is not a varnish substitute. Use only vinyl paint over epoxy sealer.

BUYING TIPS: 1 qt. of resin and 4 oz. of catalyst cover about 25 sq. ft.

INDUSTRIAL-GRADE EPOXY

DESCRIPTION: Two-part formulation of epoxy resin and catalyst, mixed approximately 4:1, resin to catalyst. Bonds to all materials, for above or below waterline use.

USE: Laminate with fiberglass cloth for repairs and patches.

USE TIPS: Harder to work than polyester resin, but makes better repair.

BUYING TIPS: 1 qt. of resin and 7 oz. of catalyst cover about 15 sq. ft.

EPOXY SYRINGE

ALSO KNOWN AS: Resin hypodermic

DESCRIPTION: Plastic 1"-diameter tube-barrel with plunger at one end and narrow straight or curved nozzle tip at the other.

USE: To inject epoxy or other resin or glue into cracks or gaps.

USE TIPS: As with a caulking gun, the syringe helps get the material into tight places.

BUYING TIPS: Inexpensive enough and difficult to clean, so replacement makes more sense than reusing.

SEALANT FOAM

DESCRIPTION: One-part urethane foam in 12-oz. aerosol can. Has tubelike nozzle extension. When foam is sprayed, it expands and hardens to a semirigid mass. Can be cut to shape.

USE: To insulate between refrigerators or iceboxes and bulkheads, fill electrical outlets, seal gaps around windows.

USE TIPS: Has no structural properties, so do not use for supporting fuel tanks or other objects. May not be compatible with fuel, so read label carefully.

BUYING TIPS: Manufacturer claims one can is equal to 25 tubes of sealant.

FIBERGLASS OXIDATION REMOVAL SYSTEM

DESCRIPTION: Three-step maintenance system includes 16-oz. bottles of fiberglass cleaner, boat polish, and yellow wax.

USE: Over time gel coat exposed to sunlight develops a chalky, whitish cast called oxidation. This cleaning system is designed to penetrate gel coat to clean away oxidation and restore luster and color by first cleaning, then polishing, then protecting with a wax that is buffed in.

USE TIPS: Gel coat can discolor and turn chalky because of manufacturing errors in the way the resin was catalyzed or allowed to cure. If that is the case with your boat, no amount of cleaning will produce permanent results. Ask the manufacturer for help if the boat is less than 5 years old. Suitable for RVs and cars too.

BUYING TIPS: Kit's components are sold separately as well.

FIBERGLASS STAIN REMOVER

DESCRIPTION: Water-soluble, nongreasy gel contains oxalic acid.

USE: Substances such as oil, fuel, and other petroleum products, as well as fish blood, rust, dirt, and scum can penetrate the gel coat, causing hard-to-remove stains. Apply stain-remover gels fairly heavy, about ⅛" thick, rub gently, then allow to stand. Sunlight can supplement stain-removing capabilities of these gels. Follow up with a water rinse and cleaning with a product of your choice.

USE TIPS: Cleaning jobs such as this can be done during a leisurely sail or while anchored in a cove for an afternoon of fishing.

BUYING TIPS: Sold in widemouthed pint-size jars with screw lids.

FIBERGLASS REPAIR KIT

ALSO KNOWN AS: Fiberglass patch kit

DESCRIPTION: Fiberglass cloth, resin, and catalyst, as well as mixing sticks, squeegee, reinforcing mesh, and instructions. May be sold in reusable plastic box.

USE: To provide all the ingredients necessary for making small, but permanent fiberglass repairs to fiberglass, wood, plastic, and metal.

USE TIPS: The materials in this kit will not cure underwater, so they should not be relied upon in an emergency. Use emergency repair tape (see page 299) when a fix is needed in a hurry.

BUYING TIPS: Very inexpensive, but contains very limited quantities of materials for limited repairs.

FIBERGLASS EPOXY MENDER ADHESIVE FILLER

DESCRIPTION: Two-part high-density epoxy resin and hardener adheres to fiberglass, wood, metal, plastic, and masonry. Allows about an hour of working time before it begins to set. Full cure overnight.

USE: To fill in dents and dings; can be sanded after it cures.

USE TIPS: Mix ratio of 1:1.

BUYING TIPS: Sold in pint set with double-ended measuring spoon.

PLASTIC FILLER

DESCRIPTION: Two-part plastic filler.

USE: Good for making small cosmetic repairs to cracks, dents, and dings. Adheres to fiberglass, wood, metal, and plastic. Can be sanded.

USE TIPS: Any extra can be used around the house.

BUYING TIPS: Sold in pints or quarts with small tube of hardener tucked under plastic mixing pot lid.

FIBERGLASS CLOTH

ALSO KNOWN AS: Glass cloth

DESCRIPTION: Any of various fabrics made of lustrous white spun-glass fibers.

Fiberglass cloth comes in various weights and resembles burlap in its weave. Cloth weight determines its strength and where it is used, but typically it is suitable for coverings, repairs, and laminates. *Fine-grained lightweight cloths* are used nearest the finished surface. Available in precut lengths of 1–3 yds. in widths of 38" and 44", but bulk rolls are available for major repair jobs or boatbuilding projects. A variation are the *multidimensional weaves,* which have diagonal threads or fibers linking the warp and the woof. The warp and woof of *woven roving* creates a grid as coarse as ⅜" × ⅜". Like cloth, roving is used

for coverings, repairs, and laminates, but in areas where its texture will not "print through" the finished surface. Commonly available in precut pieces 38" wide × 1 yd. long.

Fiberglass tape comes in the same weights as cloth, but much narrower: from 1" to 6" wide. Tape is used for repairs where structural members such as internal frames and bulkheads need to be attached or "tabbed" to the hull.

USE: To build, repair, and strengthen wood, fiberglass, and metal structures with a laminate of fiberglass cloth and polyester or epoxy resin.

USE TIPS: Avoid contact with skin; cloth fibers are extremely irritating.

BUYING TIPS: Go to a commercial supplier when you need large quantities. Prices are better in bulk.

DRY FIBER FILLER

ALSO KNOWN AS: Filler, epoxy filler, microfibers

DESCRIPTION: Short lintlike tufts of spun-glass fibers in dry form in either bags or cans.

USE: To add bulk, but not strength, to epoxy and polyester resins. This is especially useful when making repairs on a vertical surface.

USE TIPS: Other fillers are available, including spherelike microballoons.

BUYING TIPS: 1 qt. of fiber filler weighs about 1 lb.

RESIN ROLLERS

DESCRIPTION: Similar in appearance to paint rollers, only roller surface is hard plastic and usually

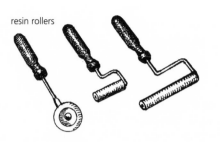

resin rollers

a maximum of 6" wide × 1" diameter. Plastic roller handles have threaded sockets. A variation is the "pizza cutter" roller with a thin circular disk.

USE: Along with a squeegee, a resin roller is an essential tool for spreading polyester or epoxy resin on cloth. This is a job that must be done carefully because "dry lay-up"—in other words areas where fiberglass cloth is not properly "wetted out" with resin—weakens the entire structure or repair patch.

USE TIPS: Use acetone to clean rollers and other resin-stained tools.

BUYING TIPS: For hard-to-reach places, you can buy a 4½' extension that screws into the roller (or you could just use your mop or scrub-brush handle, which will also fit).

Marine resin

ALSO KNOWN AS: Polyester resin

DESCRIPTION: Honey-color polyester-base resin.

USE: Mixed with hardener, marine resin is applied to fiberglass cloth and used to repair fiberglass, wood, plastic, and some metals.

USE TIPS: Polyester resin is easier to work with than epoxy resin (see page 301) because it allows considerable time before it begins to cure.

BUYING TIPS: Sometimes sold in a kit with catalyst, also known as setting agent or hardener (see below).

Setting agent

ALSO KNOWN AS: Catalyst, hardener

DESCRIPTION: Chemical added to polyester or epoxy resins. Usually the mix ratio is greatly in favor of the resin.

USE: Triggers chemical reaction that causes resin to cure and harden. Each type of resin requires its own special setting agent. Experimenting could result in a sticky mess of uncured resin.

USE TIPS: Follow manufacturer's instructions carefully when matching resin to setting agent. Use too much catalyst and not only will it "set" too quickly, it will also quickly deteriorate.

BUYING TIPS: Small bottle or tube of catalyst is often included with the resin.

Polyester gel coat

ALSO KNOWN AS: Finish gel coat, gel-coat repair kit

DESCRIPTION: Polyester-based two-part high-gloss white waterproof finish.

USE: To repair cosmetic damages to gel-coated surfaces, but do not expect the same quality of finish as your boat had when it came from the factory, where gel coats are sprayed into the mold.

USE TIPS: Small tubes of pigments are available for tinting white gel coat, but matching colors is extremely hard. Do not be disappointed or surprised if you cannot get it exactly right.

BUYING TIPS: Good for a temporary coverup, but you may want to consider repainting your hull with a one- or two-part polyurethane instead.

FAIRING COMPOUND

ALSO KNOWN AS: Surfacing compound, surfacing putty

DESCRIPTION: Very thick one-part polyester- or two-part epoxy-based putty.

USE: To fill dents or gouges prior to painting. Polyester-based material cures faster than epoxy.

USE TIPS: For boat repairs, use only fairing compounds made for marine applications. Auto-body putty absorbs water and will soon pop off.

BUYING TIPS: Polyester fairing compound is sold in pints and quarts, while two-part epoxy is sold in pint cans that combine to make a quart.

TROWEL CEMENT

DESCRIPTION: Polyester putty is applied with a putty knife over primed surfaces.

USE: Good for filling small dents, or smoothing large areas or rough wood. Can be sanded smooth. Dries hard.

USE TIPS: For use only above the waterline.

BUYING TIPS: Sold in pints.

STORAGE ACCESSORIES

BOAT COVER

ALSO KNOWN AS: Tarpaulin, tarp, storage cover

DESCRIPTION: Cotton canvas, fabric-reinforced plastic, or polyethylene rectangular sheet with reinforced seams and hem, usually has rustproof grommets every 36" to 48" along hem or may have a tunnel hem with a built-in drawstring. Sizes range from 8' long × 6' wide to a big 40' long × 25' wide. Usually available in blue, blue, or blue (to match most bootstripes), but you can get red, green, or black if you shop around. An *outboard motor cover* is also available, with an elastic hem so that it closes up tight.

USE: To cover boat when it is not in use. Run shock or other cord through grommets and under boat for a snug fit.

USE TIPS: Canvas covers "breathe" better than plastic ones, so your boat is less likely to mildew or get moldy, important if it remains covered for long periods of time. Canvas is more durable than its plastic counterparts and can be treated with protectant (see page 282) to be more waterproof. Extra care should be taken to secure covers when boats are being trailered, since they will rip or blow off otherwise. Covers that have lost their usefulness as covers because of rips or other damage can still be used as drop cloths.

BUYING TIPS: Select a size that gives good overlap down the sides of the boat. Although canvas is more expensive than plastic covers, it lasts much longer.

TARP LOCK

DESCRIPTION: Hourglass-shaped plastic-coated carbon-steel 4"-long "ring," with a hard plastic ball 1" in diameter.

tarp lock

USE: To serve as secure fastening point on boat covers or other tarplike sheets in spots where there are no grommets or where grommets have torn out. Function is similar to old-fashioned stocking garter; position the ball under the tarp and slide the ring over the tarp and ball. A cord can be tied to the ring.

USE TIPS: Kind of gimmicky—you could just add a grommet or, if it's time, buy a new tarp.

BUYING TIPS: Sold in packages of four rings and four balls; inexpensive.

COVER VENTS

DESCRIPTION: Aluminum pole ⅞"-diameter telescopes from 35" to 63".

USE: To permit air to circulate and also raises cover so that water won't pool.

USE TIPS: Vent pole does double duty as anti-pooling frame.

BUYING TIPS: Ventilation is as important during the storage of a boat as during its active use, although humidity may be lower. Go a season and see what happens before adding a vent.

BOAT COVER SUPPORT SYSTEM

ALSO KNOWN AS: Boat cover pole(s), tent pole, ridgepole

DESCRIPTION: A system of one or more one-piece or telescoping aluminum poles with protective, nonskid tips, and poly web tape or shock cord. Webbing in some systems may limit usefulness of

system only to boats up to 22' long. Some poles come with a cap that fits snugly over the tarp and pole together.

USE: To raise boat cover in the center in a tentlike manner to prevent water from accumulating, where its weight will eventually tear the cover, allowing the water to drop down and flood the boat.

USE TIPS: Especially helpful in northern climes where snow tends to build up.

BUYING TIPS: The natural profile of your boat (and boat cover) may discourage pooling; take a hose to the cover and see if it drains naturally.

STORAGE-COVER FRAMES

storage cover clamp   storage cover coupling

ALSO KNOWN AS: Boat-cover frame

DESCRIPTION: Assorted zinc-plated steel clamps, slide locks, and couplings, as well as plastic and rubber tips and end sockets. Color-coded weatherproof adhesive strips, as well as diagrams of powerboats and sailboats.

USE: Custom-build your own reusable boat-cover frame by using these fittings with ¾" EMT plastic tubing purchased separately. A cover for a 30' boat takes about 2 hours to assemble.

USE TIPS: A boat-cover frame is desirable on heavier boats, where the extra windage created by a higher cover is offset by the boat's weight. Supporting the cover with a sturdy frame keeps water from sitting on the cover and protects delicate equipment on deck.

Marking fittings and tubing with color-coded adhesive makes the frame easy to dismantle and rebuild year after year. Boat diagrams let you draw your own "blueprint" of the cover for future reference.

BUYING TIPS: Fittings are sold in multipacks. EMT tubing can be purchased at hardware stores.

INFLATABLE OR DINGHY COVER

DESCRIPTION: Rounded rectangle of canvas twill with shock cord in tunnel hem. Cord tie-down loops instead of grommets.

USE: Like a large shower cap for inflatables and other small boats—to protect boat from showers.

USE TIPS: Helpful if your dingy is left unattended for long periods, especially in the hot sun. Otherwise, why not deflate and store inside?

BUYING TIPS: Sized for 9'–11'-long dinghies and sport boats.

OUTBOARD-MOTOR COVER

DESCRIPTION: Snug-fitting, marine-grade, heavy-duty cotton canvas bag that is water-repellent and mildew- and UV-resistant. A draw cord sewn into the bottom makes it fit tightly. Sold according to engine size, by horsepower.

USE: Fits over outboard motor to protect it from sun and rain.

USE TIPS: Keep in a dry place when not in use. Supplement the draw string with shock cords or other straps to hold the cover on during storms.

BUYING TIPS: While this helps prevent fading of the motor housing, the housing itself offers excellent protection anyway.

CENTER CONSOLE COVER

DESCRIPTION: Boxlike canvas cover measures 40" wide × 25" high (front) × 40" high (back) × 30" diameter. Grommets along bottom hem. Drawstring or wrap ties at mid-height.

USE: Fits over most center consoles; raised area accommodates steering wheel or windshield.

USE TIPS: Acts like a sail cover, quickly protecting vital components while allowing you to get under way without much ado.

BUYING TIPS: Cheap protection against the elements.

— MARINE TOOLS AND ACCESSORIES —

RETRIEVER MAGNET

DESCRIPTION: Block or horseshoe magnet, usually about 6" sq., with handle, capable of lifting up to about 200 lbs. Smaller versions include cylindrical magnets on pencil-thin long handles with a universal joint near the magnet end, as well as all kinds of other sizes and shapes.

USE: A heavy-duty magnet is invaluable for locating anchors and other ferrous metal objects lost

overboard. If you are going to lift the missing item with the magnet, be sure the tether to which it is tied is secure and strong enough for the load.

Smaller magnets are useful for locating small parts that fall into the bilge or other inaccessible spots.

USE TIPS: If you store your magnet onboard, find a spot that won't interfere with the compass or other navigation gear, including electronics or autopilots.

BUYING TIPS: Prices, sizes, and styles vary widely. Kids love scavenging for underwater treasures, so a magnet can be a fun item to have around.

Tool
SAFETY STRAP

DESCRIPTION: Elastic cord ⅛" × 1'–2' long with loops and sliding cord locks at either end.

USE: To tether tools to your wrist, so that you do not lose them overboard or while you are working aloft on the mast.

USE TIPS: Always use a strap (or piece of string or line) when using a tool anywhere where it risks being dropped overboard; otherwise invest in a retriever magnet (see previous item).

BUYING TIPS: Worth having, considering the aggravation, damage, and even injuries a dropped tool can cause.

CHAPTER TWELVE

TRAILERING

ABOUT TRAILERS

The vast majority of pleasure boats in this country are trailerable. Trailers compensate for the general lack of dock and mooring space and allow the boat owner to cruise highway and byway in search of new boating and fishing grounds. The most important component, of course, is the trailer, preferably made of galvanized (zinc-plated) steel to resist water and salt-air corrosion.

Trailers are classified by maximum gross weight as follows: Class I—2,000 lbs.; Class II—3,500 lbs.; Class III—5,000 lbs.; Class IV—over 5,000 lbs. Federal law requires a sticker listing weight and other characteristics to be pasted on by the manufacturer. If your payload exceeds 85% of the listed gross weight, you should move up a class. Once a trailer is selected, you can begin choosing the many accessories that make trailering safer and more convenient.

TRAILER COMPONENTS

TRAILER WINCH

manual
trailer winch

DESCRIPTION: Stationary hoisting device with horizontal drum around which a rope or wire is wound inside a steel housing (often zinc-plated or finished with anticorrosive black powder), and steel gears (carbon 1050 steel in the better models).

TYPES:

Manual trailer winch: Open drum design, with either single- or double- ratchet action, one or two speeds, and (on most) 3-gear locking—neutral, forward, and reverse. Best models have internally lubricated drum and shaft bushings. Drum diameter ranges from ⅝" to 1½", and rated working load from 600 to about 2,600 lbs. (for boats 1,200 to about 5,200 lbs.). Many come with a detachable crank handle.

Electric trailer winch: Plastic-housed winch with steel components powered by a 12-volt battery drawing anywhere from 70 to 100 amps (with circuit breaker

built in). Better models have positive-action lock for when the motor shuts off, remote control units, and emergency manual cranks. Most come with 20' or so of wire cable. Working loads of 1,500 to 5,000 lbs. (boats 3,500 to 15,000 lbs.) are common.

USE: To pull a boat forward onto a trailer and lock it into position once it is on.

USE TIPS: Stand back from the winch and cable while operating and beware freewheeling crank handles.

BUYING TIPS: Gross boat weight should not exceed three times the rated pulling capacity of your winch.

WINCH ADAPTER PLATE

ALSO KNOWN AS: Ball-hitch adapter

DESCRIPTION: Zinc-plated steel mounting plate sized to hold most power winches; fits any ball hitch (see page 316).

USE: To allow quick removal of power winch from its stand. Multipurpose version fits over trailer ball.

USE TIPS: May not accept all winch makes. Winch should not be used for lifting purposes.

BUYING TIPS: Convenient for those who switch trailers.

V INYL WINCH COVER

DESCRIPTION: Squarish (10½" × 8" × 10½") plastic cover, open on one side.

USE: To cover electric winch or windlass.

USE TIPS: Good idea, but electric winches should be removed for security reasons when trailer is idle for extended periods.

BUYING TIPS: Good investment for keeping winches clean and dry.

W INCH CABLE

ALSO KNOWN AS: Aircraft cable, safety cable

DESCRIPTION: Galvanized-steel aircraft wire cable, often with forged snap hook attached. Commonly comes in 20', 25', and 30' lengths; diameters from ³⁄₁₆" to ⁷⁄₃₂", and working loads from 2,000 to 2,800 lbs.

USE: To join winch and boat for hauling.

USE TIPS: For larger boats. Manufacturers often rate cable or line in terms of breaking, or *tensile,* strength, rather than working strength. Safe working load is about one-half the breaking strength. Try to match maximum-load rating of cable to that of your winch.

N YLON WINCH ROPE

DESCRIPTION: Double-braided line, often sold in 20' lengths; ⅜" diameter and breaking strength of about 2,300 lbs.

USE: To winch smaller boats onto a trailer.

USE TIPS: Not recommended for boats more than 14' in length.

BUYING TIPS: Small-boat owners might keep one as a backup to a wire winch cable.

P OLYPROPYLENE WINCH ROPE

ALSO KNOWN AS: Polypro winch rope

DESCRIPTION: Braided polypropylene line; 5/16" diameter, with working load of about 500 to 600 lbs. and breaking strength of about 1,000 lbs.

USE: To winch up the smallest (500 lbs. and under) of craft.

USE TIPS: Rot-resistant but not recommended for heavy-duty work of trailering.

BUYING TIPS: Invest in a good wire cable instead.

W INCH STRAP

ALSO KNOWN AS:
Nylon web strap.

DESCRIPTION: Flat 2"–2½" wide nylon-web strap; snap hook cross-stitched on. Breaking strength of 6,000 lbs. or more. Often comes in 20' length.

USE: Trailer winch line.

USE TIPS: For hand winches only.

BUYING TIPS: It's strong and it won't tangle, but it is for smaller boats only.

Forged CABLE HOOK

ALSO KNOWN AS: Forged snap hook

DESCRIPTION: Forged anticorrosive steel snap hook, typically 25/16" × 4" with ¾" eye; working load of about 650 lbs.

USE: To hook winch cable to bow eye on boat. Cable is attached by looping end through hook eye and crimping.

USE TIPS: For manual winches.

BUYING TIPS: Make sure yours has a safety latch.

Scissor HOOK

DESCRIPTION: Plated steel hook with overlapping arms; oval in shape when closed, 3¼" × 1¾" with ½" diameter eye. Stamped hinge at bottom permits hook to open and rotate 360°. Pin holes through overlapping tops allow locking.

USE: To hook winch cable to bow eye of boat, same as forged cable hook (above) but with a working load of about 1,100 lbs., this is 30%–40% stronger.

USE TIPS: Stronger than a snap shackle, and lasts longer than a snap hook, whose springs tend to corrode.

BUYING TIPS: Helpful to have several around the boat.

90° PULLEY BLOCK

DESCRIPTION: Zinc-plated steel combination pulley/snap hook; either 3" × 8" swivel, 2½" × 7¼" nonswivel. Breaking strength of 7,500 lbs.

USE: To permit setting up a double-line winch.

USE TIPS: Almost doubles winch dead-lift capacity.

BUYING TIPS: Single-winching works for most small boats, but you can always find other onboard uses for this piece of gear.

Trailer ROLLER

DESCRIPTION: Rubber or polyurethane revolving cylinder, as small as 2" in length, up to 18" or more. Shaft hole drilled from end to end, sometimes lined with nylon or steel insert.

TYPES:

Bow roller: Small (3" long, ½" shaft hole) dumbbell-shaped roller of neoprene or polymer that fastens near front of trailer, often on winch mount, to accept bow.

Spool/keel roller: 4" or 5¼" spoollike solid black rubber roller designed to receive keel of smaller boats. Fits ⅝" shaft.

Adjusting roller: Smooth or ribbed rubber roller, fairly short in length compared with diameter (4⅜" × 3½" or 4¼" × 4⅜"), designed for support system that automatically distributes a boat's weight.

Keel roller: Longer roller, typically 8"–18", sometimes tapered to help center a keel. Made of rubber or longer-lasting (and less likely to mar) polyurethane.

Side roller: Spool or cylinder-shaped gray or black rubber roller, some with full-length plastic bushing insert. Mounted, on ⅝" shaft, at sides of trailer to guide hull in.

Wobble roller: Smooth or ribbed rubber roller, 4¼" × 4⅜", steel washer or nylon bushing insert. Sometimes mounted in pairs; "wobbles" on its shaft to conform to varying hull configurations, shapes.

bow roller   spool/keel roller   wobble roller

USE: To roll the boat up and into the trailer and to support the hull once loaded.

USE TIPS: Grease the roller shaft before installing.

BUYING TIPS: Black rubber is cheaper but deteriorates faster than polyurethane and may mark up the hull.

ROLLER BRACKET

split bracket

ALSO KNOWN AS:
Roller mount

DESCRIPTION: Galvanized-steel mounting plate, with slots for fastening to trailer supports and matching ⅝" holes to accept standard roller shaft.

TYPES:

Single-piece bracket: Galvanized-steel plate, from 8" to 12" long with right-angle end flaps ⅜" high and holes sized for standard ⅝" keel roller shaft. Mounts horizontally on cross-member with slots for up to 5" vertical adjustment.

Split bracket: Bracket consisting of two matching 7" right-angle pieces, usually mounted vertically on trailer. Separate pieces allow brackets to be positioned to accept any size roller; ⅝" holes accept standard roller shaft; 4¾"-long slot permits bracket to be adjusted vertically for better hull support. Sold in pairs.

USE: To mount roller shafts and rollers on trailer.

USE TIPS: Position brackets to provide adequate support at critical points—under the bow, the keel, the turn of the bilge, and the transom. Port and starboard rollers should be in matching positions for an even load.

BUYING TIPS: You have to buy your own ⅜" bolts for fastening these brackets.

U-BOLT

DESCRIPTION: Zinc-plated steel square or round bend bolt, from ⅜" to ½" and thread sizes from 1" to 2". Usually sold with washers and locknuts.

USE: To attach brackets to trailer frame.

USE TIPS: Not for attaching major structural parts.

BUYING TIPS: Square models are more practical.

ROLLER SHAFT

ALSO KNOWN AS: Steel shaft

DESCRIPTION: Plain or galvanized-steel rod; lengths from 4¼" to 19" and diameters of ½" or ⅝". Some come with snap-on hat-shaped *pal nuts,* but end caps are extra.

USE: To let roller roll.

USE TIPS: Keep well greased.

BUYING TIPS: Go for the galvanized.

Roller end cap

ALSO KNOWN AS: Protective end cap

DESCRIPTION: Short (2½") round rubber cap with hole (usually ⅝") in center.

USE: To slip over end of roller shaft to prevent gouging of boat hull.

USE TIPS: Check regularly for deterioration.

BUYING TIPS: Some keel rollers come with their own caps.

Bow stop

ALSO KNOWN AS: Bow guard

DESCRIPTION: V-shaped black rubber or polyurethane wedge, 2"–3" long, ½"-diameter hole in base for shaft.

USE: To attach to winch mount to cushion boat's bow during loading.

USE TIPS: Same use as bow roller.

BUYING TIPS: A fraction costlier and without the rolling action of the bow roller (see page 312), this is not a good deal.

Padded bunk board

ALSO KNOWN AS: Padded bolster, carpeted bunk board

DESCRIPTION: Carpeted 2" × 4" board in 3', 4', and 5' lengths.

USE: To provide longitudinal support to a trailered hull; padding protects against scratches and streaks.

USE TIPS: Bunk-roller combination gives best mix of support and ease of hoisting.

BUYING TIPS: Plain 2 × 4s from the lumberyard are much cheaper; just add carpet.

Trailer bunk padding

ALSO KNOWN AS: Trailer bunk carpeting

DESCRIPTION: Polypropylene carpeting with acrylic backing. Sold in 12' rolls in widths of 8", 10", and 12"; charcoal color.

USE: To provide padding for bare bunk boards.

USE TIPS: Fasten with staple gun.

BUYING TIPS: Excess can be used as area rug on boat or at home.

Bunk bracket

ALSO KNOWN AS: Bolster brackets

DESCRIPTION: Three-sided rectangular bracket, Z-shaped from side view. Zinc-plated steel. Two sizes—9½" long (with 6" vertical adjustment slot) for standard hulls, and 12⅝" (with 9" slot) for deep-V hulls.

USE: To fasten bunk boards to trailer.

USE TIPS: Adjustable, like roller brackets.

BUYING TIPS: Sold in regular hull and deep-V versions.

MOTOR SUPPORT BRACKET

ALSO KNOWN AS: Motor cradle

DESCRIPTION: Telescoping steel rod (adjusts from about 20" to 27") with either black powder or vinyl finish, topped with a polyurethane V-block; has built-in shock absorber and load meter. Attaches to rear roller or, using a bottom U-bracket, over the roller or a cross-member.

USE: Fits between trailer and upraised outboard or I/O (inboard/outboard) lower unit to brace and cushion motor during hauling.

USE TIPS: Especially useful with units that have hydraulic or manual tilt mechanisms.

BUYING TIPS: If you need a shorter strut, you can trim off the bottom end.

TRAILER HITCHES AND ACCESSORIES

ABOUT TRAILER HITCHES

Along with the coupler, the hitch makes up the critical connection point between trailer and tow vehicle. The simplest and cheapest type of hitch is the *weight-bearing hitch,* frequently called the *bumper hitch.* This kind attaches to the vehicle bumper and takes the full brunt of the tongue weight. This may work for the lightest of loads, but it is not advisable and is illegal in some states. Better is the *weight-distribution hitch,* which mounts to the frame of the towing vehicle and redistributes much of the load between the tow vehicle and the trailer wheels. Some models incorporate antisway bars, which stabilize the trailer and improve on-the-road control. Hitches are rated Class I–IV on the basis of weight.

TRAILER HITCH

ALSO KNOWN AS: Receiver hitch

DESCRIPTION: Welded steel frame, T-shaped, sometimes with a second crossbar. Base of T contains the receiver, a square 2"-diameter opening for accepting the mount that holds the hitch ball.

USE: To attach the tow vehicle to the trailer.

USE TIPS: Antisway feature saves much wear and tear on the tow vehicle.

BUYING TIPS: Check with dealer or manufacturer for the correct hitch for your make and model vehicle. Class III and IV hitches are all weight-distribution, but some Class II hitches may be weight-bearing.

Hitch Ball

ALSO KNOWN AS: Trailer ball, coupler ball, ball hitch

DESCRIPTION: One-piece 1⅞"- or 2"-diameter steel or chrome-plated steel ball, with shaft from 1½" to 2" long leading to ¾"–1"-diameter bolt; washer and locknut included. Capacities range from 2,000 to 5,000 lbs. of tongue weight.

USE: Bolts to hitch and mates with coupler (see this page) to attach trailer.

USE TIPS: Fasten with locknut or weld tight.

BUYING TIPS: A vital point in the hitch—be sure to get correct size for your load.

Reversible Hitch Ball

ALSO KNOWN AS: Converter ball

DESCRIPTION: Two versions: ¾"-diameter shank and one each 1⅞" and 2" twist-on ball; or, hollow shank with two shank balls, with safety holes for inserting a cotter pin.

USE: To be able to rapidly change ball size.

USE TIPS: Handy for vehicles that must tow different weights. Check to see ball is on tight before coupling.

BUYING TIPS: Capacity (3,500 lbs.) not as high as larger one-piece units.

Hitch Ball Mount

ALSO KNOWN AS: Trailer ball mount

DESCRIPTION: Steel bar with welded, curved-steel offset, 7" or 8" in length. Shaft inserts into 2"-diameter receiver on hitch and fastens with pull pin and clip. Curved portion has hole that takes ¾"-diameter hitch-ball shank.

USE: To mount hitch ball and attach to under-vehicle trailer hitch.

USE TIPS: Rated by one of trailer-weight classes (see page 310).

BUYING TIPS: Rise of offset varies from 2¾" to 4"; determine what degree you need (by measuring offset of undervehicle receiver).

Hitch-Ball Cover

ALSO KNOWN AS: Coupler-ball cover

DESCRIPTION: Cylindrical PVC cover, open at bottom, that slips over 1⅞" or 2" hitch ball.

USE: To keep ball clean and prevent rust.

USE TIPS: Also softens bumps and keeps grease off people moving about the rear of the car.

BUYING TIPS: A split tennis ball will do the same job.

Trailer Coupler

DESCRIPTION: Scoop-shaped steel fastener bolted to the tongue on the front end of a trailer. Sizes for 1⅞"- and 2"-diameter balls.

USE: To fit over and lock onto the hitch ball to attach trailer to towing vehicle.

USE TIPS: Quick coupler version has clamp on top that compresses locking mechanism within the scoop for precise fit against the ball.

BUYING TIPS: Check the GVWR (gross vehicle weight rating) label required by law to make sure the coupler-hitch size is correct for the trailer load.

COUPLER HANDLE

DESCRIPTION: U-shaped steel handle with padded grip; bolts to 1⅞" and 2" couplers.

USE: To provide good grip for lifting coupler.

USE TIPS: Extra leverage is helpful too.

BUYING TIPS: Helpful and inexpensive item.

COUPLER PIN

DESCRIPTION: Small rectangular steel pin (2" × 2¼"); one side is ⅜"-diameter pin that opens and snaps shut.

USE: To snap over and secure coupler-hitch connection.

USE TIPS: Just a fastener, not a lock.

BUYING TIPS: Not necessary if you have a hitch lock.

TRAILER LOCKS

ALSO KNOWN AS: Coupler lock, coupler-ball lock

DESCRIPTION: Coupler and coupler-ball locks of various designs.

TYPES:

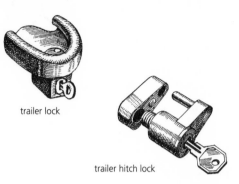

trailer lock

trailer hitch lock

Trailer lock: Y-shaped hardened-steel lock that slips over the coupler flange on an unattached trailer. The base of the lock covers the ball opening.

Trailer hitch lock: Heat-treated solid-cast-steel lock consisting of U-shaped top whose two arms lock into the base; blocks access to the coupler-locking mechanism of trailer, either on or off the hitch.

Trailer security plate: Circular steel plate with attached ball locks into and over coupler-ball opening to simulate trailer on hitch; sized for 1⅞" or 2" ball opening.

Universal locknut: Small thimble-shaped steel lock that covers the coupler-ball bolt nut, preventing ball from being unbolted from the hitch.

USE: Two purposes: to either prevent the uncoupling of trailer and tow vehicle or, in the case of an unattached trailer, to prevent its recoupling to an unauthorized vehicle, usually by covering the coupler hole.

USE TIPS: Determine whether your trailer is most at risk when hitched or unhitched and get the appropriate lock.

BUYING TIPS: Type that locks coupler onto the hitch provides extra security while towing.

TRAILER ACCESSORIES

TRAILER STAND/ PROTECTOR

DESCRIPTION: Heavy-gauge steel tripod stand 28" high. A high-tensile, solid-steel ball is welded to circular plate on top.

USE: To hold up and secure trailer tongue and coupler.

USE TIPS: Lockable.

BUYING TIPS: Lock not included.

TRAILER SAFETY CHAIN

DESCRIPTION: Welded-link steel chain (usually ⁵⁄₁₆" or ⅜"), in 32" length (for Class I loads) and 42" (for Classes II and III); comes with S-hooks.

USE: Legally required backup connection between trailer and tow vehicle.

USE TIPS: Keep attached to trailer, cross under the hitch to catch the trailer tongue should ball connection fail.

BUYING TIPS: Match chain to towing weight. Get one long enough to allow the rig to turn freely, but not so long that the chain drags.

TONGUE JACK

ALSO KNOWN AS: Dolly

DESCRIPTION: Steel jack stand on castered polyurethane wheel (6" standard) with a mounting bracket that clamps

onto trailer tongue and a hand crank. Jack range from 14" to 28", depending on the model, with lift capacities from 350 to 1,200 lbs. Some models permit jack to pivot up for better clearance and less crank time. Also available in a 12-volt electric version that can handle up to 1,000 lbs.

USE: To lift trailer tongue up to hitch.

USE TIPS: Recommended when tongue weight—the weight at the trailer coupler ball—exceeds 75 lbs.

BUYING TIPS: Double-wheel models recommended for soft or unpaved surfaces. Electric versions not really necessary.

WHEEL BEARING KIT

DESCRIPTION: Wheel's friction-reducing components—steel cones, steel cups, cotter pin, and seal. Available for axles sized ¾" to 1⅜".

USE: To provide replacement parts for seized bearings.

USE TIPS: Check bearings often (including after every long haul), and pack and repack with waterproof grease.

BUYING TIPS: Because of the stress on trailer-wheel bearings, get two kits—one for emergency repairs and one as a backup.

CAST HUB SETS

ALSO KNOWN AS: Trailer-wheel hub set, hub-replacement kit

DESCRIPTION: Kit with inner and outer bearings, grease seal, cotter pin, lug nuts, and dust cap. Will fit 4- or 5-stud wheels, with either 1" or 1¼" threaded studs.

USE: To provide a rebuilding kit for bearings, wheel hub.

USE TIPS: Dust caps are unnecessary if you are using bearing protectors.

BUYING TIPS: Bearing kit should be enough to get you through most emergencies.

Bearing protector

ALSO KNOWN AS: Bearing Buddy®

DESCRIPTION: Steel cap with interior spring and pressure-relief valve that prevents water from entering hub when wheel is suddenly submerged. Sized either for 1¾" or 2" wheel hubs.

USE: To hold grease in and keep water out, protecting bearing seal.

USE TIPS: Especially for trailers whose wheels get submerged.

BUYING TIPS: Sold in pairs, some with matching plastic covers.

Bearing protector cover

ALSO KNOWN AS: Bearing bra

DESCRIPTION: Plastic cap sized to fit over bearing protector.

USE: To catch any grease overflow from axle hub, including that squirted out by bearing-protector release valve.

USE TIPS: Better not to overgrease the axle hub.

BUYING TIPS: What's next—a bearing-protector cover protector? Get protectors with the covers included so that you don't need to buy this.

Spare-tire carrier

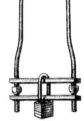

DESCRIPTION: Steel rack or bracket that clamps to trailer and can accommodate tires from 8" to 12" diameter.

locking tire carrier

TYPES:

Basic tire carrier: Tubular zinc-plated steel rack, rectangular in shape, with tray or arm on bottom to rest tire; clamps to tube or pipe from 2" sq. to 3½" × 4" and accepts 4- or 5-lug tires from 8" to 12".

Locking tire carrier: Similar design to basic except has double horizontal bars on bottom to lock tire to carrier; comes with steel lock with extralong shackles. Accepts wheels from 8" to 15" diameter.

High-mount tire carrier: Heavy-duty steel mount consisting of two plates joined by a 5" beam; one end bolts to either trailer tongue or frame; 5" offset provides ground clearance. Adjustable bolt pattern accommodates 4- or 5-bolt wheels, including larger 12", 13", and 14" sizes.

USE: Clamps to trailer to hold spare tire.

USE TIPS: Good idea, because trailer tires can be hard to find.

BUYING TIPS: Get the locking kind. Also check that your car lug wrench matches trailer lugs (sometimes they do not).

TRAILER BEARING GREASE

ALSO KNOWN AS: Wheel bearing grease

DESCRIPTION: Water insoluble, noncorrosive synthetic lubricant, often with Teflon® as a base.

USE: To lubricate wheel bearings.

USE TIPS: Also good on winches and other marine gear requiring lubrication.

BUYING TIPS: Sold in 10-oz. and 14-oz. tubes and cartridges, 14-oz. tubs.

COMPACT GREASE-GUN KIT

DESCRIPTION: One-hand grease gun that takes 3-oz. lube cartridge.

USE: To lube bearings and other tight spots.

USE TIPS: Use palm to squeeze cartridge while depressing trigger.

BUYING TIPS: Get some spare cartridges—sold in four-packs.

GALVANIZED BRAKES

ALSO KNOWN AS: Replacement brakes

DESCRIPTION: Hot-dip galvanized brakes with stainless steel springs and fasteners; other components are made of cadmium-plated steel.

USE: To provide replacement for any 2¼"-wide × 10"-diameter brake system.

USE TIPS: Unless you are a skilled mechanic, have a trailer professional check for proper adjustment before hauling.

BUYING TIPS: Sold in pairs.

FRESHWATER FLUSHING SYSTEM

ALSO KNOWN AS: Brake-flushing system

DESCRIPTION: Clear ⅜" plastic tubing, in a T or yoke shape, that installs along the axle frame of a trailer. Long end of the T has coupler that fits most garden hoses; other two ends are fitted with a barb, or nipple, and an O-ring that is inserted into wheel opening. Plastic locking ties for installation and couplers are included.

USE: To irrigate brakes with freshwater after saltwater immersion.

USE TIPS: Hooks up to garden hose.

BUYING TIPS: Good lubrication and bearing protectors should do the job. Some trailer makes may require drilling to insert barbs.

TRAILER TIE-DOWNS

transom tie-down

ALSO KNOWN AS: Hold downs, tie-down straps

DESCRIPTION: Adjustable nylon or polypropylene straps, usually in widths of 1" or 2" and lengths of up to 42" for *bow-* and *transom tie-downs,* 12' to 20' for over-the-hull gunwale straps. Usually fitted with steel S-hooks or J-hooks.

USE: To secure boat to trailer so that it won't slide off during hauling or become misaligned. Bow tie-downs hold the boat on in the event of the winch line snapping and also prevent the boat from hurtling forward if there is a sudden stop during automotive transport.

USE TIPS: Do not rely on your winch line to keep the bow fastened. Use bow and transom ties, the most critical ones. Larger boats need gunwale tie-downs.

BUYING TIPS: Nylon is stronger.

ANCHOR STRAP POINT KIT

DESCRIPTION: Zinc-plated steel eyebolts, about 4" long, with eye openings of ⅜" and ⅝". Sold with washers and locknuts.

USE: Bolts to trailer to provide fastening point for tie-down hooks.

USE TIPS: Check nuts regularly for tightness.

BUYING TIPS: Sold in twos.

TRAILER BOAT COVER

ALSO KNOWN AS: Boat cover

DESCRIPTION: 10 oz. cotton duck cover with four-ply fold-down seams and 10 or more 1"-wide nylon tie downs.

USE: Covering boats that are trailered.

USE TIPS: Provides better, snugger fit and stands up better to rigors of trailering than a generic plastic or light canvas cover or tarp.

BUYING TIPS: To ensure the best fit, first match your bow shape to that of the cover; take into ac-

count the size and style of your windshield, if any, and other protrusions (some covers are designated for a particular type of boat—walk-around cuddy, ski boat, etc.); finally, measure the overall length of the boat (in a straight line, not over the windshield). Most covers will extend another few inches, but go up one size if you suspect too tight a fit.

TRAILER ALIGNMENT SYSTEMS

ALSO KNOWN AS: Trailer guides, boat guides.

DESCRIPTION: Bright white and/or orange plastic or fiberglass markers that can be seen through rearview mirror or window of tow vehicle.

TYPES:

Trailer alignment system: Two fiberglass wands with magnetic chrome-plated bases; orange wand mounts behind trailer hitch, white, with V-top, to trailer tongue. Driver aligns them through rear mirror.

Trailer boat guides: Two white PVC tubes shaped like upside-down shepherd staffs that mount underneath trailer at the rear; arms extend up 50" and serve as guideposts. Brackets included for installing lights on top.

USE: Either to align tow vehicle with trailer or to guide boat onto trailer.

USE TIPS: Helpful but silly-looking.

BUYING TIPS: The wands are cheaper than the guides—and removable.

LAUNCH/ LOAD RAMP

ALSO KNOWN AS: Trailer walk ramp

DESCRIPTION: Galvanized-steel plate, 9½" wide and 24" or 36" in length; includes self-adhesive nonskid patches, predrilled holes, and hardware for installation.

USE: Attaches to trailer tongue and main or side beam to provide secure walkway onto the trailer while launching or loading.

USE TIPS: Paintable, but original galvanized state provides better corrosion protection.

BUYING TIPS: Sold individually, but you can combine them if you need more length.

LICENSE-PLATE BRACKET

ALSO KNOWN AS: License bracket

DESCRIPTION: Upside-down, T-shaped molded-plastic frame sized to fit standard trailer plates. Includes holes for mounting and for installing lights. White or black.

USE: To protect license plate from bending and rusting.

USE TIPS: A bargain, at under $2.

BUYING TIPS: You supply the ¼" mounting bolts nuts—preferably no-rust nylon, although stainless steel ones are available.

TRAILER FENDER

ALSO KNOWN AS: Replacement fender

DESCRIPTION: Galvanized-steel (16-gauge) arch-shaped plate, 8"–10" wide, 25¼"–64" tip-to-tip; sized to fit over 8" and 12" tires.

USE: To provide replacement for corroded trailer fender.

USE TIPS: May have to do some drilling; mounting gear extra.

BUYING TIPS: Sold individually.

TRAILER PAINT

DESCRIPTION: Primer-sealer for steel trailers.

USE: To prepare surface for topside paint.

USE TIPS: Renewing finish once each year is a good idea.

BUYING TIPS: Check manufacturer's specs to ensure primer and top coat are compatible.

TRAILER LIGHTING

ABOUT TRAILER LIGHTS

By federal law trailers must have red tail and brake lights, red or amber turn signals, as well as a white license light. Federal Motor Vehicle Safety Standard 108 also requires red and amber side lights and reflectors for trailers less than 80" wide; wider trailers need side clearance lights and three red rear I.D. lights in place of reflectors. Lights must be spaced evenly, either parallel or perpendicular to the trailer frame, and not tilted more than ¼". Tow vehicles must have a heavy-duty relay in the turn-signal circuit and a wiring harness, available from auto supply or marine stores. Lights should be mounted so that they do not get submerged; otherwise you need waterproof lights.

REFLECTORS

DESCRIPTION: Rectangular acrylic lens with adhesive backing; most common measurements are 2¼" × 2¾" or 3⅛" × 1⅜". Amber or red lens.

USE: Side and rear reflectors.

USE TIPS: Red side reflector goes as far forward as possible and must be at least 15" from the ground; amber side reflector goes behind the wheel and at least 15" up; rear red reflectors (two) are placed as far apart as feasible.

BUYING TIPS: Sold individually.

SUBMERSIBLE REAR-LIGHT KIT

DESCRIPTION: Two DOT-approved stop and taillight combos, wiring harness, and 4' trunk connector; 5" × 4½" (2⅞" deep) lenses for trailers under 80" wide, 8¼" × 3⅜" (3⅛" deep) for trailers wider than 80". Sealed for waterproofness.

USE: To protect taillights from corroding or shorting out when submerged.

USE TIPS: Swing-out socket makes changing bulbs easy.

BUYING TIPS: A must for trailer lights that go under.

SUBMERSIBLE IDENTIFICATION BAR

ALSO KNOWN AS: Submersible light bar

DESCRIPTION: Three waterproof red clearance lamps centered on 14" or 16" ABS plastic or stainless steel bar; connecting wire included.

USE: Meets DOT requirements for trailer more than 80" wide.

USE TIPS: Low profile (1¼" deep) makes mounting easy.

BUYING TIPS: Convenient way to meet the light standard.

LANDING LIGHTS

DESCRIPTION: String of six waterproof lights, with wiring harness, connectors, and mounting hardware.

USE: To illuminate trailer underwater to facilitate lining up your boat at night.

USE TIPS: Use on land while tying down hull or boat cover.

BUYING TIPS: Not necessary if you already have submersible rear lights.

TRAILER WIRING KIT

ALSO KNOWN AS: Trailer harness kit

DESCRIPTION: Kit with 25' trailer harness, 4' trunk connector, crossover wires for rear and side lights, wire tap, wire clips, and nuts. Wires are color coded.

USE: To wire trailer to tow vehicle's 12-volt system.

USE TIPS: For trailers 20' and under.

BUYING TIPS: Also available with trailer harness or trunk connector only.

BRAIDED TRUNK CONNECTOR

DESCRIPTION: Vinyl-coated braiding over internal wire; 4' long, with 48" ground wire.

USE: To connect wiring harness to tow-vehicle trunk; provides necessary grounding for system.

USE TIPS: Braided loom protects against chafing, a problem with trailer wiring.

BUYING TIPS: Most wiring kits come with a trunk connector; buy the braided one as a replacement and keep the regular connector on hand as a backup.

TAILLIGHT CONVERTER

ALSO KNOWN AS: Turn-signal converter

DESCRIPTION: Electric-current converter, either conventional or electronic, plus connectors, mounting bracket, and hardware.

USE: To change five-wire separate stop and turn lights found on foreign vehicles to three-wire single system conforming with U.S. trailer lighting.

USE TIPS: Be sure conversion kit includes a ground wire.

BUYING TIPS: A conventional converter, at half the price, does the same job.

PLUG ADAPTER

ALSO KNOWN AS: Six-way adapter, seven-way adapter

DESCRIPTION: Double plug with either six or seven prongs on one side and four slots on the other.

USE: To convert auto plugs to four-prong kind used on trailers.

USE TIPS: Don't try to use mismatched plugs.

BUYING TIPS: If you need them, you have to buy them. Don't try to fake it.

CHAPTER THIRTEEN

PERSONAL SAFETY GEAR

PERSONAL
SAFETY GEAR

ABOUT SAFETY GEAR

Federal requirements for safety equipment on boats are designed to prevent or minimize the dangers of fire, explosion, collision, and drowning. These requirements, administered by the U.S. Coast Guard, vary according to boat size and type of propulsion, as well as whether the boat is operated at night or during periods of reduced visibility. In some cases the body of water in which the boat is operated also dictates the type of equipment needed. Boats that carry passengers for hire, such as party fishing boats, ferries, and launches, must adhere to even stricter equipment requirements than recreational vessels.

Some safety equipment, such as life jackets, fire extinguishers, visual distress signals (VDS), and sound-making devices such as horns and bells are easy for the boater to purchase and bring onboard. Other mandatory safety equipment, such as bilge and engine-compartment ventilation systems and backfire flame arrestors for gas-powered boats, are installed by manufacturers and should not be removed or tampered with. The Coast Guard also requires boats to be equipped with navigation lights (see page 50).

A free brochure, "Federal Requirements for Recreational Boats," available by calling the U.S. Coast Guard's Consumer Hot Line, 1-800-368-5647, details safety-equipment requirements.

ABOUT PERSONAL FLOTATION DEVICES

Swimming ability may have little to do with your chances for survival in an emergency, but your ability to stay afloat does. In fact boating-accident statistics make it clear that wearing a personal flotation device (PFD), or life jacket, is essential for staying alive in the event of a fall overboard.

Sure, PFDs have the tradition of being bulky, sometimes uncomfortable, and often unattractive, but they are effective—only when worn—because they will keep you afloat until help arrives. In recent years many new models made of lightweight, attractive material with nonabsorbent synthetic flotation have replaced the familiar flame-orange horseshoe or bulky vest filled with kapok, an organic fiber that gets waterlogged and rots over time.

Life jackets are buoyancy-rated according to their ability to keep your head and chin above water. Buoyancy is affected by age, sex, weight, amount of body fat, and even physical condition, so it is a good idea to test your PFD in the water during a non-emergency situation, to make sure it will protect you when your life depends on it.

Buy only those life jackets that bear the "U.S. Coast Guard approved" designation. There are four types of approved life jackets. Although this is no guarantee of lifesaving performance, Coast Guard approval means that the PFD has passed standardized buoyancy tests. Every boat, regardless of size or type, must carry one Coast Guard–

approved PFD for each passenger onboard. Boats over 16' must also carry at least one throwable flotation device.

Special designs meet the needs of water-skiers, racers, offshore sailors, and jet skiers. Bright colors give best visibility for rescuers. Comfortable, fun models are available in children's and even infants' sizes. Parents should insist on their kids being properly safeguarded, while at the same time setting a good example by wearing jackets themselves. Some states require children to wear life jackets at all times. To avoid confusion, it is a good idea to mark each jacket with the wearer's name and store them in a spot that is easy for everyone to reach.

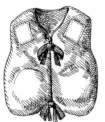
Type I
"Offshore life jacket"

Type II
"Near-shore buoyant vest"

Type III "Flotation Aid"

Life Jacket

ALSO KNOWN AS: Personal flotation device, life preserver, PFD, Mae West

DESCRIPTION: Usually a wearable device, cloth covered and filled with flotation material. A system of straps, belts, and buckles keeps a personal flotation device firmly in place. Styles include:

TYPES:

Type I "Offshore Life Jacket": Vest style—the famous Mae West—that fastens in front and may have leg straps to keep vest from riding up while wearer is in the water. Best suited for offshore cruising, racing, and fishing, especially in rough water, the *Type I* will turn most people floating faceup, important if the wearer has been injured or is unconscious. Minimum buoyancy requirements are 22 lbs. for adults and 11 lbs. for children. Wearers may find the *Type I* bulky and uncomfortable, but it is the most effective traditional model around.

Type II "Near-Shore Buoyant Vest": Collar-style with flotation pouches in front—the familiar orange life jacket—fitted around the waist with a strap and ties at the neck. Recommended for inland cruising, dinghy sailing, and dinghy racing in inland water where the chance for immediate rescue is good. Not suitable for extended survival in rough water, but will turn most unconscious wearers faceup in the water. More comfortable than *Type I* PFD, but offers less flotation, since minimum buoyancy requirement is 15½ lbs.

Type III "Flotation Aid": Zippered vest or sleeved-jacket styling, sometimes with pockets (handy for fishermen or hunters) and recommended for use during supervised activities such as sailing regattas, waterskiing, canoeing, kayaking, or jet skiing on protected inland waters where the chance for immediate rescue is good. Not suitable for extended survival in rough water or when wearer is unconscious, because you must actively tilt your head back to avoid floating facedown in the water. Most comfortable to wear. The minimum buoyancy requirement is 15½ lbs.

Type IV "Throwable Device": Buoyant cushion, ring, or horseshoe, usually with handles made of fabric or rope, tossed to overboard victim. For easy access, rings and horseshoes are often mounted on liferails on deck, while cushions do double duty as on-deck comfort. These devices are not meant to be worn but will provide additional flotation to someone already in the water. They are not suitable for use by children or nonswimmers or, obviously, unconscious persons. Buoyancy requirements are 16½ lbs. for rings and horseshoes and 18½ lbs. for cushions. Intended for use in calm inland waters where help is always nearby.

Type V "Special-Use Device": Model specially designed for specific purposes, such as sailboard harness, deck suit, commercial whitewater vest, or float coat. Type Vs must be worn while under way in order to meet Coast Guard requirements. Buoyancy ratings from 15½ lbs. to 22 lbs., depending upon use designation.

Type V Hybrid "Inflatable": PFD with 7½ lbs. of built-in buoyancy and integral CO_2 cartridge that inflates airtight suspenderlike pouches that extend down the wearer's chest. Device may inflate automatically to 22 lbs. buoyancy within 5 seconds of hitting the water, but some also activate with a rip cord or can be inflated orally through a blow-tube about 8" long. Although inflatable PFDs have not been approved for use by the Coast Guard (because they require special servicing and maintenance), they have been used for years overseas and are extremely "user-friendly" since they are lighter in weight, easy to wear, and come in universal sizes for adults and children. Type V Hybrids are much more expensive than traditional PFDs.

USE: To keep wearer afloat in the water. Can be used while in the water for recreational reasons, but more important when wearer finds himself in the water by accident.

USE TIPS: *Type I, Type II, Type III,* and *Type IV* PFDs meet Coast Guard approval. *Type Vs* do not, but the inflatable may be your best bet in a real emergency.

Store in an accessible, dry place.

BUYING TIPS: Children's and infants' versions are much more expensive than adult sizes, but their effectiveness because of proper fit more than compensates.

LIFE VEST FOR DOGS

ALSO KNOWN AS: Pet flotation device

DESCRIPTION: Saddle of flotation foam with adjustable harness that goes around dog's chest and under front arms—er, legs. Cloth handle on back of "saddle" for pickup with a boat hook or for a quick grab. Bright yellow or other colors for best visibility. Very lightweight. Sized according to dog's weight.

USE: To provide flotation protection for dog. Coast Guard requirements do not apply to animal wear.

USE TIPS: Life vest is light enough that it shouldn't annoy animals, but it is unlikely that live-aboard cats will appreciate it much. Although swimming may come naturally to dogs and cats, do not assume that they are built for endurance swimming. This is a humane way to protect your pets if you must bring them boating.

BUYING TIPS: Very inexpensive protection for what is, after all, an important member of your crew and family.

MOB (MAN OVERBOARD) GEAR

PERSONAL SAFETY LIGHT

ALSO KNOWN AS: PFD light, personal strobe, marker light, man-overboard light

DESCRIPTION: Flashlightlike in size, shape, and appearance, this item goes one step farther in that it is impact-resistant and completely waterproof—in other words, made for a dunking when someone goes overboard. All models have strong clips or pins so that they can be attached to safety harnesses, life jackets, or clothing.

Strobe flashes every second, while conventional light is enhanced by faceted "beehive" dome lens. C or D lithium or alkaline batteries give continuous light for up to 32 hours or more. Some lights self-actuate when exposed to water.

USE: Attached to a crew member overboard, safety light makes it easier to make rescues at night.

USE TIPS: Keep at least one personal safety light in life-raft emergency kit (see page 334). These lights are of no use if they are kept in the cabin instead of on deck; preferably keep on a person, where they can be put to use quickly.

BUYING TIPS: Choose a model that floats, since not all do.

AUTOMATIC STROBE LIGHT

ALSO KNOWN AS: Floating strobe light

DESCRIPTION: Larger strobe lights that produce a flash up to 250,000 lumens (at peak power), which is visible for several miles at sea. Several makes are self-activating when set afloat. Powered by 6V batteries (not included) and, depending on make, will flash from 40 hours to seven days. Mounting brackets included with some makes.

USE: Distress signal and marker during emergencies at sea.

USE TIPS: Should be kept on deck, either on a lifeline or railing, for rapid deployment. Use a lanyard—one that can be quickly unsnapped—to secure the strobe to the boat.

BUYING TIPS: A valuable addition to MOB equipment for those who go offshore or take extended cruises.

SURVIVAL WHISTLE

ALSO KNOWN AS: Audial distress signal, sound-producing distress signal

DESCRIPTION: One-piece plastic or metal "police style" whistle with ring and lanyard.

USE: To meet Coast Guard requirement for sound-producing distress signal. Use lanyard to attach whistle to life jacket, safety harness, clothing, or other safety equipment, such as throwable flotation devices, man-overboard poles, personal safety lights. Should be a part of your life-raft emergency kit.

USE TIPS: Helpful for steering rescuers to you if you are in a man-overboard situation. Bo'sun's whistles are too hard to use to be effective in an emergency.

BUYING TIPS: Another inexpensive piece of safety gear.

Heaving Line

ALSO KNOWN AS:
Retrieving line

DESCRIPTION: Length of light, "floatable" rope, usually ⅜" polypropylene, with weight, ring, knot, or float (including self-inflating devices) spliced to one end. 45'–60' long, although some versions with safety harnesses can be as long as 150'. Traditional version had a knot called a monkey's fist tied at one end. Some versions come in a nylon storage bag.

USE: Toss object at end of heaving line to person on dock or man overboard, preferably using a floating object for the person in the water. Although the light heaving line may not be heavy enough to use to pull a person in from the water or to tie your boat at the dock, you can attach a more appropriate line to the heaving line and have it pulled from the boat.

USE TIPS: Heaving lines for rescues should be located on deck in an accessible position.

BUYING TIPS: Making a dock heaving line with a monkey's fist is a fun marlinspike project (see page 92) and a good way to use otherwise unwanted lengths of rope.

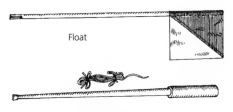

Float

weighted portion

right, with flag out of water. Pole and flag often made of reflective material visible as far as 400' at night. Backstay quick-release storage bracket provides a logical place for storage.

USE: Marks the spot when crew member falls overboard, making rescue a little easier. Required equipment on offshore racing sailboats.

USE TIPS: Man-overboard emergencies require a quick response and a cool head. Do not wait for an emergency to think out a rescue strategy. Have crew members well rehearsed and gear prepared. The man-overboard pole, for example, will be much less effective if it is not already attached to a life ring or other throwable flotation device.

BUYING TIPS: Wide range of prices below $100. Replacement "Oscar" flags are available. On smaller boats an old magazine may stand in. Just tear out pages and throw them overboard to create a paper trail (*Chapman Piloting*).

Man-overboard Pole

DESCRIPTION: One-, two-, or three-piece fiberglass or nylon pole 11'–14' long, weighted at lower end, with small foam float slightly above weight, often with red-and-yellow "Oscar" flag (see "International Signal Code Flags," page 3) attached at top end. Includes 12'-long tether for tying to throwable flotation device (see "About Personal Flotation Devices," page 326). Designed to float up-

Man-overboard ("MOB") Buoy

ALSO KNOWN AS: Throwable flotation device, Type IV personal flotation device (or PFD)

DESCRIPTION: Throwable float in ring or horseshoe shape 2'–3' in diameter, as well as double-handled cushion, designed for on-deck storage. All types may have rope or sailcloth handles or grab lines. Some horseshoe models have built-in drogues (see page 62) to slow their drift. Floats are made of rot- and mildew-resistant materials, covered in nylon, and will not retain water. Rings and horseshoes are most often bright yellow or white, but throwable cushions come in many different colors, perhaps reflecting that in their dual roles, cockpit comfort comes first before man-overboard emergencies.

USE: Stored on deck, throwable flotation devices are the first line of defense in a man-overboard situation. They are not, however, designed to provide long-term flotation, nor are they much good when the person in the water is a child or is injured or unconscious.

Also known as Type IV PFDs, throwable devices are required safety equipment on all boats over 16' long. Rings and horseshoes are designed to last and maintain their flotation. Cockpit cushions will do in a pinch, but they tend to lose their buoyancy over time.

USE TIPS: Refer to "About Personal Flotation Devices" (page 326).

BUYING TIPS: Reasonably priced.

Buoy LETTERING KIT

ALSO KNOWN AS: Stick-on reflective letters

DESCRIPTION: Complete alphabet, plus duplicates of vowels and the most often-used consonants, 2" high, blue or other colors, with adhesive backing.

USE: To label horseshoe and ring buoys as well as other objects in and around your boat.

USE TIPS: Lay out guidelines before letters are applied, since they may be difficult to lift off once they are attached.

BUYING TIPS: Quicker than stenciling. Mostly for decoration, though helpful in the case of a total disaster.

Lifesling™

ALSO KNOWN AS: Seattle sling

DESCRIPTION: MOB kit that includes a flexible yellow flotation collar/sling, an attached 150' floating polyproylene line, instructions and diagrams, and a soft cloth storage bag. The collar provides 20 lbs. buoyancy, enough for most adults.

USE: Retrieving a person who has fallen overboard.

USE TIPS: Practice deploying the sling, with crew members alternating as rescuer and rescuee. The 150-foot line enables the person on board to troll the collar past the person in the water.

BUYING TIPS: The Lifesling has been endorsed by safety-at-sea experts (many a person overboard has drowned because those on board were unable to hoist them aboard once a line was attached). An optional hard canister for storing the sling is sold separately. The sling must be used in conjunction with a hoisting harness, either one of your own devising or one designed for use with the sling (see next item).

Lifesling SAILBOAT HOISTING TACKLE

ALSO KNOWN AS: 3 to 1 sailboat hoisting tackle

DESCRIPTION: Tackle kit consisting of a fiddle block with an oversized ball to accommodate a halyard shackle, a single block with becket and attached carabiner, and 65' of 5/16" line.

USE: Snaps onto Lifesling line at onboard end and to a halyard aboard the boat, which, along with a deck winch, enables a single person to lift an overboard person back aboard. Provides 3–1 pulling power.

USE TIPS: A MOB practice session with the sling should include the hoisting aboard as well—often the most difficult part of a rescue operation.

BUYING TIPS: Unless you have a proven hoisting tackle arrangement of your own, this is a sensible complement to the sling system.

SAFETY HARNESS

ALSO KNOWN AS:
Sailing harness

DESCRIPTION: Adjustable suspenderlike straps made of 2"–2½"-wide heavy nylon webbing attached to a horizontal belt that tightens above the wearer's waistline. D-rings or easy-to-use push-lock clasps fasten horizontal belt level with wearer's solar plexus. May have leg straps. Attachment point(s) on front for hook-on safety tether. Sizes for adults and children. Some models are attached to a nylon-mesh vest, which is supposed to distribute the force of a fall over a wide area on the torso.

USE: To provide secure attachment to boat in case of falls overboard or onto slippery decks. Particularly useful when working on the foredeck in rough weather, at nighttime, and while racing. A definite must for the single-handed sailor.

USE TIPS: Like a life jacket, a safety harness makes good safety sense for children onboard. Skippers of offshore boats often set rules requiring the use of harnesses on deck.

BUYING TIPS: Another item where price indicates the level of quality, security, and comfort you can expect. Try on for comfort before purchasing.

TETHER

ALSO KNOWN AS:
Safety tether

DESCRIPTION: 6' of heavy-duty 1"-wide nylon webbing with large stainless-steel clips at either end. Some tethers have a third hook in the middle, to serve as two 3' tethers. Webbing has a breaking strength of 4,585 lbs.

USE: Clip one end of tether to a stanchion, secure fitting, or jack line (a strong safety line or web strap run fore and aft) and the other to your safety harness in case of falls overboard.

USE TIPS: Longer tethers may make it extremely difficult for someone who has fallen overboard to regain the boat and climb aboard, since the victim has to swim against the boat's speed. As you move about the deck, wear two tethers and clip one at a time to the boat, or use the double tether and move the ends. Avoid using rigging or lifeline (which really isn't strong enough) as fastening points.

BUYING TIPS: Relatively inexpensive but important piece of safety equipment.

LIFE RAFTS

ABOUT LIFE RAFTS

Unlike life jackets, which give wearers temporary flotation until help arrives, life rafts, also known as survival rafts, improve chances for survival even more because they provide shelter from the elements—cold water and air temperatures, waves, blistering sunlight—and are a more visible "target" for rescuers. This kind of protection is all the more important when your vessel is lost and help isn't near.

Life rafts are generally circular or oval in shape (they may also be roughly octagonal) but never have a bow or stern, like an inflatable boat. Multiple flotation tubes provide plenty of backup in case one is punctured or otherwise damaged. Nylon fabric is coated with urethane, frequently in a fluorescent color, such as orange, for greater visibility.

Important life-raft features include:

Ballast: Most life rafts with flat bottoms use a combination of water-filled ballast chambers and a sea anchor on a tether. Water ballast does not weigh the raft down (after all, water is weightless in water), but the filled chambers or pockets resist the lifting action of wind and waves.

Anchor: Sea anchors (see page 62) are cone-shaped bags attached to the life raft by a tether (typically 60' long). Although not a physical part of the raft itself, the sea anchor is an integral part of the raft's stability design. Once the anchor is thrown overboard, it trails behind the raft, creating drag. Usually the attachment point is on the side opposite from the raft door so that the raft's opening is turned away from oncoming waves.

Buoyancy tubes: These CO_2-filled flotation chambers inflate automatically on impact with the water.

Short-term-survival coastal rafts have one tube with two chambers to prevent complete deflation in the event of a puncture. Double tubes are found on all offshore and oceangoing rafts because they give increased freeboard, reducing the likelihood of swamping. Even if the largest flotation chamber is completely deflated, the remaining one(s) must support two-thirds of the raft's rated weight capacity.

Painter line: When a life raft is deployed, it should be tied by the painter to the boat, to keep it from floating away. Naturally if the main boat is sinking in deep water, you will need to cut the raft adrift. When the painter is pulled, this activates the inflation mechanism.

Manual inflation: Raft buoyancy tubes expand and contract, according to temperature changes. Over-inflation valves release pressure when it is hot. When cool temperatures decrease pressure, tubes must be topped off. Three types of manual pumps are available to do this: an oral inflation tube that is next to impossible to use (just picture the huge capacity of the buoyancy tube and the relatively small capacity of your lungs), a foot pump that works best on a firm floor (not likely to be found on a life raft), or an accordionlike hand pump that is efficient and the easiest of the three to use.

Canopy: Canopies serve a double purpose: They shield crew from sun, wind, and water and their typical bright orange exterior can be sighted easily by searchers. Nevertheless without large entryways, port holes and separately furled panels, the crew may feel claustrophobic and sick because of the rubber smell. Blue-lined interiors reduce glare. Canopy support arches keep the raft from inflating upside down and give passengers increased headroom. Some models require separate inflation for the canopy.

Storage container: Until they are used, life rafts must be safely stored to prevent punctures or damage that could cause malfunctions in an emergency. Rafts stowed belowdecks can be kept in specially made flexible duffel bags or, if they are kept on deck, in rigid fiberglass containers. Where you store your life raft is important, so choose a spot that is readily accessible and will allow any crew member to get to it easily.

Floor: Choose a double-floored raft, especially if you are buying an oceangoing model. Double floors insulate passengers from cold water temperatures, give better support, and lessen the impact of bumps from curious marine life. Some double-floor designs have button attachments to create depressions where water collects and can be bailed out. Other raft designers use a porous material for the floor, to keep passengers drier.

Capacity rating: Life rafts are not designed primarily with comfort in mind. Ratings specify the maximum number of people the raft will hold, based on a formula of about 4 sq. ft. per person, so do not skimp on size!

Miscellaneous equipment: Regardless of whether you buy a coastal life raft or an oceangoing one, it should be equipped with various types of safety flares, an emergency flag and whistle, and a repair kit. For offshore and ocean use, include an EPIRB (see page 339), a bailing device, sponges, paddles, waterproof flashlight, signal mirror, dye markers, sea sickness tablets, a floating knife, first aid kit, compass, fishing kit, drinking cups and water bags, life ring, survival manual, and can opener.

Survival rations: A kit for each passenger is also essential for offshore and oceangoers. These kits contain 3 days' worth of high-calorie food bars, premeasured water packets, antihypothermic ("space") blankets, which can double as emergency reflectors, as well as other useful gear.

Buying and service guidelines include the following:

Three different types of life rafts are available, *coastal, offshore,* and *oceangoing.* All are made of polyurethane-coated nylon, and each gives various levels of protection, depending on survival needs and boating environments. They come in various size and weight capacities, depending on crew size. Boaters should not count on rescue platforms (see page 335), inflatable boats (completely different animals from life rafts, see page 83), or dinghies for long-term survival, since they lack buoyancy safeguards, ballast systems, and canopies needed for rough-water use.

Coastal life rafts increase your protection from the elements by keeping you not only out of the water but shielded from the water and waves. Built-in ballast systems guard against capsizing. Nevertheless these should be considered only if you can expect to be rescued within a day, since they lack features needed for long-term survival, such as double inflation tubes.

Offshore life rafts give even more protection because freeboard (the distance from the deck of the raft to water level) is greater and there are larger ballast systems and emergency buoyancy tubes for longer-term use in heavy seas. Offshore rafts extend survival time to 4 or 5 days by including supported canopies and two buoyancy tubes so that if one deflates, the other acts as a backup.

Oceangoing life rafts are designed for long-term survival of at least 30 days and are required equipment on most commercial vessels and by some international racing authorities.

All miscellaneous equipment must be secured inside the raft. In an emergency you may not have time to gather small items, and a separate duffel bag may be lost overboard.

Life rafts should be serviced annually, whether or not they are put into use. Servicing (often required to maintain the warranty) includes removing the raft from its storage container, checking it for leaks, inspecting valves and pumps, and restocking outdated supplies. Follow the manufacturer's recommended service schedule for maintenance. If a life raft has been used, it must be inspected and repacked. This is not

a job for the do-it-yourselfer—imagine trying to fold a parachute after it has been opened. Repacking or inspection services generally cost less than $200 a year—a bargain for the peace of mind this service gives. This should be done by a factory-authorized and trained repacker; call your dealer or the manufacturer for those in your area.

BUYING TIPS: Life-raft choice should be based on how long you expect to wait before help arrives, not on distance from shore, because your chances of reaching land—even if it is only a few miles away—are minimal when you are treading water or floating in an unmaneuverable life raft.

If you need a life raft only occasionally, consider renting one. Then you can change rafts as your crew size, boating area, and the likelihood of rescue change.

Rescue Platform

DESCRIPTION: Octagonal polyurethane-coated nylon float with trampolinelike cloth span about 8'

in diameter. Grab lines are attached around the perimeter of the float, as well as handholds of nylon webbing on the inner cloth span. Inflates with CO_2, but usually equipped with manual pump for backup. Platform includes water-activated locator lights, rescue flares, emergency flag, whistle, heaving ring, and sea anchor. A soft valise or fiberglass container, as well as a deck-mount cradle, are sold separately.

USE: To enable you to abandon ship on lakes or in areas where other boats are in sight—in other words, where rescue is always imminent.

USE TIPS: Not to be confused with a life raft, since there are significant differences. Rescue platforms are not required to meet stringent U.S. Coast Guard standards.

BUYING TIPS: Good-quality life rafts do not cost much more than a rescue platform. The extra investment might be worthwhile.

VISUAL DISTRESS SIGNALS AND LOCATING DEVICES

ABOUT VISUAL DISTRESS SIGNALS

Federal safety laws require that all boats over 16' carry an array of visual distress signals (also known as VDS) when operating on coastal waters. What kind of pyrotechnic devices (more commonly known as flares), signal flags, or emergency lights you carry is determined by the size of the boat, as well as when and where you are boating.

Boats under 16' and some larger boats that are not mechanically propelled are required to carry only night signals. Signals must bear the Coast Guard–approval number or certification statement indicating that they meet visibility requirements.

Complete visual distress signal kits containing everything you need to bring your boat into compliance with the Coast Guard's minimum equipment requirements are available at ship's chandleries. Oceangoers are wise to keep a stock of visual distress signals that meet the more stringent requirements of the International Convention for Safety of Life At Sea (SOLAS). This equipment is far more expensive and difficult to use, but SOLAS-approved devices burn brighter, shoot higher, and have longer hang time than their Coast Guard–approved cousins.

VDS are classified for day (D) or night (N) use, or for both (D/N). For pyrotechnics the rule of thumb is that you must carry 3 day and 3 night distress signals—or 3 day/night combinations will suffice—but this is the minimum. Flares have a mandatory expiration date of 42 months (3½ years) after manufacture, and boat owners should make sure theirs are current. Even though a flare's shelf life may extend past this period, these devices are nevertheless prone to degradation when exposed to moisture. (On the other hand don't discard your old flares—they might serve as a lifesaver someday.)

The types of flares include handheld or aerial red flares, floating or handheld orange smoke, and pistollike launchers for aerial red meteors or parachute flares. All types must be handled with extreme caution because of the danger of burns from slag (burning flare material), ash, hot flames, and casings. Handheld devices should be held over the side because dripping slag can burn your hands and your boat. Pistollike launchers should be fired downwind and at a 60° angle above the horizon. Never shoot directly overhead—what goes up must come down! Some states and many foreign countries consider flare pistols to be firearms, which means they may be subject to licensing or other restrictions. Finally, in an emergency, do not fire flares until another vessel is in sight. Otherwise, you may use up your supply.

Because even the brightest flare is hard to see from as little as a half mile away during daylight hours, for daytime emergencies boaters should rely upon smoke signals that send forth highly visible clouds of orange smoke valued for their lengthy hang time over the emergency site. Orange and black International Distress Flags (see page 3) with square-and-disk markings are also suitable.

As with any emergency signal device, do not use flares or distress flags unless there is an immediate or potential danger to the persons onboard. Avoid false alarms. Flares are not hard to use, but it would not hurt for crew members to be familiar with lighting them. Try an on-shore test with outdated flares, but it is a good idea to first let the harbor police or other local emergency agency know what you are planning. For advice on other ways of disposing of outdated flares, call your local fire or police department.

F LARE

ALSO KNOWN AS: Signal flare, visual distress signal, pyrotechnic device, rocket flare, rocket, meteor, aerial flare, parachute safety flare, handheld flare

DESCRIPTION: Waxed cardboard or foil-wrapped cardboard cylinder about 6" long × 1" diameter containing pyrotechnic chemicals that burn with cherry-red color for 1–2 minutes. Flame for some is extremely bright—as high as 30,000 candle-power, which manufacturers claim can be seen for "over 30 miles." Plastic caps on either end conceal striker mechanism similar to striker on a book of matches. Usually come in protective pouch containing flares; may also be available in single waterproof plastic tube. Bears expiration date of 42 months after date of manufacture, as well as certification of meeting Coast Guard requirements for visual distress signals.

Air-borne *aerial* flare may be propelled skyward with a pull-chain-activated rocket or with a pistol launcher (see page 338). Small parachutes keep some aerial flares aloft longer. These VDS are called *parachute safety flares* and may rise to as high as 990', staying lit for about 40 seconds.

Handheld version comes with wooden handle and circular "collar" to prevent dripping slag or ash from burning user.

USE: Red flare flame is universally recognized as an emergency signal. Although touted as being visible by day or night, obviously flares will be more visible in darkness or in reduced-light situations.

USE TIPS: Flares are relatively easy to use, but do not wait for an emergency to test your skill at lighting and launching one. Practice on shore with old or extra flares.

Hold handheld versions away from your body and over the side of the boat. Burns from dripping slag and ash can be painful and also damage the deck of your boat. Even though these particles cool quickly, the flare itself is very hot and can start a fire if it is dropped.

Aerial flares with parachutes are intended for long-range signaling.

Refer to safety tips outlined in "About Visual Distress Signals."

Onboard, store flares in a waterproof storage box or bag (see page 338), in an easily accessible place. You can also buy kits with water-resistant plastic containers that may be refilled as needed.

BUYING TIPS: Check expiration date before purchase. Keep a stock of more than the minimum three required.

Smoke Signal

ALSO KNOWN AS: Orange smoke signal

DESCRIPTION: Handheld or floating pyrotechnic device that emits a dense, brilliant orange cloud of smoke when lit. Stubby size compared with signal flares, fit in the palm. May burn for up to 3 minutes, but slightly under a minute is more typical, especially for handheld models.

USE: To provide an emergency signal for daytime use, most effective in low-wind situations—higher winds tend to keep smoke close to the water's surface and disperse it. Ineffective at night.

USE TIPS: Position handheld or floating smoke signals downwind to avoid choking on fumes.

BUYING TIPS: Check expiration date before purchase.

Green Dye Marker

ALSO KNOWN AS: Dye marker

DESCRIPTION: Iridescent dye, usually green, nonwater soluble, that floats on water's surface. Comes in palm-sized plastic canister with cap.

USE: Spilled onto the water, the dye makes your position clear to airborne rescuers.

USE TIPS: May not be effective in very rough seas. Dye is environmentally safe.

BUYING TIPS: Sold in two-packs.

PISTOL LAUNCHER

ALSO KNOWN AS: Flare gun

DESCRIPTION: Plastic or silver metal pistol resembling a snub-nose revolver with 12-gauge or 25mm barrel that accommodates signal flares (adapter is available to make 25mm launcher accommodate 12-gauge flare).

USE: Launch aerial flares, either with or without parachutes, as high as 250'–375'. Because of their rapid descent, pistol-launched flares are less affected by winds than are slower-descending models.

USE TIPS: See tips in "About Visual Distress Signals" (see page 335). Exercise extreme caution when using. Pistol launchers are definitely not toys and should be kept out of reach of children. A signal flare fired at close range can cause serious burns. Some states regard flare launchers as handguns, and permits may be required because some models can accommodate shotgun shells. However, do not even consider trying shotgun ammo, especially with plastic launchers. The pressure from a shotgun shell could explode the pistol in your hand.

BUYING TIPS: Metal pistols will stand up longer than plastic ones, but most boaters rarely have to use theirs.

WATERTIGHT FLARE-STORAGE SYSTEM

ALSO KNOWN AS: Flare canister

DESCRIPTION: Canister, 12" long × 3" wide, made of heavy-duty PVC or ABS plastic, large enough to hold three signal flares. Equipped with brackets on canister side for mounting on bulkheads, rails, or stanchions, and a quick-release pin for easy

removal. Usually comes with label made of reflective material.

USE: Because canister is watertight, flares can be stored on deck without risk of damage or degradation.

USE TIPS: Mount canister in or near the cockpit, within easy reach.

BUYING TIPS: Not a Coast Guard equipment requirement, but handy nevertheless.

SIGNAL MIRROR

ALSO KNOWN AS: Reflecting mirror, emergency mirror, 10-mile mirror

DESCRIPTION: Palm-sized or larger glass or metal reflective plate. High-tech version contains a specially designed reflector on a plastic palm-sized rectangle.

USE: Although not a U.S. Coast Guard safety equipment requirement, signal mirrors are effective and can be seen for up to 10 miles.

USE TIPS: Though most effective in bright light conditions, these can also be used to reflect back the beams of a searchlight that is seeking you out. In a pinch any reflective object—a hand mirror, a frying pan, a pot lid, a compact mirror—may be put into use as a visual distress signal.

BUYING TIPS: Signal mirrors are relatively inexpensive and do not take up much space. A worthwhile addition to the emergency kit.

ABOUT EPIRBs

There is no adventure quite so exciting—or humbling—as being miles offshore, out of sight of land. The experience can be made safer and probably more enjoyable if you have the right kind of emergency communications gear onboard, since at around 25 miles, offshore common VHF radios can no longer be relied upon to broadcast signals back to land bases.

That is where EPIRBs, or Emergency Position-Indicating Radio Beacons, come in handy. The most common of these battery-operated devices transmit signals on two aircraft frequencies—121.5 MHz, the emergency channel of civil aviation, and 243.0 MHz, the "guard" channel for military aircraft. EPIRGs designated Class A float free and activate automatically; Class B devices are manually activated. They serve a dual function, first to alert nearby aircraft that an emergency exists and later to help rescuers pinpoint the location of the vessel in distress. If the same distress signal is picked up by more than one aircraft, a rough fix of the location can be made, aiding searchers.

Newer, more advanced Category I and Category II EPIRBs "talk" strictly with satellites on a new frequency, 406.025 MHz. These EPIRBs must be registered with the National Oceanic and Atmospheric Administration. Besides broadcasting a signal that identifies the boat it is registered to, these EPIRBs can also give their exact locations and in some cases an indication of the nature of the emergency. Satellites working in conjunction with EPIRBs are capable of storing messages until they get within range of a terminal on earth. Some 406 EPIRBs also broadcast a "homing" signal on 121.5 MHz so that they can be located more easily. They also are less prone to false alarms.

All EPIRBs are battery-operated and are required by the Federal Communications Commission (FCC) to operate continuously for 48 hours, although many will operate for as long as 1 week. EPIRBs are made for the marine environment and can be stored onboard safely for long periods of time without being damaged by moisture or salt air.

EPIRB

ALSO KNOWN AS: Emergency Position-Indicating Radio Beacon, 406 EPIRB, Coastal EPIRB, Offshore EPIRB

DESCRIPTION: Square or tubular waterproof canister, usually emergency orange in color, about the size of a heavy-duty flashlight, with a short straight or curved antenna extending from the top end.

Canister contains solid-state radio transmitter capable of broadcasting on 121.5 MHz, 243.0 MHz, and/or 406.025 MHz, powered by alkaline, magnesium, or lithium battery. Transmitter automatically activates in emergency situations. Class A, B, and C EPIRBs broadcast over 121.5 MHz and 243.0 MHz, with a power output of about 1 watt. Far more accurate Category I and II EPIRBs broadcast over those frequencies, as well as 406.025 MHz, and must be registered with NOAA.

USE: Emergency locator device to help rescuers home in on stranded boats, life rafts, or persons in the water. Not for use in inland water emergencies. Although EPIRBs are not part of the Coast Guard's required package of emergency equipment for recreational vessels, anyone sailing offshore should have one onboard. Commercial vessels, on the other hand, are required to carry EPIRBs.

Class A, B, and C EPIRBs are accurate to 12 mi., or a 144-sq.-mi. area, while Category I units are accurate to within 3 mi., or 9 sq. mi.

USE TIPS: Store in an open location, preferably on deck, in antenna-down position so that the EPIRB can float freely if the boat sinks. Category I units have automatic release brackets.

Lithium and magnesium batteries have shelf lives of 5 or 6 years, but may nevertheless need to be recharged in between. Alkaline batteries may last as long as 4 years but are required to be replaced every 2 years. Dispose of lithium and magnesium batteries in a conscientious manner, since both contain highly toxic substances. Alkaline batteries are less critical, but still, do not just toss them overboard when their time is up. Call the EPIRB manufacturer for advice on battery disposal.

BUYING TIPS: Category I and II EPIRBs cost $1,000 and up, but their accuracy is clearly desirable for the ocean cruiser or racer (and their prices inevitably are coming down). Coastal units cost considerably less, a few hundred dollars.

SART

ALSO KNOWN AS: Search and Rescue Transponder

DESCRIPTION: Electronic automatic signaling device about the size of a 406 EPIRB (but weighing just 3.3 lbs.) that is activated by incoming radio waves from a ship's radar. Its own signal is reflected as a "blip" on the corresponding radar's screen.

USE: To broadcast a distress signal: the SART continues to broadcast a signal to an active radar, pinpointing the distressed person's location.

USE TIPS: Especially valuable for anyone who must take to a life raft, which is extremely difficult to spot from air or ship.

BUYING TIPS: Fairly new on the market, the SART, like most electronic devices, is bound to come down in price from its present $1,000 or so.

PERSONAL-CARE EQUIPMENT

WRIST SEA BAND

ALSO KNOWN AS: Accupressure band

DESCRIPTION: Pair of inch-wide elastic wristbands, each with a small white plastic button.

USE: To reduce or eliminate the effects of motion sickness produced by sea, land, or air travel. Buttons press gently on spots inside each wrist.

USE TIPS: If the wristband, which draws its inspiration from the accupressure tradition, works for you, it is a great, no-side-effects cure for seasickness. Drugs and medications for this unpleasant condition can produce equally unpleasant side effects, such as drowsiness or disorientation. Besides, resisting seasickness is as much a matter of mind over matter as science. If you believe . . .

BUYING TIPS: The wristband is fairly inexpensive, but if you are prone to being seasick, a cure is worth any cost.

DENTAL EMERGENCY KIT

DESCRIPTION: Plastic box with attached snap-down cover contains temporary filling material, plastic placing sticks, analgesic, antiseptic, dental mirror, and first-aid manual for dental emergencies. Does not contain oral hygiene basics, such as toothpaste, mouthwash, dental floss, or a spare toothbrush, although these would be nice items to have onboard.

USE: To provide dental first-aid items that will serve as a stop-gap for most emergencies, such as toothaches, lost fillings, crowns, or bridges; or mouth sores.

USE TIPS: Check kit at least once a season to be sure it is complete, and do not forget to replace items that get used up.

BUYING TIPS: Should be part of the medical/first-aid kit on any boat planning to be at sea 24 hours or more.

BREATH ALCOHOL TEST

ALSO KNOWN AS: Breathalizer test, B.A.T.

DESCRIPTION: Clear plastic tube contains balloon with attached mouthpiece and small capped tube with reactive test strip. Instructions for use.

USE: If you wonder whether you have had too much to drink to operate your boat safely, this simple test can measure if blood alcohol content exceeds the legal limit, which varies from .05% to 0.1% depending on the jurisdiction. Test is accurate to .02% blood alcohol concentration.

USE TIPS: The combination of alcohol, unsteady movement of the boat, bright sunlight, fatigue, and a number of other factors adds up to a level of impaired judgment and reaction time exceeding that normally found on land. Coast Guard statistics show that the majority of boating accidents and fatalities are directly related to alcohol use, so boaters should restrict their alcohol intake to those times when the boat is moored or anchored. And don't rely on the "designated driver" concept as a way around boating under the influence. Studies show that a single unimpaired crew member may not be able to deal with the demands of both boat handling and possible medical or mechanical emergencies.

Boaters should also be aware that state and federal laws provide for civil and criminal penalties, including stiff fines and prison terms, when boat operators are convicted of operating a boat under the influence of alcohol or drugs. In addition, drunk boating convictions may carry over onto your onshore automobile driving record.

BUYING TIPS: The breath alcohol test kit is good for a single test. Its low price is a bargain compared with possible DUI fines or accidents.

COMPRESS

ALSO KNOWN AS: Ice pack, heat pad

DESCRIPTION: Sealed plastic pouch, 11" long × 4" wide, contains liquid chemicals that, when squeezed and shaken, turn cold and stay cold for up to 15 minutes. Some brands are reusable. Reusable refrigerated versions come in similar sealed pouches but may not stay as intensely cold for as long. Similar products are available that produce heat for a short period of time.

USE: To apply to bruises, sprains, strains, and other injuries where cold or heat therapy is needed to reduce pain and swelling. Cold compresses can be refreshing when the weather is hot, while heat compresses are a treat for cold hands and feet.

USE TIPS: Contents of compress pouches can be toxic, so do not open them to see what is inside.

BUYING TIPS: An inexpensive treatment for many of the types of injuries that occur on a boat—a must-have for the first-aid kit.

FIRST-AID KIT

ALSO KNOWN AS: Medical kit, marine medical kit, boat medical kit

DESCRIPTION: Plastic- or metal-covered compartmentalized box containing supplies such as adhesive strips, sterile gauze pads, bandages, bandage tape, Ace bandages, antiseptic ointments and wipes, ammonia inhalants, aspirin or other pain-relief medication, motion-sickness tablets, instant cold or heat packs, scissors, eye cups, tweezers, fishhook removers, sterile gloves, hypothermia (space) blanket, emergency signaling device, first-aid book. Box often marked with a red cross or other similar emergency-medical logo.

USE: To keep first-aid supplies clean, dry, and handy for an emergency. Basic kits contain only basic equipment, such as adhesive bandages and the like. Oceangoing kits are equipped for more serious medical situations that may arise far from land or rescuers.

USE TIPS: First-aid kits should be stored onboard in an accessible place, inside the companionway, for example. If you carry a life raft onboard, a separate well-stocked kit should be securely stored inside the raft. All boaters should take a first-aid class sponsored by the Red Cross or other emergency agency.

BUYING TIPS: Kits are fairly inexpensive, so buy the best you can find. Be sure to replenish supplies as they are used. Boaters going offshore or on extended cruises should also be sure to bring along any prescription medicines required, and if seasickness is a real threat, inquire about obtaining Transderm Scop®, the antiseasickness patch (but try it on land first for possible side effects).

FIRE-SAFETY EQUIPMENT

ABOUT FIRE AND FIRE EXTINGUISHERS

When a fire breaks out onboard a boat, help is often hours away, if it is available at all. Fuel, engine oil, stove alcohol, and propane, to say nothing of fiberglass itself, which is highly flammable, up the fire ante considerably. And although there is plenty of water around, the types of fires you are likely to encounter on a boat often cannot be extinguished with water.

The Coast Guard requires that all boats up to 26' long carry one fire extinguisher capable of putting out fires involving oil, gas, diesel, and other flammable substances. Larger boats are required to carry two and sometimes three extinguishers, depending on their size. Onboard firefighting tests show, however, that Coast Guard requirements are minimal. Boaters stand a better chance against fires if they carry additional equipment.

Fires on boats spread quickly, so your best bet is to strike early—within the first two minutes of the blaze—while the fire is confined to a small area. Watch your back! Position yourself so that there is an escape route behind you in case the fire gets out of hand. Make sure you are using the right kind of extinguisher, as some types are not effective against petroleum-product fires. If it looks like the fire is getting the upper hand, get out, but first radio a Mayday call so that rescuers know where to find you. Abandoning ship is a radical step, but it may be the only safe one in a real blaze. Make sure everyone is wearing a life jacket (see page 327).

As with all emergencies, being prepared is half the battle for dealing with them successfully. Locate portable fire extinguishers in accessible spots in engine compartments, galley areas, on-deck lockers, and inside the companionway. Make sure all crew members know how to use them and, as part of monthly maintenance, check that portable extinguishers have the proper charge so that they will work when you need them. Larger boats should have automatic systems in engine compartments. These systems activate automatically when heat or smoke is present and are usually wired to an alarm at the console station, which shuts the engine down.

FIRE EXTINGUISHER

DESCRIPTION: Pressurized cylinder or canister containing dry chemicals or Halon®, or CO_2, with straight or flared nozzle sometimes on a hose and squeeze-trigger release valve located at cylinder's head. Red or white with large fire-emergency markings, including black flame symbol, and ratings indicating what types of fires extinguisher can han-

dle. Fitted with shoulder strap and quick-release wall-mount bracket.

USE: To put out fires by smothering them with a dry chemical cloud, which often leaves a sticky powder residue.

Fires are divided into types: Type A involving burning wood, cloth, and trash; Type B involving petroleum products, such as gasoline, diesel, oil, paint, thinners; and Type C involving electrical fires. Rating numbers listed before Type letters indicate what volume of fire the extinguisher can handle: higher numbers mean bigger fires.

Fire extinguishers are broken down into categories according to what kind of fire they will put out. A triclass ABC extinguisher will put out all kinds of blazes. Try to stock your boat with triclass units, since hunting for the right firefighting tool is the last thing you will want to do in an emergency.

Halon® fire extinguishers are available either in the familiar portable manually activated format or in automatic systems fitted with temperature-release switches. Halon 1211 discharges as a liquid and turns into a vapor, while Halon 1301 discharges as a vapor. Neither type leaves a residue. The bad news is that the federal government banned production of Halon® after Jan. 1, 1994 (as an ozone-depleter), although you are permitted to keep any units you already have or stock up on any existing retail supplies. A "clean" replacement likely will involve a halocarbon cousin that will exhibit similar properties but not damage the atmosphere.

USE TIPS: Have extinguishers checked and recharged every time they are used. At the very least, take extinguishers to a qualified service center once a year for a routine checkup.

BUYING TIPS: Triclass dry chemical extinguishers are more expensive than ones with limited coverage, but they are effective against all fires. In addition, they meet and exceed Coast Guard requirements for firefighting equipment.

Halon® units are more expensive than dry chemical ones, but they are superior for putting out engine-room fires. Halon® systems are especially well suited for the engine compartment, since Halon® does not gum up internal or external engine parts.

Replacement halocarbon extinguishers will also be expensive as well as bulkier and heavier. Existing Halon® units will last indefinitely, as long as the canister retains its integrity.

ENGINE-SHUT-DOWN/ OVERRIDE SYSTEM WITH ALARM

ALSO KNOWN AS: Kill switch

DESCRIPTION: Engine shut-down switch keyed into Halon® fire-extinguisher system, emits audible and visual alarms. Override feature allows for engine start-up. Control box is installed at helm station. Can handle up to three separate engines (for example, two propulsion engines and one generator).

USE: When Halon® fire-extinguisher system activates, this switch instantly shuts the engine down. There are two good reasons for not wanting the engine running. First, fuel being fed to the engine is shut off so that there is less to burn, and second, when the engine is not running, it will not "breathe in" Halon® fumes, soot, ashes, or other potentially harmful substances.

USE TIPS: Can be installed at every helm station.

BUYING TIPS: A natural companion for automatic fire extinguishers.

FIRE ALARM

ALSO KNOWN AS: Smoke alarm

DESCRIPTION: Audible and/or visual warning device wired to automatic fire-extinguisher system. Runs on 12-volt DC.

USE: To sound an alarm and flash a light at helm station.

USE TIPS: Acquaint all guests with the existence—and significance—of the alarm, especially if they are staying overnight.

BUYING TIPS: Should be installed if you do not have an engine shut-down/override system.

GASOLINE-FUME DETECTOR

ALSO KNOWN AS: Gas sniffer, sniffer, gas alarm

DESCRIPTION: Sensor with visual light alarm that automatically brightens in daylight. Detects battery hydrogen and exhaust fumes, in addition to gasoline fumes. 2" circular display installed at helm station. Runs on 12-volt DC. Sensor is connected to display by 20'-long lead.

USE: Install sensor in bilge adjacent to engine; light alarm flashes when dangerous fumes are detected. Some versions will automatically start bilge blowers when fumes are present.

USE TIPS: Gas fumes from leaking tanks and hoses present a very real threat of fire and explosion. Immediate ventilation is the best approach to take. Extinguish all flames immediately, including cigarettes and barbecue fires.

BUYING TIPS: Any boat with an inboard gasoline engine should have a fume detector.

CABIN-SAFETY INSTRUMENTS AND ACCESSORIES

CARBON MONOXIDE DETECTOR

DESCRIPTION: Sensor detects traces of carbon monoxide (CO) and some other gases, sets off audio and visual alarms. Runs on 12-volt DC and is installed at helm station.

USE: Place sensors in cabins and engine compartments, since dangerous levels of CO build up quickly and can be fatal or cause serious injury to those onboard.

The symptoms of CO poisoning include nausea, vomiting, dizziness, drowsiness, flushed appearance, and disorientation—in short, symptoms very similar to seasickness, but with far more deadly effects. One of the worst aspects is that the victim frequently is unaware of the problem. The simplest cure is to get the victim into fresh air.

USE TIPS: Do not disconnect fume detectors if they sound frequently. They may be annoying (so much so that ABYC until recently hesitated recommending their installation), but they may be trying to tell you something that will save your life.

BUYING TIPS: Any boat that has equipment with the potential of creating carbon monoxide, such as a propane-fired hot-water heater, definitely should have a detector and/or alarm. Look for one that meets Underwriters Laboratory (UL) Standard 1524 for detectors.

DEAD-STOP

ALSO KNOWN AS: CO detector

DESCRIPTION: Small stick-up button with an orange feltlike membrane in the center that turns black when exposed to carbon monoxide.

USE: To detect carbon monoxide in a closed environment.

USE TIPS: Pilots have used these for years in cockpits as a quick, simple warning device for CO. Dead-stops last for about 2 months in use, 3 years in a sealed package.

BUYING TIPS: Available at pilot supply shops or through the well-known pilots' supplier Sportys Shop at the Claremont County Airport in Batavia, OH (1-800-543-8633). For about $3 this is a cheap lifesaving item.

FUME, FIRE, AND HIGH BILGEWATER ALERT

DESCRIPTION: Square console mount has LED displays for fume, fire, and high bilge readings. Sounds audio alarm, in addition to visual alarm, when activated by any one or all conditions. Accommodates two fume-detector sensors and as many bilge switches and heat sensors.

USE: One-stop for important safety-alarm displays.

USE TIPS: Self-test button lets you know alarm is working properly.

BUYING TIPS: Finding a device that can detect various gasses but not be tripped repeatedly into false alarms can be difficult; check with fellow boat owners for their experiences to determine the best multipurpose detector for your boat.

GLOW-IN-THE-DARK SAFETY LABELS

DESCRIPTION: Red-on-yellow 2¾" sq. adhesive labels bear glow-in-the-dark inscriptions such as "First Aid" (with cross), "Life Vests," "Flash-light" (with picture), as well as a picture of a fire extinguisher; larger 5½" long × 2¾" wide label bears the inscription "Emergency Flares." Glow green in the dark for several hours, may be recharged simply by shining a flashlight on them.

USE: To make it easy to spot emergency gear in the daytime or at night.

USE TIPS: Always store emergency equipment in accessible places.

BUYING TIPS: Labels are inexpensive.

Weather-Resistant Utility Boxes

DESCRIPTION: Stackable heavy-duty plastic box with fold-down handle and aluminum lift-and-latch hardware. Gasketed to keep water out. 13½" long × 7½" wide × 6½" high or 13½" long × 7½" wide × 11½" high.

USE: To store delicate items such as cameras, watches, or jewelry. Hard walls prevent crushing.

USE TIPS: Can be padlocked for extra security.

BUYING TIPS: Inexpensive, roomy storage system.

High-Intensity Safety Reflector

ALSO KNOWN AS: Reflective patch

DESCRIPTION: Stickerlike square or rectangle of reflective material, can be cut to shape with scissors.

USE: To apply to safety equipment, docks, floats, dinghies, boat trailers, or just about anything else that needs to be seen clearly in dark places.

USE TIPS: Operates on same principle as reflective patches worn by joggers or attached to bicycles. Makes object eight to ten times more visible than otherwise, so patch onto anything you think may require it someday.

BUYING TIPS: Sold in packages of a variety of shapes and sizes.

CLOTHING

Foul-Weather Gear

ALSO KNOWN AS: Slickers, oilskins, oilies

DESCRIPTION: Set of garments that includes a jacket with drawstring hood, overlapping placket over zipper, wrist cinches on long sleeves, and may have drawstring belt at waist and air-vent grommets

under arms, and also pants, with a drawstring waist or bib with elastic suspenders, as well as adjustable-tape ankle cinches. Both garments have numerous "cargo" pockets, usually with covering flaps held down by hook-and-loop material. Seams are reinforced and/or welded. One-piece rainsuit combines the features of both jacket and pants into a jumpsuit with a long zipper up the front.

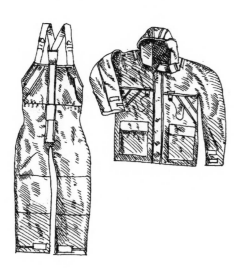

Waterproof fabric used for both items is made of nylon oxford cloth or polyester knit coated on the outside with PVC or polyurethane. Models may be solid or "breathable." Available in a variety of bright colors, in addition to traditional bright yellow. Some models feature stripes of reflective material on sleeves, back, and shoulders. Sized for men, women, and children, but do not expect a stylish fit. Form follows function with this item!

USE: To protect wearer against spray, rain, and wind. Although foul-weather gear should be strong enough to hold up in rough conditions, it must be supple enough to allow the freedom of movement needed to work on deck.

USE TIPS: Today's foul-weather gear has come a long way from the "oilskin" era, when protective clothing for sailors was made of calico coated with linseed oil—smelly, messy, and hot!

BUYING TIPS: Foul-weather gear comes in a variety of types—light-duty, racing, offshore sailing. Choose the kind that best fits your sailing needs. One that is designed to breathe so that you do not end up getting soaked in sweat, as opposed to rain, is usually preferable, but cold-weather sailors may prefer the solid PVC type. This trade-off is endlessly debatable.

SOU' WESTER

ALSO KNOWN AS:
Oilskin cap,
foul-weather cap

DESCRIPTION: Loose-fitting soft crowned hat with reinforced brim that is shorter in front and longer in back. Nylon tapes tie under chin. Crown may be lined. Made of polyester coated with PVC. Yellow is the traditional color.

USE: Traditional gear for keeping rain and spray off your head. Front brim can fold up, creating a trough to lead water down the long brim in back. The back brim should extend past the collar of your jacket to keep water from going down your neck.

USE TIPS: Ideal headgear for rainy weather on a boat; downright amusing the farther inland you get.

BUYING TIPS: Since foul-weather jackets these days tend to come with hoods, the sou'wester, alas, may eventually become extinct. However, many offshore sailors eschew their hoods and swear by their sou'westers.

SEAM SEALER

DESCRIPTION: Roll-on adhesive in 2-oz. plastic bottle with screw cap.

USE: Run sealer-adhesive over leaky seams on foul-weather gear or sou'westers, boots, bimini tops, or umbrellas.

USE TIPS: Seal stays flexible even after washing and dry cleaning.

BUYING TIPS: Effective though this product may be, you will eventually reach a point with your foul-weather gear where no amount of patching will help.

Jacket

ALSO KNOWN AS: Sailing jacket

DESCRIPTION: Lightweight, loose-fitting semi-waterproof waist- or hip-length outerwear closed by a front zipper. Waist-length models have knitted waistband to keep out drafts. May also have a partial zipper, with the rest of the front closed, in which case it is called an anorak. May have lightweight fleece lining. All colors available.

USE: Useful when it is a little chilly but not wet on the water or elsewhere. Some models are remarkably water-resistant and also dry quickly.

USE TIPS: A good heavy-duty, fleece-lined sailing jacket is also the best skiing or all-around winter jacket you can find.

BUYING TIPS: Wide range of styles and prices available to suit everyone.

Sailing Gloves

ALSO KNOWN AS:
Racing gloves

DESCRIPTION: Half-gloves with cut-away fingers and thumbs, with leather, suede, or synthetic grips on palms. "Body" of glove sometimes made of nylon mesh or, for cold weather, insulated fleece.

USE: To protect hands from rope burns, splinters, chafe, and injuries without limiting dexterity. Full-hand models are made for cold-weather sailing.

USE TIPS: Particularly useful for racing crews, who are often asked to sacrifice skin for speed with the sheets.

BUYING TIPS: Wide range of prices and styles to suit everyone's needs.

Yachting Boots

DESCRIPTION: Heavy rubber boots with knee-high or over-the-ankle shanks, light color, heavy nonskid treaded soles, reinforced toes, and cemented seams to minimize leaks. Usually come with removable, washable inner liners. Another version features similar heavy nonskid treads, but boot uppers are lightweight nylon with lace or hook-and-loop closures.

USE: To wear when the weather is dirty on deck to prevent slipping and foot injuries. Rubber styles are loose-fitting enough to kick off easily if you fall overboard.

USE TIPS: These boots will not keep your feet warm in cold weather, so keep some wool socks handy.

BUYING TIPS: Men's sizes are most commonly available; it may be hard to fit women with small feet.

Hat

DESCRIPTION: Various styles of headwear, including the traditional *watch cap,* a close-fitting knitted hat made of wool and/or synthetic blends. Turned-up ribbed rim covers ears with double layer for extra warmth. Navy blue is the traditional color, but many others are available.

TYPES:

Long-billed marlin cap: Ernest Hemingway made the long-billed marlin cap a staple for fishermen wanting to shade their eyes from the sun. To follow in "Papa's" footsteps, choose a cap with a leather visor and khaki cotton crown with grommet vent holes. *Visor*

Greek fisherman's cap

Caribe hat

caps, also known as *baseball caps,* are also popular and comfortable for hot-weather wear.

Greek fisherman's cap: popular with skippers of trawlers, although you see these black melton wool or cotton beretlike caps, with matching braiding and small visors, on and along the docks in many ports of call outside the Mediterranean.

The *Caribe hat:* similar in style to a sou'wester, although it has a broader brim all around and a flat crown. Made of white or light-color cotton; underside of brim is lined in dark green fabric to reduce sun glare. String tie keeps hat in place. Wide brim protects the face from harmful UV rays.

Collapsible hat: Also known as an *Offshore hat* or *Tilley hat,* after a popular brand name, this is a soft canvas topper with all-around brim and four or more grommets for ventillation. Dries quickly and can be folded up and stuffed anywhere.

USE: To protect your head from the sun, shield your eyes for better vision, and keep you warm in cold weather. Remember your mother's advice: Most heat is lost from your head in cold weather, and a watch cap is your best protection. In summer, hot sun beating on your head can muddle your senses fairly quickly.

USE TIPS: Don't get caught in the classic *yacht cap,* the kind with an emblem on the front and scrambled eggs on the visor, unless, of course, you have the rank to back it up. Depending on how much you value your hat, one lost overboard makes for a helpful MOB drill.

BUYING TIPS: Variety of styles matched only by variety of price ranges and taste.

SUNGLASSES

ALSO KNOWN AS: Polarized sunglasses, 100% UV sunglasses, shades

DESCRIPTION: Sunglasses of various materials and designs with tinted and polarized lenses usually made of glass.

USE: To reduce glare and protecting the eyes from damaging UVA and UVB rays.

USE TIPS: The water is a very hostile place for the eye. Glare can reduce visibility and cause headaches and fatigue. Even more insidious is the irreversible cornea damage caused by UV rays, whose effect is multiplied by reflection off the water. Sailors should wear their sunglasses at all times, even on hazy or slightly overcast days.

BUYING TIPS: Aviator or "bomber" style glasses with curved earpieces are much less likely to slip off and overboard. You can pay a lot for trendy designer glasses or a lot less for equal protection.

EYEGLASS RETAINER

ALSO KNOWN AS: Croakies (brand name)

DESCRIPTION: Cotton or neoprene strap, usually brightly colored, that hooks to ends of sunglasses to create a headband.

USE: To prevent the loss of your sunglasses and hold them around your neck when not in use.

USE TIPS: If your glasses don't have curved earpieces, then you should use the retainer, at least while onboard.

BUYING TIPS: Inexpensive protection for expensive glasses.

Zipper lanyard

ALSO KNOWN AS: Zipper pull

DESCRIPTION: Knotted cord or leather strip with loop at one end, 2"–3" long.

USE: To make it easier to work the zipper on jackets, clothing, and sail bags.

USE TIPS: Thread loop through metal zipper pull tab. Lanyard making is a favorite project for Boy and Girl Scouts.

BUYING TIPS: Inexpensive, but another easy-to-make item. Many jackets come already equipped with lanyards.

ABOUT WATER-RESISTANT WATCH SPECIFICATIONS

Sports-style watches are often advertised as being water-resistant to 80'–100' or 30 m. This sounds impressive, but does it really mean that you can dive to depths of 100' and still have a reliable timepiece? Not really. When you are in the market for a watch, particularly if you plan to go diving, it is important to be aware that watches marked "water-*resistant* to 80'–100' (30m)" will withstand some splashing, but not much else. Likewise, those marked "water-resistant to 165'" can be worn while you do the dishes or take a shower, but not when you go snorkeling, much less deep-sea diving. They are not waterproof. If you want a watch to wear in the pool, at the beach, or while snorkeling, look for one marked "water-resistant to 330'." Surfers and most divers should choose watches resistant or waterproof to 660', adequate for all types of water activities, except for when you dive deep enough to require helium gas in your tank.

Dive watch

DESCRIPTION: Rugged analog timepiece with separate dial for day and date, as well as adjustable outer ring serving as a timer. Crystal over watch face may have magnifying dome areas to make it easier to read day and date information. Hour, minute, and second hands, as well as watch face, are sometimes luminous. Watch band is made of flexible plastic or stainless steel.

USE: Designed for use while diving, when it is important to time dives to maintain an adequate supply of oxygen. Dive watches also allow the diver to time ascents, in order to avoid the bends.

USE TIPS: Works just as well above sea level as below.

BUYING TIPS: Available in both men's and women's styles.

Racing/ countdown watch

ALSO KNOWN AS:
Digital stopwatch

DESCRIPTION: LCD digital watch driven by lithium battery; accurate to 1/100 second, includes 24-hour stopwatch feature, as well as daily and hourly alarms, calendar, and 12/24-hour formats. Usually plastic with matching band.

USE: To time races, time yourself over a course, or use as an alarm clock.

USE TIPS: Not a particularly attractive timepiece, but easy to use and useful.

BUYING TIPS: You don't have to spring for a $1,000 model; fairly accurate but cheap equivalents are available at discount stores everywhere.

APPENDIX A

MATERIALS

ABOUT METALS AND METAL FINISHES

Marine metals come in a bewildering array of grades, exotic-sounding alloys, and a variety of finishes. As to the quality of a metal itself, it is more good sense than mere patriotism to buy products made in the United States, where the technology to produce top-grade marine metals exists. Good, uniform machining is probably the easiest characteristic for the consumer to identify, as well as an indication of superior quality.

ABOUT OTHER MARINE MATERIALS

Plastics, aramids, and other synthetic materials are much used in the marine industry because of their light weight, their versatlity in being molded to different shapes, their nonconductive nature, and their resistance to corrosion. The newer generation of synthetic sail fibers are as much as 30%–40% lighter than materials such as Dacron—an important consideration for sailors trying to reduce weight aloft. They also tear less easily in many cases and tend to hold their shape longer.

However, the best high-tech material will not perform as expected if it is undersized (as often is the case with stock boat equipment); when buying a part or a piece of gear, follow manufacturer's recommendations as to size and working load. The following information should help demystify the material maze and make buying decisions a little easier:

ABS <u>A</u>crylonitrile <u>b</u>utadiene <u>s</u>tyrene, a very common thermoplastic used for such things as building hulls, lining refrigerators, and making battens.

ACRYLIC Exceptionally clear lightweight thermoplastic that is frequently used for such things as windows (ports) or instrument panels. Although cheaper and more scratch-resistant than Lexan™, it is less strong and more prone to shattering. Sometimes known by its trademark name Plexiglas® (Rohm & Hass) or Lucite (Du Pont).

ALUMINUM What is known as aluminum is usually an aluminum alloy, with other metals, such as magnesium and copper, added to resist corrosion. Aluminum is lightweight—always a consideration on boats—but fairly weak. It is best used for anchors, masts, bimini-top frames, and the like that are not heavily stressed. Any aluminum part subjected to seawater should be *anodized* (subjected to an electrolytic process that forms a corrosive-resistant oxide film).

ANTRON™ Du Pont trade name for polyamide fibers used to make rope.

ARAMID A synthetic fiber produced from long-chain polyamides (nylons) that are extremely stable, stiff, and strong (about two to three times stronger than nylon). Kevlar®, used in sails, ropes, and hulls, is one of the best-known aramids. Subject to UV degradation and thus must be protected, as in rope with a polyester jacket.

BAKELITE™ Trademark name for a group of thermoplastics having high electrical and chemical resistance; used for such items as electrical connectors.

BRASS Copper-zinc alloy that is high in conductivity but subject to degradation in the marine environment. Used for various electrical applications, including battery terminals and switch components. Brass is still used to make such nautical items as lanterns and sextants, in which case its use is more decorative than practical.

BRONZE Alloys of differing composition (copper and tin are the core materials) that are corrosion-resistant and thus often used for underwater applications, seacocks in particular. Old salts swear by bronze and prefer it for such things as turnbuckles and other deck fittings; there is no evidence, however, that bronze is superior to stainless steel.

Sintered bronze is created when bronze powder is welded together but not completely and without being melted. The result is a clump that has about 50% porosity. Used to make sacrificial bronze anodes, which protect other metals against galvanic corrosion by deteriorating first.

CARBON FIBER Fibrous material made by pyrolyzing (charring) various spun or woven materials at very high temperatures (700°–1,800° C). Carbon fiber, developed originally for the aerospace industry, is prized for its high strength-to-weight properties—it has twice the strength at one-quarter the weight of high-tensile steel. In the marine industry, carbon fiber is used in such diverse things as masts, rudder posts, winch and wheel pedestals, and hulls.

CAST Generic term for a manufacturing process in which hot metal is poured into a mold and allowed to cool. *Investment cast* refers to a process in which a wax tree is used to form a series of ceramic molds that produce accurate and precise copies. *Drop-forged* is a form of casting in which a drop hammer is lowered on molten metal to compress it in its mold, creating an extra-strong item. A uniform look to articles is an indication that a particular series of items has been investment cast.

CHROME Used mainly as a plating agent for the various copper alloys (usually with a nickel underlayer) to resist tarnishing and corrosion. Although "chrome-plated" has a nice ring to it, stainless steel is hardier.

COPPER Copper, because of its low resistance to electricity (but high resistance to corrosion), is the material of choice for all wiring on a boat, including coaxial cable. Tinned copper provides even better corrosion resistance. Copper, in the form of cuprous oxide, is also the antifoulant of choice in most bottom paints. Copper cladding of the bottom, a practice that dates back to the Middle Ages, is undergoing a revival.

DELRIN™ Plastic resin from Du Pont. Somewhat waxy to the touch with some self-lubricating properties. Used for such light-load applications as ball and roller bearings in cam cleats and smaller furling-gear systems.

GALVANIZED Metal coated with zinc for weatherproofing. The two main types of galvanizing are coated and hot-dipped, in which an item is dipped into molten zinc after fabrication. Hot-dip is preferred because a thicker layer of zinc is achieved. Galvanizing is important for such items as boat trailers or anchors that are made of corrosion-prone steel. Note: Because the quality of galvanizing varies around the world, this is one area where "Made in the U.S.A." makes a difference.

KEVLAR® Du Pont aramid, noted for its strength and stiffness. Originally used to make bulletproof vests, Kevlar is suited for such marine items as racing sails (because it enables them to hold their shape well), ropes, cables, and hull construction.

LEXAN™ Trademark rigid plastic sheet from G.E. Plastics Group often used for ports and hatches. Subject to scratching, so it should be washed gently with soap and water using a soft cloth or towel, never toothpaste, which will abrade it, or acetone, which will devour it. To protect Lexan from crazing or cracking with age and exposure to sunlight, you can coat it with a noncommercial car wax.

MACHINED Refers to metal that has been cut, ground, bent, or polished as part of the after-manufacture working. Good, clean machining is an indication of a quality product.

MARELON® Glass-reinforced nylon (often mistakenly described as a plastic) with excellent strength-to-weight properties. Often used to make "plastic" seacocks, Y-valves, and other plumbing fixtures.

MARINIUM® An alloy of magnesium, aluminum, titanium, and beryllium, Marinium is lightweight but dense and strong and extremely resistant to corrosion from the elements. Because it doesn't tarnish, it is suited for such items as cleats.

MARITHANE™ A carbon fiber-polymer composite used for such things as spinnaker pole-end fittings; Marithane is strong, corrosion-resistant, and about one-half the weight of a comparable aluminum part.

MONEL™ Nickel-based alloy that is extremely corrosion-resistant. "Monel" in the marine field usually refers to Monel K-500, which is even more corrosion-resistant. Used for such items as seizing wire, propeller shafts, and water-pump components.

MYLAR® A plastic film made by Du Pont and used in the marine industry to coat sails (or serve as the sail laminate itself) and, cut into fibers, to make rope that has about twice the breaking strength of similar-sized manila rope. Mylar is prized for its isotropic qualities—its ability to handle stretch in all directions.

PRECIPITATION HARDENING Postmanufacture heat treatment of a special grade of stainless steel that produces extremely tough metal, called 17-4PH steel. This is used for such high-load items as snap shackles.

SPECTRA® A polyamide fiber by Allied Signal that is stronger and more abrasion-resistant than Kevlar. Boatbuilders are finding many uses for Spectra, including rope halyards and sailcloth. Also combined with graphite to make fishing rods.

STAINLESS STEEL Hard, strong, and corrosion-resistant, stainless steel has many marine uses. *Marine-grade* stainless steel usually refers to either American Iron & Steel Institute (AISI)–designated types 304 or 316, also known respectively as 18/8 and 18/10/3 for the percentage of chrome-nickel content (plus molybdenum in the case of 316), which is sometimes referred to as *molybdenum stabilized* stainless steel. Both kinds are subject to stress corrosion (a combination of constant stress and erosive corrosion) when exposed to saltwater and therefore should be reserved for above-the-waterline uses, such as deck

fittings. Type 304 is also susceptible to weld failure, 316 less so because of its molybdenum content, which toughens the alloy. When heat-treated during the manufacturing process, these types become 304L and 316L, denoting low carbon content, which protects against weld failure. Also suitable for welding are types 321 and 347, in which carbon content has been stabilized by the addition of titanium or niobium (columbium).

Here's a user tip for stainless: As with galvanized products, stainless steel varies widely in quality. The grade is more important than the simple claim something is made of stainless steel. Once again, U.S. stainless is a good bet. Not sure how "stainless" a product is? Bring a magnet along to check before buying—stainless steel is nonmagnetic.

TECHNORA™ A new and extremely strong Japanese-made aramid fiber with a distinctive black appearance (Teijin, the manufacturer, dies the thread as it is extruded) that protects it from UV rays. Most often used for composite sails (usually with Mylar® coating) and rope.

TITANIUM Inert metal that is extremely strong for its weight—it has about one-half the density of steel. Titanium is used in place of stainless steel for such things as swivel blocks and shackles, but it is expensive and considered "exotic" for the average boat.

TORLON™ Plastic resin from Amoco similar to but much stronger than Delrin. Noted for its great stiffness, strength, and resistance to heat. Often used for ball bearings in furling gear, blocks, and batten car systems. Torlon offers low friction and does not require lubrication, although a little nongreasy kind, such as silicone spray, helps.

VALOX® Polyester resin by G.E. Plastics, one of the class of thermoplastics, with excellent electrical and chemical resistance that is still able to be molded into precise shapes. Can be impregnated with fiberglass for extra strength. Used to make such things as nonconductive cable (telephone, TV) inlets.

VECTRAN® A liquid crystal polymer (LCP) from Hoechst-Celanese that is used to make rope. Vectran exhibits high strength, low stretch, great chafe resistance, and does not absorb water. Like Spectra-cored line (see above), Vectran is usually enclosed in a polyester jacket. Used most often on racing boats, it costs about seven times more per foot than nylon braid.

ZINC Metal used to protect more noble (and important) metal parts from galvanic corrosion. Used for plating or as anodes on such vulnerable items as propellers and prop shafts, rudder stocks, and through-hull fittings. *Zamac,* a zinc-aluminum alloy, used for such things as antenna mounts, is strong, corrosion-resistant, and platable for extra weather-proofing. Its main advantages are for the manufacturer—zamac is extremely castable and machinable, making it an ideal material for threaded mounts and small items such as running light casings. "Zinc" is fast becoming a generic term, as aluminum and magnesium replace it as the material of choice for sacrificial anodes for saltwater and freshwater applications.

MAIL ORDER SOURCES

It is not always possible to have a great ship's chandlery around the corner from your home or boat, so mail-order catalogs come in handy. Be sure to shop among them, too, and don't hesitate to ask for help from customer service.

Many mail-order companies will meet or match prices by competitors—send along a tear sheet showing the competitor's price. Check to see if the item you want is in stock—some of the smaller-staffed houses experience back-order problems from time to time. Some discounters will custom-order items that are not in stock. And some items, such as electronics, inflatable boats, videos, or books, are often nonreturnable, so buy them with extra care. Toll-free numbers are generally for orders only; call the regular number for product information and general assistance.

Often large manufacturers produce their own catalogs, not only for their own products but also for those they distribute. Some are quite extensive and well produced, with exquisite detail. It may be worthwhile to contact the company directly for a copy; advertisements or your local marine supply store should be able to provide you with information on how to reach them.

Following (in alphabetical order) is a list of some mail-order sources for most of the items listed in this book (they all cover power and sailing equipment unless otherwise noted). These catalogs carry items by a wide variety of manufacturers. Inclusion here is not meant to be an endorsement, nor is it exclusive.

Boater's World
671 Ritz Way
Beltsville, MD 20705
(301) 419-3131
(800) 826-2628

Boater's World, just six years into the marine gear business, has been expanding rapidly, evolving from a powerboat-oriented house to an all-around marine equipment supplier. Its full-color catalog, just under 100 pages in 1994, will be expanding as well.

BOAT/U.S.
880 South Pickett Street
Alexandria, VA 22304-4606
(703) 823-9550
(800) 937-2628
Fax (703) 461-2854

One of the most comprehensive, well-produced, and well-written catalogs. BOAT/U.S. is a membership organization, sort of an AAA for the waterways, and members get a discount on all items (both "list" and "member" prices are quoted). Helpful consumer tips on some items and systems. Over 660 pages long.

Consumer Marine Electronics
1771 Highway 34 South
Wall, NJ 07719
(800) 332-2628
Fax (908) 681-1498

Almost 100 pages of marine electronics. Good source for the single-minded con-

Defender Industries, Inc.
255 Main Street
New Rochelle, NY 10801-0820
(914) 632-3001
(800) 628-8225
Fax (800) 654-1616

Defender is one of the country's largest discount houses for marine gear. Its catalog contains over 300 pages of items, some difficult to find elsewhere. The mostly black-and-white catalog contains many drawings instead of photos, which sometimes makes it difficult to judge the construction or finish of a specific brand.

E & B Discount Marine/Goldbergs' Marine
201 Meadow Road
P.O. Box 3138
Edison, NJ 08818-3138
Customer service: (800) 634-6382
(800) 533-5007
Fax (908) 819-9222

No-frills catalog with more than 300 pages of boating gear, slanted toward power but with shared and sail items also. Lots of drawings, few photos. Goldbergs' Marine, an old favorite, is now part of the E & B operation.

Fawcett Boat Supplies
110 Compromise Street, City Dock
Annapolis, MD 21403
(410) 267-8681
(800) 456-9151
Fax (410) 267-7547

Some generic boating items, but the emphasis is on sailing gear sold by a staff that is small, attentive, and extremely well versed in the sport.

Freeport Marine Supply, Inc.
47 West Merrick Road
Freeport, NY 11520
(800) 645-2565
Fax (516) 379-2909

250-page catalog is devoted mostly to powerboat items, including parts that may be hard to find in more general catalogs.

Hamilton Marine
P.O. Box 227
Searsport, ME 04974
(207) 548-6302
(800) 639-2715
Fax (800) 548-6352

Hamilton got its start as a supplier to Maine boatbuilders and commercial fishermen, so it is no surprise that the emphasis remains on nuts and bolts and other hardware items, with fewer just-for-fun accessories. Hamilton encourages calls for items not in the catalog.

Jamestown Distributors
28 Narragansett Avenue
Jamestown, RI 02835
(800) 423-0030
Fax (800) 423-0542

Huge inventory of fasteners, fittings, and nuts and bolts that are hard to find else-where—including your local chandlery. Boatbuilders are among Jamestown's customers.

JSI The Sailing Source
3000 Gandy Boulevard
St. Petersburg, FL 33702
(800) 234-3220

Strictly sailboat gear. With its deep inventory (especially of rigging items), this is a good source for go-fast specialty gear and hard-to-find gilhickeys.

Landfall Navigation
354 West Putnam Avenue
Greenwich, CT 06830
(203) 661-3176
Fax (203) 661-9613

Navigation instruments, safety equipment, electronics, charts, and books for serious offshore sailors and powerboaters.

M & E Marine Supply
P.O Box 601
Camden, NJ 08101
(800) 541-6501
Fax (609) 757-9175

Mainstream catalog with lots of hardware and gear. Average prices, with no price-matching provision.

Marine Exchange
128 Newbury Street, Route 1
South Peabody, MA 01960
(508) 535-3212
(800) 888-8699
Fax (508) 535-3702

Family-owned business that trades in new and used equipment, with the emphasis on sail. Not an extensive inventory, but you might find what you want at a good price.

Outer Banks
1010 West Fort Macon Road
Atlantic Beach, NC 28512
(919) 240-2500
(800) 682-2225 and manual fax
Fax Info Service (919) 240-2243 ext. 1000

Powerboat and fishing supplies only—no sailing stuff.

Overton's
111 Red Banks Road
P.O. Box 8228
Greenville, NC 27835
(800) 334-6541
Fax (919) 355-2923

Colorful, small catalog with gear and accessories for powerboats, trailers, kayaks, and water sports in general.

Post Marine Supply
111 Cedar Street
New Rochelle, NY 10801
(914) 235-9800
(800) 922-4837
Fax (914) 235-9008

Fairly small operation that concentrates on the powerboat owner. Simple black-and-white catalog.

Shoreway Marine
Highway 73
Berlin, NJ 08009
(800) 443-5408
Fax (609) 768-2409

Equipment and accessories for the powerboater and fisherman.

Skipper Marine Electronics
3170 Commercial Avenue
Northbrook, IL 60062
(708) 272-4700
(800) 754-7737
Fax (708) 291-0244

One of the pioneers in marine electronics catalog sales. For prices comparable with competitors', go with their price-beater option rather than their pretuning and calibration packages.

West Marine
P.O. Box 50050
Watsonville, CA 95077-5050
(800) 538-0775
Fax (408) 728-4360

Possibly the largest marine-gear mail-order house, with a beautiful, 700-page, full-color catalog listing some 18,000 items. Includes excellent consumer-advice sections on technical subjects.

INDEX